Cànan & Cultar/
Language & Culture
Rannsachadh na Gàidhlig 8

ALSO AVAILABLE FROM DUNEDIN ACADEMIC PRESS

Cànan & Cultar/Language & Culture: Rannsachadh na Gàidhlig 4
Edited by Gillian Munro and Richard A. V. Cox (2010) ISBN: 9781903765869

Coimhearsnachd na Gàidhlig an-Diugh/Gaelic Communities Today
Edited by Gillian Munro and Ian Mac an Tàilleir (2010) ISBN: 9781903765852

Lainnir a' Bhùirn/The Gleaming Water: Essays on Modern Gaelic Literature
Edited by Emma Dymock and Wilson McLeod (2011) ISBN: 9781906716349

*By Poetic Authority: The Rhetoric of Panegyric in
Gaelic Poetry of Scotland to c.1700*
By Pia Coira (2012) ISBN: 9781780460031

See www.dunedinacademicpress.co.uk for details

Cànan & Cultar/
Language & Culture
Rannsachadh na Gàidhlig 8

edited by

Wilson McLeod, Anja Gunderloch and Rob Dunbar

DUNEDIN
EDINBURGH ◆ LONDON

First published in 2016 by Dunedin Academic Press Ltd.
Head Office: Hudson House, 8 Albany Street, Edinburgh EH1 3QB
London Office: 352 Cromwell Tower, Barbican, London EC2Y 8NB

ISBNs
9781780460581 (Paperback)
9781780465531 (ePub)
9781780465548 (Kindle)

Shelfie

A **bundled** eBook edition is available with the purchase of this print book.

CLEARLY PRINT YOUR NAME ABOVE IN UPPER CASE

Instructions to claim your eBook edition:
1. Download the Shelfie app for Android or iOS
2. Write your name in **UPPER CASE** above
3. Add your book in the Shelfie app
4. Download your eBook to any device

© 2016 Dunedin Academic Press

The rights of Wilson McLeod, Anja Gunderloch and Rob Dunbar and the contributors to be identified as the authors of their contributions to this book have been asserted by them in accordance with sections 77 & 78 of the Copyright, Designs and Patents Act 1988

All rights reserved.
No part of this publication may be reproduced or transmitted in any form or by any means or stored in any retrieval system of any nature without prior written permission, except for fair dealing under the Copyright, Designs and Patents Act 1988 or in accordance with a licence issued b the Copyright Licensing Society in respect of photocopying or reprographic reproduction. Full acknowledgment as to author, publisher and source must be given. Application for permission for any other use of copyright material should be made in writing to the publisher.

British Library Cataloguing in Publication Data
A catalogue record for this book is available from the British Library

Typeset by Makar Publishing Production
Printed in Great Britain by CPI Antony Rowe

Clàr-innse/Contents

	Clàr ghiorrachaidhean	vii
	Ro-ràdh	ix
1	Uinneag dhan Àird an Iar: leanailteachd crutha ann an dùthchas nan Gàidheal *Meg Bateman agus John Purser*	1
2	Manuscript and print in Gaelic Scotland and Ireland, 1689–1832 *Richard Sharpe*	31
3	The Gaelic manuscripts at Inveraray Castle *Ronald Black*	55
4	'Bean-Chomuinn nam Bàrd': Exploring common ground in the lives and perspectives of the Gaelic poets Mary MacPherson and Mary MacKellar *Priscilla Scott*	71
5	'Dh'fhalbh na gillean grinn': spiritual perspectives in women's songs of the Great War *Anne Macleod Hill*	85
6	The passion of George Campbell Hay for Gaelic and the Gaels *Sandra Malley*	103
7	*Fuaran Sléibh*: The poet's main copy *Kyriakos Kalorkoti*	117
8	The Gaelic writer, Iain Crichton Smith… *Moray Watson*	135
9	The massacre of Eigg in 1577 *Ross Crawford*	157
10	Haggis agus: Gaelic Scotland through the minibus window *Coinneach MacLean*	171

11 Nàisean cultarach nan Gàidheal: Ath-chruthachadh
    tìr-dhùthchasaich ann an Albainn Nuaidh 183
    Seumas Watson agus Marlene Ivey

12 Celtic Colours: cultural sustainability 195
    Jean S. Forward

13 Selling a language to save it? The business-oriented
    promotion of Gaelic and Irish 203
    Sara C. Brennan, Michael Danson and Bernadette O'Rourke

14 Camanachd – fada bharrachd na dìreach gèam 221
    Grant Jarvie agus Ùisdean MacIllInnein

15 Syntactic innovation in Manx and Sutherland Gaelic 237
    Christopher Lewin

16 A' suathadh ri iomadh rud: Comas is cothrom faclaireachd
    a leudachadh tro bhriathrachas a' chultair dhùthchasaich 251
    Hugh Cheape

17 Briathrachas an iasgaich ann an Eilean Bharraigh: faclan airson
    nan sgothan 271
    Ciorstaidh NicLeòid

18 Gàidheil, Goill agus coimhearsnachd na Gàidhlig: Ideòlasan cànain
    am measg inbhich a fhuair foghlam tro mheadhan na Gàidhlig 285
    Stiùbhart S. Dunmore

19 Cuimseachadh air cruth ann am foghlam tro mheadhan na Gàidhlig:
    A' leasachadh chomasan cànain le ceartachadh iomchaidh 299
    Sìleas NicLeòid

Clàr ghiorrachaidhean

CUP	Cambridge University Press
DIAS	Dublin Institute for Advanced Studies
EUP	Edinburgh University Press
HMSO	Her/His Majesty's Stationery Office
NLS	National Library of Scotland
OUP	Oxford University Press
SA (SSSA)	Sound Archive (School of Scottish Studies)
SGS	*Scottish Gaelic Studies*
SGTS	Scottish Gaelic Texts Society
TGSI	*Transactions of the Gaelic Society of Inverness*

Ro-ràdh

Chaidh a' cho-labhairt Rannsachadh na Gàidhlig 8 a chumail anns an Informatics Forum aig Oilthigh Dhùn Èideann air 23-26mh an Ògmhios 2014. B' e seo an dàrna uair a thàinig a' cho-labhairt chudromach seo chun a' phrìomh bhaile, an dèidh a' chruinneachaidh shoirbheachail a chùm sinn ann an 2004. Uile-gu-lèir, chaidh còrr is 60 pàipear a thoirt seachad aig a' cho-labhairt, air raon farsaing chuspairean, eadar litreachas, eachdraidh, dualchas, cànanachas, teicneòlas cànain, foghlam, eòlas na meadhanan, eaconomachd agus turasachd. Chuala sinn còig prìomh òraidean, leis an Dr Meg Bateman agus an Dr John Purser, an Ollamh Hugh Cheape, an Ollamh Richard Sharpe agus an Dr Moray Watson. Tha na prìomh òraidean uile air am foillseachadh anns an leabhar seo, maille ri còig deug pàipearan eile. Thugadh cuireadh don a h-uile sgoilear a leugh pàipear aig a' cho-labhairt pàipear a chur air adhart airson foillseachadh ann an gnìomharran na co-labhairt, agus fhuair a h-uile pàipear a chuireadh thugainn sgrùdadh bho leughadair neo-eisimileach. Gun teagamh, tha na pàipearan anns an leabhar ghnìomharran seo a' nochdadh farsaingeachd na co-labhairt agus farsaingeachd is fallaineachd 'Rannsachadh na Gàidhlig' anns an aonamh linn fichead.

Am measg nan tachartasan co-cheangailte ris a' cho-labhairt bha nochdadh plac do Dhonnchadh Bàn Mac an t-Saoir (le Alba Aosmhor) ann an Clòs Roxburgh anns an t-Seann Bhaile, far an robh am bàrd a' fuireach fad grunn bhliadhnaichean. Sheinn an Dr Gary West a' phìob aig an tachartas, ghabh Seumas Watson aon de dh'òrain Dhonnchaidh Bhàin agus thàinig an t-athchruthaiche eachdraidheil Arron Johnston ann an èideadh Geàrd Bhaile Dhùn Èideann, anns an robh am bàrd an sàs aig aon àm.

Fhuair sinn taic-airgid glè luachmhor airson na co-labhairt bho Bhòrd na Gàidhlig agus bho Shoillse (an com-pàirteachas eadar-oilthigh a tha a' brosnachadh rannsachadh a tha ag amas air ath-nuadhachadh na Gàidhlig ann an Alba), agus tha sinn fada nan comain. Chuir Comhairle Bhaile Dhùn Èideann fàilteachadh sònraichte air dòigh dhuinn air Talla Bhaile Dhùn Èideann. Sheinn Còisir Dhùn Èideann dhuinn ann an dìnnear na co-labhairt. A thaobh planadh is rianachd na co-labhairt tha sinn cuideachd an comain an Dr

Kyriakos Kalorkoti anns an Sgoil Coimpiutaireachd (Informatics), Christine Lennie, Rùnaire Ceiltis is Eòlas na h-Alba agus Neil Young, an t-Oifigear Coimpiutaireachd anns an Sgoil Litreachasan, Chànanan is Chultaran. Fhuair sinn cuideachadh luachmhor aig a' cho-labhairt fhèin bho Ellen Beard, Alison Buck, Matthew Dziennik, Anne Macleod Hill agus Alastair Scouller. Tha sinn a' toirt taing chridheil dhuibh uile.

Wilson McLeod, Anja Gunderloch agus Rob Dunbar

1

Uinneag dhan Àird an Iar: Leanailteachd Crutha ann an Dùthchas nan Gàidheal

Meg Bateman agus John Purser

Sabhal Mòr Ostaig

Bho chionn grunn bhliadhnachan a-nis tha mi-fhìn is John Purser an sàs ann am pròiseact, 'Uinneag dhan Àird an Iar', eadar oilthigh Dhùn Dè agus Sabhal Mòr Ostaig, is sinne a' rannsachadh ealain na Gàidhealtachd. Fhad 's a bhiodh ar co-obraichean a' cnuasachd ceist mar 'Ciamar a chunnacas am boireannach anns an dealbh *An Islay Woman*?' le càch,[1] bha sinne a' cnuasachd mar a chitheadh am boireannach fhèin an saoghal.

Tha sinn a' feuchainn ris na structaran smaoineachaidh a shònrachadh leis am biodh na Gàidheil tro na linntean a' faicinn an t-saoghail. Chan eil sinn ag ràdh gu bheil feart sam bith riatanach do lèirsinn nan Gàidheal, ach, aig an aon àm, chan eil sinn ag iarraidh sealladh dùthchasach fa leth a leigeil seachad. Ged nach rachadh mòran le Sapir agus Whorf san latha an-diugh nach gabh smuaintean eadar-theangachadh eadar cànain, tha e do-sheachanta gu bheil gach cànan a' daingneachadh dhòighean smaoineachaidh fa leth (Deutscher, 2011). Mar eisimpleir, ma nì sinn coimeas eadar cha mhòr peantair sam bith bho thaobh a-muigh na Gàidhealtachd agus Uilleam Mac an t-Sagairt (1835-1910), Gàidheal à Cinn Tìre, chì sinn gu bheil an t-àite aig na daoine anns na dealbhan aigesan gu math eadar-dhealaichte. Anns na dealbhan aig càch, tha na daoine faisg oirnn ann am meadhan an deilbh; anns na dealbhan aig Mac an t-Sagairt tha rudan mòra a' tachairt fad às – mòr do dhaoine, ach de bheagshuim do nàdar, agus tha na daoine gu tric mar fhaileas air an dùthaich (faic, mar eisimpleir, *The Emigrant Ship, The Coming of Saint Columba* no *Running for Shelter*).[2] An e gu bheil cultar na Beurla agus cultar na Gàidhlig a' riochdachadh an àite aig mac-an-duine san àrainneachd ann an dòighean eadar-dhealaichte?

Ghabh am pròiseact ainm bhon dàn 'Hallaig' aig Somhairle MacGill-Eain (1991, td. 226):

> Tha bùird is tàirnean air an uinneig
> trom faca mi an Àird an Iar
> 's tha mo ghaol aig Allt Hallaig
> 'na craoibh bheithe …

Tha sinn a' dèanamh oidhirp ris na bùird a thoirt far na h-uinneige seo. Ann am meadhan an fhicheadamh linn, tha Somhairle MacGill-Eain a' bruidhinn mu làthaireachd nam marbh san eilean agus mu bheatha choitchinn a bhith a' ruith eadar daoine agus craobhan. Tha tuigse gu math diofraichte ag obair an seo seach tuigse dhùbailteach Descartes air dà shusbaint, stuth agus smuain. Ged nach aithnicheadh reusanaichean an t-Soilleireachaidh i, 's dòcha nach biodh an dàn cho neònach do Ghàidheal bho chionn mìle bliadhna, mas e a' bheatha choitcheann a tha air a riochdachadh ann an atharrachadh crutha is obair snaidhm a' dol eadar lusan, beathaichean is daoine. 'S dòcha nach biodh e neònach nas motha don fhiosaigiche David Bohm (1917-92) no don fheallsanaiche Alfred North Whitehead (1861-1947) dham bheil an dà chuid inntinn agus stuth an sàs anns na h-uile. Fhuair an sealladh seo spreigeadh ùr nuair a thàinig innleachdas *quantum* am follais anns nach eil sgaradh soilleir eadar stuth agus spionnadh agus leis mar a chithear mìrean fo-dhadamach gan giùlan ann an dòighean mì-chinnteach (Seager agus Hermanson-Allen, 2012; Whitehead, 1929).

Tha an cànan fhèin a' toirt seachad fianais a thaobh na dòigh anns am faiceadh na Gàidheil an saoghal. Tha ainm a' ghille-bhrìghde a' sealltainn gu bheil ceangal aig an eun leis an naomh den ainm cheudna, agus tha Alasdair Alpin MacGregor (1937, td. 122) a' dèanamh aithris air an sgeul gun deach a chomharradh le comharra na croise thar nan sgiathan mar thaing dha airson Crìosd fhalachadh ann am feamainn nuair a bha e teicheadh eadar na h-eileanan. Tha a' chrois seo doirbh a dhèanamh a-mach, ach nuair a leughar obair an àrc-eòlaiche Lituàinianaich, Marija Gimbutas, is i a' sònrachadh cruth saighid no *chevron* mar chomharra na ban-dia ann an cultar Linn na Cloiche air feadh na Roinn Eòrpa, nochdaidh car eile san sgeul (Gimbutas, 1989, passim). Chan e a-mhàin gu bheil na comharran geala air na sgiathan gu soilleir ann an cruth saighid ach cuideachd gun robh Brìghde na ban-dia mus robh i na naomh. A bheil an t-ainm Gàidhlig a' dèanamh ceangal le cànan lèirsinneach Linn na Cloiche?

Tha tòrr air a sgrìobhadh mu dhathan sa Ghàidhlig agus mar a tha an speactram air a roinn aig diofar chànain. Tha dath an tuirceis air an Lochan Uaine sa Mhonadh Ruadh mar thoradh air meinnearan san uisge. Ach cha bu chòir dha seo a bhith na annas dha na Gàidheil oir tha am facal 'uaine' a' cur an cèill nach e dath an fheòir (glas) mun cuairt air an loch a tha san amharc an seo, ach dath deàlrach lèig no dath fuadain a dhèanadh mac-an-duine (Lazar-Meyn, 1994).

Ach feumaidh sinn na h-eisimpleirean ud fhàgail aig an sin, oir 's ann air 'leanailteachd crutha ann an dùthchas nan Gàidheal' a tha am pàipear seo; tha sin ri ràdh air structaran a nochdas uair 's a-rithist ann an rudan, ann an smaoineachadh agus ann an ealain.

> *I listen with my eyes and see through that*
> *Mellifluous din of shapes my masterpiece*
> *Of masterpieces:*
> *One sandstone chord that holds up time in space*
> *Sforzando Suilven reared on his ground bass* (MacCaig, 1973, td. 31).

Bha 'èisteachd leis na sùilean' ceart gu leòr do Thormod MacCaoig ach an urrainn dhuinne a bhith a' bruidhinn mu dheidhinn cheanglaichean ann an structair no cruth tarsainn air diofar mheadhanan ann an dòigh nach eil dìreach bàrdail? Bidh luchd-ciùil aig a bheil comas leughadh nan notaichean ag èisteachd leis na sùilean agus a' faicinn leis na cluasan, agus gun teagamh tha ceanglaichean structarail eadar rannaigheachd agus ceòl bunaiteach ann an òrain. Ann an dùthchas nan Gàidheal, ruigidh a leithid de cheanglaichean sàr-àirde ann an òrain mar 'Moladh Beinn Dòbhrain' a tha stèidhichte air structair ceòl mòr na pìoba.

Faodar ceanglaichean structarail (eadar ceòl is rannaigheachd) a bhith air an cur an gnìomh ann an òrain nas iriosaile, agus nochdaidh iad ann an dùthchas nan Gàidheal aig gach ìre. Tha eisimpleir sìmplidh ann an 'Tàladh do MhacFhionghain', a rèir coltais o àm nam Fuadaichean.

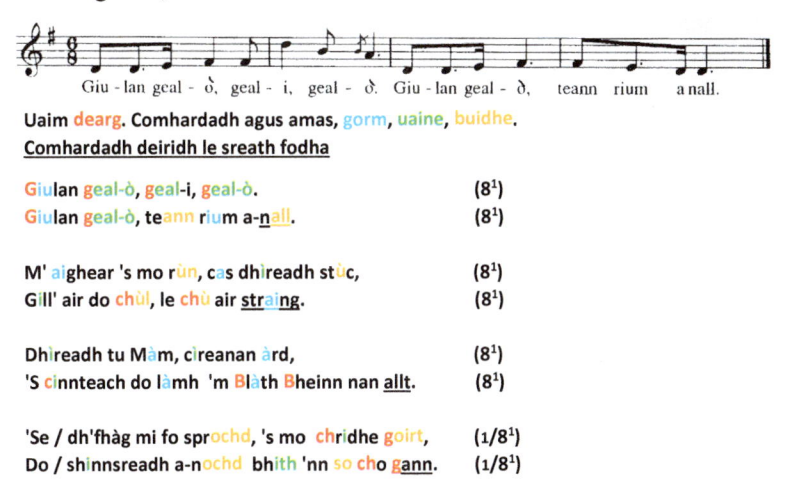

Giu-lan geal - ò, geal - i, geal - ò. Giu-lan geal - ò, teann rium a nall.

Uaim dearg. Comhardadh agus amas, gorm, uaine, buidhe.
Comhardadh deiridh le sreath fodha

Giulan geal-ò, geal-i, geal-ò.	(8¹)
Giulan geal-ò, teann rium a-nall.	(8¹)
M' aighear 's mo rùn, cas dhìreadh stùc,	(8¹)
Gill' air do chùl, le chù air straing.	(8¹)
Dhìreadh tu Mam, cìreanan àrd,	(8¹)
'S cinnteach do làmh 'm Blàth Bheinn nan allt.	(8¹)
'Se / dh'fhàg mi fo sprochd, 's mo chridhe goirt,	(1/8¹)
Do / shinnsreadh a-nochd bhith 'nn so cho gann.	(1/8¹)

Refrain Precious little lad, turn to me.
Verses 1. My joy and love, climber of peaks, A boy following thee, with his dog on a leash. 2. You would climb the Mam, high crests, Sure is your hand in Blaven of the streams. 3. What has left my mind sorrowful, and my heart sore Is (the fact) that your ancestors are here so scarce.

Dealbh 1. Structair, Tàladh MhicFhionghain.

Tha na faclan air an sgeadachadh le tòrr amais agus uaim, cho math ri comhardadh aicill. Tha structair an rainn coltach ri structair sìmplidh a' chiùil ABA«A«. Tha an dàn a' samhlachadh a' phàiste is e air dhol na dhuine mòr a' sreap nam beann. Tha cruth a' chiùil ag èirigh 's a' laighe a' dèanamh dealbh dhuinn. Tha am pong as àirde daonnan a' dol le fuaimreig chaoil; ach nuair a thèid tilleadh ainmeachadh aig deireadh na sèiste, tha sin a' dol le tionndadh – *reverse* – a' chiad fhràs A, a' chiall agus an ceòl co-shìnte mar gum b' eadh.

Le linn a bhith dèanamh ceòl, tha e cumanta gu leòr fràs a ghluasad suas no sìos, no a chur bun-os-cionn no a thionndadh gus am bi an deireadh air thoiseach. Bithear a' cleachdadh nan dòighean-obrach seo gu tric gun mhothachadh aig ìre mhìn no mhòr, agus cha leig na fràsan ùra a leas a bhith buileach ceart. Faodar smaoineachadh mun deidhinn mar fhaileas ann an sgàthan no ìomhaigh air a cur mun cuairt.

Gun teagamh rachadh an aon seòrsa sgrùdadh ri seo a dhèanamh air òrain thraidiseanta Ghàidhealach eile gus fuinn a shònrachadh air an tar-shuidheachadh, air an cur bun-os-cionn agus air an tionndadh – agus sa Laidinn lorgaidh sinn rudeigin coltach ri seo a thaobh structaran fighte-fuaighte anns an *Inchcolm Antiphoner* (Leabharlann Oilthigh Dhùn Èideann MS 211.iv) bho dheireadh an treas linn deug.

B' e manachainn le ceangal ri Dùn Chailleann a bha ann an Innis Cholm, coisrigte gu nàdarra do Cholum Cille. Anns an antiphon 'Tuis Pater', nach eil ri lorg ann an àite eile, tha ceithir eileamaidean aig a' phìos seo, trì dhiubh stèidhichte mun eileamaid mheadhanaich ag iarraidh slànachadh mar thoradh air subhailcean Cholum Chille. Tha structair a' chiùil ga fhighe le structair na bàrdachd, a' toirt a-steach an Evovae (Gloria Patri … . sEcUlOrUm AmEn), agus e a' tarraing gach rud còmhla.

> Athar, gum biodh a' choisir gad mholadh gun sòradh. Gum biodh ar canntaireachd ceòlmhor. Oir creididh sinn gu bheil sinn air ar sàbhaladh tromhad agus gum bi sinn beannaichte san t-saoghal ri teachd (EUL MS 211.iv f3r – f2r [àireamhan ùra] (eadar-theangachadh le Meg Bateman).

'S dòcha gum buin fear no dhà de na laoidhean anns an *Inchcolm Antiphoner* do linn Adhamhnain, a bha a' sgrìobhadh aig deireadh an t-seachdamh linn mu bheatha an Naoimh Colum Cille.

'S e eisimpleirean tràtha Laidinn a th' ann an seo, ach tha eisimpleirean coltach riutha anns a' Ghàidhlig, a chaidh a chumail chun an t-seachdamh linn deug, ach is gann na fuinn a th' againn dhaibh.

Thàinig am fonn seo fo chomhair 'An Duanag Ullamh' bho làmh-sgrìobhainn bhon ochdamh linn deug. Gun teagamh tha buaidh air a' cheòl aig na sreathan

Leanailteachd crutha ann an dùthchas nan Gàidheal   *Meg Bateman agus John Purser*

Tuis Pater laudibus   (7)

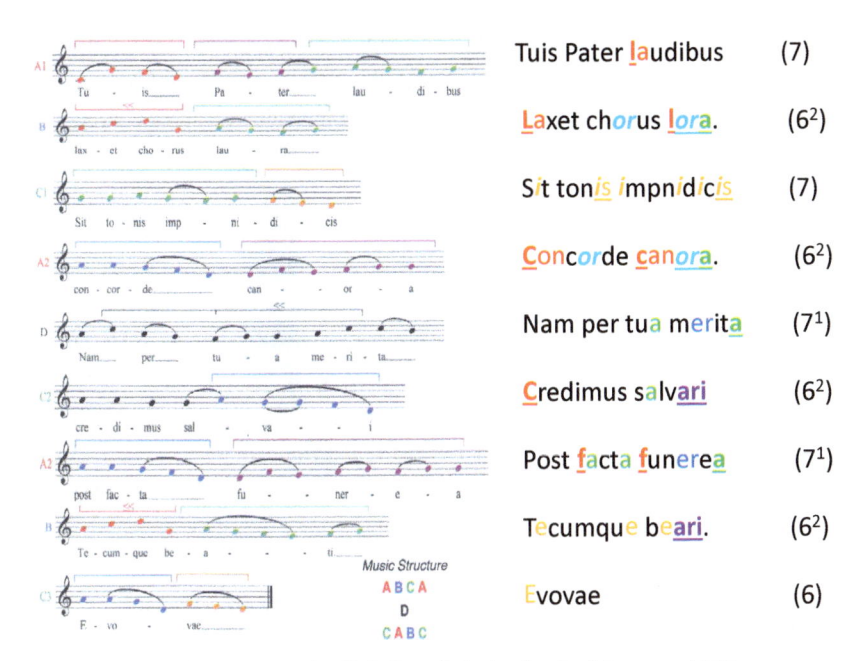

Laxet chorus lora.   (6²)

Sit tonis impnidicis   (7)

Concorde canora.   (6²)

Nam per tua merita   (7¹)

Credimus salvari   (6²)

Post facta funerea   (7¹)

Tecumque beari.   (6²)

Music Structure
A B C A
D
C A B C

Evovae   (6)

Dealbh 2. Structair, 'Tuis Pater', Inchcolm Antiphoner, *c.*1300.

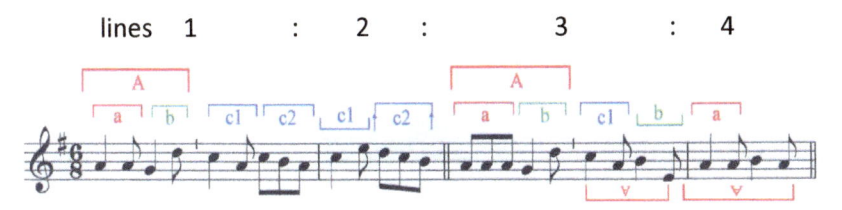

lines   1   :   2   :   3   :   4

Structair a' chiùil
A x 4, dà uair co-ionann, dà uair air a chur bun-os-cionn le mion-atharrachaidhean
a x 3
b x 3, an treas uair air a chur bun-os-cionn agus air a ghluasad
c^1 x 3, an dàrna uair air a chur bun-os-cionn agus air a ghluasad
c^2 x 2, an dàrna uair air a ghluasad

Structair na bàrdachd Snéadhbhairdne 2(8² + 4²) – 'small or swift-flowing verse'
Abhal uasal farsaing freumhach   (8²)
Do'n cubhaidh molad   (4²)
Crann as ùire dh'fhàs troimh thalamh   (8²)
Làn de thoradh   (4²)

Dealbh 3. Structair, 'An Duanag Ullamh', *c.*1550.

5

ochd- agus ceithir-lideach mu seach, ach feumar saorsa gus buillean nam facal amas sna h-àiteachan ceart – cuspair a chaidh a dheasbad le Virginia Blankenhorn (2010). Co-dhiù, tha cumadh an fhuinn teann agus cleachdar structaran bun-os-cionn agus a chomhair an cùil an seo cuideachd.

A' gluasad bho òrain le cumadh teann gu ceòl-ionnsramaid le cumadh teann, coimheadaidh sinn a-nis air ceòl mòr, seach gum buin e o thùs dhan Ghàidhealtachd. B' e an Seanalair Thomason fear de na ciad daoine a dh'aithnich an ceangal eadar bàrdachd agus ceòl mòr:

> *I have not now the shadow of a doubt as to every piobaireachd being the music of a poem* (Thomason, 1893, td. viii).

Dh'fhoillsich Thomason an leabhar *Ceòl Mòr* ann an 1893, ach tha a leithid a smuain nàdarrach do dhùthchas nan Ceilteach san fharsaingeachd.

Tha an 'Campbell Canntaireachd' bho 1815 (NLS LSS 3714-5) a' taisbeanadh ceòl mar fhaclan air an eagrachadh mar sreathan de bhàrdachd. Tha na faclan air an cruthachadh gus na notaichean agus na gearraidhean a riochdachadh. Tha an structair soilleir fiù 's ann an comharrachadh-clàir no *staff notation*.

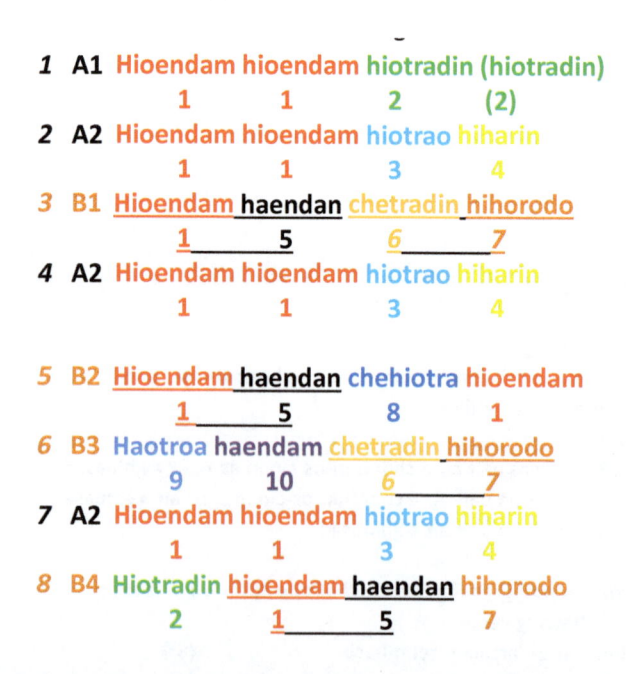

1 **A1** Hioendam hioendam hiotradin (hiotradin)
     1   1   2   (2)
2 **A2** Hioendam hioendam hiotrao hiharin
     1   1   3   4
3 **B1** Hioendam haendan chetradin hihorodo
     1   5   6   7
4 **A2** Hioendam hioendam hiotrao hiharin
     1   1   3   4

5 **B2** Hioendam haendan chehiotra hioendam
     1   5   8   1
6 **B3** Haotroa haendam chetradin hihorodo
     9   10   6   7
7 **A2** Hioendam hioendam hiotrao hiharin
     1   1   3   4
8 **B4** Hiotradin hioendam haendan hihorodo
       2   1   5   7

Tha a' chiad leth de shreathan A1,2,4,7 co-ionann agus tha sreathan A2,4,7 uile-gu-lèir co-ionann
Tha càraidean de dh'eileamaidean ann an sreathan B3,5,6,8 nach cluinnear ann an sreathan 1,2,4,7
Tha 'comhardadh' eadar a' chiad dà 'fhacal' ann an sreathan 3,5 agus ann am meadhan sreath 8
Tha 'comhardadh' eadar an dà 'fhacal' dheireannach ann an sreathan 3,6 agus am 'facal' mu dheireadh ann an sreath 8

Dealbh 4. Structair, 'Cumha MhicFhionghain', Canntaireachd agus Ùrlar.

Tha brìgh aig faclan canntaireachd, ach chan e brìgh chiallachail a th' ann. Tha iad air an eagrachadh ann an sreathan fada a tha air an roinn eadar sreathan ochd- agus seachd-lideach. Tha an structair air a shoilleireachadh an seo, leis na dathan air na faclan. Anns an ùrlar, tha deich faclan no eileamaidean.

Is ionann sreathan a dhà, a ceithir agus a seachd. Tòisichidh sreathan a trì agus a còig, mar gum b' eadh le comhardadh dà-lideach. Tha sreathan 3 agus 6 a' crìochnachadh mar gum biodh le comhardadh deiridh dà-lideach, agus tha sreath 8 cuideachd a' dèanamh comhardadh leis an lide mu dheireadh aca. Tha gach sreath ach na dhà a' tòiseachadh leis an aon fhuaim.

'S ann san t-siathamh sreath a-mhàin a nochdas fuaimean nach buin dhan chòrr de na sreathan. Tòisichidh an sreath seo ann am bad glè fhaisg air Meadhan an Òir. Tha na siùbhlaichean stèidhichte no – ma thograr – air an tarraing on ùrlar.

Aig a' char as sìmplidh, 's e AABA BBAB structair a' chumha seo. Tha an dàrna leth mar fhaileas-sgàthain den a' chiad leth. Canaidh Barnaby Brown gur e structair 'fighte-fuaighte' a tha seo, agus esan a' cumail a-mach gur e seo an structar as cumanta ann an ceòl mòr (Brown, 2004, td. 22).

Ma thogas sinn ceist leanailteachd a leithid a structar, chan eil fianais sgrìobhte againn a' dol nas fhaide air ais na an ochdamh linn deug. Ach tha fianais againn ann am pìosan ceòl mòr fhèin a tha fada nas sine.

A1 Himdaridto Himdaridto Himdaridda Himdaridda
A2 Himdaridto Himdaridto Himdaridda Hiharin
B1 Hindaridto Hindaridda Hindarride Hihorodo
A2 Himdaridto Himdaridto Himdaridda Hiharin

B2 Hindaridto Hindaridda Hindarride Hindaridda
B3 Hindaridda Hindaridto Hindarride Hihorodo
A2 Himdaridto Himdaridto Himdaridda Hiharin
B4 Hindaridde Hindaridto Hindaridda Hihorodo

	A1	1122
	A2	1123
	B1	4567
Mar an t-ùrlar, tha na sreathan A seasmhach,	A2	1123
agus tha na sreathan B nas caochlaidich.		
	B2	4565
Anns gach sreath tha dà chàraid de dh'fhaclan le ochd no seachd lidean,	B3	5467
anns a' cho-roinn 9:5 san ùrlar agus 13:3 sna siùbhlaichean.	A2	1123
	B4	6457

Dealbh 5. Structair Cumha MhicFhionghain, Canntaireachd agus Siùbhlaichean.

Bheir làmh-sgrìobhainn Ap Huw bho 1613 bunait structair co-sheirme dhuinn a tha stèidhichte air clàrsaireachd sa Chuimrigh aig deireadh nam meadhan aoisean. Tha e coltach gun robh buaidh aig cleachdaidhean ciùil agus bàrdachd taobh a-muigh crìochan na Cuimrigh orra, mar a sgrìobh Gruffudd Hiraethog ann an 1561:

> *Mwrthan [Murrough O'Brien] ... commanded everyone to secure and correctly classify the twenty-four [musical] measures and to keep them authentically, un-muddled, and to classify the gamut each one together, no more strange than for a good reader to recognize when a letter or word or syllable is left out from sense* (Harper, 2007, tdd. 110-11).

Ann an làmh-sgrìobhainn Ap Huw nochdaidh na h-aon chumaidhean 's a nochdas ann am pìobaireachd, ach tha iad air an riochdachadh an seo le seòrsa de 'binary code' leis na h-àireamhan aon agus neoni.

'S urrainn dhan 'binary code' seo caochladh shreathan de co-sheirm a riochdachadh le nota eatarra, an 'double tonic' a tha na bhun-stèidh do na ceudan de dh'fhuinn traidiseanta Albannach, gun iomradh air ceòl mòr. Tha seo a' cur an cèill gun robh prionnsabalan structarail gan stèidheachadh tràth anns an dùthchas Cheilteach ann an dòigh buileach eas-chruthach, pàtranan bun-os-cionn agus fo chomhair an cùil nam measg.

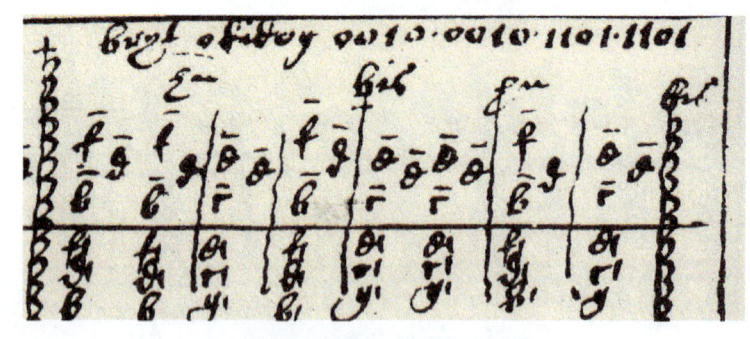

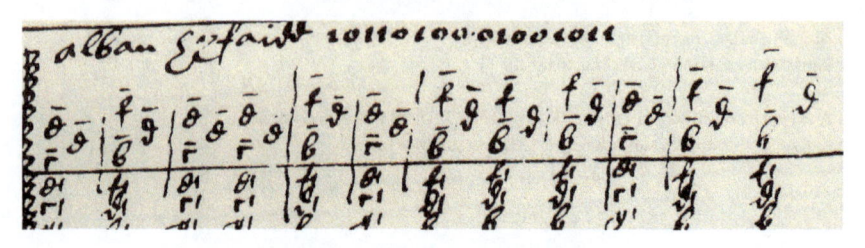

Dealbh 6. Structaran, Ap Huw MS.

Às dèidh dhuinn pàtranan cumanta a shònrachadh ann an òran sìmplidh Gàidhealach agus ann an ceòl mòr na pìoba – an ionnstramaid as suaicheanta dhan Ghàidhealtachd – a bheil teans ann gu bheil na h-aon structaran rim faicinn anns an stuth lèirsinneach as suaicheanta dhan Ghàidhealtachd?

Tòisichidh sinn le leanailteachd – eagal 's gu bheil daoine fhathast fo bhuaidh Hugh Trevor-Roper (1983, tdd. 15-41). Chaidh clò, 'twill 2:1', coltach ri tartan san latha an-diugh, a lorg an Loch Tatha ged nach robh an dath maireannach. Chaidh a dhèanamh mun cuairt air ceithir ceud bliadhna ro Chrìosd (Dixon, 2004, tdd. 134, 155).

'S e eisimpleir eile, pìos tartain bhon Eaglais Bhric anns an deach dathan na clòimhe fhèin a chleachdadh. Tha seo cha mhòr an aon rud ri plaide buachaille ar linne fhèin, ach chaidh a dhèanamh mu dhà cheud bliadhna às dèidh Chrìosd (Cheape, 2006, td. 7).

Bhathar a' meas aig an àm ud, timcheall air AD 200, gun robh clò mar sin, far a bheil dà dhath gan cleachdadh gus trì no ceithir dathan a dhèanamh, a' sònrachadh nan Cailleanach àrsaidh. Thug an Dr Fraser Hunter, aig Taigh-Tasgaidh Nàiseanta na h-Alba, an dealbh-camara seo dhuinn, a thog e de ghaisgeach Cailleanach ann am braighdeanas air a bheil briogais bhreac. Nochdaidh e air an aon phàirt mhaireannach de dh'ìomhaigh thomadach umha Caracalla ann am Morocco, a chaidh a dhèanamh cuideachd mu dhà cheud bhliadhna às dèidh Chrìosd.

Bha an dealbhadair air a chur thuige am breacan a riochdachadh. Chleachd e ceàrnagan beaga de mheatailtean diofraichte. Dhèanamaid dheth gun robh am breacan na shuaicheantas dha na Cailleanaich agus na annas mòr. Tha e coltach gun robh pàtran diofraichte air gach òsan. Gu mì-fhortanach chan eil fianais

Dealbh 7. Triubhas Breacain air Brat Umha Caracalla *c.*AD 200. Dealbh le Fraser Hunter le a chead.

nitheil eile againn mu bhreacan eadar an t-àm ud agus an t-seachdamh linn deug. Ach nach àghmhor gu bheil am meud sin againn?

Airson fianais sgrìobhte air na Gàidheil agus tartan, feumaidh sinn feitheamh gus deireadh a' cheathramh linn deug, ach chan eil adhbhar a bhith sireadh tuilleadh fianaise às dèidh sin.

> 1500 *Item, for iii elnis of Heland tertane ... a velvet heland coit ... variant cullorit* (Balfour Paul, 1905, td. 436)
>
> 1581 *They use party-coloured garments, and especially striped plaids ... Their ancestors wore party-coloured plaids, variously striped, which custom some of them still retain* (Watkins, 1822, td. 11).
>
> 1594 Ba suichnidh on ietsomh hi tréchumuscc Fer Fene la saine a narm a nerraidh a naladh ... oircnib a ccresa tara náirdnibh allamuigh dia mbrataibh.
>
> *(They were recognised among the Irish soldiers by the distinction of their arms and clothing ... for their exterior dress was mottled cloaks of many colours)* (Walsh and Ó Lochlainn, 1948, td. 72).
>
> 1618 *a warm stuff of divers colours, which they call tartane ...* (Taylor, 1618, td. 49).
>
> 1689 *Tot chlamyde intextos ostentat et ille colores/ Sole quot adverso curvata in nubibus iris (He displays as many colours woven into his plaid as the rainbow ...)* (Murdoch, 1888, td. 145).

Ach ciamar a tha seo a' bualadh air ceist structair? Chan eil sinn a' cumail a-mach gu bheil dàimh adhbharach (*causal*) eadar pìobaireachd agus breacan, ach anns an dà ealain, a tha nan dlùth 's nan inneach air a' Ghàidhealtachd, tha an aon smachd cruthachail ri fhaicinn. Chì sinn an eugsamhlachd as motha de bhuaidh an co-bhuinn leis an eugsamhlachd as lugha de bhun-stuth.

Chan eil ach ceithir dathan anns a' phàtran ris an canar san latha an-diugh Breacan MhicFhionghain, ach tha suidheachadh nan dathan mun cuairt air a' mheadhan, an tricead agus an leathad a rèir àireamh nan snàithlean air an riaghladh gu faiceallach. Tha breacan air a chruthachadh le bhith a' dèanamh faileas-sgàthain de dh'òrdugh nan snàithlean dathte san dlùth, agus an uair sin le bhith a' fighe an aon òrdugh san inneach. 'S e faileas-sgàthain dùbailte a th' ann le cuartachadh mar a bhun-stèidh, le innleachd sheòlta.

'S e faileas-sgàthain cuideachd a tha ann an Cumha MhicFhionghain, ach chan ann dhen aon seòrsa. Ma ghabhar ri sreath nan dathan agus ma smaoinichear air gach dath mar snàithlean sa bhreacan, nochdaidh cumadh mar a tha san dealbh.

'S dòcha gu bheil cus dhathan diofraichte sa bhreacan seo. Ach ma choimheadar air an structair fhèin, tha e simplidh is breagha.

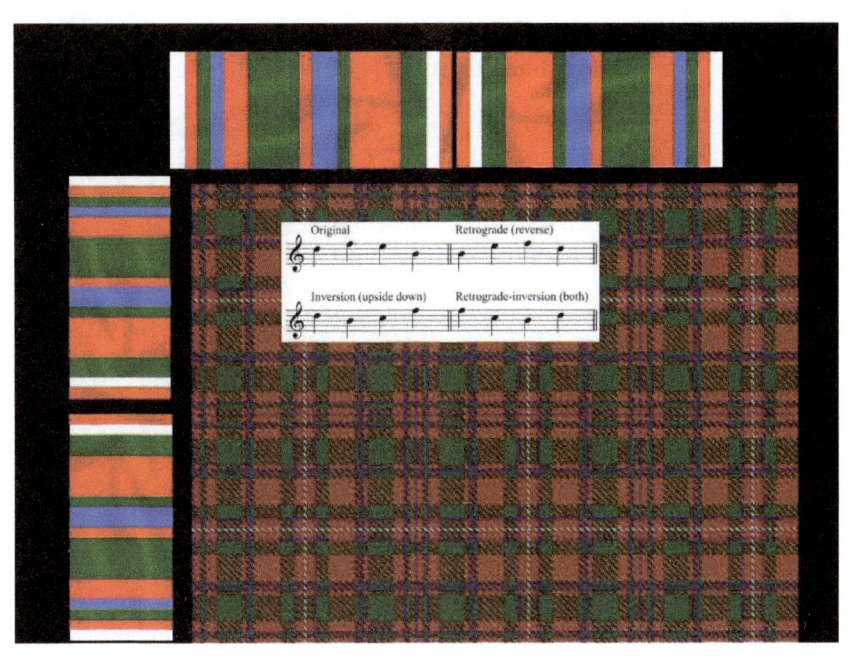

Leanailteachd crutha ann an dùthchas nan Gàidheal   *Meg Bateman agus John Purser*

Dealbh 8. Cruth Breacan MhicFhionghain – *Leabhar Comunn nam Fìor Ghael* II.

A **Himdaridto**	B **Hindaridto**	B **Hindaridto**	A **Himdaridto**
Himdaridto	**Hindaridda**	**Hindaridda**	**Himdaridto**
Himdaridda	Hindarride	Hindarride	**Himdaridda**
Himdaridda	**Hihorodo**	**Hindaridda**	**Hiharin**

A **Himdaridto**	A **Himdaridto**	B **Hindaridda**	B Hindaridde
Himdaridto	**Himdaridto**	**Hindaridto**	**Hindaridto**
Himdaridda	**Himdaridda**	Hindarride	**Hindaridda**
Hiharin	**Hiharin**	**Hihorodo**	**Hihorodo**

Dealbh 9. Canntaireachd Cumha MhicFhionghain air a chur mun cuairt agus air fhighe.

11

**An structair as cumanta aig ceòl mòr, AABA BBAB,
air a chur mun cuairt agus air fhighe**

```
A   A   B   A   B   B   A   B
A  aa aa  ab aa ab  ab aa ab
A  aa aa  ab aa ab  ab aa ab
B  ba ba  bb ba  bb bb ba bb
A  aa aa  ab aa ab  ab aa ab
B  ba ba  bb ba  bb bb ba bb
B  ba ba  bb ba  bb bb ba bb
A  aa aa  ab aa ab  ab aa ab
B  ba ba  bb ba  bb bb ba bb
```

Dealbh 10. Structair na Pìobaireachd as Cumanta mar Bhreacan.

Feumaidh sinn daingneachadh nach eil sinn a' cumail a-mach gu bheil ceangal adhbharach no buaidh dhìreach sam bith eadar ceòl mòr agus am breacan. Ach tha sinn a' tagradh gu bheil dàimh eadar teannachadh agus caochladh, no eadar lughad nan structaran bunaiteach agus meud nan tionndaidhean tron tèid iad, a tha air a toirt gu buil le innleachdachd a tha an urra ri structaran bun-os-cionn, fo chomhair an cùl, agus air an cuartachadh.

Tha sinn air a bhith a' coimhead air leanailteachd crutha ann am bàrdachd agus ann an ceòl, Gàidhlig is Laidinn, agus ann an clò, agus sinn a' dèanamh tagradh gu bheil coltas eatarra ann an structair. Ach tha rudan nas doimhne rin cnuasachd – geoimeatraidh agus co-roinn nan structaran.

Aig a' char as sìmplidh, tha co-roinn an urra ri àireamh nan lidean san t-sreath, agus tòrr eisimpleirean bho linn nam bàrd proifeiseanta dan rèir. Ann an ceòl, tha co-roinn stèidhichte, airson a' mhòr-chuid, air tìm – cò na h-àiteachan aig a bheil an t-atharrachadh as follaisiche, ann an àirde, ruitheam, luathas, no ann an gleusadh a' chiùil (*harmonic implications*) – ann an càs ceòl mòr a rèir nan dos.

Sna h-ealain lèirsinneach, faodar an craiceann no an leac a bhith air an taghadh agus an dealbhadh ron àm. Às dèidh sin, chaidh an roinn a rèir cunntasachd geo-imeatraidh mhionaidich. Chaidh geoimeatraidh ionnsachadh ann an Èirinn tràth sna meadhan aoisean, agus 's dòcha, gun do thachair an aon rud an Alba cuideachd (m.e. Dicuil, 1967; Lozovsky, 2004). Bha an rùilear agus an gobhal-roinn riatanach, gun teagamh.

Bha sgoilearan mar Carl Nordenfalk agus Robert Stevick a' sealltainn sin, agus am measg an luchd-ealain phractaigich, bha John Cargill, George agus Iain Bain, agus Aidan Meehan (m.e. Bain, 1951; Meehan, 1995). Ann an 1930,

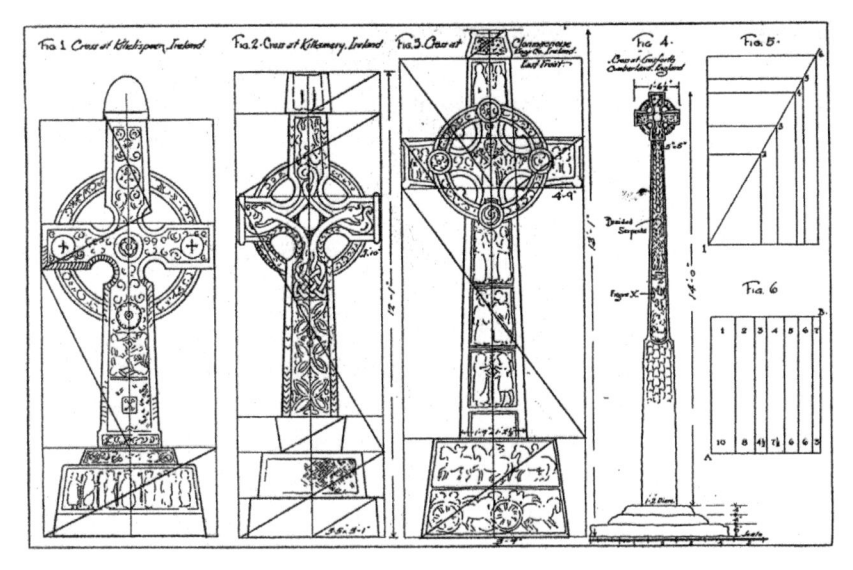

Dealbh 11. Dealbhan Chargill.

dh'aithnich Cargill, clachair ann an Chicago, gun robh co-roinn nan croisean Ceilteach air an robh e ag obair air nòs Pythagoras (Cargill, 1930; Blake 1933, tdd. 1-16).

A rèir Robert Stevick, b' e Bruce-Mitford a b' fheàrr a thuig co-chur an dealbhachaidh (Stevick, 1994, td. 146 agus faic Kendrick et al., 1956, 1960). Seo na tha aig Nordenfalk ri ràdh mu shoilleireachadh Ceilteach:

> *Thanks to its geometric regularity this controlling framework strikes the eye immediately. By contrast, the ornamental fillings are... at first sight difficult to disentangle. However, on closer inspection they too follow an orderly scheme – carefully worked out with compass and ruler.... Calculated down to their smallest details, they are sometimes as complex as any mathematical group theorem* (Nordenfalk, 1977, td. 16).

Ann an rannsachadh Robert Stevick chì sinn dòigh-obrach shaidheansail fo chomhair dealbhachaidh agus co-roinn, is e a' toirt a-steach samhlachas àir-eamhail, mar a rinn John MacQueen (Stevick, 1994). Ann an 1903 thuirt Romilly Allen:

> *It is characteristic of the Celtic treatment of the symbol of the cross both in Scotland and Ireland that the form is subjected to artistic variations, breaking the baldness of its outlines into sweeping curves ... The 'music' produced by all these different types of pattern is very different from the tonality of Classical decorative art* (Allen, 1903, td. lvii).

Air an aon ràmh, sgrìobh Nordenfalk:
> More than any other style of decoration, with the possible exception of the fully fledged Moslem arabesque, Hiberno-Saxon art aims at kinetic effects.... The "music" produced by all these different types of pattern is very different from the tonality of Classical decorative art

(Nordenfalk, 1977, td. 17).

Faodaidh beachdan eadar-chuspaireil tòrr a shealltainn mun cheist againne. Bheir a leithid 'I listen with my eyes' aig MacCaoig dhan chuimhne.

'S e an smachd air geoimeatraidh a' chearcaill a bheir an ruitheam fileanta agus an leanailteachd do dh'ealain na Gàidhealtachd. Gabhaidh na cearcaill, na cuairteagan agus na boghachan iomadh cruth. Tha fear den fheadhainn as annasaiche le trì cuairtean anns a bheil trì fir air an cuartachadh agus an casan agus an gàirdeanan nan snaidhm. Tha e ann an Leabhar Cheanannais (Coláiste na Tríonóide, Baile Átha Cliath LS 58), f. 130r. Chuir Alan Nowell air shùilean dhuinn gur dòcha gur e riochdachadh dannsa lùth-chleasach a tha an seo. Bha teòiridh Nowell stèidhichte air an eòlas aige air dannsa Wyresdale à Northumbria. Rinn Nowell an aon seòrsa moladh a thaobh leac-uaghach às an naoidheamh linn ann am Mìgeil (Meigle, Siorr. Pheairt) (Nowell, 2005, tdd. 120-24).

Ma tha Leabhar Cheanannais, Mìgeil agus Wyresdale pìos air falbh bho Ghàidhealtachd an fhicheadamh linn, beachdaichibh air an tuairisgeul seo air An Dannsa Mhòr a chunnacas ann an Eilean Eige, mu 1950:
> The dancers join hands to form a ring, all facing inwards, the hands being held just below shoulder height, with arms straight.... During the chorus, the dancers hop round on the left foot, keeping their right legs extended towards the centre of the ring, with legs straight, and the feet about 18in from the floor

(Flett agus Flett, 1953, td. 120).

Agus eagal 's nach saoil sibh gun gabhadh an rud dèanamh idir idir, tha e ga chur an gnìomh.[3] Seallaibh cuideachd air an dealbh òirdheirc seo bho *Leabhar Comunn nam Fior Ghaël* bhon bhliadhna 1880:

Seallaidh sinn aon chearcall eile dhuibh – cearcall a chaidh a dhèanamh gus coilltean na h-Alba a shàbhaladh o bhith air an losgadh gach bliadhna le Bànrigh an Taoibh Tuath a shiùbhladh tro na speuran ann an carbad glainne. Chaidh an sgeulachd a chlàradh leis an Urr. A. Dòmhnallach ann an Uibhist (McDonald, 1901-3, td. 431).

Chan e cearcall de dhannsairean a th' againn an seo, ach naoi càraidean de phìobairean, 's gach fear a' seinn an aon phort, gach càraid a' dol mun cuairt, agus an cearcall slàn a' cuartachadh. Bha a' Bhànrigh air a beò-ghlacadh leis an t-sealladh seo chun na h-ìre gun tàinig an tuaineal oirre agus thuit i às na speuran gu a bàs.

Leanailteachd crutha ann an dùthchas nan Gàidheal *Meg Bateman agus John Purser*

Tuairisgeul air *An Dannsa Mòr* à Eige *c.*1950:
"In the chorus section, the 12 all male dancers join hands with arms straight just below shoulder height, and extend their right legs into the centre of the circle thus formed, and hop round on the left foot."

Dealbh 12. Leac Mhìgeil (9mh linn) le Dannsaircan.

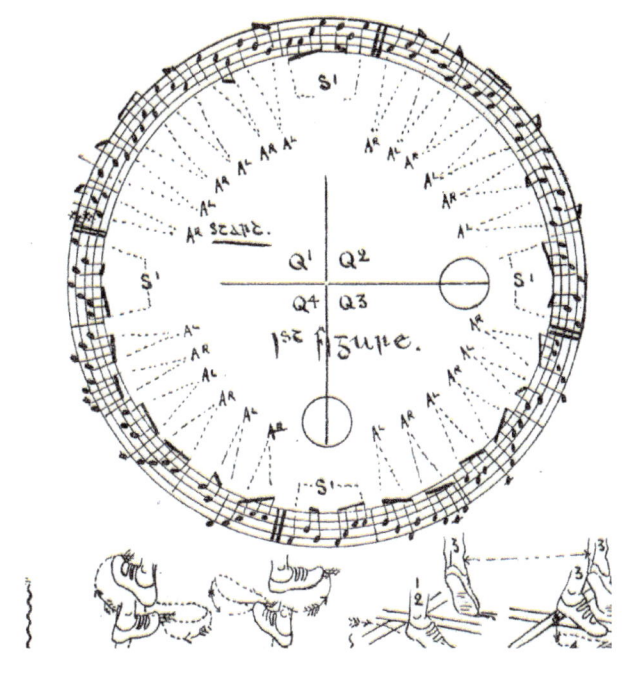

Dealbh 13. 'The sword dance', *Leabhar Comunn nam Fìor Ghaël*, Iml. II, Clàr LXVII, 1880.

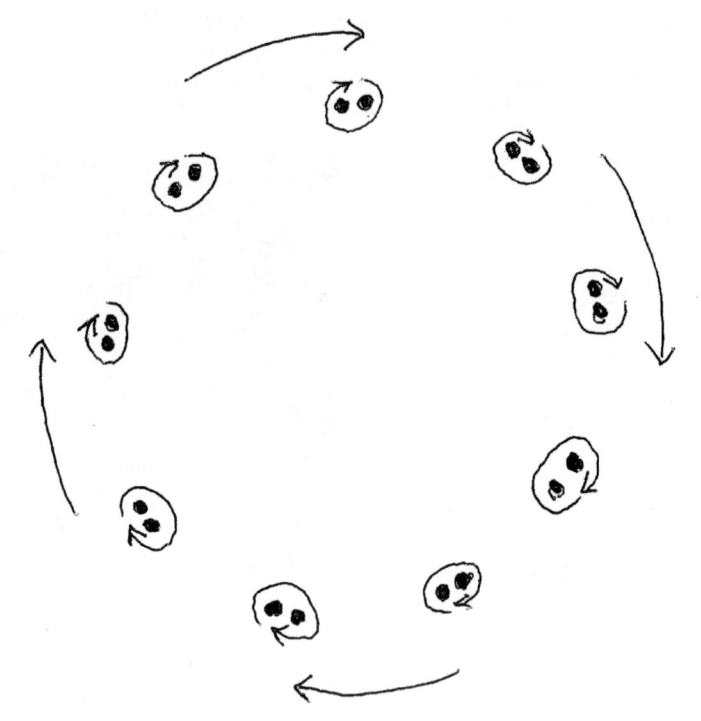

Dealbh 14. Cearcall Phìobairean.

Coimheadaidh sinn air smuaintean air a bheil structair cearcallach, fighte-fuaighte no snìomhach. Tha seanfhacal a' cur na bàidhe an cèill a bha aig na Gàidheil air cruinnead:

> Na trì rudan as brèagha air an t-saoghal: long fo h-uidheam, boireannach leatromach, agus gealach làn (Shaw, 1986, td. 33).

Ann am bàrdachd thràth, bha an domhan ri mholadh air sgàth a chruinne. Seo 'Altus Prosatur', air a chur às leth Choluim Chille (Clancy agus Márkus, 1994, tdd. 48-9):

> *Magni Dei virtutibus appenditur dialibus*
> *globus terrae et circulus abyssi magnae inditus ...*
> (Trìd feartan Dhè mhòir crochar an cruinne-cè agus cuirear an t-aigeann mòr mun cuairt air.)

Airson sgrìobhadair *An Tenga Bithnua* (9mh–10mh linn), bha e loidsigeach gum biodh gach rud fiosaigeach cruinn a chionn 's gu bheil Dia fhèin cruinn, gun tùs no èis (Stokes, 1905, td. 107):

> 'Cenco accid-si', ol se, 'is i cruinne dorraladh cach duil cid iar ndelbuib domain. Ar is i torachta chruinne doralta na nime, 7 is i torachta

doronta na secht muire immacuairt, 7 is i torachta dorónad in talam,
ocus i torachta cruinne doimchellat na renda roth cruinn in domuin,
7 iss i cruinne atchither cuairt in richidh uasail, iss i cruinne atchither
cuairt grene is esca. Is deithbeir uile sein, ar is toruchta cen tosach cen
forcend in Coimde ro bhithbhai 7 bhithbias 7 dorighne na huili sin. Is
aire is i ndeilb chruind ro damnaiged in doman'.

> *'Though you do not see it,' he said, 'it is in roundness that each element has been appointed. It is in roundness that the heavens have been appointed, and the seven seas, the lands, in roundness that the stars circle about the round wheel of the earth, in roundness the circuit of the sun and the moon, for roundness without beginning and without end is the Lord, who always was and always shall be and who made all those things. That is why the world has been embodied in round form...'* (Dillon, 1948, tdd. 141–2).

Chìthear cearcaill gan cleachdadh ann an deas-ghnàthan thairis air mìle bliadhna, mar eisimpleir bho Lorica Mhugróin a bha na aba air Eilean Idhe eadar 965 agus 981, far a bheilear a' dèanamh cearcall dìona mun cuairt air an neach-labhairt (Murphy, 1956, tdd. 34-5, rann 6):

Cros Chríst sair frim einech,
Cros Chríst síar fri fuined.
Tes, túaid cen nach n-anad,
  Cros Chríst cen nach fuirech.

Christ's Cross eastwards facing me,
Christ's Cross west towards the sunset.
South and north, unceasingly,
May Christ's Cross be immediately.

Mìle bliadhna na dhèidh, chunnaic an t-Urr. Dotair Stiùbhart cearcall loisgte ga chleachdadh san naoidheamh linn deug ann an Loch Abar aig còig boireannaich tron robh iad a' cur pàiste ann an oidhirp faighinn cuidhte agus an droch shùil. Agus san fhicheadamh linn tha Mairead Fay Shaw (1986, td. 24) a' dèanamh tuairisgeul air seunadh na bliadhn' ùire anns an robh cearcall, teine agus gluasad deiseil na lùib agus air rann a tha fhathast ga aithris san latha an-diugh.

  Mo chaisean Callaig ann nam phòcaid,
  'S math an ceò thig às an fhear ud,
  Thèid e deiseil air na pàistean
   Gu h-àraid air bean an taighe ...
  Fosgail an doras is leig a-staigh mi.

Tha *A Description of the Western Isles* aig Màrtainn MacGilleMhàrtainn (Martin, 1698) loma-làn de dh'iomraidhean air gluasad cearcallach a rèir na grèine aig bàtaichean, beathaichean agus eile.

Far a bheil cearcall, tha meadhan. Tha an dealbh ainmeil de chrùnadh an treas rìgh Alasdair an Sgàin an 1249 bho làmh-sgrìobhainn de *Scotichronicon* le Walter Bower[5] ga shealltainn air cnoc cruinn ann am meadhan na rìoghachd, faisg air na mairbh sa chladh – tha cearcall àite agus cearcall tìme an sàs an seo. 'S dòcha gum faodar coimhead air cleachdaidhean ainmeachaidh mar seòrsa de chearcall anns a bheil gach ginealach ga ath-chruthachadh san ath ghinealach. Thuirt Anne Grant (1811, td. 51):

> *No Highlander ever once thought of himself as an individual ... In the most minute, as well as the most serious concerns, he felt himself one of the many connected together by ties of the most lasting and endearing. He considered himself merely with reference to those who had gone before, and those who were to come after him; to these immortals who lived in deathless song and heroic narrative.*

Tha cearcallachd ga faicinn ann an togalaichean agus structaran ro-eachdraidheil cuideachd bho Linn na Cloiche. Gun teagamh cha b' e na Gàidheil a thog iad seo, ach tha e soilleir gun robh leanailteachd eadar an dà chultar. Tha an t-ainm Brú na Bóinne fhèin a' dearbhadh gun robh an samhlachas ga thuigsinn aig na Gàidheil. Mar a thuirt John Carey (1990, td. 30):

> *In seeking to understand the pre-Christian background of Irish civilisation we must consider, side by side with the insights afforded by the comparative study of Indo-European, the possible influence of the mysterious but impressive culture of the megalith-builders.*

Ged nach eil fios againn dè tha na comharran 'cupa is cearcaill' a' ciallachadh ann a leithid Cille Mhàrtainn, tha e soilleir gun robh an cruth cruinn cudromach. Aig Maes Howe tha an dà chuid, an càrn fhèin agus am balla mun cuairt air, cruinn. Tha sgrùdaidhean àrc-eòlach a' sealltainn gu bheil e coltach gun robh na daoine a bha fuireach san taigh-chuibhle a lorgadh sa ghainmhich ann an Uibhist a' leantail na grèine tron latha agus trom beatha, is iad a' dèanamh obair na maidne san àird an ear, a' cadal san àird an iar, agus a' tiodhlacadh nam marbh fòdhpa sa cheann a tuath (Pearson et al., 2004).

A' tionndadh gu structaran cruinne aig na Gàidheil fhèin, chì sinn ballachan cruinn mu chladhan, eaglaisean agus manachainnean air feadh na Gàidhealtachd. Tha eisimpleirean làidir mu eaglais an Naoimh Blàthan agus mun chlochar thràth aig Sgor nam Ban Naomha ann an Canaigh. Tha an aon chruth ri fhaicinn ann an crannagan agus bothanan àirigh, agus, aig an ìre as suaicheanta, mu na croisean àrda le fàinne mun cuairt orra aig na Gàidheil agus aig na Cruithnich. Dh'fhaodadh am fàinne a bhith a' samhlachadh iomadh rud fiù 's aig an aon àm: Crìosd mar *Sol Invictus*, no Dia mar nì cruinn mar a chunnacas gu h-àrd san *Tenga Bithnua*, is samhlaidhean a' chreidimh phàganaich a' dol nan samhlaidhean Crìosdail. Tha crois an Naoimh Màrtainn an Ì agus crois Chille Dhaltain an Ìle sgeadaichte le cnapan cruinn de nathraichean – samhla na h-aiseirigh is iad a' tighinn às an talamh is a' cur dhiubh an craicinn. 'S dòcha cuideachd gu bheil am fàinne a' riochdachadh na tìme, agus a h-uile sìon a' tilleadh gu Dia, mar a mhìnich Johannes Scotus Eriugena san naoidheamh linn (O'Meara, 1988, tdd. 52-3):

> *For the whole river first flows forth from its source, and through its channel the water which first wells up in the source continues to flow always without any break to whatever distance it extends. So the Divine Goodness and Essence and Life and Wisdom and everything which is in the source of all things first flow down into the primordial causes and make them to be, then through the primordial causes they descend in an ineffable way through the orders of the universe that accommodate them, flowing forth continuously through the higher to the lower; and return back again to their source through the most secret channels of nature by a most hidden course.*

Is dòcha gu bheil ceangal ri dhèanamh eadar sealladh Scotus Eriugena agus eachdraidh tùs nan Gàidheal a rèir *Lebor Gabála Érenn* agus eile a bhith gun iomradh air eachdraidh tùs an t-saoghail (Stewart Macalister, 1938-56), ged a tha na Gàidheil fhèin a' dol air ais gu Scota nighean Pharaoh, mar a b' eòl don t-seanchaidh aig crùnadh Alasdair III an Sgàin an 1249 (faic Watt et al., 1990, td. 288). 'S dòcha gu bheil beachd an seo gu bheil an saoghal ga shìor-chruthachadh aig Dia ann an tìm chearcallach. Tha tuigse gu bheil tìm cearcallach ga cur an cèill le Mìosachan Coligny aig na Gaill sa Fhraing on dàrna linn AD oir tha cuairt trithead bliadhna an sàs mus bi gluasad na grèine agus na gealaiche a' còrdadh ri chèile a-rithist. Tha modal tìm fhèin cruinn ann an inneal pàipeir ann an làmh-sgrìobhainn a bha aig Clann Mhic Bheatha bhon 15mh linn, is Aingeal Pachomius a' tomhadh Là na Càsga (McRoberts, 1968, td. 173).

Tha modal tìm cearcallaich ga fhaicinn san deas-ghnàth a tha ceangailte ri Taigh nam Bodach ann an Gleann Cailliche faisg air Gleann Lìobhainn, far am biodh an sprèidh ag ionaltradh tron t-samhradh. Thèid teaghlach de chlachan a thoirt a-mach Là Buidhe Bealltainn agus thèid an cur a-staigh a-rithist a' chiad là den t-Samhain. 'S cinnteach gu bheil ainm a' ghlinne fhèin samhlachail, is a' chailleach – no an nàdar – a' dol na màthair òg a-rithist sa Chèitean (Sjoestedt, 1982, Caib. 3; Ross, 2000, Caib. 7).

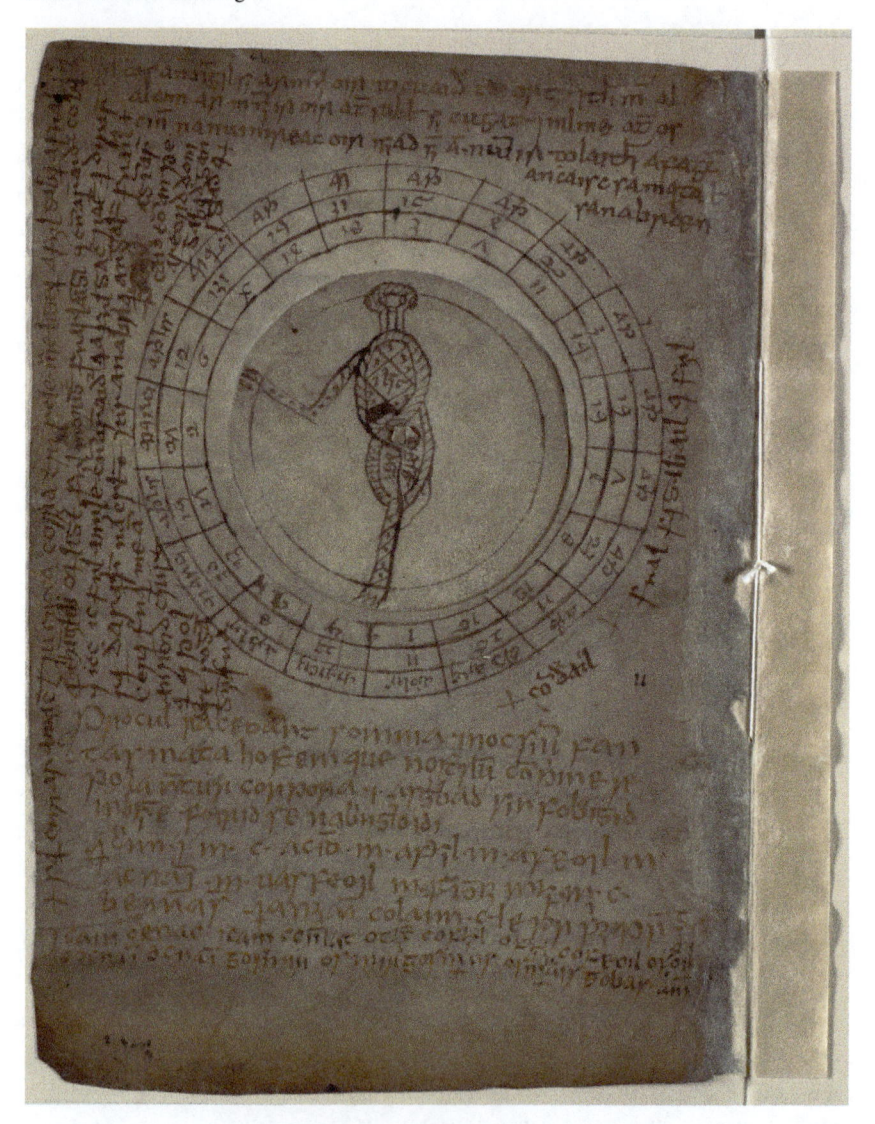

Dealbh 15. Aingeal Pachomius a' tomhadh Là na Càsga ann an LS le Clann Mhic Bheatha (NLS Adv. MS 72.1.2, f. 130 v.), 15mh linn.

Tha e coltach nach eil tìm a' sgur a ruith fiù 's san t-sìorraidheachd. Tha na seann òrain 'Crò Chinn Tàile' agus 'Dol dhan Taigh' (Stewart agus MacDonald, 1998, òrain 4 agus 10) cuideachd stèidhichte air gluasad sprèidh eadar am baile agus na h-àirighean, agus na seinneadairean a' faicinn na sìorraidheachd co-shìnte leis an àm làthaireach.

Dol dhan taigh, dol dhan taigh,
Dol dhan taigh bhuan leat,

Dealbh 16. Taigh nam Bodach; dealbh-camara le Meg Bateman.

>   Dol dhan taigh geamhraidh,
>   Dol dhan taigh samhraidh.

A bharrachd air smuaintean cearcallach, tha iomadh structair cearcallach ri fhaicinn ann an sgeadachadh buill-acainn agus ealain nan Gàidheal. A bheil dùnadh ann am bàrdachd chlasaigeach, mar eisimpleir, no siubhal cearcallach sna h-immrama no ann an ceòl mòr nuair a thilleas e dhan ùrlar às dèidh grunn shiùbhlaichean, nam faileas den tuigse gu bheil tìm agus am fìorachas fhèin cruinn?

'S ann à Babylon a thàinig ìomhaigh na *Rota Fortunae* no cuibhle an fhortain an toiseach, ceangailte ris an naoidheamh cearcall de nèamh far a bheil na rionnagan. Bha fèill mhòr air an ìomhaigh seo aig na bàird Ghàidhealach eadar An Clàrsair Dall, Iain Ruadh Stiùbhart agus Màiri Mhòr nan Òran. Sna meadhan aoisean bha daoine san Roinn Eòrpa a' smaoineachadh oirre mar chuibhle a thionndaidheadh a' bhan-dia Fortuna is cha b' fhada gus am biodh an duine a bha shuas shìos. Seach an duine fhèin a bhith gluasad, tha e sònraichte gun do lean na Gàidheil an dòigh as sine is iadsan a' samhlachadh na cuibhle ri cearcall na grèine:

>   Chaidh a' chuibhle mun cuairt,
>   ghrad thionndaidh gu fuachd am blàths (Matheson, 1970, td. 58)

Bha bràistean ann an cruth cruinn glè chumanta air a' Ghàidhealtachd do dh'fhireannaich agus do bhoireannaich, agus bha orrachan no seuntan mar an ceudna cruinn, mar eisimpleir A' Chlach Dhearg, clach criostail a bha buadhmhor an aghaidh galaran cruidh (faic Drummond, 1881, tdd. 118, 121-2).

Tha iomadh dealbh againn ann an Drummond (1881) de sgiathan Gàidhealach. 'S ann cruinn a bha iad, seach air chruth iarann-aodaich, eagraichte ann am beartas sgeadachaidh le cnapan cruinne.

Ann am beul-aithris, tha coireachan draoidheil aig an Dagda, aig Brìghde agus aig Fionn, a tha daonnan làn agus comasach air daoine ath-bheòthachadh. 'S dòcha gur e sin a tha ri fhaicinn sa chlàr de Choire Gundestrup far a bheil na gaisgich mharbha gan tumadh ann an coire agus a' marcachd air falbh, beò.[5] Chan e a-mhàin gu bheil na soithichean fhèin cruinn ach gu bheil iad an sàs ann am beatha eile a thoirt do dhaoine marbha:

> Chunnaic am Fear Beag Iosal Lapanach nis Cailleach Mhòr thar tomhais am meudachd tighinn 's stòpan ath-bheothachaidh na làimh … Chuir ise corrag às an stòpan ath-bheothachaidh ann am beul an fhir a bha làimh ris, 's leum e beò (Campbell, 1891, td. 255).

Tionndaidheamaid a-nis gu structaran fìghte-fuaighte seach cruinn. Tha obair snaidhm na dòigh sgeadachaidh cho cumanta ri gin ann an ealain na Gàidhealtachd – ann an cloich, làmh-sgrìobhainnean is obair meatailt. Chithear pàtranan eas-chruthach anns a bheil rudan diofraichte air an ceangal còmhla agus air an aonachadh. Mu leithid, thuirt Françoise Henry (1965, tdd. 210-11):

> *For an Irishman of the eighth century there were relations between the different parts of the world, between living beings of all kinds and even inanimate things which we, with our scientific categories, are no longer able to understand.*

Anns na sgeulachdan cuideachd chì sinn ceanglaichean eadar beathaichean agus daoine, lusan agus fiù 's uisge. Mar eisimpleir, bha màthair Oisein na fiadh; bha ceangal eadar clann MhicCodruim agus na ròin; agus ann an *Tochmarc Étaine*, thèid Étain ath-bhreith iomadh turas – na h-uisge, na cuileig is na h-iasg (Dillon, 1948, tdd. 54-8).

'S dòcha gu bheil obair snaidhm a' riochdachadh cheanglaichean cuideachd eadar saoghal nam beò 's nam marbh – eadar spiorad agus stuth. Bidh daoine a' dol gu furasta eadar an saoghal seo agus 'am baile ud thall', mar eisimpleir nuair a choimheadas gille tro tholl ann an sgeulachd Oisein ach am faic e cho mòr 's a bha na fèidh agus na coin aig an Fhèinn (Bruford agus MacDonald, 1994, tdd. 171-6).

Tha an aon chreideamh a' nochdadh, gu bheil na mairbh an làthair san t-saoghal, ann an sgeulachd a chaidh a chruinneachadh san fhicheadamh linn ann an Eilean Idhe (Macleod Banks, 1931, tdd. 55-60) agus anns an dàn 'A Bé Find' bhon naoidheamh linn (Murphy 1956, tdd. 106-7):

> Ghabh e iongantas agus thuirt e, 'Cò às a thàinig thu?' Thuirt e, 'Cha tàinig mi dhe cloinn Adhaimh agus cha bhuin mi dhut agus dhan dream bhon tàinig Abraham, ach bha mi an seo mus robh duine eile.' Agus thuirt e, 'Chuir thu mi à mo dhachaigh.' 'Tha mi duilich,' thuirt e, 'tha mi duilich. Cha robh mise a' ciallachadh sin idir, thuirt e, ''s e dìreach an crann gun do bhuail e air clach.'

Ad-chiam cách for cach leth,	(Chì sinne càch air gach taobh
ocus níconn-acci nech:	agus chan fhaic duine sinne:
teimel imorbais Ádaim	's e dorchadas peacadh Àdhaimh
dodon-aircheil ar áraim.	a tha gar cleith bhon dream a chunntadh sinn).

Dh'fhaodadh obair snaidhm a bhith a' riochdachadh làthaireachd Dhè sa Chruthachadh, smuain air a bheil fianais ann an litreachas. San dàn 'Meallach a bheith i n-ucht oiléin', tha Dia a' cumail smachd air a h-uile rud; san 'Hafgerdingadrápa' no 'The Lay of the Towering Waves', dàn ann an Lochlannais air a chlàradh anns an *Landnámabók* fo bhuaidh diadhachd nan Gàidheal, tha na seabhagan air spiris air làimh Dhè. Anns an dà eisimpleir seo, tha e soilleir nach eil an aon sgaradh eadar stuth agus spiorad 's a thàinig thugainn tro Phlato agus Augustine.

> Go ro bheannachainn an Coimdhe
>   con-ig uile,
> neamh go muintir gráidh go ngloine,
>   tír, tráigh, tuile.
> *I would bless the Lord Almighty*
>   *who maintains all:*
> *heaven with its pure, loving orders,*
>   *land, shore and water* (McLeod agus Bateman 2007, tdd. 14-17).

> *I pray the blameless monk-prover,*
> *Our Father, my journey to further,*
> *Heaven's Lord, may he bless and let hover*
> *his hawk-perching hand over my head* (Smyth, 1984, td. 173).

Rinn an t-Urr. Robert Kirk co-ionannachd eadar cruinnead, gluasad agus beatha anns *The Secret Commonwealth* bho 1692 (Kirk, 1976, tdd. 55-6):

> ... *nothing perisheth, but (as the Sun and Year) everie thing goes in a Circle, Lesser or Greater, and is renewed and refreshed in its revolutiones, as 'tis another, That Every Body in the Creatione,*

> moves, (which is a sort of Life:) and that nothing moves but what has another Animall moving on itt and so on, to the utmost minutest corpuscle that's capable to be a receptacle of Lyfe.

Agus chunnaic Seán Ó Tuathaláin no John Toland (1670-1722) gu bheil ath-cholainneadh – mar a dh'ainmicheadh a thaobh Étaine gu h-àrd – na phàirt den aon phròiseas:

> [We find] in these books the rites and formulations of the Druids, together with their Divinity and Philosophy; especially their two grand doctrines of the eternity and incorruptibility of the universe, and the incessant Revolution of all beings and forms, are very specially, tho' sometimes very figuratively express'd. Hence their Allanimation and Transmigration (Toland, 1813, td. 82).

Cò aige tha fios nach e an gluasad seo nuair a ghabhas spiorad na beatha diofar chruthan a tha ga riochdachadh anns na snìomhanan a chithear air na buill cloiche ro-eachdraidheil a lorgadh air feadh ceann a tuath na h-Alba?[6] Gun teagamh, tha snìomhanan cumanta ann an ealain Chrìosdail cuideachd, eadar clachan mar a' chrois aig Hilton of Cadboll agus an duilleag 'Chi Rho' an Leabhar Cheanannais, 's iad 's dòcha a' riochdachadh facal Dhè a' gabhail iomadh cruth tron chruthaidheachd.

Tha a' chlach neònach bhon 7mh-9mh linn às an Riasg Bhuidhe ann an Colbhasa doirbh a mhìneachadh. Tha coltas croise air an dàrna taobh agus bod air an taobh eile. An e fealla-dhà a tha ann no a bheil spiorad Dhè a' gluasad tro gach rud tro ath-ghineamhainn?

Tha am pàipear seo a' sireadh leanailteachd smaoineachaidh. Tha suaip den ìomhaigh a chleachd Scotus Eriugena de Dhia mar abhainn (faic td. 19 shuas) ri fhaicinn sna rannan seo à 'Coilltean Ratharsair' le Somhairle MacGill-Eain (1991, td. 182) agus ann an 'Laoidh nach eil do Lenin' le Fearghas MacFhionnlaigh (Whyte, 1991, td. 84), is iad uile a-mach air feart cumanta a' sruthadh tro gach rud:

> Tha eòl air slighe an t-snodhaich
> a' drùdhadh suas gu ghnothach,
> am fìon sìor ùrar beothail
> Gun fhios dha fhèin, gun oilean.

Agus:

> cailèideascop-Dhia
> beò-dhathan dian-loisgeach ...
>
> leatsa speictream na beatha
> leatsa a-mhàin

Dealbh 17. Riasg Buidhe, Colbhasa. Dealbh-camara clì le cead RCAHMS; dealbh-camara deas le John Purser.

    's leinne an dubhaigeann
    ma dhùnas Tu do shùilean …

Anns na h-aistidhean a sgrìobh Dòmhnall MacLaomainn (1874-1958) airson *Life and Work* eadar 1907 agus 1951, tha creideamh ann an làthaireachd Dhè air thalamh fhathast ri fhaicinn aig ministear na h-Eaglais Stèidhichte san fhicheadamh linn:

> Ciod air bith àite anns a bheil làthaireachd Dhè a' brùchdadh a-steach air cridhe duine, is e sin da-rìreadh taigh Dhè agus geata nèimh… (Murchison, 1988, td. 6).

> Tha na h-ainmhidhean nan oighreachdan air an talamh cho math ri mac an duine, is tha còir as fheàrr aca air, ma tha aois a' daing-neachadh còrach (Murchison, 1988, td. 15).

Gus am pàipear seo a thoirt gu crìoch, tha e soilleir gu bheil luchd-ealain co-aimsireil a' leantail orra a bhith a' cleachdadh structaran cruinn, fighte-fuaighte agus snìomhach, is iad ag aithneachadh dàimh air choreigin eadar iad sin agus dualchas nan Gàidheal. Bha ùidh aig Kate Whiteford ann an snìomh-anan agus ann a bhith a' sgeadachadh na talmhainn anns an obair a chruthaich i mu chuairt air Eden Court Theatre an Inbhir Nis agus air Calton Hill an Dùn Èideann an 1987. Tha leanailteachd ri faicinn eadar an seann taigh cluige ann am Breichinn agus Eaglais na h-Alba ann an Canaigh a dheasaich MacGregor Chalmers an 1914. Mar an ceudna, tha structair cruinn an dùin ri fhaicinn an Lòchran an Dòmhnallaich aig Sabhal Mòr Ostaig.

Thuirt Uilleam MacGill'Ìosa, ann an deasbad air an dàn 'Beinn Dòbhrain', 'Bardic verse ranked visualising much higher than seeing' (Gillies, 1977, td. 45). 'S dòcha gun tèid am beachd seo a leudachadh do dhualchas nan Gàidheal san fharsaingeachd, agus structaran sònraichte gan cleachdadh thairis air na mìltean de bhliadhnachan gus – mar a tha sinn a' cur air adhart an seo – tuigse dhomhainn air ceanglaichean sa chruinne-cè a chur an cèill. 'S dòcha gur e sin a tha a' fàgail nan aon structaran nam bun-stèidh de dh'iomadh seòrsa ealain Ghàidhealaich.

Eàrr-notaichean

1   Air a dhèanamh le David Forrester Wilson (1873-1950). Faic bbc.co.uk/arts/yourpaintings/artists/david-forrester-wilson/paintings/slideshow#/6 (air a ruigsinn air 7.8.15).
2   Faic bbc.co.uk/arts/yourpaintings/artists/william-mctaggart (air a ruigsinn air 7.8.15).
3   Faic https://www.youtube.com/watch?v=dMHkkYWrA1s (air a ruigsinn air 22.2.2015).
4   Faic https://commons.wikimedia.org/wiki/File:Alexander_III_and_Ollamh_R%C3%ADgh.JPG (à Corpus Christi College Cambridge LS 171, f. 206) (air a ruigsinn air 24.9.15). Tha e ri fhaicinn cuideachd ann an Watt, Taylor agus Scott (1990), mu choinneimh td. 288.
5   Faic 'The Gundestrop Cauldron', am measg 'My photos related to norse history and art', http://commons.wikimedia.org/wiki/User:Malene (air a ruigsinn air 7.8.15).
6   Faic, mar eisimpleir, 'Carved Stone Balls from Scotland', http://www.ashmolean.org/ash/britarch/highlights/stone-balls (air a ruigsinn air 7.8.15).

Tùsan

Allen, J. Romilly (1903). *The Early Christian Monuments of Scotland ... with an Introduction by Joseph Anderson*, Cuid I. Dùn Èideann: Society of Antiquaries of Scotland.
Bain, George (1951). *Celtic Art: The Methods of Construction*. Glaschu: MacLellan.
Balfour Paul, James (deas.) (1905). *Accounts of the Lord High Treasurer of Scotland*, imleabhar 6. Dùn Èideann: HMSO.
Blake, C. G. (1933). *Celtic Art*. Chicago: Charles G. Blake.
Blankenhorn, Virginia (2010). 'Observations on the Performance of Irish Syllabic Verse'. *Studia Celtica*, Iml. 44, tdd. 135-44.
Brown, Barnaby (2004). 'Making sense of pibroch', ann an *Donald MacPherson: A Living Legend* (leabhar CD). Glasgow: Siubhal.
Bruford, Alan, agus MacDonald, Donald Archie (1994). 'The Story of Ossian', ann an *Scottish Traditional Tales*, tdd. 171-6. Dùn Èideann: Polygon.
Campbell, John Grigorson (deas.) (1891). *The Fians* (*Waifs and Strays of Celtic Tradition*, IV). Lunnainn: David Nutt.

Carey, John (1990). 'Time, Memory, and the Boyne Necropolis', ann an William Mahon, (deas.), *Proceedings of the Harvard Celtic Colloquium*, Iml. 10, tdd. 24-36.
Cargill, John (1930). 'Notes on The Old Cross at Canna', ann an *The Celtic Cross and Greek Proportion*, tdd. 1-10. Chicago: Charles G. Blake.
Cheape, Hugh (2006). *Tartan: The Highland Habit*. Dùn Èideann: NMSE Publishing.
Clancy, Thomas Owen, agus Gilbert Márkus (1994). *Iona: The Earliest Poetry of a Celtic Monastery*. Dùn Èideann: EUP.
Deutscher, Guy (2011). *Through the Language Glass*. Lunnainn: Arrow House.
Dicuil (825). *Dicuili Liber de Mensura Orbis Terrae*, deas. le J. J. Tierney. Baile Àtha Cliath: Institiúid Ard-Léinn Bhaile Átha Cliath.
Dillon, Myles (1948). *Early Irish Literature*. Chicago: University of Chicago Press.
Dixon, Nicholas (2004). *The Crannogs of Scotland: An Underwater Archaeology*. Stroud: Tempus.
Drummond, James (1881). *Ancient Scottish Weapons*. Dùn Èideann: George Waterston and Sons.
Flett, J. F., and Flett, T. M. (1953). 'Some Hebridean Folk Dances'. *Journal of the English Folk Dance and Song Society*, Iml.7, tdd. 112-27, 182-4.
Gillies, William (1977). 'The Poem in Praise of Ben Dobhrain'. *Lines Review*, Àir. 63, tdd. 42-8.
Gimbutas, Marija (1989). *The Language of the Goddess*. Lunnainn: Thames and Hudson.
Grant, Anne (1811). *Essays on the Superstitions of the Highlanders of Scotland*. Lunnainn: Longman, Hurst, Rees, Orme and Brown.
Harper, Sally (2007). *Music in Welsh Culture before 1650: A Study of the Principal Sources*. Aldershot: Ashgate.
Henry, Françoise (1965). *Irish Art in the Early Christian Period*. Lunnainn: Methuen.
Kendrick, T. D., et al. (1956, 1960). *Evangeliorum Quattuor Codex Lindisfarnensis*. Olten: Urs Graf.
Lazar-Meyn, Heidi Ann (1994). 'Colour Terms in Táin Bó Cúailnge', ann an J. D. Mallory and Gerald Stockman (deas.), *Ulidia: Proceedings of the First International Conference on the Ulster Cycle of Tales*, tdd. 201-6. Beul Feirste: December Publications.
Lozovsky, Natalia (2004). *"The Earth Is Our Book" Geographical Knowledge in the Latin West c.400-1000*. Ann Arbor, MI: University of Michigan Press.
Macalister, R.A. Stewart (1938-56). *Lebor Gabála Érenn*, cuid I-V. Lunnainn: Irish Texts Society.
MacCaig, Norman (1973). 'Moment Musical in Assynt', ann an *The White Bird*, td. 31. Lunnainn: Chatto and Windus.
McDonald, Rev. A. (1901-3). 'The Norsemen in Uist Folklore'. *Saga Book of the Viking Club*, Iml. 3, tdd. 413-33.
MacGill-Eain, Somhairle (1991). *O Choille gu Bearradh/From Wood to Ridge*. Lunnainn: Vintage.
MacGregor, Alasdair Alpin (1937). *The Peat Fire Flame*. Dùn Èideann agus Lunnainn: The Moray Press.
Macleod Banks, M. (1931). 'A Hebridean Version of Colum Cille and St. Oran'. *Folklore*, Iml. 42, Àir. 1, tdd. 55-60.
McLeod, Wilson, agus Bateman, Meg (deas.), Bateman, Meg (eadar-theang.) (2007). *Duanaire na Sracaire/Songbook of the Pillagers: Anthology of Scotland's Gaelic Verse to 1600*. Dùn Èideann: Birlinn.

McRoberts, David (1968). 'Two Hebridean Liturgical Items'. *Innes Review*, 19, tdd. 170-73.
Martin, Martin (1994 [1698]). *A Description of the Western Isles of Scotland*, deas. le Donald J. Macleod. Dùn Èideann: Birlinn
Matheson, William (deas.) (1970). *The Blind Harper (An Clàrsair Dall): The Songs of Roderick Morison and his Music*. Dùn Èideann: SGTS.
Meehan, Aidan (1995). *Celtic Design: A Beginner's Manual*. Lunnainn: Thames and Hudson.
Murchison, T. M. (deas.) (1988). *The Prose Writings of Donald Lamont*. Dùn Èideann: SGTS.
Murdoch, Alexander D. (deas. agus eadar-theang.) (1888). *The Grameid – An Heroic Poem by James Philip*. Dùn Èideann: EUP.
Murphy, Gerard (1956). *Early Irish Lyrics*. Oxford: Clarendon Press.
Newell [*recte* Nowell], Alan (2005). 'An Insular Dance – the dance of the Fer Cengail?' *Archaeology Ireland*, Iml. 19, Àir. 2, tdd. 36-9.
Nordenfalk, Carl (1977). *Celtic and Anglo-Saxon Painting*. Lunnainn: Chatto and Windus.
North, C. N. McIntyre (1882). *Leabhar Comunn nam Fior Ghael: The Book of the Club of True Highlanders*, etc,. 2 iml. Lunnainn: R. Smythson.
O'Meara, J. J. (1988). *Eriugena*. Oxford: Clarendon Press.
Parker Pearson, Mike, et al. (deas.) (2004). *South Uist: Archaeology and History of a Hebridean Island*. Stroud: Tempus.
Ross, Anne, (2000). *Folklore of the Scottish Highlands*. Stroud: Tempus.
Seager, William, agus Allen-Hermanson, Sean (2012). 'Panpsychism', ann an *The Stanford Encyclopedia of Philosophy (Winter 2012 Edition)*, deas. le Edward N. Zalta. Ri fhaighinn bho URL: http://plato.stanford.edu/archives/win2012/entries/panpsychism/ (air a ruigsinn air 7.8.15)
Kirk, Robert (1976). *The Secret Common-wealth & A Short Treatise of Charms and Spels*, deas. le Stewart Sanderson. Cambridge: D. S. Brewer.
Shaw, Margaret Fay (1986 [1955]). *Folk Songs and Folklore of South Uist*. Obar Dheathain: Aberdeen University Press.
Sjoestedt, Marie-Louise, Dillon, Myles (trans.) (1982 [1941]). 'Mother Goddesses', ann an *Gods and Heroes of the Celts*, tdd. 37-51. Berkeley, CA: Turtle Island Foundation.
Smyth, A. D. (1984). *Warlords and Holy Men: Scotland AD 80-1000*. Dùn Èideann: EUP.
Stevick, Robert D. (1994). *The Earliest Irish and English Book Arts*. Philadelphia: University of Pennsylvania Press.
Stewart, Margaret, and Allan MacDonald (1998). *Fhuair mi Pòg* (CD), CDTRAX132. Cùil Choinnich: Greentrax.
Stokes, Whitley (1905). 'The Evernew Tongue'. *Ériu*, Iml. 2, tdd. 96-162.
Taylor, John (1618). *The Pennyles Pilgrimage* ... Lunnainn.
Thomason, C. S. (1893). *Ceol Mor Notation*. Glaschu: John MacKay.
Toland, John A. (1813). *Critical History of the Celtic Religion and Learning*. Obar Bhrothaig: John Findlay.
Trevor-Roper, Hugh (1983). 'The Invention of Tradition: The Highland Tradition of Scotland', ann an Hobsbawm, Eric, agus Ranger, Terence (deas.), *The Invention of Tradition*, tdd. 15-41. Cambridge: CUP.
Walsh, Paul, and Ó Lochlainn, Colm (deas.) (1948). *The Life of Aodh Ruadh Ó*

Domhnaill by Lughaidh Ó Clerigh. Baile Àtha Cliath: Irish Texts Society.
Watkins, John (deas.) (1822). *Buchanan's History of Scotland*. Lunnainn: Fisher and Jackson.
Watt, D. E. R., Taylor, Simon, agus Scott, Brian (deas.) (1990). *Scotichronicon by Walter Bower in English and Latin*, Iml. 5. Obar Dheathain: Aberdeen University Press.
Whitehead, Alfred North (1929). *Process and Reality*. Cambridge: CUP.
Whyte, Christopher (deas.) (1991). *An Aghaidh na Sìorraidheachd: Ochdnar Bhàrd Gàidhlig/In the Face of Eternity: Eight Gaelic Poets*. Dùn Èideann: Polygon.

2

Manuscript and print in Gaelic Scotland and Ireland 1689–1832

Richard Sharpe

University of Oxford

The year 1832 saw the publication in Glasgow of John Reid's *Bibliotheca Scoto-Celtica*, the first catalogue of Scottish Gaelic printing. Reid was only sixteen or seventeen, apprenticed to a bookseller in Glasgow, and learning Gaelic, when he first compiled a list from the Gaelic printed books in a friend's library in 1825. The list grew as Reid examined 'all the Gaelic books in the neighbourhood', and the author was still no more than twenty-four at the time of its publication (Reid, 1832, pp. v–vi). It is a well-organised book, listing Gaelic publications according to thematic groupings, with a synoptic list of contents at the front, allowing one to form an impression of the subjects covered, the periods of activity, and the towns where Gaelic books were produced. In September 1832 an anonymous review appeared in *The Christian Examiner and Church of Ireland Magazine*, which provides pointed reflections on the comparison of manuscripts and printed books in Scottish Gaelic and Irish. Defining the end of the period with which we are here concerned, its perspective is instructive. Apparently impressed by Reid's list of printings, the reviewer brings in a comparison of manuscript resources in the two countries:

> There is this remarkable difference at present (and Mr Reid's work, now before us, confirms the observation) between the Irish and Gaelic literature – that while the Irish is rich in ancient MSS, and poor in modern works, whether MS or printed; on the contrary, the Gaelic is poor in the former, and comparatively rich in the latter, indeed so much so, that none of the Gael can, like the Irish, complain that he must remain ignorant for lack of the means of acquiring knowledge.

His view of Irish books is entirely antiquarian, but this leads him to accuse the University of Dublin:

of being wanting to the country [...] in not making any endeavour whatsoever to support Irish literature or perpetuate the language. We would ask, of what use is it to the nation that there are Irish MSS. in abundance locked up in their MS. room, which nobody can peruse except under the immediate eye of the librarian, who is altogether ignorant of the Irish language?

I think the writer of these comments was Henry Monck Mason (1778–1858), graduate of Trinity College, librarian of the King's Inns in Dublin, and keen promoter of the Irish Society or, to give it its full name, 'the Irish Society for promoting the scriptural education and religious instruction of the Irish-speaking population chiefly through the medium of their own language'. He makes a fictitious contrast between Inverness, imagined as full of eager booksellers and energetic Gaelic printers, and Galway with neither. If he had referred to Cork, he would have found in the 1820s and '30s no fewer than four booksellers, John Connor, Thomas Geary, William Ferguson, and (especially) Charles Dillon, who offered competing editions of Tadhg Gaelach Ó Súilleabháin's *Pious Miscellany*, a little book of highly wrought Irish poems, the work of a Waterford poet of the late eighteenth century (Sharpe, 2014). Dillon produced a number of Irish titles, while Ferguson advertised for Irish works of a devotional nature, inviting translations of works such as Bishop Challoner's *Think well on't* or Thomas à Kempis' *Imitatio Christi*, translations that were soon forthcoming, though from other printers in Dublin. Mason knew these books, produced for Catholic laymen and their priests (Mason, 1837, p. 629). What he knew about Scottish Gaelic printing included testaments and catechisms, naturally, and, for example, translated works of the English writer John Bunyan, all set out in Reid's book. His mention of Irish manuscripts was as selective and slanted as his reference to printing. In 1821 he had bought at auction a few Irish manuscripts from the library of Fr Paul O'Brien (1763–1820), poet-turned-priest and first professor of Irish in the seminary at Maynooth (de Brún, 1972; de Brún, 1977; Mac Gabhann, 1999). In 1830 and 1831 the Royal Irish Academy had started to buy Irish manuscripts, and Mason was well acquainted with Owen Connellan, who had some role in the Academy to act as scribe and who contributed a list of manuscripts to the review of John Reid's book. And Reid himself says much more, revealing things about Irish literature and Irish manuscripts that the reviewer chose to pass over in silence. For example, Reid mentions the abundance of texts by some four hundred Irish authors before 1750 as catalogued from the manuscripts by Edward O'Reilly in 1820. Some of the readership of *The Christian Examiner* may, indeed, have been acquainted with O'Reilly's book, published for the Iberno-Celtic Society.[1] Rather than devote space to repeating what O'Reilly shows from manuscripts, Reid went on to provide the first history of printing in the Irish language and in Irish types (Reid, 1832, pp. xxiii–xxix). He was apologetic in his preface that he did not devote more space to books in Irish. Again the reviewer passes over all this. And, as one would expect, Reid was the source for Mason's remarks about Gaelic Scotland's poverty in manuscripts.

Context helps us to make sense of this review. Mason belonged to an upper tier of Anglo-Irish society and to a forward-thinking segment of that society. He was a modern evangelical who, like others of his class, saw the linguistic interest of Irish and its literature in antiquarian terms. It served both philology and romance. Modern Irish was to be taken seriously in order to save souls through the Bible rather than through the mass, but Mason was no supporter of practical Irish books that might have educated the Irish-speaking underclass with whom his contact cannot have been close. The young Reid was less educated and less experienced but hardly less evangelical: his family belonged to the Secession Church, and he blamed a perceived decline in Gaelic on steam-boats, stage-coaches, and the listlessness of the Highland clergy of the Established Church (Reid, 1832, p. lviii). Mason had some knowledge of Irish, learnt from recent grammar books, though he could not converse in the language.[2] As librarian of the King's Inns he knew about books. Yet what he really knew of books in Irish is not revealed. Reid was a trainee bookseller who was learning Gaelic through contact with native speakers in Glasgow, not from labourers in town for casual work or the purchase of supplies, but from educated people who owned and valued books printed in Gaelic. His argument was that Gaelic books were interesting for their own sake, and even his short survey of books printed in Irish strikes me as remarkably well informed. Mason must have read it, but he chose not to acknowledge that such books existed.

*****

Books are still intensely familiar, and they provide a vehicle that helps to bridge both cultures and centuries. It requires only elementary curiosity to learn how books are made – we know how they are used because we use them – and if we use books that are a hundred or two hundred years old, we can easily assimilate how they differ from the books of our own day. There is an additional challenge, however, in what we call the early modern period. Before 1455 we are usually clear about the difference between manuscript books and other handwritten documents that are not books, but the rapid spread of printing, first in Latin, and then in both vernacular and learned languages, opened up a gap. For much of Europe it was a big bang with at least 26,000 editions produced in the first fifty years of printing with types.[3] Before then all books were manuscripts, though not all manuscripts were books. Book comes to mean a printed book, manuscript becomes a confused category that includes private papers whether finished and retained or completely ephemeral, formal records or informal material of record interest, and so on. Add the range of possible languages and the picture is more complicated. In print-heavy English, there were still handwritten books in niche circulation in the late seventeenth century: so-called libertine verse, for example, could not be printed for reasons of moral censorship, but there was a readership for it. In languages for which printing was slow to develop, the making of handwritten books could continue for many years. In Irish handwritten books were normal until the end of the eighteenth century and in Icelandic until the end of the nineteenth century.

My business today is to air some questions about books, handwritten or printed, in Irish and in Scottish Gaelic in the period between the shipwreck, *an longbhriseadh* (to use Dáibhidh Ó Bruadair's word), of the old classical Gaelic culture, represented by the date 1689, a year that carries related significance in Scotland and Ireland, and the more notional date, 1832, when Reid and Mason looked back at what was a time of development for both languages.

Reid presented a fairly simple contrast with Irish, represented by old manuscripts, and Scottish Gaelic, well established in print. Mason turned this into something simplistic by cutting out what Reid had said about print in Irish. For Mason there was a stark contrast. Manuscripts made Irish an old language, not a modern language, and for him the link between the language and Catholicism was just one of the ways in which Irish was out of date. He presented Scottish Gaelic as thriving in print, modern, dynamic, and Protestant. There is a long-established argument linking print and Protestantism, an argument that goes back to Martin Luther and his contemporaries. His German translation of the New Testament was printed and reprinted in great numbers, feeding the Reformation throughout northern Germany. Print took Protestantism to the masses. In the Celtic languages Victor Durkacz made this into an argument about the strength of language-resilience, setting out the case that the Protestant revival in the Highlands and Islands helped Scottish Gaelic remain in majority use, albeit in a defined territory, while Welsh remained the national language in most of non-conformist Wales (Durkacz, 1983). In Ireland the rapid decline of the use of Irish is associated with Catholicism, though the link is not nearly so direct; there was far more going on than is reflected in the very limited use of print in the language. The role of Breton in peasant Catholic Brittany through the nineteenth century would have provided a counterweight against this line of reasoning. There was little printing in Breton, but this did not set back the use of the language and did not serve the argument.

Comparisons need to be much more complex. Book-culture was changing in both Ireland and Scotland at the start of our period, but they were hardly alike in 1689. There is first a comparison between manuscripts in one language or the other. In Ireland an old culture of aristocratic patronage was destroyed, and with it the manuscripts of the old order lost their value and their place. In Scotland manuscripts appear to have played a far smaller role in Gaelic culture in the seventeenth century. There is a second comparison between the history of printing in either language, though in both countries we must allow that the role of print cannot be discussed without including also widespread printing in English and in other languages, in particular Latin books used in education. Differences in the transition from manuscript to print are associated with a quite different interface between manuscript and print in Scottish Gaelic from what can be observed in Irish. If this were not complex enough, there are further complicating factors. The conditions influencing the preservation of manuscripts were different in Ireland and in Scotland, shaping the evidence on which we base our conclusions. In the years towards the end of the period under consideration and after it, perceptions of what manuscripts were and are have been very different in Ireland and Scotland, and we need to avoid allowing our comparisons to be swayed merely by established habits of thought. It is certainly the case that awareness of the role of print in Scottish Gaelic has been greater than is the case with Irish: Reid's book is the first of several such catalogues of printing in Scottish Gaelic, but the nearest comparable work for Irish, by Dix and Ó Casaide (1905), is both limited and out of date. Students of the language in Scotland are far more accustomed to working with older vernacular printed books than students in Ireland, and this reinforces the relative invisibility of Irish printing. There is a need to control for the difference between material preservation and literary preservation: in Scotland many texts are known by a slender thread of evidence, in Ireland there are texts that are known in dozens of manuscript copies, but unless we control for the difference in material preservation, we are liable to draw false conclusions from superficial facts. What we know of the interaction between oral literary culture and written literary culture is different for the two languages: with Irish the number of late manuscripts can lead us to underestimate the role of memory and recitation in the circulation of texts. In Ireland our starting point was an age of both oral and manuscript literature, but a major change in the written culture caused a major change in the literary culture. Perhaps the new vernacular literature was emerging from the written shadow of classical literary culture, perhaps it was coming into being for the first time. In Scotland the spoken language had certainly been distinct from the written use of Irish, and in the course of the eighteenth century Gaelic was becoming a written language, finding its orthography in the process. In Ireland all this is expressed through the work of professional scribes; in Scotland the interaction with print, even with Irish print, played a bigger part. To do full justice to this complexity would take far more space than an article and demand skills that at this time perhaps no one fully commands.

So what are the real facts about handwritten and printed books in the two languages over this period?

*****

Before 1689 we can look back to a Common Gaelic world of shared texts and shared manuscripts. The literary language facilitated such exchange, but it was only a literary language (Ó Cuív, 1986, p. 387). It is illustrated by the inclusion of the work of Irish poets in the Book of the Dean of Lismore; by the poem of Piaras Feiritéir, celebrating the Scottish poet Maol Domhnaigh Ó Muirgheasáin, who visited schools of poetry in all four provinces of Ireland around 1642.[4] The use and preservation of Irish medical manuscripts in Scotland is another indication of that shared community. But that world of learned poets, physicians, lawyers, genealogists, who served and were sustained by the Gaelic elite, came to an end. Its demise was long forecast. Br Mícheál Ó Cléirigh in the 1620s and '30s saw himself as working against the hand of time to copy texts before that culture vanished. Others speak of its impending disappearance again and again in later decades. The Williamite conquest was the death-blow, leaving survivors such as Tadhg Ó Rodaighe and Ruaidhrí Ó Flaithbheartaigh to cling as best they could to the flotsam. But their contemporaries who owned learned books in Irish were not concerned to retain them. In a few months in Ireland in 1699 and 1700, and with no real money to offer in return, Edward Lhwyd picked up the largest collection of older manuscripts now known, both vellum and paper (O'Sullivan, 1962). He acquired the Book of Leinster and the Yellow Book of Lecan and more brehon law-books than anyone else collected, and all because their former custodians were no longer interested. The survival of older books in Irish depends quite heavily on collections formed in the seventeenth century and shipped out of Ireland. The three most substantial sources of vellum and older paper books are the collections formed before and after 1630 by Mícheál Ó Cléirigh and his Franciscan colleagues, which were shipped to Louvain; by

James Ware, antiquary in Dublin, sold by his son to the Earl of Clarendon in 1686 and taken to England in 1688; and by Lhwyd in 1699 and 1700, taken to Oxford, sold by Lhwyd's executors to Sir Thomas Sebright, and returned to Ireland in the 1780s, where they form the core of the collection in Trinity College. Left in Ireland, these books would most likely have quickly perished.

In Scotland Edward Lhwyd provides the odd glimpse by his acquiring a little handwritten book[5] made in 1698 by Eoghan Mac Gilleòin, of Kilchenzie, in Kintyre, for the use of the young Lachlan Campbell a few miles away in Campbeltown. One of the old metrical glossaries he copied is also found among the pages added to the Book of Leinster in the sixteenth century (Sharpe, 2013b). And one of Eoghan's other productions, written in 1690–91, includes texts as diverse as a poem on the lineage of Archibald Campbell (1607–1661), marquis of Argyll, and a modern version of the Old Irish *Scéla muicce Mac Dá Thó*.[6] MacGilleòin's only letter to Lhwyd quotes an epigram from the early seventeenth-century cycle of poems *Iomarbhadh na bhFileadh* (Sharpe, 2013a, p. 301n). All this reflects the Common Gaelic culture. And yet Campbell's letters to Lhwyd a few years later suggest that he looked on that old scribal culture as already extinct. He was making an almost antiquarian effort to learn Irish script and to acquaint himself with the writings of the older generation (Sharpe, 2013b). While barely one generation later, and only twenty miles north along the Kintyre peninsula at Largie, Uilleam Mac Murchaidh (d. 1778), was teaching a school, composing capable verse, and still writing a Gaelic hand.[7] He bears comparison with what followed the old Gaelic order in Ireland, a sign that in both countries the same successor culture might have flourished.

*****

In the last decades of the seventeenth and through the eighteenth century in Ireland a new vernacular literary culture flowers, with prose literature (mostly still relatively little known) and large quantities of poetry, all of it preserved by a thriving manuscript culture, sustained by scribes who, for the most part, earned a living by taking in school pupils, and who copied books on Sundays for themselves and for a market that is all but entirely hidden from our view. Scribes regularly signed and dated their copies, and some scribes' books have come down to us in considerable numbers. Twenty-seven manuscripts in the handwriting of Seán Ó Murchadha na Ráithíneach, for example, written between 1721 and his death in 1762, have survived by a variety of different routes (Ó Conchúir 1982, pp. 167–72). The actual number of handwritten books – a few of them imitating the appearance of printed books – surviving from this period is hard to estimate but very substantial, certainly over a thousand from the eighteenth century, and with late seventeenth-century books included and a relaxed view on the end of the tradition – say to 1820? – it may be nearer to two thousand. It is not the work of a few minutes to count them. Such books are treated as quarries for texts but they are little studied. I might almost say they are not studied as books at all. What has attracted attention is the identification of scribes, a challenging task sometimes brilliantly practised. Despite our having so many handwritten books, their survival should not be judged inevitable.

In 1821 and 1822 the first book auctions to include collections of Irish manuscripts took place in Dublin, the libraries of Paul O'Brien, already mentioned, at which Henry Monck Mason was a buyer, and of the solicitor John MacNamara (Sharpe, forthcoming). The prices fetched by manuscripts were pitiful. These were poor people's books of interest almost exclusively to the Irish-speaking countryman and to schoolmasters who carried the torch of Irish literacy, all of them people with little or no money. Few Dublin buyers were bidding.

I note here that the only eighteenth-century collection to have survived in reasonable shape, that of Charles O'Conor, of Belanagare in Co. Roscommon, a collection formed after 1730, transported to Stowe House in Buckinghamshire by his grandson in 1799, and after two sales restored to Ireland in 1883, has surprisingly little of this vernacular literature. Why is that? His collecting was dominated by his antiquarian interests, perhaps. Did he not also have a modern interest in current Irish literature? Perhaps he disdained peasant entertainments? Or perhaps his enjoyment of modern vernacular poetry needed no support from books? He learnt the songs he heard but did not need the written text? Or, tentatively, I wonder, was Roscommon not like Munster or south-east Ulster where manuscript culture flourished? Was there actually less of it on the ground?

Breandán Ó Conchúir did a great service with his catalogue of scribes and their works from Co. Cork, but such catalogues from most counties in Ireland would be much smaller, and from some counties there would be little indeed, even where Irish was in widespread use.[8] The culture of the handwritten book was not universal in eighteenth-century Ireland, though it is often tempting to generalize as if it were. There is a real need for the completion of the collection catalogues in the major holding libraries of Irish manuscripts, from which one can derive catalogues of scribes and their productions, enabling an atlas of late manuscript production. I venture to add that such an atlas also needs a timescale, because the picture might change decade by decade through the eighteenth century, and as the tradition faded, much discrimination is needed before nineteenth-century manuscripts are counted at all.

*****

Turning again to Scotland, I make two observations. The preservation of older manuscripts, books from the seventeenth century and earlier, is thin – Ronald Black has counted 83 of them against more than 500 in Ireland – and it depends on internal survival in collections, either institutional in origin like that of the Highland Society, or that crossed from private to institutional in the early nineteenth century.[9] If the books retained by the MacLachlans of Kilbride in Seil had been lost, the number of surviving older books would have been severely reduced (Bannerman, 1977). Collections such as theirs might have been replicated many times across the Highlands, but the eighteenth century saw them slip from obscurity into non-existence. That may have been happening later in Scotland than in Ireland, and perhaps more from obsolescence than from regime-change, but happening it surely was. As late as 1805 Lachlan MacMhuirich was alive to make a statement to the Highland Society's committee on Ossian that his family's manuscripts were disposed of because no one could read them any longer; he even came out with the cliché of a tailor's cutting the vellums into strips (Mackenzie, 1805, pp. 276, 278–9).

From after 1689, or after 1700, the near complete invisibility of early eighteenth-century handwritten books in Scotland makes a striking contrast with what we find in Ireland, where even in Dublin there were active scribes, the leading ones authors in their own right, such as the father and son, Seán and Tadhg Ó Neachtain (O'Rahilly, 1913; Ní Shéaghdha, 1989). Perhaps books exist in Scotland, and it is my lack of research, or the state of the catalogues, that hinders my view. But if the books are hard to find, the poetry certainly exists from Gaelic Scotland in the first half of the eighteenth century. Some weight can surely be attached to the title given by the most famous poet of the period, Alasdair mac Mhaighstir Alasdair, to his collection, printed in 1751, under the title *Ais-eiridh na Sean Chánoin Albannaich* 'The resurrection of the old Scottish language'. After a time other poets followed his example and saw their own work into print, among them Duncan Macintyre, Kenneth Mackenzie, Angus Campbell, and Duncan Campbell. Much secular poetry of the early eighteenth century, and earlier, was also written down, collected, and printed as a series of later eighteenth-century anthologies, often referred to by short titles, such as the Eigg Collection, Gillies Collection, Stewart Collection, which were the mainstay for approaching the great Gaelic poets of the period until well into the twentieth century. It is only from the 1930s that scholars have sought out manuscript copies to improve our understanding of textual histories and of reception. The character of those manuscripts, however, needs careful consideration.

In the later eighteenth century we do not find much in the way of handwritten books, though there are certainly manuscripts. The manuscripts of Donald MacNicol (1735–1802), minister in Lismore, are now – through the intervention of George Henderson (1866–1912) – in the university library in Glasgow, where they amount to nearly one hundred items in their archival numbering, but they are almost entirely his own copies of his own sermons, written on half-sheets of paper folded twice to give quires of eight pages, usually three or four such quires, sewn, per sermon. These are personal papers, not handwritten books; they were retained so that he might reuse a sermon from time to time, not for circulation among his fellow ministers. His main manuscript collections were lost at sea in the nineteenth century, but from what we know of them, they were his personal or working papers, the result of his collecting texts: interesting, no doubt, as a quarry but not in themselves evidence of any late manuscript culture. That question is pushed back to his sources: did he collect from handwritten copies? Or from reciters? I have floated the notion that in quoting a phrase from an old poem about St Columba and his howling dog, *Donnalaich chon chinain*, he may have had a bad reading from manuscript, since memory would not retain what could not be understood (Sharpe, 2012, pp. 182, 201–2). We do have a manuscript copy of the same poem that once belonged to Dr John Smith (1747–1807), like MacNicol from Glenorchy, and like MacNicol known as a minister on the west coast, in his case at Campbeltown. It is a sixteenth-century vellum booklet of only fourteen leaves, NLS MS 72.1.41 (Gael. XLI), which passed through the hands of John Mackenzie to the Highland Society and so into the National Library. Where it was written or how it reached Smith are unknown to me, and the poem is jotted into a blank space, not a planned part of the content. Smith's reading in older Gaelic literature is generally something that has to be inferred from his writings: it is not easily seen in its material context. If, as Joseph Flahive points out (Flahive, forthcoming), he had read *Cath Fionntragha* rather than heard the story, it is hard to say how such a written text came into his hands. Around 1800 older manuscripts had reached the heritage stage of being collected, a few by the Advocates' Library, others by the Highland Society, but the eighteenth-century manuscripts are by and large collections of papers. The papers of James McLagan (1728–1805) form the largest, with 254 items 'at collection level' (as the archival expression goes). How far such a collection typifies a widespread interest is hard to know, for no other collection on this scale exists. McLagan was an active intermediary between the living literature and the preserved text. But we may reasonably ask,were there so few handwritten books that McLagan, actively interested from his early twenties, could not find any to add to his collection?

*****

What we do see in Scotland is Gaelic printing, and from the publication of Alasdair Mac Mhaighstir Alasdair's *Ais-eiridh* in 1751, it is visibly the dominant medium.

The beginnings of printing in Gaelic and in Irish are not far apart in date. Carswell's version of the Book of Common Order (1567) and Seán Ó Cearnaigh's *Aibidil agus Caiticiosma* (1571) represent the same kind of entry into print, intended to serve the needs of the Protestant church. Yet Ó Cearnaigh used the same Irish type to produce a broadside of Irish Franciscan poetry.[10] And church books remained dominant, indeed almost exclusive, in Gaelic printing for nearly two hundred years. The books were almost always produced by printers in Edinburgh or Glasgow with the dominance of one city over the other changing from time to time according to where there was a more energetic business. How far such books travelled I have no idea. The various catalogues of editions from Reid to Black do not provide a census of where copies are now found, so there is no ready means to see whether individual copies carry evidence of past owners.[11] The English Short Title Catalogue records copies in libraries, though its coverage of editions, and one suspects its listing of copies too, is far from thorough. Present location,

NUMBERS OF PRINTED EDITIONS (INCL. BROADSIDES) BEFORE 1801

SCOTTISH GAELIC	(gla)	16th Cent.	1	Black lists 231
		17th Cent.	5	but he includes
		18th Cent.	101	some items with
	(gae)	18th Cent.	2	words in Gaelic
		total	**109**	but not wholly in Gaelic.
IRISH	(gle)	16th Cent.	3	Dix lists about
		17th Cent.	16	100 editions
		18th Cent.	28	before 1801
		total	**47**	
MANX	(glv)	17th Cent.	1	incomplete list
		18th Cent.	15	
		total	**16**	
SCOTS	(sco)	16th Cent.	65	
		17th Cent.	16	
		18th Cent.	7	
		total	**88**	
WELSH	(wel)	16th Cent.	21	
		17th Cent.	166	
		18th Cent.	768	
		total	**954**	

however, is not much guide to the circulation of the books in the sixteenth, seventeenth or earlier eighteenth century. Historic evidence of ownership, sale, or use would be valuable, but it may be all too hard to find.

The profile of printing in Irish is very different from what is seen in Scotland. Ó Cearnaigh's Elizabethan fount was little used after the early seventeenth century, when the government in Dublin ceased to support Protestant outreach in the Irish language. In 1685 Robert Boyle sponsored the casting of an Irish fount in London, used for the Irish Bible and for quotations in O'Flaherty's *Ogygia*, published in the same year. The Catholic presses enjoyed brief periods of activity, first in the hands of the Franciscans of Louvain in the reign of James VI and I, again in Rome in the 1670s and beyond, and finally among Jacobites in Paris in the middle decades of the eighteenth century. They produced few editions and they had little means of distribution. Take, for example, Proinsias Ó Maoilmhuaidhe's *Lucerna Fidelium* (Rome, 1676): it is not known how many copies were printed of this elaborated catechism, but they are now very rare. In 1842 J. P. Lyons visited Rome and found some 278 copies still in stock, which account for most of those now known in Ireland (Ó Casaide, 1912). Any edition still in stock after 165 years is not a good seller.

The Elizabethan Irish fount was an unsightly hybrid, while the three Continental presses and the London printer used elaborate *cló Gaelach* typefaces, including some contractions. A few eighteenth-century Protestant editions in Ireland used a roman fount, and this continued even in some Catholic books despite the availability of Irish founts from 1787 onwards, but the choice between the two styles remained much debated until the Irish government abandoned the *cló Gaelach* around 1960. Many have taken the view that adherence to this distinct fount retarded the printing of Irish through the eighteenth century and reduced its use in the nineteenth century.[12]

Scottish Gaelic editions were more numerous, though not very much more numerous before 1750, and copies of the books may have achieved better distribution. They were produced more economically, I dare say almost commercially, in Glasgow and Edinburgh, and the number of editions printing the same recurrent works, catechisms and testaments, suggests that there were sales, that there was demand, that there was reception. But there is nothing quite as appealing to literary interest as the Louvain edition, thirty-two pages in sextodecimo, of three religious poems in Irish by Br Bonaventura O'Hussey in 1614, now exceedingly rare. Although he had included some verses in his catechism in 1611, the poems that came out around the same time as its second edition are pleasing to read and substantial in length, printed in a form aimed at a popular readership. The main evidence of an audience in Ireland is now copies in manuscript derived from the edition.

Printing in Gaelic increases significantly after 1751, however, and, in contrast to printing in Irish, it is carried on for the Gaelic-speaking community in a way that cannot be paralleled in Irish before the 1790s. By 1801 the Scottish Gaelic Bible was complete, religious books were printed in some numbers, secular poetry was printed in a relatively small number of editions but – in the case of the 1790 edition of Donnchadh Bàn's poems – with a high print-run and presumably high distribution.

In Ireland Henry Monck Mason serves to remind us of the historic link between print and Protestantism, and there were Protestant efforts in the early nineteenth century to print booklets in Irish to induce the reading of scripture. Dr Whitley Stokes's edition of the Dundalk Catechism was produced in considerable numbers with a print-run of 3000 copies. In 1809 one activist, the Revd William Neilson, even considered using the modern Scottish Gaelic Bible, a reverse of the influence of Kirk's 1690 Irish Bible in eighteenth-century Scotland.[13] There were also some few Catholic books printed, especially catechisms, of which *The Spiritual Rose* (Monaghan, 1800) is an elaboration. The bestseller of cheap Catholic print was Tadhg Gaelach Ó Súilleabháin's *Pious Miscellany*. Tadhg died at an advanced age in 1795, and in 1802 twenty-five religious poems were printed by subscription in Clonmel, Co. Tipperary. Some 350 copies were subscribed by 277 individuals and two convents. This looks slight compared to nearly 1500 subscribers to the 1790 edition of Donnchadh Bàn's poems, who are thought to have paid 3/– per copy. Editions of the *Pious Miscellany* would usually sell for 3d or 4d, and I doubt whether the original subscription edition could have cost very much more, but have found no means of knowing. Between 1802 and 1841, however, Tadhg's book went through not fewer than twenty-seven printings with booksellers, first in Clonmel, from 1817 in Cork, with one pirated edition from Limerick in 1832, all vying for a share of the market. It was 'a work at the present day in the hands of almost every peasant in Munster', according to the scribe and bookseller Seán Ó Dálaigh, who was living in Munster through the years when these books were pouring out in their thousands of copies (O'Daly, 1849, 29).

The 1820s were a boom-time for provincial printing in Ireland, albeit chiefly in English, perhaps a shade earlier than in Scotland. This phenomenon was caused by the falling cost of hand-press printing-machines, which made the investment viable for smaller businesses.

In Scotland John Reid catalogued the Gaelic editions available to him in Glasgow just as the boom began to accelerate. The later listing by Donald

Maclean is too cumbersome to use as a means of studying this, since he organized it alphabetically rather than by year or by town and printer. It obscures the story.

In Ireland there is no listing before that by Dix and Ó Casaide (1905), which is not well made and stops in 1820. Why? Dix collected and studied a lot of Irish provincial printing of the eighteenth and very early nineteenth century – Ó Casaide brought the Irish-language interest into their collaboration – but Dix generally stopped at 1800, 1820, or 1825, because after that he reckoned there was too much material. Since provincial printing in Ireland collapsed with the Famine and never recovered, it would not have been an open-ended increase if he had continued to 1850. And the material actually printed in Irish was never large. But to this day I know no listing of Irish-language imprints between 1820 and 1850, when Risteard de Hae's *Clár Litridheacht* (1938–40) begins, and that is just a librarian's tool, an author–title catalogue with no sense at all of printing history.

This material is scarce. Something like nine editions of the *Pious Miscellany* are now represented by no copies at all, others by a single copy. If only the National Library in Dublin would follow the example of Edinburgh, digitizing its truly vernacular Irish printed books! But the fact is that no one has shown much interest in early Irish printing, though the period between 1790 and the Famine strikes me as one of extraordinary interest. These little printed books, even catechisms, are proxy evidence for vernacular literacy, and they present a complex picture of the interaction between daily use of Irish and elementary education in English.

Scottish Gaelic recognizes its printing history, Irish does not, though even here in Scotland more attention could be paid to the printers, especially in the early nineteenth century, and to the reception of these books. It would be good to see Black's catalogue continued beyond 1800, in relation to its subject a meaningless date imposed by the *Edinburgh History*. The Inveraray chapbooks, for example, produced in the first years of the nineteenth century and published by Peter Turner of Inveraray, are an important element in the picture.

Irish scholarship treats handwritten books as sources for texts, not as books, but Scottish Gaelic has yet to discover how much there may exist – or may have existed – of late handwritten books. If it remains the case that they appear always to have been rare, then the questions must be addressed, Why did vernacular culture in Ireland, and especially in Munster and parts of Ulster, continue to cultivate the handwritten book? Why did Gaelic Scotland cease to do so?

Considered categorization of manuscripts is really fundamental here.

The people who made and used books are surely different between Ireland and Scotland. In Scotland we see ministers and schoolmasters who take an interest in the literature, more often collecting what appears 'old' (a generation or two before the present) than what is new. Donald McNicol's acting as amanuensis to Donnchadh Bàn in 1766–7 is an exception, and its purpose was to get Donnchadh Bàn's poems into print, not into handwritten currency. Ministers' and schoolmasters' interest was scholarly, touching on antiquarian, perhaps preservative, and in some cases clearly aimed at printing. In the latter part of the eighteenth century the quest to authenticate James Macpherson's compositions produced that strange aberration, retroversions from English into Gaelic. This was a perverse outcome from the failure to find and exhibit true manuscripts of Ossian. In this context the Englishman Thomas Ford Hill in 1780 and the Irishman Matthew Young in 1784 provide non-partisan testimony to those like Alexander MacNab and John Gillies who collected ballads orally and wrote them down in the absence of an evident written tradition (Hill, 1783; Young, 1787). By the time Young was preparing his lecture for press, he could compare Gillies's printed texts with written texts of Irish *fiannaigheacht* in manuscript.

In Ireland, on the other hand, scribes, supported by other paid work, usually taking on pupils, kept a record of their literary tradition as well of their own time as of the past. Quite how far their handwritten books were used is uncertain. Prose texts may have been read aloud when people gathered – some of them would make for lengthy reading – while verse texts, which represent a large majority, were very often known to their hearers and might be sung or recited rather than read in Ireland just as much as in Scotland. The experience of knowing from hearing or repeating may relate to the written text in either of two ways, either the written text existed to prompt memory or resulted from the writing down of words learnt from speech.

The poetic literatures of Ireland – should I say parts of Ireland? – and Gaelic Scotland may bear much comparison, and their *viva voce* character was surely important, but their written manifestations in manuscript or print appear to me challengingly different.

Writing has played an important role in preserving the literature of the late seventeenth and eighteenth centuries to our own time in both countries. In a largely oral world, however, a change of taste would lead to extinction, and Scottish Gaelic may have lost rather more than Munster has where the written word was more widely used. It is impossible to say whether regional differences in our atlas of scribes would equate to difference in the use of writing or difference in fundamental literary culture, but the tendency is to generalize Irish and not to look at the question county by county or province by province. Such local questions must surely have a real relevance in Scotland too, especially as the territory of spoken Gaelic was contracting even more noticeably than in Ireland.

The rise of printing in the 1810s and 1820s in Ireland gave rise to a brief period of prose translations, Catholic for the most part, such as Thomas à Kempis' *Imitatio Christi* or Bishop Richard Challoner's *Think well on't*. In 1837 Monck Mason said that such books – he at least admitted to their existence – were too expensive to have real impact on the Irish speakers who might have benefited, though he says nothing of how such people were to read them. By now Catholics as well as Protestants were seeking to promote reading, and there is a focus on boys' learning to read in second-language English at school and then practising reading Irish, so that they can read aloud for illiterate families and neighbours. But by the time this was happening the remarkable vernacular culture of late seventeenth- and eighteenth-century Ireland was on life-support, dead but not allowed to die.

Post-traditional handwritten books, produced at high prices by entrepreneurial scribes for patrons with little or no Irish are a curiosity of the 1810s to 1840s. The collection formed by Bishop John Murphy, now in the library at Maynooth, is the largest example.

To stay with a late example familiar to me, the reception history of Tadhg Gaelach's *Pious Miscellany* has been distorted by a failure to recognize the complexity of the book-culture that preserved it. Tadhg was illiterate, or nearly so, in Irish. He composed and recited by memory. The written texts, it is said, were achieved not by dictation – as I understand to be the case with Donnchadh Bàn – but by literate hearers' learning the poems and then writing them down. One manuscript of 1792 has preserved a fair number, written while the poet was still alive, and it serves as the basis for the 2001 edition of those poems. Yet no editor in the last 160 years has paid attention to the twenty-seven or more Munster editions of the *Pious Miscellany*. In 1889 John Fleming, editor of *Irisleabhar na Gaedhilge*, did not contemplate recourse to manuscripts, and he supposed that 1802 was the best edition and that reprints added errors (Sharpe, 2014, pp. 250–51). Comparison proves him wrong. Improvements to readings characterize the first half-dozen printings from 1802 to 1817, and I very much doubt whether those improvements resulted from anyone's seeking out better manuscripts. Some of it was simply reducing typographical error, but much of it came from unnamed editors who knew the poems and could correct – or at least alter – from memory. Memory tends only to preserve intelligible readings. At least they understood the texts: I am not at all sure that the compositors could read any Irish at all.

So, in the early nineteenth century, we see a curious crossover between a late handwritten tradition and print, but almost all the self-appointed guardians of the dying or dead tradition saw manuscripts and Irish script as an integral part of it.

Between 1840 and 1880 or so, printing in Irish was predominantly antiquarian, carried out by the Dublin University Press using the famous Petrie types. O'Donovan's 1842 edition of the ?late Middle Irish *Fled Dúin na nGéd* together with the late medieval *Cath Maighe Ráth* started the trend.

Between 1830 and 1860 or so, Irish vernacular manuscripts made that vital transition, already mentioned, from peasant chattels, made for and used by people with no spare money, to national heritage, collected by nationalist members of the middle or upper class, both Protestant and Catholic. I shall argue in a book on Irish manuscripts in the sale room (Sharpe, forthcoming) that auctions held in Dublin in 1830 and 1831 played a significant part in this transition, leading booksellers Hodges and Smith to form the largest collection of vernacular manuscripts – 227 of them – sold in 1843–4 to the Royal Irish Academy for a fantastic price, 1250 guineas. Hodges and Smith made more money out of Irish manuscripts than anyone else ever did.

By then Irish literature was in a parlous state. Little if anything was being created, manuscripts had fossilised, print was focused on the oldest texts anyone at that date could understand–and thanks to the work of Zeuss and Stokes, study became ever more focused on Old and Middle Irish. A few stalwart individuals such as Seán Ó Dálaigh tried to keep Irish-language books afloat, but he never produced a monolingual Irish book. His *Poets and Poetry of Munster* (1849) was very influential, but by the time Daniel Corkery (1924) came to revisit this literature through the later editions of Torna and others, Ó Dálaigh's work was beneath his notice. He used neither manuscripts nor older printed editions.

Scottish Gaelic by contrast seems to have cast off handwritten books long since. It seems to me an interesting question to ask how much circulation of such books continued after 1689, but handwritten books are distinct from transcripts made for private consumption, after all, though these may have been vital in the preservation of texts.

Though the use of print did not progress rapidly in Gaelic in the late eighteenth century, by 1800 it was well established even for contemporary writers. In 1798 we have a striking instance of a failed opportunity, when the Cork subscription edition(s) of Duncan Campbell's poems did not noticeably inspire Irish authors to follow his example of printing his poems.

In the early nineteenth century, and most noticeably with the increase in Gaelic printing in Inverness after 1830 (which Mason appears to have foreknown), there is something modern about Gaelic books that cannot be said about Irish books before 1922.

I wonder how much more can be learnt about Highland book-culture in the eighteenth century and after by approaching it in the light of these issues. It strikes me as a happy boon that Donald Macintosh, author of the *Gaelic Proverbs* printed in 1785, bequeathed his library to the town of Dunkeld, long ago transferred to Perth, where nearly 900 books that belonged to him remain in the A. K. Bell Library and are retrievably listed in the English Short Title Catalogue. It shows how much someone publishing in Gaelic was accustomed to a world of printed books and periodicals in English and Latin.

I have taken only two closely related language-cultures in this discussion, but questions about how the written word is used apply to all languages. After the big bang of European printing in the fifteenth century, handwritten books become restricted to specific niches and to smaller language communities – though the number of speakers of Irish in the eighteenth and early nineteenth centuries was sufficient to support a much bigger printed book-trade than it did. Limited literacy is not peculiar to Ireland and does not favour the handwritten book, and the English colonial restrictions are only part of the reasons for the long-lived and fascinating vernacular manuscript culture that thrived in the absence of an Irish press.

Let me briefly compare and contrast Welsh and Icelandic.

In the seventeenth century Wales – not a separate kingdom like Scotland and Ireland – had no printers at all, because the Licensing Acts in England and Wales restricted the craft to members of the London Stationers Company and printers working under letters patent granted to the universities of Oxford and Cambridge. Yet the number of books printed in Welsh before 1700 is close to 200, three quarters of them printed in London. After 1695 other towns, notably Shrewsbury but also Dublin, printed for the Welsh-language market, cheap books carried by chapmen, such as could have flourished in Ireland or Gaelic Scotland. There were well over 700 Welsh-language editions during the eighteenth century. Welsh scholarship has little idea what to make of Welsh manuscripts of the seventeenth and eighteenth centuries, yet it is obvious that the patronage of manuscripts by Welsh gentry fell away dramatically in the seventeenth century – and we may see another literary comparison with Ireland in the decline of strict metres and the rise of free metres (Jones, 1998). I have not found any secure evidence for any handwritten books within my definition in this period. So, with far fewer speakers than Irish, and despite the lack of pre-industrial towns in Wales, Welsh flourished in print.

Iceland's very small population benefited from an episcopal printing press producing church books in Icelandic: print-runs must have been small, I imagine, but the detail is inaccessible, for the catalogue is only now nearing completion. Literary texts of a secular appeal were widely available as handwritten books in Icelandic, while Danish printed books filled the space that English occupied in Gaelic Scotland and Ireland. Today there are some 18,000 literary manuscripts of the eighteenth, nineteenth and twentieth centuries in Icelandic in the national collections of Iceland, a nation with 330,000 speakers now and just 50,000 at the beginning of the eighteenth century.

From the same late period, Irish has more than 3000 handwritten books surviving from an Irish-speaking population of several millions in the nineteenth century. Scottish Gaelic manuscripts may number 1000, but only by dint of counting anything written in Gaelic in Scotland. The number that can be defined as handwritten books is small. The number of speakers peaked at around 300,000 in the early nineteenth century, probably *c.* 1830–40.

My period began with the *de facto* end of the Stuart monarchy and of classical Gaelic learning in both kingdoms. Since then language and literature have taken divergent courses, materially reflected in book-culture. In 1832, when Mason saw the Irish language as a tool for converting the mass of the population to Protestantism and the modern world, the living vernacular tradition was extinct, and an antiquarian concern had taken over, with print failing to maintain much foothold, and handwritten books becoming heritage. In Scotland Gaelic was well on the road to having completed its antiquarian phase by 1832 – one may perhaps thank Macpherson for that. What manuscripts could be saved had been saved, and print seems to have thrived in Gaelic alongside English. And young John Reid had catalogued Gaelic books and surveyed the history of both Gaelic and Irish printing.

Wherever languages have – pick a number – five million users or fewer, these issues must have been real. Irish, Gaelic, Welsh, and Icelandic all followed different courses. It would be fitting to address such questions in the context of many other languages in Europe, but that is work for another day.

Endnotes

1 Members were mostly though by no means exclusively Protestant. Indeed Henry Monck Mason and Fr Paul O'Brien were both members of the committee at St Patrick's Day 1820.
2 'Let it not be objected, that I am not acquainted with the Irish as a colloquial, but only as a written, language; I admit it. […] I have compared Molloy's, Vallancey's, Neilson's, Halliday's, O'Brien's, and O'Reilly's grammars; and not neglected others' (Mason, 1830, p. [iii]).

3 The number is deduced from the Incunable Short-Title Catalogue (istc.bl.uk), which records some 30,000 editions, a number that includes broadsides that are not books and post-incunables once thought to be earlier than they are.
4 O'Rahilly, 1942 identifies three poems by the Scottish poet, all apparently composed in West Munster, apparently in 1642; edited by Black, 1976–81. A fourth poem of the same date was added by Ó Riain, 1970.
5 Now Trinity College Dublin MS MS 1307 (H. 2. 12, no. 6).
6 NLS Adv. MS 72.1.36; see Mackinnon, 1912, pp. 116-17 and 144.
7 NLS Adv. MS 72.2.13; see MacKinnon, 1912 p. 211 and Ó Macháin, 2006.
8 Ó Conchúir, 1982, with at its core a list of scribes and manuscripts assigned to them, pp. 3–190. For lists from Kilkenny and Waterford, see Ó hÓgáin, 1990, Ó Súilleabháin, 1992.
9 Black, 1983. A looser definition was adopted in Black, 1989, resulting in a larger number.
10 The broadside *Duan ann so Philip Mhac Cuinn Chrosaigh ann* (1571) is reproduced as part of the modern edition of *Aibidil Gaoidheilge & Caiticiosma* (Ó Cuív, 1994).
11 Ferguson & Matheson, 1984 is a very basic finding-list.
12 Mason, 1837 took this view; it later became part of the case for abandoning a distinct national type.
13 de Brún, 2009, 108, citing a letter from William Neilson to the British and Foreign Bible Society.

Bibliography

An asterisk indicates that the writer has an entry in the *Dictionary of Irish Biography* (2009), while a dagger refers to the *Oxford Dictionary of National Biography* (2004).

Bannerman, John (1977). 'The MacLachlans of Kilbride and their manuscripts'. *Scottish Studies*, Vol. 21, pp. 1–34.
Black, Ronald (1976–81). 'Poems by Maol Domhnaigh Ó Muirgheasáin'. *SGS*, Vol. 12, pp. 194–208, Vol. 13, pp. 46–55, 289–91.
Black, Ronald (1983). 'Manuscripts, medical', in Derick S. Thomson (ed.), *The Companion to Gaelic Scotland*, pp. 195–6. Oxford: Basil Blackwell.
Black, Ronald (1989). 'The Gaelic manuscripts of Scotland'. in William Gillies (ed.), *Gaelic and Scotland/Alba agus a' Ghàidhlig*, pp. 146-74. Edinburgh: EUP.
Black, Ronald (2009). 'A handlist of Gaelic printed books 1567–1800'. *SGS*, Vol. 25, pp. 35–93.
Black, Ronald (2012a). 'The Gaelic book', in Stephen W. Brown and Warren McDougall (eds), *The Edinburgh History of the Book in Scotland* 2 *Enlightenment and Expansion 1707–1800*, pp. 177–87. Edinburgh: EUP.
Black, Ronald (2012b). 'Gaelic secular publishing', in Stephen W. Brown and Warren McDougall, *The Edinburgh History of the Book in Scotland* 2 *Enlightenment and Expansion 1707–1800*, pp. 595–612. Edinburgh: EUP.
Black, Ronald (forthcoming). 'Gaelic manuscripts: a survey', in Alastair Mann and Sally Mapstone (eds), *The Edinburgh History of the Book in Scotland* 1 *From the Earliest Times to 1707* (forthcoming).
Corkery, Daniel (1924) [*al.* Domhnall Ó Corcora, 1878–1964*]. *The Hidden Ireland: A Study of Gaelic Munster in the eighteenth century*. Dublin, M. H. Gill; 2nd edn, Dublin, M.H. Gill, 1925.

de Brún, Pádraig (1972). *Catalogue of Irish Manuscripts in King's Inns Library*. Dublin: DIAS.
de Brún, Pádraig (1977). 'Father Paul O'Brien's Irish manuscripts: a note'. *Éigse*, Vol. 17, 220.
de Brún, Pádraig (2009). *Scriptural Instruction in the Vernacular: The Irish Society and its Teachers 1818–1827*. Dublin: DIAS.
de Hae, Risteard and Ní Dhonnchadha, Brighid (1938–40) [al. Richard Hayes, 1902–1976*]. *Clár Litridheacht na Nua-Ghaedhilge 1850–1936*. 3 vols. Dublin: Oifig Dhíolta Foillseacháin Rialtais.
Dix, Ernest McClintock [1857–1936*], and Ua Casaide, Séamus [1877–1943*] (1905; new and enlarged edition, Section 1, 1913). *List of books, pamphlets, &c., printed wholly, or partly, in Irish from the earliest period to 1820*. Dublin: Hanna & Neale.
Durkacz, Victor (1983). *The Decline of the Celtic Languages: A Study of Linguistic and Cultural Conflict in Scotland, Wales, and Ireland from the Reformation to the Twentieth Century*. Edinburgh: John Donald.
Ferguson, Mary, and Matheson, Ann (1984). Edinburgh: NLS. *Scottish Gaelic Union Catalogue: A List of Books Printed in Scottish Gaelic from 1567 to 1973*
Flahive, Joseph (forthcoming). *An Fhiannaigheacht: The Fenian Literature of Ireland and Gaelic Scotland*.
Gunderloch, Anja (forthcoming). 'Donnchadh Bàn and his Subscribers', in *Proceedings of the Gaelic Networks Symposium* (University of Glasgow).
Hill, Thomas Ford (1783). *Antient Erse poems, collected among the Scottish Highlands, in order to illustrate the Ossian of Mr Macpherson*. London.
Jones, J. Gwynfor (1998). 'Scribes and patrons in the seventeenth century', in Eiluned Rees and Philip Henry Jones (eds), *A Nation and its Books: A History of the Book in Wales*, pp. 83–9. Aberystwyth: National Library of Wales.
Mac Gabhann, Séamus (1999). 'Dr Paul O'Brien of Cormeen (1763–1820), folk poet and Maynooth professor'. *Ríocht na Midhe*, Vol. 10, pp. 125–51.
Mackechnie, John (1973). *Catalogue of Gaelic Manuscripts in Selected Libraries in Great Britain and Ireland*. 2 vols. Boston: G. K. Hall.
Mackenzie, Henry [1745–1831†] (1805). *Report of the Committee of the Highland Society of Scotland, appointed to inquire into the nature and authenticity of the poems of Ossian*. Edinburgh: A. Constable & Co.
Mackinnon, Donald [1839–1914†] (1912). *A Descriptive Catalogue of Gaelic Manuscripts in the Advocates' Library, Edinburgh, and elsewhere in Scotland*. Edinburgh: T. & A. Constable for W. Brown.
Maclean, Donald (1915). *Typographia Scoto-Gadelica; or, Books printed in the Gaelic of Scotland from the year 1567 to the year 1914, with bibliographical and biographical notes*. Edinburgh: John Grant.
Mason, Henry [Henry Joseph Monck Mason, 1778–1858*†] (1830). *A Grammar of the Irish Language, compiled from the best authorities*. Dublin: Goodwin & Nethercott.
Mason, Henry (1832). Review of Reid's *Bibliotheca Scoto-Celtica*, *The Christian Examiner and Church of Ireland Magazine*, new ser. 1 (No. 9, September 1832), pp. 627–40.
Mason, Henry (1833). 'On the Irish language'. *The Christian Examiner and Church of Ireland Magazine*, new ser. 2 (No. 22, September 1833), pp. 618–32.
Mason, Henry (1837). 'Practical observations respecting the use of the Irish language, as a medium of scriptural instruction'. *The Christian Examiner and Church of Ireland Magazine*, 3rd ser. 2 (No. 22, September 1837), pp. 621–32.

Meek, Donald E. (2007a). 'Gaelic printing and publishing', in Bill Bell (ed.), *The Edinburgh History of the Book in Scotland* 3: *Ambition and Industry, 1800–1880*, pp. 107–22. Edinburgh: EUP.

Meek, Donald E. (2007b). 'Gaelic communities and the use of texts', in Bill Bell (ed.) *The Edinburgh History of the Book in Scotland* 3: *Ambition and Industry, 1800–1880*, Edinburgh: EUP, pp. 153–72.

Ní Shéaghda, Nessa [1916–1993] (1989). 'Irish scholars and scribes in eighteenth-century Dublin'. *Eighteenth-Century Ireland*, Vol. 4, pp. 41–54.

Ó Casaide [Séamus Ua Casaide, 1877–1943*] (1912–13). 'Dean Lyons'. *Irish Book Lover*, Vol. 4, 57–9.

Ó Casaide, Séamus (1938). 'An tAthair Pól Ó Briain'. *Irish Book Lover*, Vol. 26, pp. 63–4.

Ó Ciosáin, Niall (2012). 'Pious miscellanies and spiritual songs: devotional publishing and reading in Irish and Scottish Gaelic, 1760–1900', in James Kelly and Ciarán Mac Murchaidh (eds), *Irish and English: Essays on the Irish Linguistic and Cultural Frontier, 1600–1900*, pp. 267–82. Dublin: Four Courts Press.

Ó Ciosáin, Niall (2013a). 'Popular song, readers, and language: printed anthologies of songs in Irish and Scottish Gaelic, 1780–1820', in John M. Kirk, Michael Brown and Andrew Noble, *Cultures of Radicalism in Britain and Ireland*, pp. 129–44. London: Pickering & Chatto.

Ó Ciosáin, Niall (2013b). 'The print cultures of the Celtic languages, 1700–1900'. *Cultural and Social History*, Vol. 10, pp. 347–67.

Ó Conchúir, Breandán (1982). *Scríobhaithe Chorcaí 1700–1850*. Cork: An Clóchomhar.

Ó Cuív, Brian [1916–1999*] (1976). 'The Irish language in the early modern period', in T. W. Moody, F. X. Martin and F. J. Byrne (eds). *A New History of Ireland* 3: *Early Modern Ireland, 1534–1691*, pp. 509–545. Oxford: OUP.

Ó Cuív, Brian (1984). 'Ireland's manuscript heritage'. *Éire–Ireland. A Journal of Irish Studies* 19 (1984), pp. 87–110.

Ó Cuív, Brian (1994). *Aibidil Gaoidheilge & Caiticiosma. Seán Ó Cearnaigh's Irish Primer of Religion published in 1571*. Dublin, DIAS.

Ó Cuív, Brian (1996). 'Irish language and literature: 1691–1845', in T. W. Moody and W. E. Vaughan (eds), *A New History of Ireland* 4: *Eighteenth-Century Ireland, 1691–1800*, pp. 374–423. Oxford: OUP.

O'Daly, John [1800–1878*] (1849). *The Poets and Poetry of Munster*. Dublin: J. O'Daly.

Ó hÓgáin, Éamonn (1990). 'Scríobhaithe lámhscríbhinní i gCill Chainnigh, 1700–1850', in William Nolan and Kevin Whelan (eds), *Kilkenny: History and Society*, pp. 405–36. Dublin: Geography Publications.

Ó Macháin, Pádraig (1997). 'Irish and Scottish traditions concerning *Ceathrar do bhí ar uaigh an fhir*'. *Éigse*, Vol. 30 , pp. 7–17.

Ó Macháin, Pádraig (2006). 'Scribal practice and textual suvival: the example of Uilliam Mac Mhurchaidh'. *SGS*, Vol. 22, pp. 95–122.

O'Rahilly, Thomas F. [1883–1953*] (1913). 'Irish scholars in Dublin in the early eighteenth century'. *Gadelica*, Vol. 1 , pp. 157–62, 302–3.

O'Rahilly, Thomas F. (1942). 'A poem by Piaras Feiritír'. *Ériu*, Vol. 13, pp. 113–18.

O'Reilly, Edward [1768–1830*†] (1820). *A Chronological Account of Nearly Four Hundred Irish Writers, commencing with the earliest account of Irish history, and carried down to the year of our Lord 1750, with a Descriptive Catalogue of such* of their Works as are still extant in Verse or Prose, consisting of upwards of one thousand separate tracts. Issued as *Transactions of the Iberno-Celtic Society*, Vol. 1, Part I.

Ó Riain, Pádraig (1970). 'A poem on Séafraidh Ó Donnchadha an Ghleanna'. *Journal of the Kerry Historical and Archaeological Society*, Vol. 3, pp. 48–58.

Ó Súilleabháin, Eoghan (1992). 'Scríobhaithe Phort Láirge, 1700–1900', in William Nolan and Thomas P. Power (eds), *Waterford: History and Society*, pp. 265–308. Dublin: Geography Publications.

O'Sullivan, William [1920–2000] and O'Sullivan, Anne (*al.* Áine Ní Chróinín, 1910–1984 (1962). 'Edward Lhuyd's collection of Irish manuscripts'. *Transactions of the Honourable Society of Cymmrodorion*, 1962, pp. 57–76.

Reid, John [1808–1841/2†] (1832). *Bibliotheca Scoto-Celtica; or, An account of all the books which have been printed in the Gaelic language*. Glasgow: J. Reid & Co.

Sharpe, Richard (2012). 'Iona in 1771: Gaelic tradition and visitors' experience'. *Innes Review*, Vol. 63, pp. 161–259.

Sharpe, Richard (2013a). *Roderick O'Flaherty's Letters to William Molyneux, Edward Lhwyd, and Samuel Molyneux 1696–1709*. Dublin: Royal Irish Academy.

Sharpe, Richard (2013b). 'Lachlan Campbell's letters to Edward Lhwyd, 1704–7'. *SGS*, Vol. 29, pp. 244–81.

Sharpe, Richard (2014). 'Tadhg Gaelach Ó Súilleabháin's *Pious Miscellany*: editions of the Munster bestseller of the early nineteenth century'. *Proceedings of the Royal Irish Academy*, Vol. 114C, pp. 235–93.

Sharpe, Richard (forthcoming). *Irish Manuscript Sales*.

Young, Matthew [1750–1800*†] (1787). 'Ancient Gaelic poems respecting the race of the Fians, collected in the Highlands of Scotland in the Year 1784'. *Transactions of the Royal Irish Academy*, Vol. 1, pp. 43–119

The Argyll–O'Donnell Treaty.

3

The Gaelic manuscripts at Inveraray Castle

Ronald Black

Peebles

Over the past few years the 13th Duke of Argyll's massive archives at Inveraray Castle have been opened up to the public as never before. Under the control of an enthusiastic professional archivist, Ishbel MacKinnon, they are now located in an eighteenth-century farm steading in the Castle grounds known as Cherry Park, and are known as 'The Argyll Papers'. The catalogues are still those compiled by the National Register of Archives in the 1960s and 1980s, however, and are rather basic; future development depends on funding (MacKinnon and Black, 2014, pp. 5–6).

The aim of this paper is to describe the Argyll Papers' principal Gaelic holdings. These are nine in number, and I will approach them chronologically. I will try to put down a few markers for future research, in the hope that these will be of some use.

As Gaelic scholars, our knowledge of the Inveraray Castle holdings relevant to our trade has always been hazy, to put it mildly. We were aware of the existence of two of the most important items, nos. 1 and 6, but we have never known what no. 1 looked like, and the riches of no. 6 have never been placed before us. The other seven are *terra incognita*.

1. Argyll–O'Donnell Treaty

This was contracted by the 4th Earl of Argyll in 1555 and renewed by the 5th Earl in 1560. It was in Classical Gaelic, presumably because this was the only written language that Argyll and O'Donnell had in common. The 1555 version does not survive, but the 1560 version is in the Argyll Papers (no reference number). There is also a contemporary English version (no reference number). This material is pretty well known to historians, Gaelic scholars and ethnologists alike (Macphail, 1934, pp. 212–16; Mackechnie, 1953; Black, 2012, pp. 22–3); as mentioned above, the only qualification is the lack of a facsimile or photograph. It is in an attractive hand, but I am unable to identify the scribe.

There is additional material in bundle 731, mostly in the hand of the 10th Duke of Argyll – notes about the treaty, a transcript of the Gaelic original, a transcript of the English abstract of 1670–80, and the translation of the original made for the Duke by the Rev. Dr Charles Plummer of Corpus Christi College, Oxford.

I have just one minor criticism to make of the published editions, and that is with reference to O'Donnell's signature. In Plummer's translation it was rendered 'AN NO DOMNALL' (Macphail, 1934, p. 216). Mackechnie made it 'ANNODOMN.', and added insult to injury by remarking that O'Donnell 'certainly was not in the habit of writing' (1953, pp. 96, 99). I now find that it is in fact 'Misi O Domn*uill*' ('I am O'Donnell'), very carefully written.

It would be well worth while to revisit the text as a whole, identifying all the signatories, bringing the Gaelic and English versions together, and presenting them in the context of the advances that have been made since 1953 in our understanding of the relationships between the West Highlands and Ulster in the sixteenth century.

2. Collection of Gaelic proverbs

The records of the Synod of Argyll consist of two series of bundles, 535–609 and 1751–1761. Among them, in bundle 545, is what appears to be the earliest known collection of Scottish Gaelic proverbs. They are written in Gaelic script on both sides of a double sheet of paper which has suffered much from folding, damp-staining and crumbling. Half of one side (i.e. one of the four pages) is taken up with a different text in English, which I will discuss below. There are five portions of paroemiography, each of which is scored out with a huge cross, suggesting that the manuscript has only survived because of its usefulness as spare paper on which to write the English text.

There are about ninety-three proverbs. It is difficult to be exact about the total number. The damage to the manuscript has left many acephalous and a few incomplete, so that it is not always possible to tell where a new one has begun. Of the sixty-seven which are complete, many are certainly unique, but some are broadly familiar from other sources, and this gives me hope that it will be possible in due course to reconstruct parts of the lost or damaged text.

The material is entertaining and thought-provoking, as proverbs should be. Examples of those which I believe to be unique are *S diuid bean a ngcuilidh mna eile* 'Shy is the woman in another woman's clothes' and *Déanad gach duine dho féin chuaidh Mc Cailen do Shruiledh* 'Let every man fend for himself – Mac

Cailein has gone to Stirling'. For 'fend for himself' we might perhaps read 'do as he likes'. Examples of those which I have come across elsewhere are *S gioraid an Gall an ceann a chur dheth* 'The Lowlander is the shorter of being beheaded' and *Cho nann a mBód uile bhios an tolc* 'Not all the evil is in Bute'. When quoted elsewhere the latter is sometimes given a sting in the tail: *tha cuid dheth sa Chumradh bheag làimh ris* 'some of it is in little Cumbrae nearby' (Nicolson, 1951, pp. 106, 254).

I do not recognise the hand. Our only clue to the authorship, date or provenance of the collection lies in the accompanying English text. It is in a seventeenth-century secretary hand; most of the heading has gone, but the words 'be sent to the north' and 'Inverness' have survived, and the text itself is in good shape: it consists of nine numbered reasons why ministers should not be sent to the north. There are in fact two other copies of it in bundle 545, one by a later-looking hand, probably that of a younger man. Although neither is undamaged, enough survives to show that the heading is 'Reasons why no minister within the Synod of Argyll should be sent to the north', and that there are in fact eleven numbered arguments, followed by this resounding conclusion:

> By all which reasons and considerations your wisdoms may see the great and unsupportable work that lyes upon our hands, both publick and personal, and how unreasonable it were to remove any of our ministers to the north, or especiallie to Inverness, and some few places adjacent thereto, who generallie have both languages, & so may be supplied by ministers from the Lowlands, whereas our parishes doe all requyre ministers of the Irish language, as is known.

It will be possible to reconstruct the entire text from the three copies, but I have cited enough here to show what was afoot – the fundamental issue was the Gaelic language itself!

In fact, the rest of bundle 545 explains what was happening. In the years after the Revolution of 1689 the Synod of Argyll was the most active ecclesiastical body in the Highlands. They reactivated their old plan to publish all 150 psalms in Gaelic verse. The Rev. John Maclaurin (1658–98), minister of Kilmodan (Glendaruel), spent the months from December 1693 to April 1694 in Edinburgh, correcting the press for *Sailm Dhaibhidh A Meadar Dhàna Gaoidheilg*, which was then published to great acclaim. The General Assembly promptly backed a call to Maclaurin from the Gaelic congregation of Inverness. On 6 September the Assembly's commission wrote to him emphasising that that important town was much disadvantaged 'for want of one who can preach in the Irish tongue'. They wrote again on 5 April 1695, begging him to go and exercise his ministry in Inverness for at least a quarter of a year, and remarking that their previous letter must have 'miscarried'. It had by no means 'miscarried', as the Synod was already conducting a defensive war against them to hold on to its brethren. In bundle 580 we find a specific statement of reasons why John Munro (Rothesay), Robert Duncanson (Campbeltown) and John Maclaurin (Kilmodan) should not visit Inverness, referring to Duncanson's work on the *Paraphrases* and Maclaurin's on the *Confession of Faith*, which was ultimately published in 1725. The row subsided when Munro died in March 1696, to be followed to the grave by Duncanson, 'a man of rare gifts', in 1697, and Maclaurin in 1698 (Scott, 1923, pp. 31, 40, 49).

John MacLaurin, born in Inveraray, was the father of Prof. Colin Maclaurin, the celebrated mathematician (1698–1746). Colin, who was born the month before his father died, possessed Gaelic manuscripts which had come down to him from his forebears in Tiree (Mackinnon, 1912, pp. 72, 309; Campbell and Thomson 1963: 11). We need look no further, I think, than John Maclaurin as the collector and scribe of our proverbs.

3. 'An Duanag Ullamh'

In bundles 743 and 818 are two copies of 'An Duanag Ullamh' ('The Finished Verses') with English translation. This remarkably vigorous praise-poem has appeared frequently in published anthologies, beginning with the so-called 'Eigg Collection' (Macdomhnuill, 1776, pp. 253–57). The latest scholarship on it (McLeod and Bateman, 2007, pp. 372–87) distinguishes between two versions: A, twenty-five quatrains seemingly addressed to Colin, 3rd Earl of Argyll (d. 1529), and B, twenty quatrains to Archibald, 4th Earl (d. 1558). Ours has twenty-five quatrains and is a variant of Version A. It is not, however, the same as in the 'Eigg Collection'.

The two copies of the basic text and translation were written by the same late eighteenth-century hand. They are identical, even to corrections and deletions. Both include this introduction:

> An ode or sonnet composed by a Highland bard in honour of Colin 3d Earl of Argyll in the Reign of K. James 5th Anno 1528, upon his being appointed by the King to command an expedition against the Douglasses, then in rebellion on the Borders. Buchannan B. 14. Ch. [*blank*] gives account of this expedition – with a beautiful and noble character of this Colin.

There are, however, differences in other respects. The copy in bundle 743 has sixteen pages. At p. 14 the tune is given in staff notation, making it perhaps the oldest surviving example of a Gaelic song set to written music. The melody is remarkably close to that sung by my late friend and colleague the Rev. William Matheson. At p. 15 is an end-note on the Mackintoshes (referred to in verse 15). Also in bundle 743 is the cover formerly used to hold the manuscript: it bears a note signed by J. F. Campbell, informing us that it was from 'Sonachan's Papers' and that he had made a copy of it on 30 Oct. 1872. The copy in bundle 818 has fourteen pages and contains no music or end-note. Also in bundle 818 is a separate sheet containing no Gaelic but an edited version of the translation, backed 'Mr John Campbell's translation of the poem composed in Gaelic to Colin Earl of Argyll anno 1528'. Who this John Campbell was I have no idea; nor do I know of any member of the Sonachan family who is likely to have written the Gaelic text.

This Inveraray text of the 'Duanag Ullamh' has independent value and deserves careful study. As an illustration, here is the first verse.

> *Trialfa me le m' Dhuanaig ullamh*
> *Go Riogh Ghaoidheal*
> *Fear ag am bi 'm baile toitheamhil*
> *Sonna Saidhbhir.*

Anonymous translation: 'Travel I will, with my Sonnet, to a Highland Prince, whose Court, where Plenty vies with Prosperity, is always crouded with a numerous Train of Attendants.' John Campbell's translation: 'Go I will with my Song unto a Highland King, a Man whose Court is always crouded with a Throng of Attendants and where Plenty vies with Prosperity.' My own translation might be: 'I will bring my finished verses to the King of the Gael, a man who has the wealthy homestead, rich and happy.' The word *toitheamhil* does not appear in any other version that I know of; as Prof. William Gillies points out to me, it may represent *toiceamhail* 'wealthy' with an Argyllshire pronunciation. The usual word here is *dùmhail* 'thronging'.

4. 'An Duan Albanach'

In bundle 945, amongst the papers of Lady Charlotte Campbell (1775–1861), is a version of the 'Duan Albanach' in a nineteenth-century hand, with English translation. This poem, probably composed by an Irishman *c.* 1093, provides the names of the alleged kings of Scotland from legendary times to Malcolm Canmore. Twenty-seven verses are known; here there are seventeen. Our copy begins:

> *A eolcha Alban uile,*
> *A sluagh feta* falt-bhuidhe;*   **leta?*
> *Cia ceud ghabhail an eol duibh,*
> *Ro ghabhsadar Alban bruigh.*

> O all ye learned of Alban
> Ye host of yellow locks* (*see foot-note)
> Whose first possessions, for your information,
> They took in the Albanian hills.

Lady Charlotte, a famous beauty in her day, was a daughter of the 5th Duke of Argyll. Known as Lady Bury following her marriage to the Rev. Edward Bury in 1818, she took to writing romantic novels and was the author of a celebrated diary of the court of Queen Caroline. She is not known as an antiquarian, but Sir Walter Scott was a guest at her parties. This copy of the poem deserves close scrutiny, as it may reflect a lost manuscript. It is preceded by an introduction, the following part of which seems to offer some clues to the writer's identity:

> From such historical poems, favorite Chiefs were selected for the subjects of *Heroic* poetry, in which chronology and truth were as much disregarded by the Highland Bards as by those of other countries, and many of the Gaelic poems ascribed to Ossian by McPherson and others (in their rage for antiquity) can be proven to have been compositions of much later times. All Ardgail, and especially Lochow, is Classic ground – from the names of *heroes* of Gaelic poetry, and of *places* derived from them, *both* can, in many instances, be traced to the race of Caomhal, connected thereby with names recorded in the Irish Annals, as chronological proofs. This subject is noticed in my MS., but may be traced much further by searching the "Annals of Ulster", "O'Flaherty's Ogygia", and "Ogygia vindicated", which are not within my reach, further than I find quotations from them in other publications. I am also inclined to believe that further notices of the race of Caomhal are to be found in these Irish Annals, between the reign of Kenneth Mac Alpin and that of Malcolm Ceanmor, a space of little more than 200 years – and that period is the only dark part of the history of Argyll, from the year 503 – it is the period of the Danish and Norwegian invasions, of whom not a trace is to be found within the bounds of Ardgail, or Lorn, which never were subdued by these Barbarians. In this period flourished Diarmid O Duin, from whom the Campbells are, to this day, called "Siol Diarmid", (the offspring of Diarmid) – all his exploits were against the Lochlinites (Scandinavians) whose invasions of Scotland in the *ninth* century could neither have been foreseen nor sung by the Bards of earlier times. Every

---

* The Gael were *yellow* haired – the Danes, in the Irish annals are called the *fair*, or *white Gentiles* (Strangers); the Norwegians, *black* Gentiles. – The different races may be traced by the colour of their hair, at this day.

thing I found on this subject that appeared to me worth transcribing, will be found in my MS. and will afford ample scope for that particular style of writing to which Lady Charlotte Bury is partial.

This final remark dates the material to after 1826, when Lady Charlotte published her first work of prose, a romantic novel called *"Alla Giornata;" or, To the Day*. The writer has a manuscript, clearly, but I think he means one written by himself, compiled from a variety of sources. He refers to Lady Charlotte in the third person, appears not to be one of the Irish scholars, says much of Argyll and the Campbells, and knows Gaelic, but is sceptical of Macpherson's Ossian. He goes on:

> The "Report on the authenticity of Ossian, by a Committee of the Highland Society of Scotland" will be found useful, and can easily be got – but, like all Highlanders, the Committee argue strongly in support of the antiquity of the poems – they make Diarmid a cotemporary [*sic*] of Ossian, and yet assert that "it is a general belief, over all the Highlands and western Isles of Scotland, that the Campbells are descended from *this very Diarmid* . . .

He may be an Englishman, more likely a Lowlander; indeed he could well be addressing his remarks to Sir Walter Scott (1771–1832). But he is a more than competent Gaelic scholar, and is perfectly familiar with the edition of the poem in Pinkerton's *Enquiry into the History of Scotland* (1789, 1794, 1814), vol. 2.

> The kings from Kenneth 2d to Malcolm Ceanmor are included in the poem, but it is unnecessary to copy that part of it – being unconnected with the race of Comhal . . . This translation is as literal as the sense admits of – it is not altogether copied from Pinkerton, as there are several blunders both in the Gaelic poem, and translation. Enq. 2. 321–2–3–4 and 6.

His page-references to the *Enquiry* are true for all three editions.

Other than Pinkerton, the editions of the 'Duan' known to me are O'Conor, 1814 (pp. cxxii–cxxx); Skene, 1847; Todd, 1848; Skene, 1867; Jackson, 1956 and 1957. In none does the text correspond to ours, nor is the Inveraray manuscript mentioned. Conversely, our anonymous scholar does not mention Skene or Todd, so we may conclude that he was writing between 1826 and 1847, when Lady Charlotte was between 51 and 72 years old. Nor does he mention O'Conor, which underlines that he was no Irishman. Identification of him will come down to a comparison of handwriting; the most likely candidates, I think, are the likes of David Laing (1793–1878), Cosmo Innes (1798–1874), James Browne (1793–1841), possibly James Logan (*c*. 1794–1872).

5. Sermons and letter by Rev. Duncan Clerk

In bundle 573, amongst the papers of the Synod of Argyll, are two Gaelic sermons in a nineteenth-century hand. The first is entitled 'Cionnus, ma ta, a shaorar duine aig Dia? Creid anns an Tighearn Iosa Criosd' ('How, then, is a man redeemed by God? Believe in the Lord Jesus Christ'). The second is 'Oidhirp air Freagairt a thoirt Do'n Cheist Chudthromaich sin Cionnus a dh' fhireanaichear am peacach ann am fianuis Dhe?' ('An Attempt to Answer that Important Question: How is the sinner justified in the sight of God?').

Elsewhere in the Synod papers, but in the same handwriting (bundle 570), is a letter written in Gaelic – a rarity in itself. First we find a sheet of paper folded to form an envelope, as was common down to the early nineteenth century. It is inscribed:

> Do
> > Sheanadh EarraGhael
> *"'S mòr an t-eolas bho leirsinn ar 'n aineolas"*
> *'S fuathach leis an dorchadas an solus*

('To / The Synod of Argyll / "Great is the knowledge from the vision of our ignorance" / Darkness abhors light')

The letter is a brief covering note, undated.
> *A Sheanaidh Urramaich*
> > *Sgrìobhadh an òraid a tha dol 'an cuideachd na litreach so le*
> > > *'ur Seirbhiseach Umhal*
> > > > *Donnacha Clèireach*

('Reverend Synod / The lecture that accompanies this letter was written by / your Humble Servant / Duncan Clerk')

This gives us the name of the writer of the two sermons: Duncan Clerk.

Duncan Clerk or Clark was born in Campbeltown in 1790, the son of Duncan Clerk, a carpenter, and Mary Stevenson. The parish minister of his childhood was the Rev. Dr John Smith (1747–1807), an enthusiastic Gaelic scholar who has been described as 'the ablest minister we ever had, not only in Campbeltown, but in Argyllshire' (MacVicar, 1933–34, p. 9). Thanks presumably to Dr Smith, young Duncan was educated at the University of Edinburgh. Licensed by the Presbytery of Dunoon on 4 April 1821, he was presented by the 6th Duke of Argyll to the Mull parish of Torosay in September 1828, and was ordained on 9 April 1829; he died on 13 December 1878 (Scott, 1923, p. 124). He is not himself known for his scholarship, his only publication being the description of his parish in the *New Statistical Account* (Clerk, 1845).

It seems likely that the occasion of the delivery of the sermons in writing to the Synod was Clerk's presentation to Torosay in 1828. Torosay was a 'Gaelic essential' parish, but Campbeltown was not a wholly Gaelic-speaking community, and the Synod was entitled to satisfy itself that the Duke's candidate was competent to preach in the language. A parallel is found in the case of the Rev. John Gregorson Campbell, whose presentation to Tiree by the 8th Duke in 1860 was hotly contested, resulting in the printing of six of his sermons, three English and three Gaelic, of which only the three Gaelic have survived (Black, 2005, pp. 620, 624–25).

Clerk's sermons deserve examination, either in their own right or in the context of an overall assessment of the historical development of Gaelic preaching. Gaelic sermons survive from the seventeenth century onwards, but not in large quantities (Ó Baoill 1983, p. 96; Thomson, 1962).

6. The Dewar MSS

The Dewar MSS are certainly more important than all the other manuscripts described here put together. They consist of a huge body of historical tales gathered from the mouths of the people and written down in Gaelic during the years 1862 to 1866 by a man from Cowal, John Dewar (1802–72). He was paid to do so by the 8th Duke of Argyll at the suggestion of J. F. Campbell. The area covered is Argyllshire, Arran, West Perthshire and Lochaber. Seven of the volumes are in the Argyll Papers; the other three are amongst Campbell's papers in the National Library of Scotland, shelfmarked Adv. MSS 50.2.18, 50.2.19 and 50.2.20. All ten volumes contain copious notes by Campbell which are of little real value today.

Also in the Argyll Papers are the twenty volumes of the Hector MacLean MSS. This is a translation of the Dewar MSS into English, commissioned by Lord Lorne from the Islay schoolmaster Hector MacLean in 1879 and completed in 1881. The reason why twenty volumes of MacLean correspond to ten of Dewar is simply that MacLean sent in his work in twenty batches. These were subsequently bound into six tomes.

Very little of the material has appeared in print, and some of what has appeared has been unsatisfactory. Members of the Argyll family made use of the MacLean MSS in various publications without acknowledging their source, allowing their readers to assume that they were personally familiar with the popular traditions of Argyllshire; this paper trail should be fully researched, also taking account of more recent 'leaks' (e.g. Budge, 1960, pp. 177, 185–86). Various Gaelic texts from Adv. MSS 50.2.18–19 were published by Prof. Angus Matheson (1939, 1958) without mentioning Dewar's name. The first tome of the MacLean MSS has been reproduced in a book misleadingly called *The Dewar Manuscripts Volume One* (Mackechnie. 1963). The material consists of about two-thirds of Dewar MSS vol. 1, but in English only. Its editor made amends, however, by publishing a valuable catalogue of Adv. MSS 50.2.18–20 (Mackechnie, 1973, pp. 91–98). There is also a draft catalogue of six of the seven other Dewar MSS, but it remains unpublished (Wiseman, 2002). Again there is compensation: its compiler has published a general account of the manuscripts which is of great value (Wiseman, 2006).

The Argyll Papers contain some related items. In bundle 3626 is a memorandum of agreement, 16 September 1959, between the 11th Duke of Argyll and William MacLellan Ltd., publishers, regarding Mackechnie's proposed *The Dewar Manuscripts*. In the same bundle is correspondence relating to a dispute about the book that rumbled on from September 1962 to January 1967. The correspondents were the Duke, J. Gordon Williamson C.A., W. H. F. Smith of the law firm Donaldson and Alexander, and William MacLellan. The Duke was dissatisfied with Mackechnie's editorship in general and his introductory essay in particular. I should add that this was not the only such dispute. Mackechnie himself threatened an academic colleague of mine with legal action over a perfectly fair review of the work, taking particular exception to the remark that 'one could scarcely anticipate that a note on the execution of two Jacobite officers after Culloden would culminate in a bibliography on Sir Roger Casement' (MacDonald, 1966, p. 135).

Also in the archive (no reference number) is an eight-page typescript report on the Dewar MSS, dated 10 December 1987, by Donald Archie MacDonald (1929–99) of the School of Scottish Studies. This reveals that, in the years immediately before his death in 1973, the 11th Duke tried to persuade Donald Archie 'to edit and translate the whole collection for publication'. Robin Lorimer (1918–96) was involved in various schemes for publication, first as agent for Irish Universities Press, then on behalf of his own firm Southside Publishers. None came to fruition, but we may see the reprint of *Leabhar na Feinne* (Campbell, 1972) as a positive result of this activity. In 1987 Alastair Campbell, yr of Airds, as chief executive for the Argyll Estates, enrolled Donald Archie as editor and translator of a fresh project. The result was the report, which suggested optimistically that the aims of the project could be achieved in ten published volumes appearing 'at, perhaps, nine monthly or yearly intervals'. Again the burst of activity led to a different outcome – Airds's own history of his clan (Campbell, 2000–04).

There is no evidence in Donald Archie's report that he had ever thought of abandoning the 'Mackechnie model' of publishing the texts in the order in which they stand in the manuscripts. The alternative, arising out of careful study of the materials, is to prepare a detailed catalogue (which reveals that different versions of the same stories are scattered here and there throughout the ten manuscript volumes), then to reorganise the texts thematically. We may call this the 'Wiseman model', as it was first suggested by the appropriately-named author of the 'Overview'. Wiseman also reveals that by 1999 the plan had mutated into a proposal for a series of volumes edited by Donald Archie with historical notes by Dr John Shaw, to be published, like Airds's *History of Clan Campbell*, by Edinburgh University Press. This proposal came to an end with Donald Archie's untimely death in that year (Wiseman, 2006, pp. 163, 173 n. 12). Dr Wiseman tells me that a subsequent attempt by himself and Dr Shaw to obtain funding for a fresh project came to nothing.

The most promising focus for future activity looks like being the Friends of the Argyll Papers (see below). One of the first aims is to prepare a searchable on-line catalogue of the Dewar and MacLean MSS. This is already under way. A set of themes should arise organically; some examples might be 'The Oldest Songs and Stories', 'The Montrose Wars', 'The Earls and Dukes of Argyll', 'The Clans of Argyll', 'The People of Argyll', 'Cowal, Lennox and Perthshire', 'Kintyre and Arran', 'Appin and Glencoe', 'The Islands and the North'.

The fundamental principle of all these schemes, fully accepted by all parties, has been that the Gaelic text must be published as well as a translation.

7. MSS of J. F. Campbell

These consist of three bundles of notes made by the above-mentioned John Francis Campbell of Islay, *Iain Òg Ìle* (1822–85), as follows: bundle 748, Gaelic tales and folklore, 1870–82; bundle 749, extracts from the Dewar MSS, *c*. 1870; bundle 750, mainly extracts from the Dewar MSS, *c*. 1870, including a poem 'Oran gaoil le MacCailean do inghean Mhic Dhonuill Ile, nuair a bha e chomhnuidh ann Dun-naomhaig'.

The notes have not been catalogued. They should, however, be seen in the overall context of the very substantial survival of Campbell's folklore papers elsewhere. The principal holdings of such material are in the National Library of Scotland, consisting of three main categories: contributions to, and correspondence on, his *Popular Tales of the West Highlands* (1860–62), Adv. MSS 50.1.1–50.2.1, 50.2.3, 50.2.18–20, 51.2.3, 51.2.6–7 (twenty-two volumes); manuscripts and proofs of, and correspondence on, his *Leabhar na Feinne* (1872), Adv. MSS 50.2.5–17 (thirteen volumes); collections of songs and tales, Adv. MSS 50.2.21, 50.3.1–5 (six volumes).

8. *Waifs & Strays*

Amongst the Argyll Papers are what appear to be final handwritten drafts of four of the five published volumes of Lord Archibald Campbell's *Waifs & Strays of Celtic Tradition*, published between 1889 and 1895 by the folklorist Alfred Nutt (no reference number). These constitute one of the classics of Scottish Gaelic folklore. They may be described as follows:

> I. Lord Archibald Campbell, *Waifs and Strays* I (often referred to as 'Craignish Tales'), 1889. White leather volume. Tales collected from several sources, including John Gregorson Campbell, George Clark, gamekeeper, Rosneath (previously of Glen Shira), Mrs Thorpe, and others. The volume also includes reviews of the published work, May–June 1889, and a note on the war dress of the Celts by Lord Archibald. Annotated with brief binding and publication notes referring to David Nutt, publishers, 270 Strand, London, and Messrs Whiting, printers, 30 Sardinia Street, Lincolns Inn Fields.

> II. Rev. Duncan MacInnes, *Folk and Hero Tales*, 1890. Brown leather volume with gilt edge. In addition to MacInnes's manuscript notes, this volume contains proof printed copies of his Introduction and Nutt's introductory essay 'Development of Ossianic Saga'.

> III. Rev. James MacDougall, *Folk and Hero Tales*, 1891. Brown leather volume with detached front cover. Tales collected by Rev. James MacDougall, Duror, from Alexander Cameron, roadman between Duror and Ballachulish, summer 1889 and spring 1890. MacDougall's introductory notes state that Alexander Cameron, a native of Ardnamurchan, learned the tales from Donald McPhie and other old men whom he knew in his boyhood. Other people in the district who partly remembered some of the tales are also noted in his appendix/index.

> IV. Rev. John Gregorson Campbell, *The Fians*, 1891. Brown leather volume with gilt edge. Tales collected by J. G. Campbell 'made over to Lord Archibald Campbell for his Argyleshire series ... in appreciation of his Lordship's ardent and judicious services to Gaelic literature in continuing the work well began [*sic*] by J. F. Campbell of Islay', June 1891.

> V. Rev. John Gregorson Campbell, *Clan Traditions and Popular Tales*, 1895.

A word about the series as contextualised by Richard Dorson, the historian of British folklore (1968, pp. 406, 413), may not be out of place here. Dorson described it as 'conceived by Lord Archibald Campbell but given its direction by Alfred Nutt, the publisher, who inevitably contributed essays and notes'. Lord Archibald (1846–1913), brother of the 9th Duke, father of the 10th, was the general editor. Dorson concluded:

> Without the essays and notes of Nutt, the *Waifs and Strays* would have remained a parochial series of local collections, valuable in content but amateurish in format. Nutt gave the materials intellectual significance, bringing them into the orbit of international scholarship, indicating their values for the cultural historian of the Celt, defining the enigmatic problems they presented. An Englishman, he sounded a trumpet call to Scottish nationalists to repossess their heritage, forget the silly distraction of the Ossianic controversy, and concentrate on the genuine oral riches at their disposal. The often naïve prefaces and observations of the well-intentioned clergymen – Campbell ended *The Fians* with acclaim for Macpherson – faded into the background before the broad learning of Nutt, whom no one could accuse of narrow Highland filiopietism.

In light of this, the Inveraray drafts should be carefully examined to see if anything further may be elucidated about Nutt's engagement with the material. Ishbel MacKinnon believes that the fifth of the five volumes may be lying unidentified elsewhere in the archive.

9. 'Balg Tionail'

'Balg Tionail' (NRAS6/125) is a short collection of Scottish Gaelic rhymes and sayings originally made by Donald C. MacPherson of the Advocates' Library (1838–80), and transcribed in 1893 by Duncan MacIsaac, Oban, for a *Waifs & Strays* volume which never appeared. The collection, which is carefully written out as printers' copy, would have been very much at home in *Carmina Gadelica*. It should certainly be published. On lined paper, it consists of a biography of MacPherson (3 pp.), texts (23 pp.), and notes (4 pp.). The texts may be characterised as: sayings and rhymes from or about particular places (Lochaber, Glencoe, Rannoch, Badenoch, Atholl, Glen Falloch, Knoydart); seven versions of a 'hiding the button' game; a saying about women attributed to King Cormac, headed 'Na Boirionnaich a dh'iarr Cormac an seachnadh'; sheiling rhymes, animal sayings, tongue-twisters, riddles, wit ('Beuradaireachd'); a triad; a curse on a thief ('A Mhic a's ogha Bhrian á Eirinn…'); etc. Most, but not quite all, are accompanied by English translations. Of particular interest, perhaps, is the

67

memorate 'Am balbhan-caileige' ('The Dumb Lass'), a variant of the ingenious tale about inhospitality characterised by Barbara Hillers (2001) as 'Oidhche Rionnagach Reulagach'.

The manuscript is backed 'MacPherson's / Balg Tionail / (Collecting Wallet) / Copied (Gaelic) from the / original MS. – / Received from / Mr. Henry Whyte ("Fionn") / Glasgow / For / "Waifs and Strays of / Celtic Tradition"'. It is accompanied by two letters which help explain its transmission. The first is:

1 Albany Street
Oban 28th April 1893.

Dear Mr. Nutt,

I have just put the last word to the late D. C. MacPherson's "Balg Tionail", and I now send it to you herewith.

The Rev. D. M. Campbell, Cumlodden, has not yet forwarded to me his outstanding tale. I have word from Lord Archibald that the Miscellany volume is to be put past in the meantime, and I am writing to Mr. Campbell to ask him not to hurry with his tale.

If there is any Gaelic in the new material, and that I can be of use in dealing with it, I shall be glad to do what I may.

Yours sincerely
Dun. McIsaac

P.S. I have to write to you about the old chap-book forwarded to me for perusal by Mr. A. Sinclair, Glasgow. It has none of the poems contained in the Inveraray chap-book.

I hope to discuss the 'Inveraray Chapbooks' on another occasion. There are three of them in the Argyll Papers (bundle 829). The second letter is:

270. Strand. London. W.C.
15/6/1896

Dear Lord Archibald

Here is another lot of Ms for Vol VI which I have turned up. You had better keep it I think.

Faithfully
Alfred Nutt

We may deduce that the course of transmission was D. C. MacPherson > Henry Whyte > Duncan MacIsaac > Alfred Nutt > Lord Archibald Campbell.

Contact details

The address of The Argyll Papers is Cherry Park, Inveraray, Argyll, PA32 8XE (archives@inveraray-castle.com). The archive is currently staffed part-time.

The catalogues (survey lists) may also be consulted at the National Register of Archives for Scotland, HM General Register House, 2 Princes St., Edinburgh, EH1 3YY (nra@nas.gov.uk), or Argyll and Bute Council Archives, Manse Brae, Lochgilphead, PA31 8QU (archives@argyll-bute.gov.uk).

A charitable organisation called 'The Friends of the Argyll Papers' was set up in 2015 to support the development of the archive and promote its use and enjoyment to a wide audience. There is a website (http://friendsoftheargyllpapers.ab-12.co.uk/), a Facebook page (https://www.facebook.com/friendsoftheargyllpapers), a biannual newsletter, lectures and visits. New members will be welcome (individual £15, corporate £25).

Acknowledgements

I am grateful to the 13th Duke of Argyll for permission to quote from the above documents, and to my enthusiastic audience at Rannsachadh na Gàidhlig, from whom I learned much of value. I would like to thank Dr Aonghas MacCoinnich and Prof. William Gillies for additional help on nos. 2 and 3 respectively. Above all, I could have done nothing without Ishbel MacKinnon, who produced the manuscripts, read and commented on a draft, answered my tiresome questions, and patiently plugged the gaps in my knowledge. For all surviving errors I am solely responsible.

Bibliography

Black, Ronald (2012). 'Gaelic Law as Literature', in *Scottish Life and Society: A Compendium of Scottish Ethnology: The Law*, ed. by Mark A. Mulhern, pp. 11–46. Edinburgh: John Donald.
Budge, Donald (1960). *Jura: An Island of Argyll*. Glasgow: John Smith.
Campbell, Alastair, of Airds (3 vols, Edinburgh, 2000–04). *A History of Clan Campbell*. Edinburgh: EUP.
Campbell, J. F. (1972 [1872]). *Leabhar na Feinne*. Shannon: Irish University Press.
Campbell, J. L., and Thomson, Derick (1963). *Edward Lhuyd in the Scottish Highlands 1699–1700*. Oxford: OUP.
Clerk, Rev. Duncan (1845). 'Parish of Torosay', in *The New Statistical Account of Scotland*, vol. 7 (1845), part 2, pp. 277–96. Edinburgh: William Blackwood & Sons.
Dorson, Richard (1968). *The British Folklorists: A History*. London: University of Chicago Press.
Hillers, Barbara (2001). 'Oidhche Rionnagach Reulagach – A Tale with a Sting', in *Northern Lights: Aistí in Adhnó do Bho Almqvist*, ed. by Séamas Ó Catháin. pp. 72–86. Dublin: University College Dublin Press.
Jackson, Kenneth (1956). 'The Poem *A Eolcha Alban Uile*'. *Celtica*, vol. 3, pp. 149–67.
Jackson, Kenneth (1957). 'The Duan Albanach'. *Scottish Historical Review*, vol. 36, pp. 125–37.
Macdomhnuill, Raonuill (1776). *Comh-Chruinneachidh Orannaigh Gaidhealach*. Edinburgh: W. Runciman.

MacDonald, Kenneth D. (1966). Review of *The Dewar Manuscripts*, Vol. I, in *SGS*, vol. 11, part 1 (1966), pp. 133–35.
Mackechnie, John (ed.) (1953). 'Treaty between Argyll and O'Donnell'. *SGS*, vol. 7, pp. 94–102.
Mackechnie, John (ed.) (1963). *The Dewar Manuscripts Volume One*. Glasgow: William MacLellan.
Mackechnie, John (1973). *Catalogue of Gaelic Manuscripts in Selected Libraries in Great Britain and Ireland*, vol. 1. Boston, MA: G. K. Hall.
Mackinnon, Donald (1912). *A Descriptive Catalogue of Gaelic Manuscripts in the Advocates' Library Edinburgh, and Elsewhere in Scotland*. Edinburgh: W. Brown.
MacKinnon, Ishbel, and Black, Ronald (2014). 'The Inveraray Castle Archives as a Source for the History of Tiree', in [Alayne Barton (ed.)], *The Secret Island: Towards a History of Tiree*, pp. 5–32. Kershader, Isle of Lewis: Islands Books Trust.
McLeod, Wilson, and Bateman, Meg, eds (2007). *Duanaire na Sracaire/Songbook of the Pillagers: Anthology of Scotland's Gaelic Verse to 1600*. Edinburgh: Birlinn.
Macphail, J. R. N. (ed.) (1934). *Highland Papers*, vol. 4. Edinburgh: Scottish History Society.
MacVicar, Rev. Angus J. (1933-4). *The Rev. Dr John Smith of Campbeltown*. Campbeltown: Kintyre Antiquarian Society.
Matheson, Angus (1939). 'A Traditional Account of the Appin Murder'. *TGSI*, vol. 35, pp. 343–404.
Matheson, Angus (1958). 'Traditions of Alasdair Mac Colla'. *Transactions of the Gaelic Society of Glasgow*, vol. 5, pp. 9–93.
Nicolson, Alexander (1951). *Gaelic Proverbs*. Glasgow: Caledonian Press.
Ó Baoill, Colm (1983). 'Gaelic Manuscripts in the Colin Campbell Collection'. *SGS*, vol. 14, part 1, pp. 83–99.
O'Conor, Charles (ed.) (1814). *Rerum Hibernicarum Scriptores Veteres, Prolegomena, pars 1*. London: J. Seeley.
Pinkerton, John (1814). *An Enquiry into the History of Scotland*, 2 vols. London, 1789, 2nd edn 1794, 3rd edn 1814.
Scott, Hew (1923). *Fasti Ecclesiæ Scoticanæ*, new edn, vol. 4. Edinburgh: Oliver & Boyd.
Skene, William F. (1847). 'The Gaelic Poem, "A Eolcha Albain Uile"', in *Collectanea de Rebus Albanicis*, pp. 70–79. Edinburgh: The Iona Club.
Skene, William F. (1867). *Chronicles of the Picts, Chronicles of the Scots*. Edinburgh: H. M. General Register House.
[Thomson, Derick S. (1962)] 'The Rev. John Mackay's Gaelic Sermons', *SGS*, vol. 9, part 2, pp. 176–202.
Todd, James Henthorn (ed.) (1848). *The Irish Version of the Historia Britonum of Nennius*. Dublin: Irish Archæological Society.
Wiseman, Andrew E. M. (2002). 'A Descriptive List of the Dewar Manuscripts 1862–66, Inverary Castle'. Aberdeen: unpublished.
Wiseman, Andrew E. M. (2006). 'The Dewar Manuscripts: An Overview', in Michel Byrne, Thomas Owen Clancy and Sheila Kidd (eds), *Litreachas & Eachdraidh/ Literature & History: Papers from the Second Conference of Scottish Gaelic Studies, Glasgow 2002*, pp. 161–82. Glasgow: Department of Celtic, University of Glasgow.

4

'Bean-Chomuinn nam Bàrd': Exploring common ground in the lives and perspectives of the Gaelic poets Mary MacPherson and Mary MacKellar

Priscilla Scott

University of Edinburgh

On the penultimate day of October, 1890, the *Scottish Highlander* published a lament for the Lochaber writer and poet, Mary MacKellar, who had died the previous month. Entitled 'Cumha do Mhairi Chamshron, Bana-Bhard nan Camshronach', it was composed by another poet, the well-known Mary MacPherson or Màiri Mhòr nan Òran[1] who, as the paper stated, had composed the lament for 'her friend and fellow-poetess, Mary MacKellar'. Both women had been increasingly prominent in Gaelic circles during the previous two decades, and were conspicuous as women in Gaelic cultural and political arenas that were dominated by men. Although there was an age difference of some fourteen years between them, their creative period was almost parallel, from *c.* 1870 to 1890, and it is therefore not surprising that both women at times addressed the same subject-matter in their songs. However, while the paths of their lives often ran close, there is little evidence to suggest that they interacted socially to any great extent. Was the lament from one Mary to the other, therefore, simply a public duty acknowledging a Gaelic compatriot and sister-poet, or was it a personal response reflecting female solidarity and shared experience? This specific question will be addressed at the end of the paper, but it prompts the more general question that will be explored here concerning the relationship between the two Marys and what their songs might reveal about the similarity or difference in their individual perspectives on the Gaelic world in the second half of the nineteenth century.

Biographical connections

In their song-making Mary MacKellar (1834–90) and Màiri Mhòr (*c.* 1821–98) both drew on an intimate knowledge of the Gaelic song tradition absorbed from their upbringing in Lochaber and Skye respectively. A fundamental difference between the two in their early years was that Mary MacKellar was more fortunate in her schooling and, remarkably for her gender and class, gained literacy in Gaelic and English. She was therefore able to write poetry and prose in both languages, and she also undertook translation work from English into Gaelic. Màiri Mhòr, in contrast, was non-literate, at least until she moved to Glasgow around 1872 at the age of 51 when she began her training as a nurse (Meek, 1998, p. 27), and whatever degree of literacy she was able to achieve at that stage in her life was likely to have been at a fairly basic level. However, although her poetry was composed orally, in performing her own songs at large Highland gatherings, her work reached her audience very directly, and more effectively than in print, although a number of her songs were published in the Highland press. Both women in fact saw collections of their songs published in their own lifetime: Mary MacKellar's volume, *Gaelic and English Poems*, in 1880, and Màiri Mhòr's, *Dàin agus Òrain Ghàidhlig*, in 1891.

Both women were married but, as a result of widowhood or divorce, they were single in the period that concerns us here (*c.* 1870–90), and therefore faced the not inconsiderable challenge of supporting themselves financially by whatever means they could. At critical moments in their lives, they both had experience of a court of law, and while the circumstances of their appearances were quite different, they both suffered the consequent humiliation of having the personal details of their respective cases reported in the press. Màiri Mhòr, as is well known, found herself in court in Inverness in 1872 on an accusation of theft and was sent to prison, although influential friends were subsequently able to secure her release (Meek, 1998, pp. 23–7). It was an experience that not only unleashed her poetic voice but also awoke her sense of the injustice of the circumstances faced by her kinspeople in the Highlands as a result of changing land-use policies. In Mary MacKellar's situation, she herself took the initiative to go to court in December 1880 to seek legal separation from her husband and indeed won her case, but this earned her little sympathy from those reporting on the matter. As single women, the two Marys were living in the Lowlands – Màiri Mhòr in Greenock and Glasgow and Mary MacKellar in Edinburgh – although they still maintained strong ties with their home areas and returned to and travelled within the Gàidhealtachd fairly regularly. Their Gaelic involvement and networks reflected in general the differences in the Gaelic communities of Glasgow and Edinburgh, although they did have influential and supportive friends in common, and of these Professor John Stuart Blackie and John Murdoch were particularly important.

The general scope of the subject-matter that the two women addressed in their poetry was broadly similar, with the notable exception of the political output of Màiri Mhòr. They both commented on various events of their day that had an impact on the Gaelic world; they praised and lamented public figures and, more informally, less-prominent individuals; and they celebrated their particular clan affiliations and their individual sense of place in Skye and Lochaber. Within the scope of this paper, I want to consider more closely three specific subject overlaps in their poetry, all of which reflected circumstances and concerns relevant to the Gaelic-speaking community in the second half of the nineteenth century: clan loyalties, Highland regiments, and the 'Land Question' in the Highlands.

Clan loyalties

For both Mary Cameron MacKellar and Mary MacPherson, *née* MacDonald, the historical connection to the clan whose name they bore was a strong part of their Gaelic identity. In the case of Màiri Mhòr, her loyalty was to both her own clan and that of her husband; addressing, for example, the MacPherson chief in one song as, '''Chluainidh, mo luchd-iùil' (Nic-a'-Phearsain, p. 129). It is clear that both women had a fairly partisan streak in their devotion to clan. In a poem marking a gathering of influential dignitaries in support of the proposed Celtic Chair for the University of Edinburgh in 1873,[2] a 'Grand Celtic Conversatione', as the *Scotsman* described it (16 April 1873), Mary MacKellar noted the presence of Cluny MacPherson,[3] pointing out that he had 'fuil uasal bho 'mhàthair ag eiridh na 'phòr'. This was a reference to the fact that his mother was a Cameron, daughter of Ewen Cameron of Fassiefern, and having made this link, Mary MacKellar could not resist adding a verse in praise of her own clan, despite the fact that Locheil was not in fact present. She composed a celebratory song for her chief, Donald Cameron of Lochiel,[4] on the occasion of his marriage to a daughter of the Duke of Buccleuch in 1875 ('Fàilte do Lochial agus d'a Mhnaoi Oig do Lochabar', MacKellar, 1880, pp. 103–5).[5] In another poem, 'Cumha le Lochial' (MacKellar, pp. 10–11), she reflected on the response of the 19th chief (the 'Gentle Locheil') to the burning of the clan seat, Achnacarry, in 1746, an indication of her vivid engagement with the history of her clan.[6] In her clan eulogies she did not, however, make any mention of the Cameron lands that were cleared in the early decades of the nineteenth century, and indeed it may have been that her own family on both her paternal and maternal sides, who were settled on the shores of Loch Eil, arrived there as a result of this displacement.[7] Màiri Mhòr, on the other hand, was willing to 'name and shame' clan leaders with respect to their position on the issue of the land, and in 'Òran Loch-Iall', first published in *The Highlander* newspaper (8 August 1874), she challenged with typical directness the views expressed by Donald Cameron of Lochiel in 1874 in relation to the Highland deer forests:

> O tha Camronach Loch-iall,
> Cur an sgiala os àird
> Gur e frìthean nam fiadh,
> Tha cur dìon air ar n-àl.
>
> Their gach duine chual an sgial,
> Gur beag ciall a tha na d'ràdh,
> Bho nach b'aithne dhuitse trian
> Cor is rian mo luchd-gràidh.
> [...]
> 'S iomadh duine còir le sprèidh,
> 'S le chuid fèudail air blàr,
> Chuireadh fad o dhuthaich fhèin,
> Air son fèidh 's caoirich bhàn'
> (Nic-a'-Phearsain, 1891, pp. 267–8).

Màiri Mhòr, however, also produced clan eulogy and elegy when required as, for example, her verses on the marriage of the youngest daughter of Cluny MacPherson in October 1874,[8] and her lament on the death of the chief himself in 1885.[9] Although these are on the whole conventional panegyric exercises, this did not deter Màiri Mhòr from including personal comment. In her song on the MacPherson wedding noted above, she suggests that the happy occasion had lifted her spirits and provided a joyful distraction from her distress at what was taking place in some crofting communities at the time:

> Ged is aon mi tha 'm ònar
> 'S mi 'n còmhnaidh fo ghruaim,
> 'S mo chridhe air a leònadh,
> Le fòirneart an t-sluaigh,
> Ghluais m' aigne le sòlas,
> 'S chaidh bròn air an ruaig,
> 'N uair a bha Liusaidh 's Fitzroy,
> Air am pòsadh le buaidh
> (Nic-a'-Phearsain, 1891, p. 298).

The lines "'S mo chridhe air a leònadh/ le fòirneart an t-sluaigh' probably refer to the attempt in the spring of that year by crofters in Bernera, Lewis, to resist eviction, in what became known as the Bernera Riot, an event about which Màiri Mhòr had already composed a song, 'Daoine Còire Bheàrnara',[10] published in *The Highlander* three months previously (4 July 1874).

In contrast, Mary MacKellar's song composed the following year in celebration of Cameron of Locheil's marriage contained no such contemporary comment but emphasises, in richly evocative language, the traditional Gaelic understanding of the connection between clan ancestry and hereditary lands, and her own acute sensibility to that relationship:

O dhuthaich Chloinn-Chamshroin, dream mheanmnach mo ghaoil,
Cha choigreach le leannan tha 'tarruing na d' ghaoith,
Ach meangan de'n Daraig ann 'ad thalamh tha aosd'
'Tighinn dachaidh le 'bhaintighearn' gu teampul na h-aoidh'
('Fàilte do Lochial agus d'a Mhnaoi Oig do Lochabar', MacKellar, 1880, p. 103).

It should be noted, however, that Màiri Mhòr was not always consistent in her 'naming and shaming', and compared to her panegyric output for her husband's clan, she was selective in her praise for her own MacDonald leaders, and the clan on the whole escaped her censure.

Highland regiments

Given the personal clan affiliations that Mary MacKellar and Màiri Mhòr both clearly subscribed to, it should be no surprise that they also celebrated the military involvement of their clans in the Highland regiments. There were two contexts in particular that both women commented on in their verse. The first was the successful British campaign led by Sir Garnet Wolseley in 1874 to quell an uprising in Ashantee (Ashanti) on the Gold Coast of Africa (what is now South Ghana), and to capture, and indeed destroy, the capital, Coomassie (Kumasi). In this mission, the soldiers of the 42nd Highlanders, the Black Watch, were seen as the heroes of the hour.[11] Màiri Mhòr's poem on the subject, 'Oighre Chluainidh an uair a chaidh a leòn ann an Ashantee' (Nic-a'-Phearsain, 1891, pp. 262–3), was addressed to the son and heir of Cluny MacPherson, Major Duncan MacPherson, who was seriously wounded at Amoaful during a particularly difficult exchange (Schofield, 2012, p. 498). In the song, Màiri Mhòr offers a loyal nod to Queen Victoria, who honoured Major MacPherson for his bravery, but she extends this to make the point that such honourable conduct was his inheritance from his father, referring to the chief's good record as a non-clearing landlord:

Rinn a' Bhan-righ chaomh ruibh còmhradh,
'S chuir i onair oirbh le mòrachd,
Mac an athar nach d'rinn fòirneart,
'S nach tug an còir o shluagh le foill
(Nic-a'-Phearsain, 1891, p. 263).

Although the subject of this song was not directly connected to the land issue in the Highlands, Màiri Mhòr was once again able to make a connection and to praise Cluny MacPherson as a chief 'nach d'rinn fòirneart' and 'nach tug an còir o shluagh le foill'. However, she also had a closer personal connection to this particular campaign as her only son, aged nineteen at the time, was with the 71st Highlanders[12] and the song provided her with an opportunity to comment on this, and express her desire that he should be in MacPherson's own regiment:

> Tha m' aona mhac 's an arm a chòmhnuidh,
> A' dìon ar Rioghachd bho luchd-fòirneart,
> 'S na'm faighinn gach ni fo m' òrdugh,
> Bhiodh e còmhla riut 's a' champ
> (Nic-a'-Phearsain, 1891, p. 263).

In contrast to this personal approach focussing on individuals, Mary MacKellar's poem on the same subject, 'Oran air an 42nd air dhoibh bhi Buadhar an Cogadh Ashantee', (MacKellar, 1880, pp. 67–9) addresses the 42nd Highlanders collectively. The overriding tone is celebratory, praising the regiment's military reputation, and in significant imagery suggesting their upholding of the hereditary honour and bravery of the Gael:

> Thàinig sgeul à tìr na grèine,
> 'S gur mòr m'èibhneas, 's mo chùis mhànrain,
> Freiceadan Dubh nan ceum èutrom,
> 'Bhi gu h-èuchdach mar a b'àbhaist.
> [...]
> B'èutrom ur cèum anns gach cruadal,
> Mar bu dual do mhic nan Gàidheal
>   'Bha mar fhèidh nam beannaibh fuara,
> Gun chuing, gun bhuaraich, gun sgàth orr'
> (MacKellar, 1880, p. 68).

Both Mary MacKellar and Màiri Mhòr were supportive of the Imperial campaign, as was the case with most of the Gaelic-speaking poets in the nineteenth century (McLeod, 2013), and they indicate no sympathy for those at the receiving end of the military prowess that they praise so highly in their songs.

Another issue with a military connection that both women took up in their poetry was the proposal by the War Office in 1881 to abolish the distinctive tartans of the Highland regiments. The Gaelic Society of Inverness was quick to react against this and to harness the support of prominent individuals and members of the Highland gentry and aristocracy to back Lord Archibald Campbell, who took a leading role in the protest. Mary MacKellar had been Bard to the Gaelic Society of Inverness since 1876 and in that role it was natural that she should reflect the Society's activism in this matter in a composition that was sung at its Annual Assembly in July 1881. The song summarises the protest and highlights Lord Archibald's part in securing the positive outcome, while in addition stressing the iconic place of the tartan in the heritage of the Highland soldier:

> C' àite 'm facas riamh air faiche,
> 'N àm tarruing nan cruaidh-lann
> Fir cho sgairteil ris na gaisgich
> G'an robh 'm breacan dualach!
> [...]
> Am bliadhna thainig fios a Lunainn [*sic*]
> Chuir oirnn uile buaireas,
> Na breacain ur ga'n d'thug iad gaol
> Ga'n toirt o laoich nam fuar-bheann;
>
> Dh' èirich an Caimbeulach òg
> A's e aig mòd nan uaislean;
> Phòg e bhiodag, 's thug e bòid
> Gu'm biodh a' chòir an uachdar.
> ('Fleasgach an Fhuilt Chraobhaich, Chais', *TGSI*, Vol. 10, 1881–3, pp. 72–3)

For Màiri Mhòr the subject provoked a strong, personal reaction. She herself was a skilled maker of tweed and tartan, and her symbolic use of the 'breacan' in both song and gesture is an aspect of her Gaelic activism worthy of closer scrutiny. She understood the tartan as empowering the men who wore it in their military campaigns, but she also claimed a role for herself and for women in that narrative. Her song on the issue of the regimental tartans, 'Caoidh nam Ban Gaidhealach' an uair a chaidh bagar a dheanamh gun rachadh an deise bhreacain a thoirt bho na Saighdearan Gaidhealach' (Nic-a'-Phearsain, 1891, pp. 77–84), is composed in the voice of Highland women lamenting the loss of this distinctive feature of the Highland soldier. Màiri Mhòr eulogises the tartan across thirty-six verses in which she cites significant moments in military and clan history when the tartan empowered those wearing it to achieve success and glory:

> Gur e chùm gun chadal sinn
> Is airtneal air ar n-inntinn
> 'N uair thainig fios a Sasunn
> Gus am breacan thoirt o'n t-saighdear,
>   'S e sud a chùm gun chadal sinn

> A shaighdearan na Gàidhealtachd
> A chùm fo smàig gach rioghachd,
> Na gluaisibh fo na bhrataich
> Gun am breacan air ur druim ann,
> > 'S e sud a chùm gun chadal sinn
> (Nic-a'-Phearsain, 1891, p. 77).

Màiri Mhòr's engagement with this matter was so intense that when, eleven years later, she took to the stage in Oban to inaugurate the first Mòd of An Comunn Gàidhealach, she began by praising Lord Archibald Campbell, who was present, for his part in saving the regimental tartans. She then proceeded to sing a song in praise of the qualities and powers of the 'breacan', while her amply proportioned body acted as a visual aid for her message, clothed from shoulder to heel as she was in the 'breacan' of her own making (*Oban Express*, 14 September 1892). One of the recipients of Màiri Mhòr's cloth-making handiwork was Professor John Stuart Blackie, for whom she designed a special patterned plaid and which covered his coffin at his funeral (*Inverness Courier*, 11 November 1898). This was not just a personal token of her appreciation, but honoured his activism in support of the Gaelic language and the Highland crofters with cloth that was symbolic of the history and heroism of the Gael, and also in its very fabric represented the close association between the people and the land.

Professor Blackie was also a friend and patron of Mary MacKellar, the two having come together in Gaelic circles in Edinburgh – 'An t-ard-fheallsanach, Blackie nam buadh, / Ceannard uasal 'measg nan ceud!' as she referred to him in her first official composition for the Gaelic Society of Inverness in 1876 ('Còmhradh eadar am Bàrd 's a Chlàrsach', *TGSI*, Vol. 6 (1876–7), pp. 13–16). When her collection of poetry was published in 1880, it was dedicated to the Professor and it is possible that it was Blackie who financed the publication. Four of his own poems were included in the book, which Mary MacKellar had translated into Gaelic. She refers to him in the dedication as 'caraid dileas', but also significantly as 'Fear-Tagraidh mo dhùthcha, mo shluaigh agus mo chànain', acknowledging, it would seem, not just his enthusiastic support for the Gaelic language and culture, but also his activism in support of the crofters.

Highland Land Struggle

Màiri Mhòr's position on the subject of the crofters' struggle for the land is well-documented in her songs where she articulates with such resonance the sentiments of the Gaelic-speaking population during the important years of land protest and resistance. Indeed, the matter was never far from her mind in whatever subject she was addressing in her songs, as has already been noted. Mary MacKellar's position is more ambiguous, although she does comment on the land situation in a number of poems, reworking the well-used imagery from earlier in the century of the alien Lowland shepherds with their dogs and large numbers of sheep that had replaced the Gaelic-speaking communities:

> Ach mar dhuilleach nan craobh no moll air ghaoith,
>   Chaidh muinntir mo ghaoil fhogradh;
> 'S gheobhar ar sluagh, deas agus tuath,
>   Gu iomall nan cuan bocach.
> 'N ait uaislean mo ghaoil a bha daimheil ri'n daoin,
>   Thainig Goill le'n cuid chaorach mora,
> Agus Sasunnaich chiar a shealgach nam fiadh,
>   Feadh gharbhlach nan sliabh snodhar
> ('Duan Gairdeachais do Chomuinn Gàidhlig Inbhirnis', MacKellar, pp. 106–8 (p. 107)).

Mary MacKellar's lack of incisive political comment on the land situation in the Highlands was referred to in a number of commentaries written at the time of her death.[13] An obituary in the *Scottish Highlander*, for example, in addition to declaring that she was 'one of the most companionable, the best and most agreeable conversationalists we have ever met', also fairly categorically stated:

> In one important respect her poetry is defective. We are not aware of a single line she has ever written in which she gave voice to the aspirations of the Highlanders of her own time ('Death of Mrs Mary MacKellar', *Scottish Highlander*, 11 September 1890).

Mary MacKellar's most direct commentary on the land situation is found in a prose article in English with the title 'A Lay Sermon – "How Much is a Man better than a Sheep"' (*Scottish Highlander*, 9 February 1888), where she concluded that:

> Freewill emigration to better their condition and give better prospects to their families – that is laudable, but insomuch as men are better than sheep, we object to their being turned like dumb driven cattle out of the land of their forefathers by the arbitrary will of any interested individual or by oppressive measures.

The article was published at a time of renewed unrest in connection with the land; although the Crofters' Holdings (Scotland) Act had been passed in June of the previous year, there were still many concerns, in particular the circumstances of the landless cottars, who had no opportunity to obtain land while there were still large tracts under sheep (Hunter, 2000, p. 236). The language and tone in Mary MacKellar's article closely echoes that of Rev.

Thomas MacLauchlan, minister of the Free Gaelic Church in Edinburgh, the church that Mary MacKellar attended, and indeed he was the minister who had officiated at her marriage in 1855. However, she was reluctant or unwilling to follow through this perspective, as MacLauchlan had done:

> Men talked of the Sutherland Clearances. Had they forgotten the Glengarry evictions, and those of Lochiel? Large tracts of land along the Spean and its tributaries were waste, so were the southern banks of Loch Lochy. […] The population had been drained by an unrelenting avarice, […] as short-sighted as it was unjust and selfish.[14]

The more circumspect approach of Mary MacKellar to the land question compared to that of Màiri Mhòr can be illustrated by a comparison of two songs in which they both touch on a common argument in Gaelic poetry with reference to the Clearances – namely that the clearing of the people would effectively reduce the numbers of men available to sustain the much-lauded Highland regiments. In Mary MacKellar's song, she seems to be both making the argument and refuting it at the same time. She highlights the presence of the sheep and the fact that the people are not on the land in the numbers that there was previously, but she then implies that those that are left will still be a match for any enemy:

> 'Us ma thig nàmhaid ort nall thair sàile
> Bheir mic nan Gàidheal dha blàr 'bhios cruaidh,
> Ged 's gann an àireamh, 'us caoraich bhàna,
> 'S gach gleannan àrd anns am b'àbhaist tuath
> ('Òran do Bhan-Rìgh Victoria', MacKellar, 1880, p. 3).

Màiri Mhòr, on the other hand, addresses the argument directly to the landlords and urges those left on the land to stand firm against signing up for military service in lieu of their rent.

> Ach sibhs' tha fuadach ar clann,
> As gach gleann an robh'n tàmh,
> Ma thig nàimhdean a nall
> Thig an ceann dibh gun dàil.
>
> Na tha fuireach dhibh 's an tìr,
> Bithibh dìleas a chàch,
> Tha mi'n dùil nach tog sibh àrm
> Chur air falbh luchd a mhàil
> ('Òran Loch-Iall', Nic-a'-Phearsain, 1891, p. 268).

The Gaelic journalist John Whyte expressed the opinion that Mary MacKellar was 'deeply imbued with a spirit of admiration for the chiefs and chieftains of her native north' ('Funeral of Mary MacKellar', *Oban Times*, 20 September 1890). However, in the same article, he also referred to her as being deeply interested in the cause of the Highland people and an 'active sympathiser' with 'all that related to their advancement and the proper recognition of their language and their legitimate aspirations'. While the latter assessment recognises Mary MacKellar's commitment to the Gaelic language and the Gaelic-speaking people, the first comment suggests at least an understanding of her reticence with regard to the land question, a view that was possibly also shared by John Murdoch, the most radical of land activists, who remained a loyal friend to Mary MacKellar, to the extent that he was a pall-bearer at her funeral.[15]

While it is evident from Mary MacKellar's poems that she lamented the empty glens and decried forced emigration, she made no comment on the land protests taking place in her day. Her position was not unlike that of a number of prominent Edinburgh Gaels with whom she interacted, and while her own minister, as already noted, was strong in his condemnation of the clearance undertaken by the clan chiefs, MacLauchlan was not in fact an advocate of active protest, stating that 'the land in this country must be devoted to the support of the people, and that could be done without any revolutionary touching of any interests'.[16]

Since presenting this paper at Rannsachadh na Gàidhlig in 2014, some personal letters written by Mary MacKellar have come to light and in which we are privy to her private opinions on the land issues in the Highlands in a more candid context.[17] It is very clear that she was politically minded and at the 'conservative' end of the spectrum of views on the Highland Land Question, writing in a letter to Cameron of Locheil: 'I am proud to be a native of the only county in the north that has not gone in for rowdyism and cadocracy – Hurrah!'.[18] In this perspective she may have been influenced by the opinions of prominent individuals with whom she interacted as has already been suggested,[19] but as a woman of independent mind, she had her own reasons for taking such a stance. Her experience of the political situation in parts of Europe during the period she was travelling with her husband on his trading vessel was also a factor, as she indicated in her letter to her chief:

> I who have been abroad a good deal – especially in Germany and Russia and every day I spent in these countries made me more and more Conservative, and after seeing a good deal of the occupants of the slums in St Petersburg nothing seemed to me more ridiculous than the Sovereign of that country going abroad as the apostle of civilisation.[20]

Conclusion

While there were a number of overlaps in the lives and perspectives of Màiri Mhòr and Mary MacKellar, it is not known to what extent, if any, the two women came together socially. In comparing their songs, it is clear that whereas Màiri Mhòr gave free reign to her heartfelt feelings, a fact which makes her best songs so immediate and convincing, Mary MacKellar was much less-inclined to bare her soul in that way, and was generally more reserved in revealing her private opinions. To a degree this contrast reflects the different personalities of the two women, but also their personal circumstances. Mary MacKellar's economic situation was always precarious, her livelihood fully dependent on patronage for her literary work and in that position she was possibly more circumspect in revealing her private opinions. Although it is clear from their songs that their approach to the Highland land question differed both in perspective and priority, Mary MacKellar's private letters reveal that their positions were more polarised than the song evidence might suggest. Mary MacKellar had an unshifting loyalty to her own Cameron clan, its history so implicit a part of her deep-rooted connection to Lochaber. There can be no doubt that Màiri Mhòr would have empathised with this territorial attachment; her 'glorious pride' (MacLean, 1985, p. 71) in her native island of Skye was a touchstone in her songs and in her land activism. In her case, though, the intuitive understanding of this relationship was more immediately focused on the people and community life that the land had supported in her own living memory.

To return finally to Màiri Mhòr's lament for Mary MacKellar – was it composed from a sense of public duty or from personal sentiment? As has been noted, the public and the personal are not easily separated in the songs of Màiri Mhòr, and both dimensions interact in the lament. Màiri Mhòr acknowledges on the one hand the honour and pride of the public position they shared as female Gaelic poets, but also the trials and tribulations of their personal lives:

> Bho'n tha onair nam bàrd
> Air fhàgail dhuinne le uaill,
> Ga gleidheadh gu bràth,
> Cho làn 's a chumas a' chuach,
> Ged gheobhadh iad tàire,
> 'S tàmailt iomadach uair,
> 'N uair thigeadh am bàs,
> Rachadh càrn is clach air an uaigh.
> (Nic-a-Phearsain, 1891, p. 314)

The choice of the word 'tàmailt' is significant, echoing Màiri Mhòr's defiant statement regarding her own experience of 'humiliation'.[21] In another verse, the lines – 'Tha'n fhìrinn cho fior – / Bheir diachainn cuid gus an ùir' – reflect on the fact that the trials of life had taken their toll on Mary MacKellar's health, hastening her untimely death at the age of fifty-seven. In her inclusive choice of pronouns, as illustrated in the verse quoted above, Màiri Mhòr appears to be consciously affirming their shared experience of testing times as well as their common bond as female Gaelic poets. Having that very year (1890) reached the allotted biblical span of three score years and ten,[22] although still in good health, Màiri Mhòr may also have been pondering on her own mortality, and therefore on how posterity would remember them both.

Endnotes

1 Mary MacPherson will be referred to as 'Màiri Mhòr' unless there is a specific reason to use 'Mary MacPherson'.
2 'Oran mu'n Choinnimh-Chomhraidh 'bha ann an DunÉideann air son Cathar Ghàidhlig fhaotuinn anns an Ard Oil-Thigh' (MacKellar, 1880, pp. 59–60).
3 Cluny MacPherson (1804–85), 14th chief.
4 Donald Cameron, 24th of Locheil (1835–1905), Conservative MP for Inverness-shire from 1868–85, and a member of the Napier Commission.
5 Donald Cameron married Margaret Elizabeth Scott, daughter of the 5th Duke of Buccleuch, in 1875.
6 The Cameron homestead of Achnacarry was burnt to the ground by Hanoverian forces on 28 May 1746.
7 'Lord MacDonald, MacLeod of Dunvegan, MacDonald of Clanranald, Cameron of Locheil, the Sutherland family: all […] had by the end of the nineteenth century's second decade, settled the coastal fringes of their estates with crofters, large numbers of whom had been evicted from older farms which were by that time under sheep' (Hunter, 2000, p. 66).
8 Lucy Janetta Julia MacPherson married Edward Albert Fitzroy on 29 October 1874.
9 Ewen MacPherson (1804–1885), 14th chief.
10 In *Dàin agus Orain Ghàidhlig*, this song has the title 'Ceatharnaich Bhearnaraidh' (Nic-a'-Phearsain, 1891, pp. 272–4).
11 For a description of the crucial role of the Black Watch in the Ashantee War see Watson, 1915, pp. 178–86; Schofield, 2012, pp. 490–503. Watson writes: 'The 42nd pushed steadily and irresistibly forward. To that regiment belong, of course, the chief honours' (Watson, 1915, p. 183).
12 See note in Nic-a'-Phearsain, 1891, p. 263.
13 'Mary MacKellar, Bard and Seanachie', *Highland Monthly* (1890–1), Vol. 2, pp. 434–7; 'Death of Mrs Mary MacKellar', *Scottish Highlander*, 11 September 1890, p. 5; 'Mary MacKellar – The Lochaber Bard', *Scots Magazine* (1890–91), pp. 451–63.
14 Quoted in Leask, 1905, p. 104.
15 'Funeral of Mrs Mary Mackellar', *Oban Times*, 20 September 1890.
16 Quoted in Leask, 1905, p. 104.
17 I am grateful to Alex du Toit, archivist at Lochaber Archive Centre, Fort William, for alerting me to the existence of these letters.
18 Mary MacKellar to Cameron of Locheil, 10 April 1880 (Highland Archives,

Lochaber, CL/3/15/2/2/6).
19 Another friend was Alexander Nicolson, who was publicly outspoken in his opposition to any form of active protest. See, for example, his letters in the *Oban Times*, 29 April 1882.
20 Mary MacKellar to Cameron of Locheil, 10 April 1880 (Highland Archives, Lochaber, CL/3/15/2/2/6).
21 'S e na dh' fhuiling mi de thàmailt, / A thug mo bhàrdachd beò' ('Eilean a' Cheò', Nic-a'-Phearsain, 1891, pp. 3–9 (p. 9)).
22 Assuming that her year of birth was in fact 1821 (see Meek, 1998, pp. 20–21).

Bibliography

Hunter, James (rev. edn. 2000). *The Making of The Crofting Community*. Edinburgh: John Donald.

Leask, W. K. (1905). *Thomas McLauchlan, MA, LLD*. Edinburgh: Oliphant, Anderson & Ferrier.

MacLean, Sorley (1985). 'The Poetry of the Clearances', in William Gillies (ed.), *Ris a' Bhruthaich: The Criticism and Prose Writings of Sorley MacLean*, pp. 48–74. Stornoway: Acair.

McLeod, Wilson (2013). 'Gaelic Poetry and the British Military Enterprise, 1756–1945', in Carla Sassi and Theo Van Heijnsbergen (eds), *Within and Without Empire: Scotland Across the (Post)colonial Borderline*, pp. 61–76. Newcastle: Cambridge Scholars Publishing.

MacKellar, Mary (1880). *Gaelic and English Poems*. Inverness: MacLachlan & Stewart.

Meek, Dòmhnall Eachann (ed.) (1998). *Màiri Mhòr nan Òran: Taghadh de a h-Òrain*. Edinburgh: SGTS.

Nic-a'-Phearsain, Màiri (1891). *Dàin agus Orain Ghàidhlig*. Inverness, A. & U. Mac-Coinnich.

Schofield, Victoria (2012). *'The Highland Furies': The Black Watch 1738–1899*. London: Quercus.

Watson, Frederick (1915). *The Story of the Highland Regiments*. London: A & C Black.

5

Dh'fhalbh na gillean grinn: spiritual perspectives in women's songs of the Great War

Anne Macleod Hill

University of Edinburgh

This paper is based on a group of Gaelic songs composed during the Great War by women in the Isle of Lewis and in Harris. There are songs from Losgaintir, Tarasaigh and Orasaigh; Sildinis, Baile Ailein and Cromòr; Sgìre a' Bhac and Tolastadh bho Thuath; Pabail Ìosal, Brèinis Uig, Càrlabhagh and Baile an Truiseil, each poet responding to the war as it unfolds, with no idea of when, how or even if it would end. They belong to a time and a place where no distinct separation was made between the spiritual and the secular, where the one was understood in the light of the other. The songs draw freely on each other. Each tune and chorus has a specific emotional register. Each has a life of its own, deeply embedded in communal memory, surviving through generations, surfacing as and when required to carry forward something less tangible yet stronger than any individual song.

Of the fifteen songs found from this period, twelve show poets setting out a framework within which war can be comprehended and its impact mitigated, accepting it as having been preordained, affecting humanity at large, rather than just their own villages. Seven songs have been selected as representing different points on this spiritual/secular spectrum. By their proximity in time and place, and their similarity in theme, they allow a clear picture to emerge of the systematic sharing of tunes, verses and choruses, intensifying and contextualising each individual's message. This thread of contextualisation also runs through the work of war poets such as Dòmhnall Ruadh Chorùna who, amidst the indiscriminate slaughter of the Somme, uses the *dùthchas* implicit in patronymics and in songs such as 'Dh'fhalbh na gillean grinn' and 'Tha mi duilich, cianail duilich' to assert the identity of the individual soldier (Black, 1999, pp. 126-31, 134-9).

Four days after the declaration of war the *Highland News* of 8 August 1914 reported, 'The mobilisation of the Militias and the Territorials, after the Naval Reservists, has practically denuded Lewis of its able-bodied male population'. The absence of the men had an immediate effect on crofting and fishing, and on domestic, social and spiritual life. This is clearly reflected in women's songs. In Losgaintir, the sub-postmistress Mary Galbraith puts new words to the old recruiting song 'Dh'fhalbh na gillean grinn' telling of the sudden call-up of the Militia, men returning wounded, men lost or missing in action, young girls giving up hope of marrying:

'S ann an taigh a' chladaich
Fhuair sinn òrdan batail,
Thog na gillean gasda
Cas mu seach 's gun dh'fhalbh iad.
Dh'fhalbh na gillean grinn fo 'n chuid armachd. (v. 2)[1]

Of six versions of this song, three are thought to date to the Peninsular War of 1807-14; one to the Boer War; two to the Great War.[2] They show recruits from different islands, heading for different destinations, some armed with swords, some with guns. In one of the early versions, the *gillean grinn* are Mrs MacLeod of Losgaintir's sons, John, Bannatyne, William, Donald and Ewan, all of whom were serving soldiers.[3] In Mairead NicAoidh's version, thought to relate to the Boer War, the cries of cormorants and seagulls mingle with the women's tears as their men leave An Tairbeart.[4] A version from Mòr NicAmhlaidh in Toronto reflects the patriotism of Canadians and emigrant Highlanders flocking to join the British forces.[5] Dòmhnall Ruadh Chorùna, himself one of the *gillean grinn*, leaves a version grimly evocative of the horrors of trench warfare, yet somehow preserving the cheerful camaraderie of the frontline soldiers – even when listing the names of the fallen (Black, 1999, pp. 126-31; SSSA SA 1966.068).

In Tarasaigh, a grandmother takes up a well-known campaigning song for her own protest, 'Is làithean brònach a th' ann'.[6] In Orasaigh and Baile Ailein, the love song 'Tha mi tinn, tinn, tinn' becomes a lament and an appeal that Christ as *An Lighiche* bring peace and healing.[7] In Brèinis, Baile an Truiseil and Cromòr, even in the trenches of the Somme, the old *cianalas* song 'Tha mi duilich, duilich, duilich' re-materialises to mourn sons, brothers and brothers-in-arms.[8] As the unprecedented scale and inhumanity of the war become apparent, some poets rationalise it in terms of an unchangeable providence, some as the last great battle between good and evil. A single voice speaks of war in purely secular terms – if malediction can be considered to be a secular concept.

Ceit Anna Domhnullach, Ceann a muigh a' Bhaic, Leòdhas, 'Tha mo mhallachd aig a' Chaiseir'

Ceit Anna Domhnullach [*sic*] was in Fraserburgh, possibly working as a herring girl, when the call-up came. With the men gone, the herring trade collapsed and the women were left to make their way home to Lewis, unpaid. Everyone had expected the boys of the Militia and the Reserve to be back by New Year, but it soon became clear that the Naval ports of Chatham and Portsmouth were little better than *bailtean faing*, sheep fanks where men were herded together to be sent to the slaughter:

> Tha mo mhallachd aig a' Chaiseir
> Choisin an Reserve thoirt uainne,
> 'S am Militia mar an ceudna
> Gu Brigade a chuir thar chuain. (v. 1)

> Dh'fhalbh an traine leibh do Chatham
> Is do Phortsmouth, bailtean faing,
> Sgap iad sibh an sin bho chèile
> Thìrean cèin is dhan a' Fhràing. (v. 3)

> Tha mo mhallachd aig a' Chaiseir
> 'S iomadh cridhe rinn e tinn,
> 'S iomadh fiùran maiseach àluinn
> Chaidh a chàradh ri a linn. (v. 7)[9]

Her condemnation of the Kaiser is absolutely unequivocal, and is unique within the context of these songs in that she depicts him as being wholly responsible for a war which he himself has instigated. The other poets consistently represent war as being above and beyond human control. The Kaiser may be depicted as Satan, allowed to trouble the world for a fixed period, but is just playing out his part in an unchangeable providence, as they themselves are. The understanding is that wars are ordained by God himself, and that neither side can prevail over the other, nor peace be won except with His consent. Iain MacLeòid of Siabost had set this out very clearly in his 'Òran a' Chogaidh', composed while serving in the Transvaal in 1899:

> 'S e Dia tha riaghladh an domhainn,
> 'S ann Leis a tha còmhairl' gach rìgh,
> 'S ann Leis a tha bhuaidh anns a' chogadh,
> 'S E dh'ordaich an claidheamh o thìm. (v. 1)

(MacLeod, 1998, pp. 239-47, p. 239).

As war returned in 1914, his song was still fresh in local memory, with stray couplets and verses clearly traceable in these songs of the Great War.

Raonaid NicFhearghais, Tarasaigh, 'Is làithean brònach a th' ann'

MacLeòid's cataloguing of the heavy losses and dubious victories of the Boer War shares both tune and chorus with Iain MacMhathain's 'Òran mu 'n Eaglais' (1843), castigating worldly ministers, and Rob MacDougall's condemnation of hard-drinking Highland emigrants, 'Comunn na Stuamachd'.[10] In each, the optimism of the chorus, 'Tha buaidh aig comunn mo ghaoil' rises above the darkness of the subject, making it a natural choice for Raonaid NicFhearghais' wartime song, 'Is làithean brònach a th' ann' (MacLeod 1916, p. 95). In 1915 Raonaid was eighty-two years old, with her son and two grandsons on active service in France. Her song shows her to be practical, angry and well-informed. She complains that with most able-bodied men away, Tarasaigh was facing real difficulties in feeding the women and children. There was no work, just a steady stream of official papers as the Government spread its net ever wider, taking in older men, and boys who had been too young for the first call to arms. The newspapers were filled with reports of war and notifications of those lost, or missing in action:

> Is làithean brònach a th' ann
> Dh'fhannaich gach cosnadh a bh' ann,
> Cha 'n fhaic mi an diugh tighinn do 'n àite
> Ach eallaich de phàipeirean Galld'. (v. 1)

> Cha bheathaich sud mnathan is clann
> Feumaidh sinn Creideamh 's an àm,
> 'S iad ìnnleachdan mallaichte a' Chésair
> A tharruing gu léir oirnn an call. (v. 2)

> Chuala sibh uile 's gach àit'
> Mu 'n chroich a rinn Haman mar thà,
> Tha an César a' togail dhuibh t' éile
> Ach cha 'n eil i gu léir aig a h-àrd. (v. 3)

This was the year of Ypres and the Battle of Loos and whether from newspapers, from men invalided out or from men returning on leave, Raonaid had a clear perception of this war as going beyond all other wars. It was not just the difficulty of feeding local children which concerned her, but that as thousands of men fell, an unimaginable number of children all over Europe were being left fatherless:

> Cha do chruthaicheadh teang' ann an ceann
> A dh'innseadh mu 'n chogadh a th' ann,
> Na tharruing e dh'olc air gach rìoghachd
> Is na dh'fhàg e de dhìlleachdain annt'. (v. 4)

As with MacLeòid's 'Òran a' Chogaidh', her understanding was that it was not only the soldiers on the battle front who would affect the outcome, but also those who recognise the cause behind war and who pray for peace. While soldiers faced *an nàmhaid* in the trenches, spiritual leaders confronted *Nàmhaid Dhaoine*, man's old enemy Satan, in a war which was just as real:

> Thàinig an glaodh ud chum bàis
> Ràinig e ìosal is àrd,
> Dh'fhàg iad an dachaidhean rìomhach
> Is leagadh na mìltean 's na blàir. (v. 5)

> Is iomadh bliadhna is linn
> Bho dh'innis an Fhìrinn sud duinn,
> Gu 'n èirich cogadh 's gach rìoghachd
> Mu 'n ruig sìth sinn a mhàireas a-chaoidh. (v. 7)

> Na smuainichibh idir an ràdh
> Nach eil iomadh Maois anns gach àit',
> Tha tagradh a là is a dh'oidhche
> Cho dìleas ri saighdear aig blàr. (v. 8)

> Mo chluas ri clàistinn gach tràth
> Chluinntinn na sìth 'tighinn bho 'n Àird,
> Oir cha dèan innleachdan rìghrean
> An Nàmhaid a chlaoidh anns na blàr. (v. 11)

In a society which accepted the Bible as the source of all authority, her biblical references would have been immediately recognised and understood. Citing Old Testament precedent, she compares the Kaiser to Haman (Esther, 8.5–10), showing that those who try to destroy their neighbours will themselves be destroyed. Her reference to Moses was a reminder that their own ministers and elders were also in the forefront of battle, praying night and day that evil would be overcome and peace be restored. Iain MacLeòid had used exactly the same illustration to make the same point:

> Tha Maois ann an iomadach àite
> 'S luchd-cumail a làmhan a-suas. (v. 16)
> (Macleod, 1998, p. 244).

She sees the whole world at war, interpreting this as a fulfilment of the biblical prophecies of the 'last days' when there would be wars and rumours of wars, when nation would rise against nation. Listening for news of peace, she longs for some sign of comprehension on the part of governments that war is an affliction visited equally on both sides and that neither enemy forces nor Satan himself can be overcome by strength of arms alone. She hears reports from the trenches; the poison gas, the wounded shot on the battlefield, crowded field hospitals, shell-holes becoming graves for men drowning in mud, and she despairs of her son and grandsons returning:

> Is mìorbhuil iongantach th' ann
> Ma thilleas sibh chugainn a nall,
> Am measg nan lasraichean puinsein
> 'S na peileirean dian ruith mu 'r ceann. (v. 12)

> Gur iomadh cridh' tha fo chàs
> Cluinntinn thighean-leighis bhi làn,
> Is a chuid dhiubh nach gabhadh an giùlan
> Chuir an nàmhaid gu brùideil gu bàs. (v. 13)

> Cha d' àraicheadh cridh' ann an com
> Nach leaghadh an sealladh tha trom,
> Tha spreadhadh nam peilear mòr ùra
> A dùsgadh dhoibh uaighean 's a' pholl. (v. 14)

Having said what she can, with all the dignity of her eighty-two years, she steps back from this world and turns her face to the next, waiting patiently for the *aiseag*, not from Tarasaigh to Harris, but to carry her soul over Jordan:

> Cha chuala mi leithid 'nam là
> 'S mi nise ceithir fichead 's a dhà,
> Is m' aghaidh gu dlùth air mo dhachaidh
> A' feitheamh an aiseig gach tràth. (v. 15)

Mrs Ceanadaidh, Orasaigh, 'Tha mi tinn, tinn, tinn'

By the spring of 1916 Loos and Ypres were over. The Battle of Verdun was well under way and set to continue until winter. Casualties on the Western Front alone were being counted in their hundreds of thousands by both sides. In Orasaigh, South Lochs, another poet, Mrs Ceanadaidh goes far beyond Raonaid NicFhearghais in explaining war as being under divine rather than human control. From her very first verse, Mrs Ceanadaidh's words mark her out as one of the *mathraichean an Israel*, devout women respected for their biblical knowledge and spiritual insight. She acknowledges immediately that peace can only come from *Rìgh nam Buadh*, from virtue rather than power alone. Though evangelical song often depicts Christ as *An Gaisgeach*, no such imagery appears in these songs of actual war.[11] *Gaisgeach Treun nam Buadh* and *Armailt Neàmh* do not fight in earthly wars and cannot be called upon by either side. The whole message of Mrs Ceanadaidh's song is that both sides are equally culpable, and all must suffer the consequences of defying God's Law.

Both tune and chorus, 'Tha mi tinn, tinn, tinn', traditionally associated with songs of unrequited love or spiritual longing, transfer effortlessly to wartime laments where the sickness of love gives way to the sickness of anxiety and grief. 'Tha mi tinn, tinn, tinn' had appeared in the Elizabeth Ross Manuscript of 1812 (Cooke, MacLeod and Ó Baoill 2011, p. 62), Iain MacLennan, the 'Brisbane Bàrd', made it into a *cianalas* song as he emigrated to Australia in 1885:

> Tha mi tinn, tinn, tinn,
> Tha mi tinn gun bhith slàn,
> Mi bhi fàgail an tìr
> Gun fhios an till mi gu bràth.
> (MacLennan, 1937, p. 2).

John MacRae of Kintail's version was an old man's love song to his young wife (SSSA SA1980. 026). In Scalpaigh, Calum MacSuain transformed it into an evangelical song, 'Tha mi tinn leis A ghràidh'.[12] For Bean Chaluim Dhòmhnuill Alasdair of Baile Ailein it became 'Caoidh Iain MacLeòid', mourning a young soldier lost on the Western Front in 1917.[13] By changing *gràdh* to *Gràs* Mrs Ceanadaidh emphasises her evangelical message, depicting war and sorrow as disease, healing as Salvation, with Christ as *An Lighiche*, the Physician. Loneliness, anxiety and grief are as poignant in her song as in any secular lament as she explains her own situation and that of the local community:

> *Sèist*
> Tha mi tinn, tinn, tinn,
> Tha mi tinn, gun bhi slàn,
> 'S cha 'n eil lighich fo 'n a' ghréin
> A nì feum dhomh ach Gràs.[14]
>
> Dh'fhàgadh mis' an so air tuath
> 'Am baile aig gualainn na Pàirc',
> 'S mar tig Thu Rìgh nam Buadh
> Cha bhi suaimhneas an càil. (v. 1)
>
> Thugadh taobh mo leapa bhuam
> Bha mi lòm anns an àit,
> Ach na 'm biodh e a chum Glòir Chriosd,
> Bhithinn riaraicht' le 'làimh. (v. 2)

Unlike Raonaid NicFhearghais, she makes no complaint of domestic hardship. Her bleak statement that her husband has been taken and that she lies in an empty bed is all that she claims of sympathy for herself, quickly covering her weakness with a willingness to accept even this if it is part of God's purpose:

> Tha mi 'g ionndrain Do shluaigh
> 'Bha dèanamh suaimhneach an àit,
> Tha cuid sgapt' ac' anns a' chuan
> 'S cuid aig cruadal 's a bhlàr. (v. 3)

> Tha e duilich ri 'luaidh
> Gu 'n d' thuit cuid fuar anns a' bhlàr,
> Tha iadsan 'nis an sonas buan
> 'Snàmh a' chuan 'tha gun tràigh. (v. 5)

She speaks of missing, not her own family, but the spiritual family of the church. The term *Do shluagh* indicates members rather than adherents, and her confidence that those friends lost in battle or at sea are now *an sonas buan, a' snàmh a' chuan tha gun tràigh* is a clear statement of this distinction. The *cuan gun tràigh* was not the North Atlantic or the South China Sea, where so many lost their lives, but one of evangelical song's many names for eternity: in this case, *Cuan A ghràidh*, the sea of unbounded love as opposed to *Cuan feirge*, the sea of wrath. In the absence of the men who made up the backbone of the congregation, Mrs Ceanadaidh takes on the task of those whom Iain MacLeòid and Raonaid NicFhearghais had depicted as Moses, the spiritual leaders who pray for peace. Her song amounts almost to an evangelical sermon, warning against politicians who think that military strength brings victory:

> 'S ann tha ceann'rdan ar sluaigh-n'
> Ann an suain cadail bàis,
> Suil ri Breatainn airson buaidh
> 'S air Rìgh nan Sluagh 'dèanamh tàir. (v. 39)

An underlying convention of evangelical preaching, prayer and song is that every assertion must be supported by *dearbhadh an Fhocail*, a biblical text used to validate each statement made and justify each hope expressed. Mrs Ceanadaidh would naturally support her message at every point with the appropriate *dearbhadh*. For those facing insurmountable odds in battle she cites the case of David, the shepherd boy armed with a sling who defeated Goliath and the whole of the Philistine army (I Samuel 17.50). For those under enemy fire, there were Shadrach, Meshach and Abednego who came unharmed from Nebuchadnezzar's fiery furnace (Daniel 3.26). For those hemmed in by the enemy, there was the account of the Israelites escaping

Pharaoh's army by the parting of the Red Sea (Exodus 14.29). For those at sea, there was the story of Jonah brought safely to shore in the belly of the whale (Jonah 2.10). Her central example is that of the King of Nineveh, whose penitence turned aside God's anger (Jonah 3.5-10). This is exactly what Mrs Ceanadaidh hopes for and what her song is intended to bring about. She petitions The King of Kings on behalf of the kings of Europe, looking to a time when the Gospel of Peace will be declared throughout the world; when Satan's power will be broken; when nations recognise that peace is in the hands of God himself and is beyond the power of any earthly leader:

> Na 'n tigeadh Tu a dh'eubhach sìth
> 'Measg na rìghrean an dràsd',
> Deidheadh an cumhachdan 'neo-bhrìgh
> Cha d' dheidheadh nì dheth thar T' Ainm. (v. 43)

> Sin an là air am bi prìs
> 'S cha bhi nì mar a bha,
> Rachadh Soisgeul na Sìth'
> Chraobh-sgaoileadh 's gach àit'. (v. 44)

> Ma 's e sin tha 'na Do rùn
> Bheir Thu daoine gu àit',
> Bheir thu dhaibh aon chridhe
> 'S cha bhith cìs orr' aig Nàmh. (v. 45)

Màiread NicLeòid, Tolastadh bho Thuath, 'Òran air a' Chogadh: 1914-18'

In Tolastadh bho Thuath, Màiread NicLeòid is tired of lonely nights, sleeping and waking alone in her empty bed while her husband Seonaidh Choinnich is at sea.

> *Sèist*
> O nach mise tha sgìth ag èirigh 's a' laighe leam fhìn,
> 'S nach urrainn dhomh gun a bhith 'g ionndrainn
> Gu h-àraid mo chompanach fhìn.[15]

With two hundred and thirty men from Tolastadh bho Thuath away on active service, the village is empty. Scouring the newspapers for news of her husband's ship, the *HMS Invincible*, Màiread is quietly proud as she hears of Admiral Sturdee's victory in the Falklands, then, feeling torn between her husband and her brother, she excuses herself for having her heart at sea with Seonaidh Choinnich rather than in France with her brother:

> Feuch an gabh sibh bhur tìd'
> Anns an rìoghachd ri strì aig an àm,
> Ach, O bhiodh bhur sùil ris an Rìgh
> Aig am bheil iuchair na sìth 'n A làimh. (v. 9)
>
> O, ged dh'fhàg mi mo bhràthair
> Chan e nach cuimhnich mi e,
> Oir tha e muigh anns gach gàbhadh is cunnart
> A ghràidh as do dhèidh. (v. 10)
>
> Ach is ann air a' mhuir 'tha mo chrìdhse
> Is èiginn dhomh innse sin dhuibh,
> O gu 'n tilleadh iad sàbhailt
> Le beannachd nan Gràs air an cinn. (v. 11)

She becomes convinced that this is Armageddon. The Kaiser is to her, and to many others, the Beast depicted in the Book of Revelation. He is to be given power for a certain time, but will be overcome and imprisoned by the King of Kings:

> O cha b' fhair orm Kaisear
> A thuirt air A' Bhéisd mar ainm,
> Is iomadh cridh' rinn e 'reubadh
> A bha glè threubhant a' falbh. (v. 14)
>
> Ma 's e gum faigh sibh gu Bherlin
> 'S ar brataichean féin chur air seilbh,
> Cha chreid mi nach cuir sibh e am prìosan
> Às nach fhaigh e ri shaoghal air falbh. (v. 15)

Màiread makes no separation between the reality of war and the reality of evil. She reminds servicemen and prisoners of war caught up in this conflict between the King and the Beast, the great struggle between good and evil, that they must be in constant readiness for the coming of 'an Rìgh aig am bheil iuchair na sìth 'n A làimh' (v. 9). In one sense this would be their own death: in another, the return of Christ and the end of the world. Physical and non-physical worlds are again barely distinguishable in her expectation that it is in Berlin that this incarnation of evil, the Beast, will be imprisoned. As she lies in her own warm bed, she thinks of local boys out in the trenches, soaking wet, sleepless, with neither blanket nor pillow:

> O chàirdean, nach sibh a tha suaimhneach
> 'N ur laigh' air a' chluasaig troi 'n oidhch',

>An uair a tha balaich ur dùthcha
>A-muigh fo 'n bhùirn anns an trainns'. (v. 20)

Unlike Mrs Ceanadaidh, Màiread does not deliver a sermon. Her song simply reflects the perspective of a woman for whom life is contextualised in terms of biblical teaching. Longing for life to return to normal, she quotes the prophet Isaiah's description of the reign of peace and justice, where there would be no more destruction and where the outcast and the exile would be gathered home from the four corners of the earth:

>Is truagh nach tigeadh an latha
>Às am bitheadh gach bail' ann an sìth,
>Is gu 'n cluicheadh an leòghann 's an leanabh
>Aig toll na nathrach 's an raon. (v. 24)

>Is gu 'n itheadh a' bho 's am math-ghamhainn
>Sìol às an amar mar aon,
>Is gu 'n sguireadh gach rìoghachd a' chòmhstri
>Is iomradh air cogadh nach bi. (v. 25)

Though the text is from Isaiah 11. 7-8, her paraphrasing of it imitates Iain MacLeòid's 'Òran a' Chogaidh'. Her mirroring of MacLeòid's verse suggests a possibility at least, that she may also have been using his tune, just as Raonaid NicFhearghais had done:

>O, nach tigeadh an latha
>Sam biodh gach bail' ann an sìth!
>A chluicheadh an naoidhean 's an leanabh
>An comann nan nathrach is rìgh;
>A dh'itheadh an leòmhann 's am math-ghamhainn
>An sìol anns an amar mar aon;
>A sguireadh gach rìoghachd da còmhraig
>Is iomradh air cogadh nach biodh!
>(MacLeod, 1998, pp. 239-47 (p. 240, v. 4)).

'An Leave mu Dheireadh'

Màiread's second song, 'An Leave mu Dheireadh' (Comann Eachdraidh Tholastaidh bho Thuath, 2005, pp. 88-9), goes beyond biblical prophecy and enters the realm of preordination, the concept that the world and everything in it, every living creature and all human life follow a course ordained for them before the universe itself came into being. In the Battle of Jutland, on the last day of May 1916, her husband's ship the *HMS Invincible* took a direct hit to the munitions store and went down with the loss of over a thousand men, Seonaidh Choinnich amongst them. Màiread, now a widow with four children, is tormented not just by the loss of her husband, but by the thought that he has no grave. A year and more after his death she cannot keep from watching the shore, thinking of him amongst the waves or on the bed of the sea. If she could lay him in his coffin, stand at his grave, put a stone at his head, she believes she could at least be free from this endless watching:

> Nam faighinn do an ùir thu
> Is ciste dhùinte ort a ghràidh,
> Gun tugadh sin dhomh saorsa
> Gun mo shùil bhith air an tràigh. (v. 6)

Looking back on his last leave, Màiread has come to believe that her husband had foreknowledge of his own death. After visiting a fellow Naval Reservist who had been invalided out and was close to death, he had said that he would rather be dying there with him, if he could be sure of a place in heaven. As though his words had somehow attracted death's attention, on the very day that his friend Iain Dòmhnallach died at home in Tolastadh, Seonaidh Choinnich's ship was lost:

> B' iongantach mar a dh'òrdaich Thu
> 'S gun deònaicheadh dhuit e,
> 'S tu sealltain air do charaid
> 'S tu aig an taigh air 'leave'. (v. 1)
>
> Is e thuirt thu nuair a dh'fhàg thu e
> Gum b' fheàrr gun robh thu fhèin,
> Còmhla ris a' bàsachadh
> Nam biodh d' àit air Nèamh. (v. 2)
>
> Is ann mar sin a thachair
> Chaidh a choimhlionadh dhuit fèin,
> Bha e rèir nam briathran
> Mar a dh'iarr thu às do bheul. (v. 3)

In describing what happened, Màiread uses the words *òrdaich*, *deònaich* and *coimhlionadh*, words bound up with the concept of preordination and to a path set out for Seonaidh Choinnich which he must inevitably follow. Her understanding of his having known the place and time of his own death, and that he went back to sea knowing that he would not return, sits somewhere between local belief in foreknowledge and Reformed teaching on preordination, but it is to the Bible that she turns for words to express her anguish:

> Cha robh ach beagan uairean
> Anns a' cheum bha sibh bho chèil',

Gus an robh sibh anns an t-sìorraidheachd
'S gun iadh oirbh an t-eug. (v. 4)

Nuair a bhios mi stigh leam fhìn
Bidh mi smaoineachadh a ghràidh,
Cho òg 's a chaidh ar dealachadh
Ann an toileachas ar là. (v. 11)

An cupan chaidh a lìonadh dhuinn
Air iarraidh a bhith tràight',
Is gun dh'òl mi deoch bha searbh dheth
'S cha chaill mi bhlàs gu bràth. (v. 12)

O tha mis an dòchas
Nach robh do lòchran gann,
Is gun d' fhuair thu 'measg nan òighean
'Steach còmhl' ri Fear na Bainnse. (v. 13)

The *cupan searbh*, symbolising acceptance of God's will in the face of grief and adversity, appears again and again in Gaelic spiritual song.[16] For Màiread, the *deoch bha searbh* which she could never lose the taste of was widowhood. For Seonaidh Choinnich, it was that he would die far from home. In her first song, with her husband still living, Màiread hopes for peace in this world. In her second, she can only hope that he has passed safely to the next. Using the conventional symbolism of evangelical laments; *an lòchran*, the lamp which must always be kept in readiness; *na h-òighean*, those who watch and wait faithfully for the coming of *Fear na Bainnse*, and *an t-aiseag* which carries the soul over Jordan, she hopes that death had not caught him unprepared:

Is ma fhuair thu 'n aiseag shòlasach
A thug do Ghlòir thu null,
Cha chaoidh thu gun do dh'fhàg thu
An saoghal ànradhach seo tha ann. (v. 14)

Catrìona Mhoireasdan, Brèinis, 'Tha mi duilich, duilich, duilich'

By the spring of 1917, unrestricted submarine warfare was sinking one in every four merchant ships coming to Britain, and in the village of Brèinis, Catrìona Mhoireasdan was mourning her brother Dòmhnall. His ship, the *HMS Jason*, had hit a mine twenty miles off the Irish Coast and gone down with the loss of twenty-five men. Though Catrìona's lament is essentially secular, it shares the same perspective as the most spiritual of these poems.[17] She reconciles herself to the loss of her brother in virtually the same words as Mrs Ceanadaidh accepts the loss of her husband, '*bhiodh sinn riaraicht' leis an àmhghar*' and '*bhithinn riaraicht' le 'làimh*'. Both the tune and the chorus, 'Tha mi duilich, duilich, duilich' were known throughout the islands, in men's songs and women's songs, secular and spiritual alike. Originally associated with physical and spiritual exile, they came to typify wartime laments. Uilleam MacCoinnich, Bàrd Cnoc Chùsbaig had used these words as he left Siadar for Ontario in 1907:

>Tha mi duilich, duilich, duilich,
>Tha mi duilich, duilich thà,
>Tha mi duilich, duilich, brònach,
>Fàgail Steòrnabhagh mo ghràidh.
>(Comunn Gaidhealach Leòdhais, 1982, pp. 41-2, *sèist*).

In Beàrnaraigh, the evangelical poet Eachann MacFhionghain, dreading exclusion from God's presence, adopts them for 'Cait an Taisbean Mi?'

>Tha mi duilich, cianail duilich,
>Tha mi duilich dol tron fhàsach;
>Tha mi duilich 's trom fo smuaintean
>An téid m' fhuadachadh bho làthair.
>(MacFhionghain, 1990, pp. 77-80, *sèist*)

Peigi NicLeòid of Cromòr takes them for 'Amhran Peigi Eachainn', mourning her son John who was lost in action in Cairo:

>Tha mi duilich, duilich, duilich,
>Tha mi duilich dol tron fhàsach,
>Tha mo chridhe tùrsach cianail,
>Cha b' e an aois a liath cho tràth mi.
>(Smith, 2010, p. 79, *sèist*)

Dòmhnall Ruadh Chorùna transforms them into a lament for fellow soldiers lost in the trenches of the Somme:

>Tha mi duilich, cianail duilich,
>Tha mi duilich 's cianail tha mi,
>Bhon a chunna mi le m' shùilean
>Sealladh tùrsach mo chuid bhràithrean.
>(Black, 1999, p. 134, v. 1).

Some versions pre-date Catrìona's lament for her brother, others post-date it, but the survival of at least ten published versions implies the existence of similar unpublished songs:

>*Sèist*
>Tha mi duilich, duilich, duilich,

Duilich airson mo bhràthar,
Tha mi duilich, tùrsach, cianail
Làn de chianalas a tà mi.

Bha thu measail anns gach baile
'S aig gach banabaidh is nàbaidh,
Fichead mìle mach à Èirinn
Anns an *Jason* chaidh do bhàthadh. (v. 1)

Ach cha tèid sinn dh'ionnsaidh t' uaigh
Fada bhuainn 'sa chuain a tà i,
Ach nam biodh tu ann an Criosda
Bhiodh sinn riaraicht' leis an àmhghar. (v. 2)

Everything around her reminds Catrìona of her brother; the *feannagan* which had cost him so much labour, the sound of the sea on the shore, the bed which he will never sleep in and the thought as she smooths the covers that he is lying on the bed of the sea, a bed that can never be warmed:

Nuair a thèid mi gu do leabaidh
'S a bheir mi làmh oirr' gus a càradh,
'S a chuimhnicheas mi do leabaidh fhuar-sa
Anns a' chuain a-chaoidh nach blàthaich. (v. 4)

Nuair a thèid mi chun an dorais
Oidhche ghealaich 's i an àirde,
Cianalas a' tighinn air m' inntinn
Nuair a chluinn mi fuaim na tràghad. (v. 5)

'S e thubhairt thu ri Calum do charaid,
Nach deigheadh talamh gu bràth ort,
Is nach fhaiceadh tu tuilleadh Ùige
'S nach fhaiceadh tu a-chaoidh do chàirdean. (v. 6)

Like Seonaidh Choinnich, Dòmhnall had had a premonition of his own death, confiding it to a friend the last time he had been home on leave. He was a man of forty-nine, and in this third year of the war, was well able to understand the dangers he faced and that men lost at sea rarely came home for burial. For Dòmhnall and for Seonaidh Choinnich, forewarning of their own death carries connotations of sacrifice or of being sacrificed, laying down their lives for family and friends, or of going as lambs to the slaughter. By this stage of the Great War casualties were being counted in their millions, and men being sacrificed needlessly must have been in the forefront of many minds. For the men themselves, caught up in a war over which they had no control, forewarning and preordination may have offered a way of maintaining dignity and a sense of identity. It may have helped them face the fear of death or the fear of being afraid. It may have comforted them to feel that, however indiscriminate the slaughter and however unidentifiable the bodies, each one of them was known to God.

Whatever they may have of poetic or philosophical merit, these songs are eloquently evocative of a time and place where a generation was cut off. In Losgaintir young girls lose all hope of marrying. In Tarasaigh, Raonaid NicFhearghais has little hope that her son and her grandsons will survive. In Brèinis, Catrìona Mhoireasdan mourns her only brother. In Tolastadh, Màiread is left with four fatherless children. In Orasaigh, there is no word of children, or that life may in any way continue. Tunes which used to belong to love songs are still shared and still carry their traditional associations, but are now turned to mourning, each song a formalised expression of grief where no funeral is possible, a headstone on a non-existent grave.

> Soraidh leat gus 'n tig a mhaduinn,
> 'S an teich na sgàilean tha mun cuairt,
> Soraidh leat, thèid sinne thugad,
> Ach cha till thu, ghaoil on uaigh.[18]

Endnotes

1. Mary Galbraith, 'Dh'fhalbh na gillean grinn', SSSA SA1977.182 (available from URL: www.tobarandualchais.co.uk/en/fullrecord/of/73048/1) (accessed 12 August 2015).
2. Two anonymous versions of Dh'fhalbh na gillean grinn', both very similar to Mrs MacLeod of Losgaintir's version and assumed to date from the Peninsular War, are held at SSSA SA1954.053 and SA1975.221.
3. Mrs MacLeod of Losgaintir, 'Òran le Bean Lusgintir', in MacDonald, 1911, pp. 180, xxxiii.
4. Mairead NicAoidh, 'Dh'fhalbh na gillean grinn', SSSA SA1952.114.
5. Mòr NicAmhlaidh, 'Dh'fhalbh na gillean grinn', in MacLeod, 1916, p. 96.
6. Raonaid NicFhearghais, 'Is laithean brònach a th' ann', in MacLeod, 1916, p. 95.
7. Mrs I. Ceanadaidh, 'Tha mi tinn, tinn, tinn', in *The Monthly Record of the Free Church of Scotland*, March 1916, pp. 11-12; Bean Chaluim Dhomhnuill Alasdair, 'Caoidh air Iain Macleòid', *Stornoway Gazette,* 30 November 1917.
8. Catrìona Mhoireasdan, 'Jason', in Nic a' Ghobhainn, 2009, p. 74; L. McL. 'In Memoriam Charles MacLeod', *Stornoway Gazette*, 27 April 1917; Peigi NicLeòid, 'Amhran Peigi Eachainn', in Smith, 2010, p. 79; Domhnall MacDonald, 'Tha mi duilich, cianail, duilich', in Black, 1999, pp. 134-8.
9. Ceit Anna Domhnullach, 'Tha mo mhallachd aig a' Chaiseir', *Stornoway Gazette*, 10 August 1917.

10 MacMhathain, 1843; Rob MacDhùgaill, 'Comunn na Stuamachd', in Cameron, 1892, pp. 351-5.
11 The appellations *An Gaisgeach Buadhmhor, Gaisgeach Treun nam Buadh* and *An Curaidh Treun* appear in NicDhòmhnaill, 2010, p. 24, v. 1, v. 6. For *Gaisgeach Mòr na Buaidh* and *An Gaisgeach*, see MacLeod, 1916, p. 315, v. 3, and p. 316, v. 9.
12 Calum MacSween, 'Laoidh', on Martin 1998.
13 Bean Chaluim Dhomhnuill Alasdair, 'Caoidh air Iain Macleòid', *Stornoway Gazette*, 30 November 1917.
14 Mrs I. Ceanadaidh, 'Tha mi tinn, tinn, tinn', *The Monthly Record of the Free Church of Scotland*, March 1916, pp. 11-12.
15 Màiread NicLeòid, 'Òran air a' Chogadh: 1914-18', in Comann Eachdraidh Tholastaidh bho Thuath, 2005, pp. 87-8.
16 For illustrations of the symbolism of the *cupan searbh*, see Murchadh a' Cheisdeir's 'Cliù an Uain' (MacLeod, 1962, pp. 44-5 (v. 1) ('Tuil na feirg' tha cho searbh nach gabh inns'/ 'S nach ruig mìltean de lìnntean a tràigh / Sin an cupan thug Dia dha ri òl / Gus ar dìon o gach dòruinn gu bràth') and Bean Iain Domhnullaich's 'Cumha' (Bean Iain Domhnullaich, nd, pp. 21-5 (v. 9) ('Tha 'm banntraichean le cridhe leòint' / Ag òl á cupan searbh').
17 Catrìona Mhoireasdan, 'Jason', in Nic a' Ghobhainn, 2009, p. 74.
18 C. NicLeòid, 'Marbh-Rainn do Dhomhnull MacLeòid le phiuthar', *Stornoway Gazette*, 1 June 1917.

Bibliography

Bean Iain Domhnullaich (nd). *Òrain le Bean Iain Domhnullaich*. No publisher stated.
Black, Ronald (ed.) (1999). *An Tuil: Anthology of 20th Century Scottish Gaelic Verse*. Edinburgh: Polygon.
Cameron, Paul (1892). 'Perthshire Gaelic Songs'. *TGSI*, Vol, 18, pp. 340-62.
Ceanadaidh, I. (1916). 'Tha mi tinn, tinn, tinn'. *The Monthly Record of the Free Church of Scotland,* March 1916, pp. 11-12.
Comunn Gaidhealach Leòdhais (1982). *Eilean Fraoich: Lewis Gaelic Songs and Melodies*. Stornoway: Acair.
Comann Eachdraidh Tholastaidh bho Thuath (2005). *Clachan Crìche: Taghadh de Bhàrdachd Tholastaidh – 1850-2000*. Tolsta: Comann Eachdraidh Tholastaidh bho Thuath.
Cooke, Peter, MacLeod, Morag and Ó Baoill, Colm (eds). *The Elizabeth Ross Manuscript: Original Highland Airs Collected at Raasay in 1812 by Elizabeth Jane Ross*. Edinburgh: Celtic and Scottish Studies. Available from URL: http://www.ed.ac.uk/polopoly_fs/1.100544!/fileManager/RossMS.pdf (accessed 12 August 2015).
MacDonald, Angus, and MacDonald, Archibald (eds) (1911). *The MacDonald Collection of Gaelic Poetry*. Inverness: Northern Counties Newspaper and Print and Publishing Co.
MacFhionghain, Eachann (1990). *An Neamhnaid Luachmhor*. Stornoway: Stornoway Religious Bookshop.
MacLennan, John (1937). *Duanagan agus Sgeulachdan Beaga*, ed. by Hector MacDougall. Glasgow: Alasdair MacLabhruinn.
MacLeod, Iain N. (ed.) (1998 [1916]). *Bàrdachd Leòdhais*, Stornoway: Acair.
MacLeod, Malcolm C. (ed.) (1916). *The Celtic Annual 1916: Year Book of the Dundee*

Highland Society. Dundee: Dundee Highland Society.
MacLeod, Murdo (1962). *Bardachd Mhurchaidh a' Cheisdeir*. Edinburgh: Darien Press.
MacMhathain, Iain (1843). *Òran mu 'n Eaglais*. Edinburgh: Thornton and Collie.
Martin, John Murdo (1998). *Airc a' Choimhcheangal* (CD). Perth: Smith Mearns Recordings.
Nic a' Ghobhainn, Màiri (ed.) (2009). *Sheòl mi 'n Uiridh; Òrain mun t-Seòladh*. Inverness: Clàr.
NicDhòmhnaill, Catrìona (2010). *A' Chreathall, An Crann 's An Crùn*. Staffin: Cranagan.
NicFhearghais, Raonaid 'Is laithean brònach a th' ann', in *The Celtic Annual*, 1915-16.
Smith, Maggie (ed.) (2010). *Sgìre a' Bhradain: Bàrdachd bho Cheann a' Loch, Eilean Leòdhais*. Stornoway: Comunn Eachdraidh Cheann a' Loch.

6

The passion of George Campbell Hay for Gaelic and the Gaels

Sandra Malley

University of Aberdeen

George Campbell Hay is possibly the least well known of the *Còignear Cliùiteach*, the five twentieth-century modern Gaelic poets who transformed Gaelic poetry and raised its status in the literary world (MacAulay, 1995 [1976]). Hay also wrote a number of articles concerning Gaelic, Gaelic literature and Scotland. These articles, published mainly between 1939 and 1947, were witty, erudite and allusive, and provide a fascinating insight into his views on Gaelic and poetry. He was writing at the time of the second wave of renaissance writing in Scotland and was very involved in the proselytising regarding linguistic and national identity. The major theme running through his articles was praise of Gaelic, both poetry and people, and the need to preserve the language and culture. He was not one to mince his words when giving his opinions.

Both Hay and Sorley MacLean were writing at a 'time of ideological ferment' and both were radicals and anti-imperialists (Byrne, 2003, p. 527). Both writers were concerned with promoting Gaelic and Gaelic poetry and wished to show that Gaelic literature was the equal of literature in any language. In a talk by MacLean given in 1940 but only recently published (MacGill-Eain, 2008), he cited five Gaelic poems from the late seventeenth and eighteenth centuries which he considered to be the equal of, or superior to, much European poetry of any age. He asserted that 'to those who know Gaelic the music of the poetry of England, France and Germany is a poor thin thing' (MacGill-Eain, 2008, p. 4).

Hay's prose was even more extreme. It was confident, extravagant, outspoken and at times quite vituperative. Both MacLean and Hay could be seen as extremely partisan about Gaelic poetry but Hay went further. His view of both Gaeldom and Gaelic poetry, especially work of the sixteenth, seventeenth and eighteenth centuries, was idealised and very passionate.

Hay was committed to the cause of Scottish independence and was heavily involved with prominent nationalists in Edinburgh, as can be seen from his diary entries, especially from 1938 to 1939 (NLS MS 26728). He was not, however, particularly interested in party politics. In April 1939, in a letter to Douglas Young (NLS Acc. 6419/38 (a)), he wrote 'we need ... pure nationalism. The government will be what the people wills'. On 17 February 1940 he described his disillusionment with party political manoeuvring, describing nationalists as 'numbskulls', with no idea of how government works. For Hay, nationalism seemed bound up primarily with his identity as a Scot.

Whyte (1988, p. 116), in discussing the freedom (or not) 'a writer may have in the choice of his themes', wrote that 'Hay's nationalism ... can be seen as a theme imposed on him rather than being chosen.' It can be argued, however, that Hay's brand of nationalism, and, indeed his identity, was very much a choice, and a choice which he relished. This can be seen in both his verse and prose. As Byrne noted (2003, p. 445), he 'put down his cultural and emotional roots' in Tarbert, Argyll, when he, his mother and sister moved there after the death of his father when he was four. He seemed to identify with the way of life of the fishermen there, and with the Gaelic language, which he acquired with great fluency, the first of many languages he learned through his life. From this identification there developed his identity as a Scot and a Gael.

In his first article of 1939, an article which Byrne described as his 'manifesto' (Byrne, 2003, p. 505), he used the story behind the Gaelic proverb 'Na puirt uile air an aon fhonn, mar bha iad aig seanmhair na feannaige' as an amusing introduction to a subject on which he had strong opinions, namely 'Gaelic and Literary Form' (Hay, 1939). Hay stated that 'in formlessness there is no variety' (Hay, 1939, p. 14). He felt this was especially important in relation to Gaelic poetry, as, compared to English literature, 'in Gaelic literature the fields are all white and the reapers are few' (Hay, 1939, p. 15). He was passionate about retaining Gaelic and Gaelic structures in poetry.

Hay was scathing about Gaelic writers who adopted structures and styles from English literature. He wrote, 'she [Gaelic] would be exchanging a clàrsach for a brass band' (Hay, 1939, p. 15), if Gaelic structures were set aside. He accepted borrowing, seeing this as having always happened in any literature, but was concerned that borrowing might take over from the Gaelic originals, 'jettisoning ... any fundamental native characteristic', and producing a 'wizened changeling' in place of a 'bonnie bairn' (Hay, 1939, p. 15). He thought that a fundamental characteristic of Gaelic poetry was 'a highly developed technique' (Hay, 1939, p. 15). He himself had already written a number of complex lyrics by this time, including 'An Gleannan', with ornamental structures from earlier centuries (Byrne, 2003, p. 9). Byrne considered that in his 'manifesto' Hay hoped 'to modernise Gaelic poetry by re-energising its traditional strengths' (Byrne, 2003, p. 505).

Hay considered that three European languages 'at least' had highly evolved lyrical technique, and intricate ornamentation, namely Gaelic, Welsh and Icelandic, and had suggestions for how structures and techniques from Welsh and Icelandic could be adapted for Gaelic poetry (Hay, 1939, p. 15). He outlined the need for a metre 'suitable for sustained narrative' and considered that the Irish 'caoineadh' was appropriate (Hay, 1939, p. 17). (He was to use this metre to stunning effect in his epic *Mochtàr is Dùghall* (Hay, 1982)). This first article was a 'call to arms' for other poets writing in Gaelic.

In common with other writers of the earlier twentieth century, Hay rejected the Celtic Twilight depiction of the Highlands. MacLean (2008, p. 11) referred to 'the fozy[1] and inauthentic splendours of the Celtic Twilight'. Hay too disliked the notion that Gaelic literature was seen as 'shrouded in mists and the vapours of melancholy' (Hay, 1940a, p. 7). He saw this as the reverse of what was true, as illustrated in the following extracts:

> There is to be found in most Gaelic poetry a burning spirit which blazes equally in affection, hate, disdain or love, and a love of brightness and colour (Hay, 1940a, p. 9)

> Gaelic poetry seldom stumbles or hesitates, … It seems to blaze up, or burst out with a natural abandon, and whether it be praise or cursing, sorrow or joy, it is always satisfying (Hay, 1940b, p. 7)

> Gaelic poetry is peculiar in the manner in which it sets vividly before the eye a succession of scenes and figures as if on a bright day of sunlight. (Hay, 1940-1, p. 8)

This idealised, but clearly sincerely felt, view of earlier Gaelic poetry informed his own writing. His nature poems, in particular, are full of colourful, musical images and convey a feeling of the poet's joy in the landscape. This can be seen in poems such as 'Do Bheithe Bòidheach' (Byrne, 2003, pp. 20-21), with its intricate internal rhymes, assonance and alliteration:

> ùr bàrr-uaine gruag a' bheithe,
> leug nan leitir cas mun Lùib (ll. 3-4)

In the line 'Ceileireadh 's e binn binn' (l. 13) Byrne pointed out (2003, p. 548) that the repetition of 'binn' echoed much earlier nature poetry, including early Irish lyrics.

Although Hay did express some doubts in a letter to MacLean as to how innovative his poetry was, especially when he compared his work to MacLean's

Dàin do Eimhir (Byrne, 2002, p. 3), MacLean (1986, p. 115) wrote that, 'To me George Campbell Hay's poetry has the virtuosity of genius and is an exquisite blend of the Bardic old and the new.' Hay's creative strength was considered by contemporaries to lie in revivifying ancient poetic traditions, using themes relevant to contemporary times. Byrne (2003, p. 456) quoted a poem by Douglas Young, in which he described Hay as a being who 'lives in another realm / than our drab narrow Scotland of dull slaves.'

Hay admired early Gaelic poetry for praising leaders for honourable conduct. He criticised sharply people who put money above honour. With extreme sarcasm he wrote 'for the whole world knows now that the only proper god for a good citizen is Mammon in a tile hat' (Hay, 1940-41, p. 9). This sentiment can also be seen in his poem 'Sgairt mo Dhaoine', written in 1940 (Byrne, 2003, pp. 69-70), in which he commented:

is sibh a shealladh gu h-ìosal

brù is sporan a' sìor ghabhail rèim (ll. 5-6)

Here he castigates his fellow Scots for betrayal of their country because of greed.

It appears that Hay had written a long political piece called 'Dealbh na h-Eòrpa', of which this poem formed a part. Hay wrote to Douglas Young in September 1940 to tell him about the piece, and said that he was glad that Young liked it. Sadly only this and one other poem survived (Byrne, 2003, p. 567). Had the work survived, perhaps there would be a larger number of such poems to stand beside his opinions in his essays.

His scorn for the worship of possessions is also keenly felt in his English poem, '"S Leam fhèin an Gleann' (Byrne, 2003, p. 50), where he paints a picture of a new (upper-crust) landlord revelling in his possession of a glen which he intends to clear further. 'I skip and shout "The Glen is mine"' (l. 16). In contrast to this view of a non-Gael's cupidity, Hay considered that there was a 'kind of mean of behaviour' among Gaels. He described Gaels as disliking excess, as generous, and 'cho ciùin ri maighdinn', but as a 'fìor-bhòcan' if the need arose (Hay, 1940-41, p. 9). He was expressing the values found in the panegyric code, which he then incorporated into his own work.

This idealised view of the Gael comes across in many of his 'fisherman' poems, such as 'An t-Iasgair', where he alluded to 'faire 's fulang / 'nad shùil 's an ciùine do ghutha' (Byrne, 2003, p. 216, ll. 7-8). Although the fishermen he looked up to were real people, in these poems they seem also to be a synecdoche for the culture of the working man. The qualities Hay admired in a man were steadfastness, loyalty, and independence (Hay, 1940b, p. 7). This view was not narrowly confined to Gaels. He admired the Arabs he encountered in Tunisia during his war service in similar ways. This is clear in his poem

'Atman' (Byrne, 2003, pp. 162-4), where he described Atman, who appears to function as a synecdoche for the world of the ordinary Arab, as follows:

> dh'fhairich thu a' bheatha
> is cha do mheath thu roimpe riamh (ll. 31-2)

Hay's view of the English was often less flattering; he saw them as inclining 'to intellectual laziness, using caricatures of other nationalities, and perhaps none so fantastic as Jock and Paddy' (Hay, 1940a, p. 7). He was severely scathing about authors who interpreted Highland history falsely and propagated phony images of the Celt (Hay, 1940a, p. 7); he wrote about 'ladies with harps, a little Mayfair Gaelic and much self-assurance, who "interpret" us to a fleering world through the medium of baby-fairy-talk' (Hay, 1941, p. 10). His satirical poem 'Renaissance', written in 1939 (Byrne, 2003, p. 44), expressed similar sentiments to those in MacLean's satirical poem 'Rathad nan Eilean' (MacLean, 2011, pp. 14-15), also written in the 1930s. Like MacLean, Hay had no time for those who appropriated Gaelic culture and portrayed it in Celtic Twilight terms:

> How many still figure to themselves a Highlands peopled with Rob Roys, rigged out by the Kilt Society, and Clarsach Society ladies with buns and peculiar dresses (not to mention peculiarer Gaelic) (Hay, 1940a, p. 7).

Hay was describing the stereotypic characteristics that others projected on to Gaels, which he saw as negative and demeaning. He used stereotypes also, but the Gaelic stereotypes/archetypes he used were positive, and came from Gaelic tradition itself. Both negative and positive stereotypes are overgeneralisations, for Gaelic communities depicted by both sides could be seen as 'imagined communities' (Anderson, 1996). Both views are as much projection as reality, but given the strength of his nationalism, this concept seems particularly apposite in relation to his image of the authentic and inauthentic Gael. In 'Prìosan Da Fhèin an Duine' (Byrne, 2003, pp. 174-6) he wrote:

> An cridhe fialaidh, misneachail,
> na bu chiomach e am fròig;
>   ùraich cridh' an t-saoghail leis –
> cuir mu sgaoil e – cuir gu stròdh (ll. 33-6)

This was what an authentic Gael should do. By contrast, he then wrote of inauthentic people as

> an troichshluaigh dàicheil, rianail,
>   nach robh riamh ach leth bheò, (ll. 41-2)

From the same poem, he wrote 'Bi iomlan is bi beò' (l. 8), a phrase which could almost be his watchword.

Hay highlighted the hidden potential dependent on a sense of belonging in his work. He saw himself as attached firmly to the Gaelic world, to Kintyre, as well as to Scotland, and he made it clear he was both Highlander and Lowlander ('nam dhalt aig Gàidheal 's mi leth-Ghallda' in 'Gum Chur an Aithne' (Byrne, 2003, p. 358, l. 3).

Macleod (2009, p. 169) made the point that there was no portrayal of tension between Gael and Lowlander in his poetry. In his essays Scotland as a whole is as much a subject for praise and support as is Gaelic. In his poetry Scotland could appear as a mother, a lover, certainly the source of all good things, but as in need of nurture. In his exhortatory poem 'Na Trèig do Thalamh Dùthchais' (Byrne, 2003, p. 235), written in 1947, he pleaded with fellow Scots to support Scotland by not leaving. In common with many Gaelic poets, both in the twentieth century and earlier, he was deeply attached to his homeland.

This attachment to Scotland and to Kintyre, his adopted homeland, shone through, and formed one of the major themes of his work. The theme of home was one which concerned many writers of the nineteenth and twentieth centuries. Hay was not born in Kintyre, but he claimed it as his home. Meek (1984, p. 3) wrote that 'Kintyre and South Argyll awakened in Hay an awareness of his Gaelic heritage' and that his work was a celebration of *dùthchas* – all that is meant by heredity in the Gaelic world.

For instance in 'Cinntìre' (Byrne, 2003, pp. 24-6), written in 1938, probably not long before his earlier articles were written, Hay wrote in the metre and style of formal panegyric (Meek, 1984, p. 3):

> sòlas duit Chinntìr' is sonas –
> cuim nach molainn crìoch gun lochd? (ll. 3-4).

In this poem, he was indicating his awareness of, and desire to emulate, the long tradition of Gaelic poetry. This was only one of a number of praise poems he wrote about Kintyre between 1932 and 1938, in which he makes clear how important his adopted homeland was for him.

Hay was uncompromising about those who complained about lack of translations from Gaelic, telling them simply to 'learn the language' (Hay, 1941, p. 4). Even so, he did provide translations of much of his own poetry. He bemoaned the lack of support for the publication of Gaelic works, but was optimistic that more Gaelic writers would emerge (Hay, 1944, p. 105). His optimism, which can now be seen as well founded, was in contrast to contemporaries who described Hay and MacLean in around 1950 as 'the last gleam of the Gaelic sky' (Black, 1987-8, p. 195). Although Hay was passionately committed to the Gaelic language, he wrote all of his articles on poetry in English, except one in 1944, 'Cor Litreachas na Gàidhlige an Albainn'. It may be that he thought he could reach a wider audience for his promotion of Gaelic by writing in English, and he was encouraged by Hugh MacDiarmid, who published some of his articles in his role as editor of *The Voice of Scotland.*

Two articles in *Scottish Art and Letters,* written in 1944, probably contain his clearest statement of what he saw as the business of poetry and the role of poets in the world (Hay, 1946a,1947). Hay wrote that culture should not be seen as the prerogative of the rich, nor of intellectuals. He felt that people should be seen as 'full of unlimited potentialities' and wrote that 'The peoples have a right to Art just as they have a right to food' (Hay, 1946a, p. 57). There appears to be a strong egalitarian undercurrent running through his articles. He saw the poet as needing to be part of the people, not separate. It may be that he was making a statement about his own choice of belonging to the Kintyre community when he made this argument. His egalitarianism comes through in a number of poems, including 'Fhearaibh 's a Mhnaoi na h-Albann' (Byrne, 2003, p. 95), where he asserts his Scottish identity and kinship with the people of Scotland.

In the first of the *Scottish Art and Letters* articles, he railed against the 'ivory tower' poet, singling out André Gide as a particular villain, because he saw Gide as considering sound to be more essential than sense in verse (Hay, 1946a, p. 51). By way of rebuttal, Hay wrote that 'poetry is not made by jugglers with words, but by men who have hearts, brains and bodies, who speak to men and for them' and 'without meaning ... poetry is impossible' (Hay, 1946a, p. 52). In this article he was tapping into both the contemporary European debate about the role and function of poetry and the role of the poet, and the traditional perception of the Gaelic bard as spokesperson for the community. Hay saw poets who are indifferent about whether they can be understood as showing contempt for others, and he did not like irony; he considered it 'rots like damp and consumes like rust' (Hay, 1946a, p. 55). There is certainly little of world-weary irony in most of his poetry. There is irony in his poem about war, 'Esta Selva Selvaggia' (Byrne, 2003, pp. 211-14), but he was using the device in this poem to make a strong point about man's intolerance towards the 'other'.

His outlook in much of his writing was optimistic. The first of his *Collected Poems and Songs,* 'The Hind of Morning' (Byrne, 2003, p. 3), which he wrote in 1932, used a common symbol from classical and Gaelic poetry. However, in Hay's version of the hunt, the hind, possibly symbolising Gaelic and freedom for the Gaels, is not captured and overcome; she escapes. This optimism is also seen later in 'Stoc is Failleanan', written in 1946 (Byrne, 2003, pp. 220-22), where he uses the well-known trope of a felled tree to symbolise the possible destruction of the Gaelic language and culture. This felled stump is, however, covered by fresh growth. Although his circumstances had changed greatly towards the end of his life when he wrote the darker poems 'Am Bàta Dubh' (1983) and 'Mios a' Ghearain' (1983) (Byrne, 2003, pp. 412-15), he seemed to remain hopeful about Gaelic poetry. In the same year he wrote the beautifully constructed quatrain 'Dùrd a' Ghlinne' (Byrne, 2003, pp. 412), recalling golden days in the countryside, and produced an exuberant and cheerful poem in 'Is Mear a Bhreabas i Sàil' (Byrne, 2003, pp. 418-20), in which a ship is conceptualised as a prancing mare, free on the sea. He was drawing on well-known seventeenth-century sea imagery, as he had done in earlier poems. In a paper given in 1963, Sorley MacLean had drawn attention to 'the horse-ship contrast' in relation to his discussion of Iain Lom's 'An t-Iorram Dharaich' and Murchadh Mòr Mhic Mhurchaidh's 'An Làir Dhonn' (MacLean 1985, p. 93).

Hay's argument about the need to consider people from humble backgrounds continued in his second article in *Scottish Art and Letters* (Hay, 1947), subtitled 'The Time, the Money or the Inclination', where he likened 'a nation where culture is restricted to small scattered groups, or individuals', to an 'uncivilised desert' (Hay, 1947, p. 52). He felt that 'Life is one and poetry is part of it', and that literary and social problems could not be separated (Hay, 1947, p. 56). He quoted a wide range of authors whose views matched his on this subject, and wrote:

> If it were not for the dragging feet of the peasant behind the plough and for the sore wrists and shoulders of the fisherman there would be no human existence except of a precarious nomadic kind, not to speak of culture and civilisation (p. 53).

This sympathy and fellow-feeling for 'the people' (albeit at a distance) comes through in many of his poems, notably 'Atman' (Byrne, 2003, pp.162-4), where he compared the judge very unfavourably to Atman, seeing the judge as probably only half alive, while Atman is portrayed as an authentic, whole man, despite his poverty. Hay wrote of him 'gur bràthair dhomh thu fhèin' (l. 44). In 'An t-Eòlas nach Cruthaich' (Byrne, 2003, pp. 164-5), he made the point even more strongly, when he depicted 'Fear a' bhreithneachaidh 's an fhiosa' (l. 1):

> Chan eil òrd ann, gilb no clàrsach,
> cha snaidh, cha ghràbhail e, cha seinn ... (ll. 9-10)

He did not admire educated people who lacked passion, humanity and creativity.

In this article he quoted a writer as saying that 'a firm distinction should be made between "the pleasures of the educated – appreciation of the arts" and "the pleasures of the populace – gambling, betting, drinking"' (Hay, 1947, p. 53). This point he demolished by citing many people he considered geniuses who might not be considered 'cultivated', all the way up to Christ (p. 54). He quoted

Dante (p. 55), who also wrote against an elitist view of the 'common people', and who wrote that people lacked the time for the 'intellectual light of discernment' because they were so caught up with work. Hay's view was similar, that peoples' 'primary wants are security and leisure' (p. 55). He saw that much literature, because of its cost, was outside the reach of the working class. He thought, however, that literary and social problems could not be separated (p. 56), and warned that 'if mankind is to continue ... in ... armed conflicts the poet will soon find that it has neither time nor place for him' (p. 57).

Hay also had broader views on 'The Scotland I'd Like To See' (Hay, 1946b). He saw a clear need for Scottish self-government, and considered what he saw as the economic needs of an independent country. Most importantly, however, he considered the issue of identity, and was quite unequivocal about his viewpoint. 'For we are a nation, and mean to go on being a nation' (p. 26).

Hay was passionately anti-war. Byrne (2003, p. 532) described his poetry about war as 'arguably the harshest indictment of war by any Scottish poet'. However, he had no time for defeatism and fatalism, as could be seen in his article 'Gael Warning' in 1947 (Hay, 1947c). This attitude is mirrored in his poem 'Meftah Bâbkum es-Sabar?' (Byrne, 2003, pp.193–5), where he concluded:

   No, mur an gleacar,
 rud suarach ann an cùil ga cheiltean,
 a thraogh 's dhìochuimhnich sluagh eile (ll. 59-61).

In this article Hay started by asking if Gaels were really 'doomed or dying out, the broken ghosts of a dying race?' and went on to ask 'How much longer have we to listen to such snivelling nonsense and facile, half-informed defeatism about our language and our culture and ourselves?' (Hay, 1947c, p. 104). There was no equivocation here. For a man whose poetry was not generally self-reflective nor focused on psychological issues, it is interesting that he discussed what he called 'Difference Anxiety' in this article. He did not, however, mean quite what others have meant as fear of difference; his view was that people fear complication, such as multilingualism (Hay, 1947c, p.104). He could see the advantages of having more than one language, and promoted the cause of preserving Gaelic. 'We are not going to be the generation to let that language and culture perish' (Hay, 1947c, p. 105). A similar sentiment was outlined in his poem in English 'We Abide For Ever' (Byrne, 2003, p. 223).

Probably his most outspoken article, 'The Anglo-Scot and Gaelic Literature', published in 1947 in *The Voice of Scotland,* was described by its editor, MacDiarmid, as 'a devastating analysis ... of many of the stock attitudes of

Anglo-Scots relating to Gaelic language and literature' (Hay, 1947b, p. 31). His writing in this article was, without doubt, vituperative. He railed against the erosion of Gaelic culture. His opprobrium in this article was reserved for the 'Anglo-Scot'. He set up arguments for the anti-Gael, whom he named 'Thistle', which he then demolished (Hay, 1947b, p. 32). He possibly used the label 'Thistle' as a symbol of the maintenance of the status quo in Scotland. He was particularly exercised by the idea that interest in Gaelic was 'purely academic or sentimental', because Gaels were not more numerous, and because the social and economic conditions for Gaelic culture 'have vanished for ever' (Hay, 1947b, p. 33–4). He cited many examples to support his arguments about the breadth and depth of Gaelic literature, both past and present.

Conclusion

Hay's opinions in these articles were, more often than not, stated in extreme terms. His views were very black and white; he was not given to nuance. He was often echoing the views of others of the Scottish Renaissance. His passion for Gaelic, the Gaels and for Scotland does, however, shine through his writing. His language has to be considered in the context of its times. Clancy and Byrne quote William Gillies as making a similar point in relation to MacLean's 1940 article (Clancy & Byrne, 2008, p. ii). In the periodical *The Voice of Scotland,* at the time, MacDiarmid's voice, in particular, could be much more extreme.

Hay clearly saw his writing as a form of activism, primarily in the service of Gaelic (Byrne, 2003, p. 526) and Scottish independence. It is also notable that although Hay's collections contained many nationalist poems, he did not refer at all to nationalist party politics in his articles. His prose writing appears more ontological than political. Although his words were passionately pro-Scottish, his arguments were always focused on literature and language. Whyte (1988) made the point that his nationalism was not tied to party politics. He was primarily against the assimilation of Scots and Gaelic writing into an English culture. The poet William Neill, a great admirer of Hay, wrote:

> There are some men who hold on to their love of country because they cannot help it. George Campbell Hay is such a man and his internationalism is the mirror of his patriotism (Neill, 1974, p. 54).

A number of themes emerge in his articles, primarily relating to the depth of erudition in Gaelic culture and literature and the positive character of the (generally male) Gael. He was concerned to promote Gaelic and Gaelic poetry and to show the stature of Gaelic culture through the ages. He was passionate about a language which was not his first, and about a homeland where he was not born. Underlying his rhetoric he might be seen as a man in search of an identity, who grasped what he saw as a secure and appealing environment in Tarbert, straightforward people he could admire (the fishermen), and a language and literature with which he identified. He held on firmly to that identity throughout his life.

This may be one factor which marks Hay out as so different from the other four of the Nua-Bhàrdachd poets. He could be seen as an outsider in many senses; his experience of Gaelic and Gaels was only in specific settings, with the fishermen and his aunts in Tarbert from age four, and then only in the holidays after age ten. His education, at Fettes and Oxford, would have included little that was Scottish, let alone Gaelic. However he made himself an insider to his Gaeldom, an insider who was a learner of Gaelic. As Trosset (1986) wrote in relation to Welsh learners, learning a language is less of an intellectual endeavour than a process of entering a community and acquiring a new identity. Again this seems to fit with how Hay chose his path in life.

As Crichton Smith did in *Towards the Human* (1986), Hay did consider what he saw as the 'other's' view of Gaeldom in his articles, but, unlike Crichton Smith, this did not lead to introspection and existential crisis for him. His outlook could be quite Manichean, the 'other' was to be scorned if not in agreement with his cause.

Hay's writing, both poetry and prose, conveyed a sense of a man who chose an identity with which he was happy. He showed no sign of internal conflict regarding language and identity. His nationalism and nationalist poems demand identification, which works to create identity, but his portrayal of identity tends to refer to a social, not an individual process.

As Macleod (2009) pointed out, Hay's perception of Gaelic was 'almost uniquely associated with traditional Gaelic speakers and mostly with the traditional Gaelic speaking areas'(p. 168). She considered that in his 'poetry there is a pervading sense that language and location cannot be separated in any discussion of Gaelic identity' (p.168). She also wrote (p. 167), that 'sociologists and (linguistic) anthropologists have long believed that language is one of the key factors in determining a person's identity'. Whyte (2004, p. 88) wrote that 'by choosing to write in Gaelic, in a language used neither by his parents nor in his own social ambience, Hay had himself crossed a cultural boundary'. He also alluded to Hay's 'specific brand of "linguistic homelessness"' (Whyte, 2007, p. 157).

It could be argued, however, that the safe haven which Kintyre and Gaelic provided gave him an acquired identity, a language and tradition where he was 'at home', and from which he could express strong opinions. There is no sense in his articles and verse of his being infected by notions of inferiorisation, nor of his being troubled by becoming bi-cultural, as MacAulay suggested (1995 [1976], p. 48) was the experience of the other four *Nua-Bhàrdachd* poets. Unlike the others, Hay did not come from a background of active Gaelic speakers, or tradition bearers of Gaelic lore. He chose to continue a tradition of Gaelic poetry, reflecting both past and present. His adopted homeland of Kintyre, probably purely an 'imagined community' by the time he returned in the early 1980s, had been a source of joy and pride for most of his life. His attachment to his home country was 'uncomplicated' (Byrne, 2003, p. 538). His writing indicates a man secure in the identity he chose, and proud of that identity.

Endnote

1   *Fozy*: 'wet, moist with saliva, dribbling ... light, spongy, soft, porous; fat, bloated; stupid, dull-witted; hazy, foggy; obscured by haze or fog' (Warrack, 1930, p. 192). In one short word MacLean encapsulated his feelings for the Celtic Twilight.

Bibliography

Anderson, Benedict (1996 [1991]). *Imagined Communities*. London & New York: Verso.

Black, Ronald (1987). 'Thunder, Renaissance and Flowers: Gaelic Poetry in the Twentieth Century', in Cairns Craig (ed.), *The History of Scottish Literature, Vol. 4: Twentieth Century*, pp. 195–214. Aberdeen: Aberdeen University Press.

Byrne, Michel (2002). 'Tails o' the Comet? MacLean, Hay, Young and MacDiarmid's Renaissance'. *Scotlit,* No. 26, pp. 1–3.

Byrne, Michel (ed.) (2003). *Collected Poems and Songs of George Campbell Hay (Dèorsa Mac Iain Dhèorsa)*. Edinburgh: Edinburgh University Press.

Clancy, Thomas Owen, and Byrne, Michel (2008). 'A recently discovered critical essay by Somhairle MacGill-Eain'. *Aiste*, No. 2, pp. i-ii.

Hay, George Campbell (1939). 'Gaelic and Literary Form'. *The Voice of Scotland*, Vol. 2, No. 1, pp. 14–18.

Hay, George Campbell (1940a). 'Scots Gaelic Poetry'. *The New Alliance,* Vol. 1, No. 5, pp. 7–9.

Hay, George Campbell (1940b). 'Scots Gaelic Poetry, cont.'. *The New Alliance*. Vol. 1, No. 6, pp. 7–8.

Hay, George Campbell (1940–41). 'Scots Gaelic Poetry, cont.'. *The New Alliance,* Vol. 2, No. 1, pp. 9–11.

Hay, George Campbell (1941) 'Scots Gaelic Poetry, cont.' *The New Alliance,* Vol. 2, No. 2, p. 4.

Hay, George Campbell (1944). 'Cor Litreachas na Gàidhlige an Albainn'. *An Gàidheal*, Vol. 39, pp.104–5.

Hay, George Campbell (1946a). 'Poetry in the World or Out of It?' *Scottish Art And Letters,* Vol. 1, No. 2, pp. 49–58.

Hay, George Campbell (1946b). 'The Scotland I'd Like To See'. *New Scot,* Vol. 2. No. 10, pp. 24–6.

Hay, George Campbell (1947a). 'Poetry in the World or Out of It? II: The Time, the

Money or the Inclination'. *Scottish Art and Letters*, Vol. 2, No. 3, pp. 52–7.

Hay, George Campbell (1947b). 'The Anglo-Scot and Gaelic Literature'. *The Voice of Scotland,* Vol. 4, No. 1, pp. 31–40.

Hay, George Campbell (1947c). 'Gael Warning'. *The Scots Review,* Vol. 8, No. 7, pp. 104–5.

Hay, George Campbell (1956). 'Affinities Elsewhere'. *The Voice of Scotland,* Vol. 7, pp. 26–30.

Hay, George Campbell (1982). *Mochtàr is Dùghall*. Glasgow: Department of Celtic, University of Glasgow.

MacAulay, Donald (ed.) (1995 [1976]). *Nua-Bhàrdachd Ghàidhlig/Modern Scottish Gaelic Poems*. Edinburgh: Canongate Classics.

MacGill-Eain, Somhairle (2008). 'Five Gaelic poems – regional, national or European?' *Aiste*, No. 2, pp. 1-29.

MacLean, Sorley (1985). 'Aspects of Gaelic Poetry' and 'Notes on Sea-imagery in Seventeenth Century Gaelic Poetry', in William Gillies (ed.), *Ris a' Bhruthaich: The Criticism and Prose Writings of Sorley MacLean*, pp. 75–82 and 83-105. Stornoway: Acair.

MacLean, Sorley (2011). *Caoir Gheal Leumraich/White Leaping Flame*, ed. by Christopher Whyte and Emma Dymock. Edinburgh: Birlinn.

Macleod, Michelle (2009). 'Language and Identity in Modern Gaelic Verse', in Ian Brown and Alan Riach (eds), *The Edinburgh Companion to Twentieth Century Scottish Literature*, pp. 167–80. Edinburgh: Edinburgh University Press.

Meek, Donald (1984). 'Land and Loyalty: The Gaelic Verse of George Campbell Hay'. *Chapman,* No. 39, pp. 2-8.

Neill, William (1974). 'The Poetry of George Campbell Hay'. *Scotia Review,* 8, pp. 50–56.

Smith, Iain Crichton (1986). *Towards the Human: Selected Essays*. Edinburgh: Macdonald Publishing.

Trosset, Carol S. (1986) 'The Social Identity of Welsh Learners'. *Language in Society*, Vol. 15, pp. 165–92.

Warrack, Alexander (1930). *A Scots Dialect Dictionary*. Edinburgh: W & R Chambers.

Whyte, Christopher (1988). 'George Campbell Hay: Nationalism with a Difference', in Thomson, D. (ed.) (1988), *Gaelic and Scots in Harmony: Proceedings of the Second International Conference on the Languages of Scotland*, pp. 116–35. Glasgow: Department of Celtic, University of Glasgow.

Whyte, Christopher (2004). *Modern Scottish Poetry*. Edinburgh: Edinburgh University Press.

Whyte, Christopher (2007). 'Cultural Catalysts: Sorley MacLean and George Campbell Hay', in Ian Brown (ed.), *The Edinburgh History of Scottish Literature, Vol. 3: Modern Transformations: New Identities (from 1918)*, pp. 151–62. Edinburgh: Edinburgh University Press.

7

Fuaran Sléibh: the poet's main copy

Kyriakos Kalorkoti

University of Edinburgh

1. Introduction

George Campbell Hay (1915–84) ranks among the great Scottish twentieth-century poets. Biographical sketches are given by Martin (1984), Rankin (1984) and Byrne (2000). Kintyre, the place of his childhood, was central to his outlook. His life was blighted by mental illness, most likely triggered by an attack on him while on military service in Kavalla, Greece, during World War II.

In mid-February 2014 my wife, Jenny, found an extensively annotated copy of Hay's collection *Fuaran Sléibh* (published in March 1948) in a charity shop and bought it for me. It was soon clear that the annotations were probably by Hay. This paper discusses the evidence for this belief and some of the annotations. Throughout, *FS* will denote the copy found.

The previously known copies of Hay's own publications are quite lightly annotated long after publication; no earlier than 1960 and often much later. By contrast, the *FS* annotations, as argued below, seem to date from much nearer the time of publication.

2. Evidence that *FS* was annotated by Hay

FS is signed by Hay on the front free end-paper and p. 32. There are three phrases in Greek, some more in Icelandic, some in English and more in Gaelic. They vary from factual information, allusions to sources of inspiration, some changes or corrections of content and many changes of spelling.

Hay annotated his copies of books to varying degrees; the National Library of Scotland (NLS) holds more than 40 such glossed texts by many authors as well as a few copies of Hay's own publications. For example, source 20 is a lightly annotated copy of his 1952 collection *O Na Ceithir Àirdean*; mostly corrections probably from the 1960s. Source 21 is another such copy, annotated in 1983.

Suggestive though the preceding observations are they do not constitute proof. Hay's papers in the NLS (listed as 'Sources consulted' below) were therefore studied for comparative evidence. Throughout the following descriptive analysis, *FS* annotations will be indicated by ⟨⟩, as for example ⟨at Sea⟩$_p$ (this on p. 18 next to the translation title of 'Na Baidealan'). The subscript indicates the writing instrument: *p* for pencil, *f* for fine nib fountain pen, *i* for italic nib fountain pen and *ip* for italic nib fountain pen over pencil. Line breaks in quotations within running text are indicated by '|'. Dates from sources are given in their original format.

2.1 Comparison of handwriting

Up to the late 1940s Hay's handwriting is generally fairly neat and flowing, sometimes small but mostly medium size. Normally in fountain pen, fine nib or italic, but sometimes pencil. It tends to slant right but is often upright, slanting back rarely (e.g. source 3:18). When using the fine nib pen the handwriting was quite small at times.

In the 1950s his handwriting started to change although there are hardly any sources with a definite date. There are some oddities, e.g., source 22, a letter to Young dated October 1950 (by another hand, probably Young's). This is written in fine nib fountain pen and red ink with very small handwriting, various letters look like Greek ('b' is like 'β', 'd' like 'δ', 'e' like 'ε'). It is difficult to read and, as observed by Byrne (2000, Vol.II, p. 40), seems to have been written when Hay was not in a healthy frame of mind. In a letter sent to Young dated 23rd Oct 1950 (source 22), Hay's mother states 'he employs a good deal of writing – mostly in Gaelic…doing my best to type it all out but it is rather difficult really owing to difficult writing' (she states that she is 'sending on a letter George has written you' which must be the one referred to above). Source 25, which is undated, contains texts of 'The Sun over Athens' (published in 1957) and 'Jebel and the Dayspring' (uncollected poem) in a similar script. These are easier to read, the handwriting is rather neater and various letters (e.g., 'e', 't') are now standard. Some aspects of this handwriting are present elsewhere but rarely, e.g., at the bottom of source 2:34v, 'd' is like 'δ'.

Hay's letter to Young starts with 'thank you for your book … it is one of the best books I have read – and I don't mean simply of the genre either – pretty well since I can remember.' The book is source 18, Douglas Young's *Chasing an Ancient Greek* (1950). Hay's copy is very densely annotated, mostly with fine nib fountain pen in red ink but sometimes pencil. The handwriting is identical to that in the letter but is more difficult to read. It is soon clear just how ill Hay was at the time. There is an obsessive repetition over most of the book of the phrase '§1942 (Bône)| §1950!'; sometimes '(Bône)' is omitted. (Hay had landed at Bône [Annaba, Algiers] with the British army forces in 1942, but there seems to be no record of any event there to explain his repeated reference to it. He also added 'Bône' under the translation of the poem 'Bisearta' in source 20; given the horror of the events that inspired what is arguably his finest poem, did he view these as the seed of his breakdown? Perhaps the most poignant annotation is 'Có mise anise' inside the front cover (repeated on p. 5 and p. 162 slightly expanded). There is a possible connection with the repeated line 'Who am I? Who am I? Who am I? southward.' in 'The Sun over Athens' (published in 1957); however there seems to be no other connection between this poem and the annotations in Young's book. None of the annotations in *FS* are in any way similar to those in source 18, indicating that Hay did not annotate *FS* around late 1950.

In the 1960s Hay's handwriting starts by being very small and upright in biro or pencil with some oddities. For example, in source 7 he uses standard 'A' in places; he nearly always used script 'A'. From the 1970s onwards it becomes large, upright and quite jagged but legible; he uses mostly biro but sometimes pencil (never fountain pen).

Throughout most of his life, characteristics persist in the formation of certain letters. For example, he raises the stem of the letter 'p' rather high, 'e' often looks like 'i' without a dot and 'g' is often like 'j' without a dot, 'F' and 'T' are in script form like 'A'.

Naturally Hay's handwriting is subject to considerable variation even within a short time, especially in the wartime notebooks, e.g., in source 6. However, handwriting up to around 1950 is distinct from post 1960, especially post 1970. (One possible exception is a brief letter in Gaelic to the Rev. Dr Kenneth Macleod, dated 8/iv/52 [source 24:19], thanking him for his help with *O na Ceithir Àirdean*. The handwriting is small and neat so in some respects it shares qualities with that of the 1960s but it resembles more that of the late 1930s. Presumably he wanted to be as clear as possible in expressing his deep gratitude.)

2.2 Nature of the annotations

In various manuscripts Hay writes down words and indicates pronunciation with IPA-like notation. For example, in source 8:13v he writes 'freis (frɛʃ) 1748'. On the inside front cover of source 9 he writes various words, e.g., 'gesham (gɛʃam): rain'. He does this in *FS*, e.g., on p. 52 where he seems to be notating the Kintyre pronunciation of some Gaelic words (see Figure 3). This handwriting is not easy to date, though it seems not to be from the 1960s. Source 10 (content from the 1960s and 1980s) has various place names and words with accompanying IPA-like notation; the handwriting here is very small, in contrast to the examples in *FS* where it is larger.

Up to around 1950 he quite often wrote in pencil first and then wrote over the words in italic nib fountain pen, e.g., source 8. After 1960 he wrote over the words in biro though quite rarely: source 9 contains the poem 'Do Shomhairle MacIllethain' dated 29/8/81 written in pencil with the title and first line overwritten in biro.

The handwriting in *FS* is pre-1960. There are a few annotations in fine nib fountain pen with small upright letters. There are some in italic nib fountain pen, occasionally over pencil, many are in pencil but none in biro. They can be ascribed to roughly three phases: early in fine nib fountain pen, middle in italic fountain pen and/or pencil and later ones in pencil only with less tidy handwriting. There are no dates inscribed in the book, thus the claim is based purely on comparative evidence and is tentative (see §2.6).

2.3 Recurrence of *FS* Annotations in other manuscripts

The right hand side of source 8:1 has: ⟨hann kunne eikkje| sè, hann kunne| eikkje hitta| forðí| Hann var orðinn| til það| ðí⟩ (Icelandic with non-standard spelling). These lines do not, to my knowledge, appear in any published work. The first three appear in *FS* on p. 27 (see Figure 1). The modern spelling is 'hann kunni ekki sé| hann kunni ekki hitta' and means 'he could not see| he could not hit' (as in missing a mark, possibly in battle). The rest is slightly problematic but 'Hann var orðinn til það' means 'He had become'.

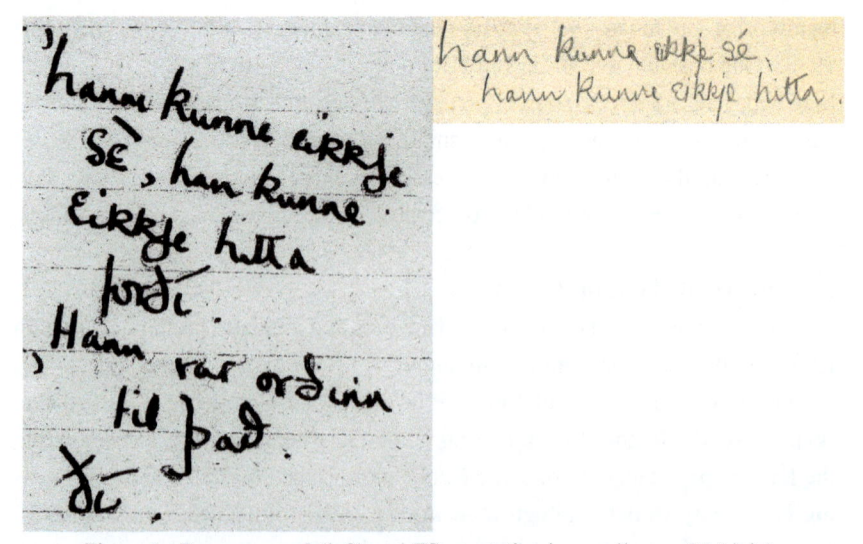

Figure 1. From source 8 (left) and *FS* annotation in pencil on p. 27 (right).

At the top of source 8:2 Hay wrote 'Sènos Brugos', which is not the title of any published work; the rest of the page is a continuation of a Gaelic poem started on the first page. The same title is written in *FS* at the bottom of p. 38. At 8:18v he has the lines 'Slabhraidh òir do'n Argalophos| Argalopha sònɛ. se ar òl an àir sa' chomhraig'. The origin of the name Argalophos is unclear but it occurs twice in *FS*, on pages 38 and 40.

2.4. Other copies of *Fuaran Sléibh*
In a letter to Angus Martin dated 22/2/74 (but most likely dating from 1978), source 16:1, Hay stated:
> I'll send you copies of Wind on Loch Fyne and O Na Ceithir Àirdean to give him. I cant [sic] manage Fuaran Sléibh because I only possess one copy of it.

Originally he had more than one copy, so he had either given away or misplaced the rest. One is source 17, with a few annotations in biro from the 1970s/1980s; Byrne (2000, Vol.II, p. 232) suggests *c*. 1983. These annotations are distinct from those in *FS*, thus it is likely that *FS* was no longer in his possession by 1974 (see §2.5 for supporting evidence that *FS* was not in Hay's hands beyond 1958). Hay gave a copy of *Fuaran Sléibh* to Professor Robert Rankin, a friend dating from schooldays, in 1976 (Byrne, 1992, p. 233). This has a few annotations (Byrne, 2014) which Byrne estimates to be from the 1960s; this is not *FS*, which Byrne examined in March 2014.

2.5 Coincidence with family history
On the dedication page ⟨acus do| Iomharr⟩$_p$ was added; Byrne (2014) informed me that Hay had a younger brother Ivor who died as a child. In a letter to Martin dated 9/12/82, source 16:56, Hay stated 'PS Information I had from my mother:-' and then drew a short family tree ending with 'Sheena Hay, George Hay, Ivor'. In a letter to Martin dated 20 August 1984, source 17:79, Rankin stated:
> He never spoke to me about his ancestry. Another interesting point is that the Glasgow Herald obituary [about Hay's father] from which you and I quote states that 'He leaves a wife and a family of three. Perhaps one child died in infancy...

On pp. 31, 42 of *FS* Iomharr appears again but it is unclear if this is the same person (see §3). No other mention of Iomharr was found in Hay's papers; Martin (2014) confirmed that Hay did not otherwise mention Ivor to him. Anne Artymiuk (2015) found the birth and death certificates of Hay's young brother. In fact he was named Duncan Ivan, born 30th April 1917 and died from bronchopneumonia on 4th June 1920. It is unclear why Hay used

Ivor in the letter to Martin, possibly this was a family name for his brother (perhaps the child mispronounced Ivan).

The Hays lived at two principal addresses in Edinburgh: 14 Carlton Street, Stockbridge, and then 6 Maxwell Street, Morningside. The latter is close to the Royal Edinburgh Hospital where Hay was a patient for some twelve years up to around 1960. A search at Meadowbank House, Edinburgh, Registers of Scotland, conducted in May 2014 showed that the deeds to 6 Maxwell Street were signed over to Hay's mother Catherine on 14 August 1958 (she rented 14 Carlton Street). *FS* was found in a charity shop on Raeburn Place, Stockbridge, very close to Carlton Street. The most likely explanation is that during the move *FS* was left behind. The shop does not keep records of donors but informed me that an individual donated *FS* in early to mid-February 2014. The Carlton Street house is now divided into four flats. I asked the residents about *FS* in June 2014 but they had no knowledge of it. However, until four years before, a lady had occupied the basement flat from 1972 and owned a large number of books. It seems likely that *FS* was found amongst them and eventually donated to the charity shop.

2.6 Conclusion of evidence

The annotations in *FS* are surely by Hay; probably started in the late 1940s and stopped before 1960, indeed not later than August 1958 (see §2.5). The late 1940s date is based on the few annotations in fine nib fountain pen; the handwriting is very similar to, e.g., that in a letter in Gaelic to Kenneth Macleod, dated 19 viii 46 (source 24:18). However, the handwriting of the letter cited resembles that of the aforementioned letter to Macleod dated 8/iv/52 (source 24:19). The writing in italic nib is very similar to that in source 8 but there is no date on this source; Byrne (2000, Vol. II) states c. 1950? The annotations in pencil often resemble those in italic nib pen but vary from tidy to untidy.

3. The annotations

Only a few annotations will be discussed due to space constraints. From p. 28 onwards Hay de-lenited all occurrences of 'fhéin' to 'féin' except on p. 34. He also amended, but not consistently, the spelling of various words to their Irish form or some form of Common (Classical) Gaelic, e.g., on p. 31 'sneachta' replaces 'sneachda'.

p. 9 An Gleannan ⟨An Gleannan anns a' Cheathramh| agus an Lethchreag.⟩$_p$ after the translation. Perhaps 'Lethchreag' is the same as the 'Creag an Fhasgaidh' of the final line. Martin (2014) informed me that Hay never mentioned

Lethchreag to him and he knows of no such place. He suggested that some of the names in the annotations might be fanciful. King (2014) located An Lethchreag to the north west of Abhainn a' Ghleannain that runs into the eastern side of Loch Long, raising the possibility that Hay associated the poem with two places. However he learnt many place names from fishermen who often had their own versions, many of which have not been recorded. This applies to several other annotations.

p. 10 Do Bheithe Bhòidheach ⟨faisg air| Daireo⟩$_p$ by the first stanza and ⟨near Daireo⟩$_p$ by the translation. The final letter might be 'd' but this seems very unlikely. The place is presumably in Kintyre or Kerry Cowal but has not been located. King (2014) suggested that the spelling might be Daireamh, but no such place has been located. Martin (2014) confirms that there is no such place in Kintyre.

p. 15 Cinntìre Line 36 'saoil nach pògainn ùir an fhuinn' bears the annotation ⟨c'uim⟩$_f$ to the left and ⟨c'uim na pògainn⟩$_f$ to the right. Surely 'na' is 'nach', as confirmed by source 12:7. In l. 40 the 'treun' of 'sliochd nan treun' is underlined with ⟨seud⟩$_f$ next to it, a variant which preserves rhyme and gains alliteration.

There seems to be no surviving manuscript of the poem predating publication, the earliest version being in *An Gàidheal* (1943). The two lines discussed appear there exactly as annotated in *FS*; these variants are not mentioned by Byrne (1992). For whatever reason l. 40 was kept in its *Fuaran Sléibh* form in the 1974 recension (source 12:7) while in l. 36 was returned to its earlier form.

p. 19 An Sealgair agus an Aois ⟨(aig Alld a'| Bheithe| really.)⟩$_p$ by the title. Hay was probably referring to Allt Beithe in Kintyre. According to Martin (2013), this burn is south of Tarbert and beside it are ruins with the same name. He provides evidence that this had been a place of some importance. The poem 'Luinneag' on p. 17 mentions Allt Beithe in the fifth stanza. The next stanza mentions Loch a' Chaorainn, which is to the northeast of Tarbert (the Ordnance Survey map calls it Loch Chaorainn); close to it is Cruach Chaorainn, which is mentioned in the third stanza of 'An Sealgair agus an Aois'. Thus, although the stream and mountain are not close to each other, Hay connected them in some way.

p. 27 Trì Rainn is Amhran (An gaol cha d'fhiosraich mi uair) in the final line 'a shon' replaces 'a son'. This changes the meaning of the line so that it refers to 'cùl' in the preceding line or 'gaol' in the title (since these are both masculine).

'Son' appears lenited in source 3:83v which has the lines 'thus a càradh do chùil bhàin| mise dol bàs air do shon' but here the lenition is not caused by gender. This draft begins with the Modern Greek line 'ἀλλοὶ δὲν με λυπᾶσας δὲν μὲ σπλαχνίζεσαι' ('alas you do not grieve for me, you do not pity me'). At 92v there is a list of titles including 'ἀλλοὶ δὲν με λυπᾶσας'; perhaps he intended to give the poem the Greek title.

A version is also included amongst poems sent to Kenneth MacLeod with a letter dated 26/9/40, source 24:16. This has some minor differences from the published one but l. 12 is the same. Thus the annotation seems to be a new idea rather than a typographical correction.

p. 31 Sguabag 1942 ⟨Iomharr's word⟩$_p$ by l. 20 referring to 'faoisgneadh', which is underlined. ⟨Ìomharr⟩$_p$ appears below the poem. The first mention of Iomharr on this page is somewhat puzzling if we assume that Hay was referring to his brother: since he died in infancy he is unlikely to have used 'faoisgneadh' either in Gaelic or English. See also the discussion for p. 42.

pp. 38–9 Prìosan da Fhèin an Duine? ⟨An Cladach Siar| mu'n Bhitti.⟩$_p$ above the title, a reference to Bitti, a municipality in the Province of Nuoro, Sardinia. Hay was posted in the region of Salerno and Naples in June 1944. He enclosed a copy of the poem in a letter to his mother dated 29.11.44, source 13:6, it is therefore possible that he wrote it in Italy.

⟨Skarpheðinn.⟩$_p$ next to ll. 21–4, a reference to the son of Njáll in the Icelandic *Njáls Saga*. In source 2:2v–3 Hay copied out two extracts from the saga, with the second mentioning Skarpheðinn. There is another short annotation about him on p. 21. His interest in Skarpheðinn was manifested most clearly in the long poem 'Seeker, Reaper', published in *Wind on Loch Fyne* (1948).

At the bottom of p. 38 there are what appear to be titles of poems; see Figure 2. ⟨Cnoc an Atha Dhuibh⟩$_p$, the Gaelicisation of an Edinburgh toponym, became the title of a poem in 1980, see (Byrne, 2000, Vol.II, p.213); the others are not titles of known poems. Argalophos is mentioned for the first time; see the discussion for pp. 40–41. To the top left, Hay seems to be playing with the word 'Brugos'; as mentioned above ⟨Senos Brugos⟩$_p$ appears in source 8:2. It also appears on the blank paper before the back free end-paper; the source language is unclear. At the bottom is ⟨Drochaid Stuic – Stoc a' Rì⟩$_p$, a reference to Stockbridge where the Hays lived (p. 51 has the annotation ⟨Gàidhlig Stoc a Rì⟩$_p$ next to the fifth stanza).

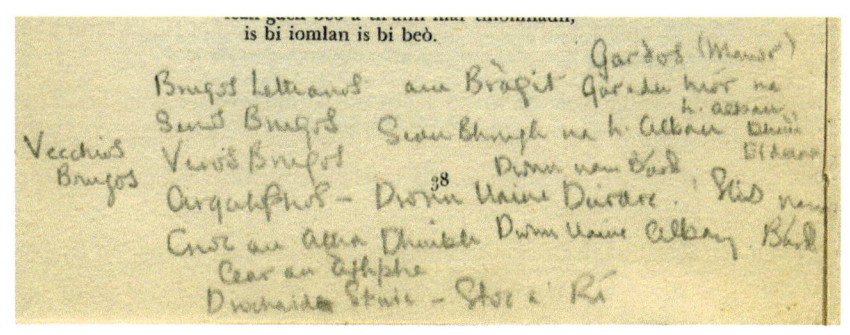

Figure 2. Possible titles at the bottom of p. 38 of *FS*.

p.40–41 An t-Òigear a' Bruidhinn o'n Ùir ⟨Argalòphos ar òl an àir⟩*ᵢ* by l. 3, 'Seall am fonn a dh'òl ar lotan'. As discussed in §2.3, source 8:18v has a similar entry, and a further verse (8:21) suggests that the name designates a mountain:

Slabhraidh oir do'n Argalòphos,

se ar òl an àir 's a' chomhraig,

coron òir do'n Argalòphos

an druim uaine, uanach, ceòlmhor

A mhórachd, Argalópha sònε

a mhóralachd, Argalópha tònε

a bhóidhchead, Argalópha ònε.

The words 'sònε', 'tònε' and 'ònε' are puzzling.

⟨Cúchonnacht O Dálaigh| – an rann a Shábhail Síth Eirend⟩*ᵢₚ* by the final line, an almost identical note occurs on p. 37; the source poem is unclear. At the end there is ⟨an aon fer do b' fheàrr ri cogadh| riamh acus bu lugha aobhar| ri cogadh riamh| – Cu Chúlann mac Coingeilt acus Cú Coingeilt⟩*ₚ*; Cú Coingeilt is a minor character in a Middle Irish tale called *Cathréim Cellaig*. Finally there is ⟨ökinn frórinn| ökinn Auster⟩*ᵢₚ* in Icelandic. 'Ökinn' means 'travelled' or 'driven' but the meaning of 'frórinn' is unclear, the rest means 'travelled/driven east'.

pp. 42–43 An Lagan ⟨Am Balachan agus| Colum Cille ocus| Módos an Ithaka⟩*ᵢₚ* on the right of the fourth stanza. The name 'Módos' seems Greek; indeed, source 8:19 has a mixture of names including Μῶδος Καβούρις, but there is no hint as to who this might be. Intriguingly, he also wrote 'mise Ἀλκιβιαδής', 'mise Ἕκτωρ' and 'mise Skarphedinn'.

⟨Iomharr| o'n Chearo⟩*ᵢₚ* on the left of ll. 23–24. Byrne (2014) suggested that 'Cearo' might be a Kintyre pronunciation of 'Ceathramh'. King (2014) confirmed that the Kintyre pronunciation was 'keru'. Martin (2014) agrees that it 'corresponds to the pronunciation in place names with that element'. Hence it seems likely that either the Iomharr of the dedication was not Hay's brother or there were two different people.

⟨GC Hay⟩$_{ip}$ on the left of ll. 26–8, of an autobiographical nature. ⟨GC Hay⟩$_p$ on the right of the thirteenth stanza. ⟨GC Hay air fad⟩$_p$ after the final stanza; indicating that the poem relates to Hay throughout which is not surprising. See also the comments to pp. 44–5 on this and 'Módos'.

⟨Hòmer⟩$_{ip}$ on the left of stanza 8 and ⟨the Englishman on the| NTB⟩$_{ip}$ on the right (the acronym is not entirely clear). No further reference to the Englishman has been found, so he remains a mystery; there might be a connection with this annotation and two in source 18:162,164. 'NTB' was a World War II acronym for 'Norwegian Training Base' that moved from near Toronto, Canada, to Devon, England, in 1945. However, apart from Hay's affinity with Norway there seems to be no connection. The mention of Homer makes sense as the stanza refers to the triremes of ancient Greece. ⟨Ὅμηρος Ἀρχ⟩$_p$ to the right of the twelfth stanza is another reference to Homer.

⟨Am Balachan⟩$_f$ on the right of the ninth stanza and ⟨Am Balachan⟩$_p$ to the right of the final stanza. The second occurrence is well in keeping with the nature of the stanza but the first is somewhat at odds (perhaps it was intended as a stark contrast).

pp. 44–5 Tilleadh Uiliseis ⟨módos⟩$_f$ at the left of the line 'Iotaca is tràighean 'òige' which is underlined in pencil. ⟨Módos Ithakys⟩$_p$ at the end of the poem, see the comments to pp. 42–3. Below this is ⟨G C Hay air fad..⟩$_p$ as on p. 43. The typescript in source 1:4v–5 states 'Salerno 23.5.45'; perhaps Hay, feeling far from home against his wishes and with a strong desire to return, identified with Ulysses and his own attempts to avoid going to war. Due to his strong Nationalist stance, Hay had tried to evade conscription by taking to the hills of Argyll; see (Byrne, 2000, Vol.II, p.27). This poem contrasts peaceful nature and human violence, as does 'An Lagan'.

pp. 51–3 Ùrnuigh Oisein as Ùr See Figure 3 for most of the annotations to p. 52. The handwriting of ⟨Bail' a' Bheòlaigh⟩$_f$ is characteristic of a few other annotations in fine nib fountain pen. As elsewhere no place with the given name has been identified; see the discussion to p. 9.

To the right of the last line of stanza 14 is ⟨Leig díot a' shiodag| s dèan greim air an tàl⟩$_f$, probably an early annotation. To the right of the penultimate line 'Bidh mi réidh riut Mhic Alpein' is ⟨Calphuirn⟩$_p$. It has been suggested that 'Mac Calphuirn' is the origin of 'Mac Alpine': see (Calder, 1923, p. 146).

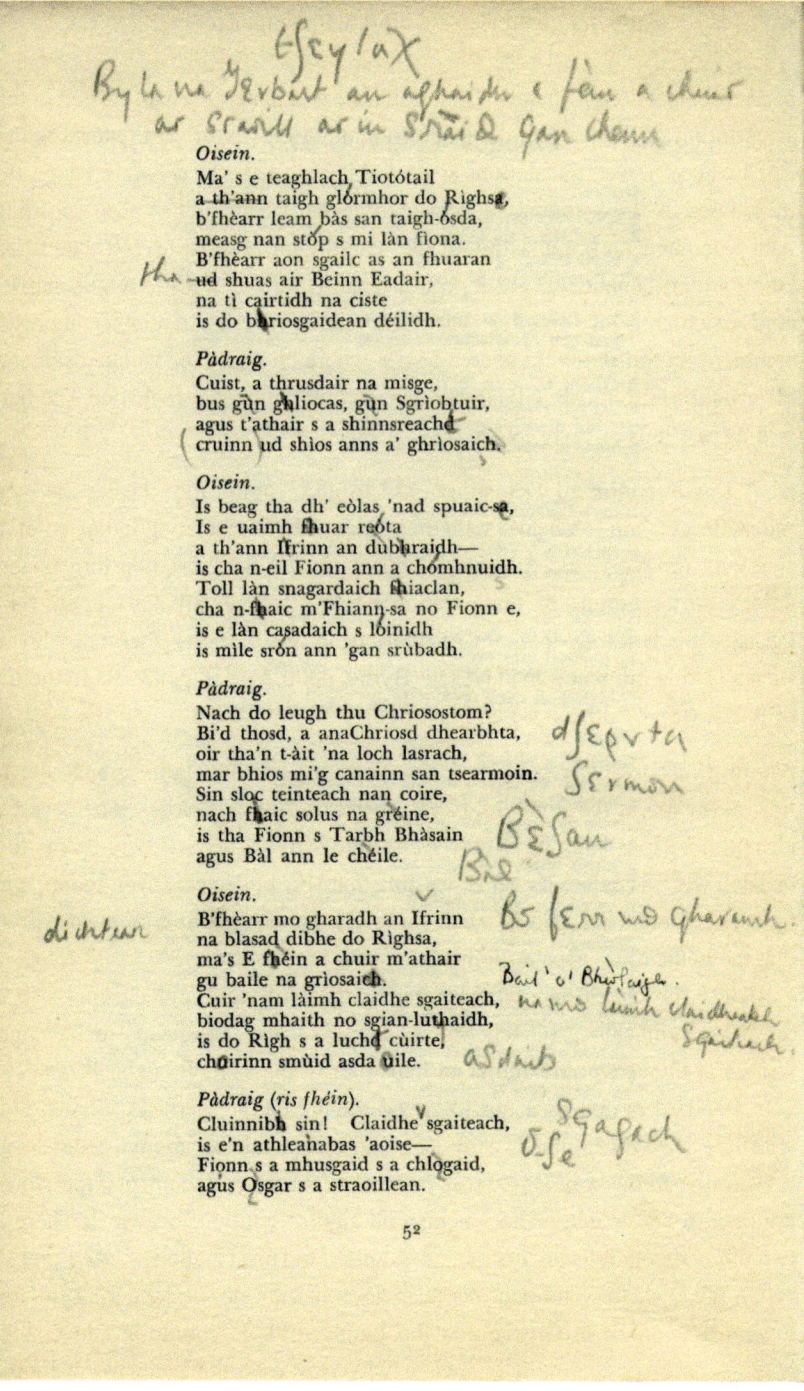

Bylana Jerbert an aghaidh e fèin a chuir
ar sraoill ar in sràid gan cheann
tsεylax

Oisein.
Ma' s e teaghlach Tiotótail
a th'ann taigh glòrmhor do Rìghsa,
b'fhèarr leam bàs san taigh-òsda,
measg nan stòp s mi làn fiona.
B'fhèarr aon sgaile as an fhuaran
tha ud shuas air Beinn Eadair,
na tì cairtidh na ciste
is do bhriosgaidean déilidh.

Pàdraig.
Cuist, a thrusdair na misge,
bus gùn ghliocas, gùn Sgrìobtuir,
agus t'athair s a shinnsreachd
cruinn ud shìos anns a' ghrìosaich.

Oisein.
Is beag tha dh' eòlas, 'nad spuaic-sa,
Is e uaimh fhuar reòta
a th'ann Ifrinn an dubhraidh—
is cha n-eil Fionn ann a chòmhnuidh.
Toll làn snagardaich fhiaclan,
cha n-fhaic m'Fhiann-sa no Fionn e,
is e làn casadaich s lòinidh
is mìle sròn ann 'gan srùbadh.

Pàdraig.
Nach do leugh thu Chriosostom?
Bi'd thosd, a anaChriosd dhearbhta,   *dʒɛpvta*
oir tha'n t-àit 'na loch lasrach,
mar bhios mi'g canainn san tsearmoin. *Sεrmon*
Sin sloc teinteach nan coire,
nach fhaic solus na gréine,
is tha Fionn s Tarbh Bhàsain   *Bɛ̀ San*
agus Bàl ann le chéile.   *Bæl*

Oisein.
dichtear   B'fhèarr mo gharadh an Ifrinn   *Bs fεrr mo gharamh*
na blasad dibhe do Rìghsa,
ma's E fhéin a chuir m'athair
gu baile na grìosaich.   *Bail' o' Bhrìsaigh.*
Cuir 'nam làimh claidhe sgaiteach,   *na mo làimh claidheakh*
biodag mhaith no sgian-luthaidh,   *Sgaiteach.*
is do Rìgh s a luchd cùirte,
chuirinn smùid asda ùile.   *aSdaib*

Pàdraig (ris fhéin).
Cluinnibh sin! Claidhe sgaiteach,   *Sgaθach*
is e'n athleanabas 'aoise—   *oSe*
Fionn s a mhusgaid s a chlogaid,
agus Osgar s a straoillean.

52

Figure 3. Page 52 of *FS* (stanzas from Ùrnuigh Oisein as Ùr).

p. 54 An Ceangal ⟨aigne chànain...⟩_p below the final line of the poem which seems particularly apt given Hay's facility with languages.

p. 55 ⟨(Translations)⟩_p below 'Dàin Eadartheangaichte'. Perhaps he had in mind a reprinting of the book and wished to make things clearer to readers without Gaelic. Hay viewed translations as desirable. In a letter to Douglas Young from Italy dated 29/3/44, source 22, he stated: 'Sam, I believe, has been confronted with a demand for a translation of the 'Cuilthionn.' I think myself that a translation would enhance it, but it would make it bulkier and more expensive of course (which is anything but what Sam wants)'. He made another interesting comment on translation in source 5:41v, where he wrote the isolated sentences 'Translation in English. Given the current situation that is realistic.' The handwriting is 1960s or early 1970s.

p. 61 Lasso, Amor mi Transporta ov' Io non Voglio. Line 11 has the words 'gheamhradh' and 'oidhche', with their intended pronunciation indicated on the side with ⟨ghevra⟩_p and ⟨ídhche⟩_p. After the poem there are two further annotations. At the bottom is ⟨Fuair Calum e fèin| 'ga ghabhail| agus an ath fer'⟩_p. Perhaps this is a reference to Calum Johnson, the Tarbert fisherman who was such a lasting influence on Hay; see (Byrne, 2000, Vol. II, pp. 3, 5). To the right of this is ⟨(San Tairbeart)| ⁊ an Eadailtis.⟩_p.

Annotations on the free end-papers. There are two annotations in Greek. The first, at the top of the front end-paper, is ⟨τίς εἶναι (επίδελφος)⟩_f. The phrase τίς εἶναι can be translated as 'who/which/what is it?' However there seems to be no such word as επίδελφος. It is possible that Hay elided επί (over, to, on, upon, in, under, for, during) and ἀδελφός (brother). This would fit with the possibility that the dedication 'acus do Iomharr' was to his brother.

Below the Greek annotation is ⟨Fuair mi thall aig a' chlach thu,| s tu mo gheansa de macaib...| (Clach Mór Gleann Loin)⟩_f. This seems to have been written at the same time and is perhaps part of the same thought. It is unclear why standard grammar is not followed for the dative; perhaps 'i' was elided with 'c'. The word 'chlach' is quite clear except for the internal letter 'c' but it is similar to the way Hay wrote internal 'c' in many documents; the word is unlikely to be 'chladh'. There is also no sign of lenition for 'Mór'. There are two more annotations on this page in addition to Hay's signature; see Figure 4.

On the back free end-paper is ⟨Σούνιο προμοντόριο⟩_i, a rendering in Greek letters of Sounion in Greece and the Latin word 'promontorio'; in Greek it is ακροτήριον or ἄκρον. It is unclear why Hay used the Latin word; he used ακροτήριον in a letter to Douglas Young dated 2/1/46, source 22.

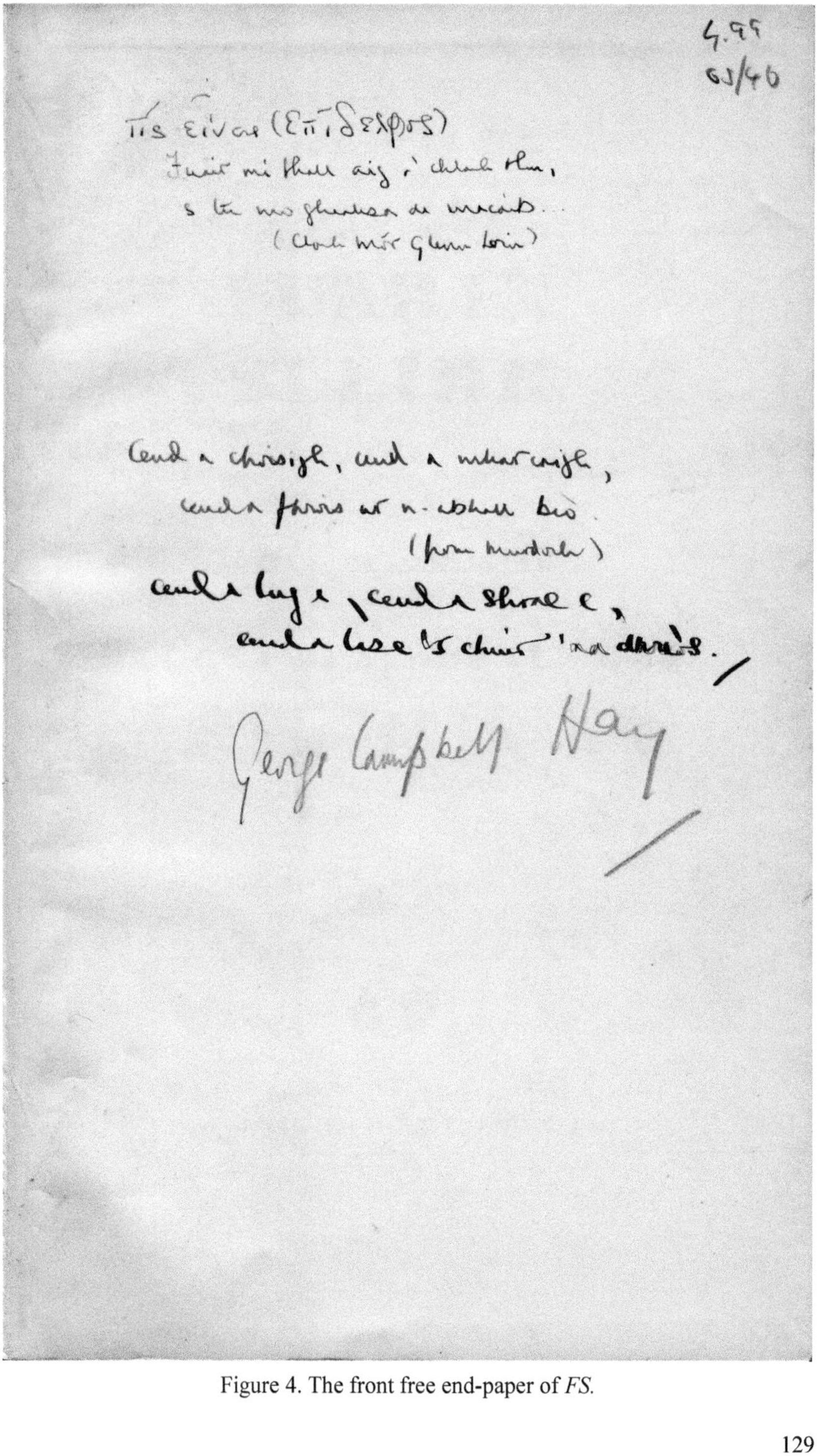

Figure 4. The front free end-paper of *FS*.

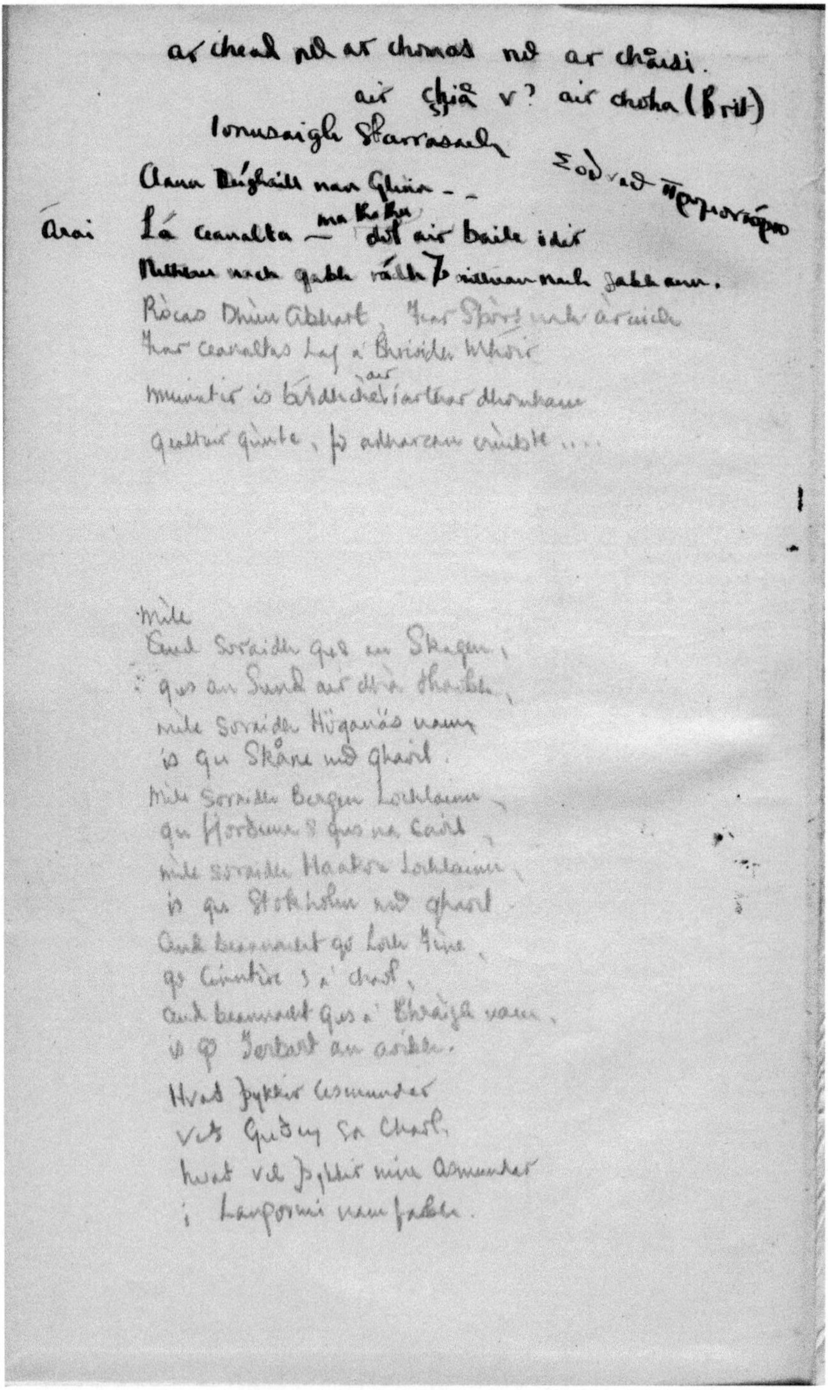

Figure 5. The back free end-paper of *FS*.

The most notable annotation is the valedictory poem on the back:
Mìle soraidh gus an Skagen,
gus an Sund air dà thaobh,
mìle soraidh Hügenäs uain
is gu Skåne mo ghaoil.
Mìle soraidh Bergen Lochlainn,
gu Hörðum s gus na caoil,
mìle soraidh Haakon Lochlainn,
is gu Stokholm mo ghaoil.
Ceud beannacht go Loch Fìne,
go Cinntìre s a' chaol,
ceud beannacht gus a' Bhràigh uain,
is go Tarbart an aoibh.
Hvað þykkir Asmundar
Við Guðey sa chaol,
hvað vil þykkir mire Asmundar
i Lanpormi nam faobh

Lines 13–15 are mostly in Icelandic and translate roughly as 'What does Asmundur| About Guðey (sa chaol)| What does my Asmundur'. In the last line 'Lanpormi' is presumably a place name in Scandinavia. Since 'i' can mean 'in' in Norwegian, Hay might be referring to a place name learnt from his sailing trips around Norway. In the Icelandic part, he might be playing with the fact that Asmunder in Old Norse means 'Divine Hand' and tying this with 'God's Island', one meaning of Guðey (the Norse name for Gigha).

There are various other annotations on the back free end-paper, with some words that are difficult to decipher, see Figure 5.

Acknowledgements

It is a pleasure to thank all of the following for their help. Michel Byrne gave me very useful information on several matters. Ian Stark pointed me in the right direction for Scandinavian topics and Hlin Davidsdottir helped with the Icelandic texts. Jake King helped with place names. Angus Martin responded fully to various questions. Peadar Ó Muircheartaigh helped with Irish matters. Anne Artymiuk kindly shared her information on Hay's younger brother. I am also very grateful to the referee whose insightful comments led to several improvements of the paper. Finally the W. L. Lorimer Memorial Trust Fund granted permission to reproduce from Hay's work.

Sources consulted

The descriptions here are mostly the same as Byrne (2000, Vol. 2).

1. NLS MS 14968, wartime poetry notebook, 1945–6 (Italy, Greece, Scotland).
2. NLS MS 26722, quarto notebook, late 1930s, some 1970s content, possibly some 1950s content.
3. NLS MS 26723, quarto notebook, late 1930s.
4. NLS MS 26728, quarto notebook, includes diary 1938–41.
5. NLS MS 26730, wartime notebook, 1944–5, 1972, 1980.
6. NLS MS 26731, quarto notebook, 1946.
7. NLS MS 26733, quarto notebook, notes on Norwegian poetry mainly $c.$1961.
8. NLS MS 26732, jotter of traditional and original poetry in Gaelic and Icelandic, $c.$1938–$c.$1947, possibly early 1950.
9. NLS MS 26734, quarto notebook, mid 1970s.
10. NLS MS 26736, quarto notebook, early 1960s; poetry content 1980s.
11. NLS MS 26744, folder of miscellaneous poems, 1920s–1980s.
12. NLS MS 26745, typescript of Hay's collected Gaelic poems, with English translations, 1974.
13. NLS MS26748, folder of correspondence 1941–83.
14. NLS MS26752, miscellaneous papers of Angus Martin, $c.$1980–84.
15. NLS MS 26751, transcripts of recordings in Martin, 1979.
16. NLS MS 26753, folder of correspondence with Angus Martin, 1974–83.
17. NLS MS 26777, copy of *Fuaran Sléibh*, annotated $c.$1983.
18. NLS MS 26780, copy of *Chasing an Ancient Greek* by Douglas Young (1950).
19. NLS MS 26781, copy of *An Dealbh Briste* by Derick S. Thomson (1951).
20. NLS MS 26783, copy of *O na Ceithir Àirdean*, annotated 1960s?
21. NLS MS 26784, copy of *O na Ceithir Àirdean*, annotated 1983.
22. NLS Acc 6419/38. Douglas Young papers. Letters from Hay to Young, mainly 1939–46.
23. NLS Acc 10105, letters mostly from Hay to Prof. Robert A. Rankin, mainly 1934–39.
24. NLS Acc 9927/6, letters to the Rev. Kenneth Dr MacLeod.
25. NLS Acc 13211, undated texts of 'The Sun over Athens' and 'Jebel and the Dayspring' in Hay's handwriting.

Bibliography

Artymiuk, Anne (2015). Private communication.
Campbell Hay, George (1943). 'Cinntìre', *An Gàidheal*, Vol. 39, p. 9.
Byrne, Michel (1992). 'Bàrdachd Mhic Iain Dheòrsa: The Original Poems of George Campbell Hay – An Annotated Edition'. Unpublished PhD thesis, University of Edinburgh.
Byrne, Michel (ed.) (2000). *Collected Poems and Songs of George Campbell Hay (Deòrsa Mac Iain Dheòrsa)*. 2 vols. Edinburgh: EUP.
Byrne, Michel (2014). Private communication.
Calder, George (1923). *A Gaelic Grammar*. Glasgow: MacLaren & Sons.
King, Jake (2014). Private communication.
Martin, Angus (1980). *Celtic and Scottish Studies Archives, Edinburgh, recordings of*

George Campbell Hay and Angus Martin, 14 May 1979, 3 October 1980 and 15 November 1980.

Martin, Angus (1984). *Kintyre: The Hidden Past*. Edinburgh: John Donald.

Martin, A. (2013). *Kintyre Places and Place-names*. Edinburgh: Grimsay Press.

Martin, Angus (2014). Letter to the author, 14 May 2014.

Rankin, Robert A. (1984) 'George Campbell Hay as I knew him'. *Chapman*, 40, pp.1–12.

8

The Gaelic writer, Iain Crichton Smith...

Moray Watson

University of Aberdeen

1 Introduction: half of my seeing

> 'Feeling,' they said,
> 'that's the important thing'–
> those poets who write in English over in Ireland.
> (Smith 1995 [1992])

These lines come from Iain Crichton Smith's inspired (yet inelegantly titled) 'For Poets Writing in English Over in Ireland'.[1] They may seem a surprising choice as the opening salvo in a paper about Gaelic literature; on the contrary, these lines, and the poem in general, cut straight to the point of this paper. My title slightly playfully points to the duality that has often been noted in the bilingual writer who is known as both Iain Crichton Smith and Iain Mac a' Ghobhainn: in this paper, to signal which of his two literary identities is in play at any given moment, I use both of his publishing names, and I hope the reader can excuse any potential confusion caused by this practice.[2] In this essay, I argue that this duality is not something that is restricted to Smith/Mac a' Ghobhainn, but that he usefully exemplifies it. What is immediately obvious about 'For Poets...' is that it is about that same kind of existential question of choice that so famously exercised Somhairle MacGill-Eain and that underpins a good deal of Mac a' Ghobhainn's other writing, regardless of whether he is being Mac a' Ghobhainn or Smith at the time. It is a kind of choice, and often the specific choice, that sits in the background of much of our contemporary Gaelic literature, sometimes noted and remarked upon, sometimes ignored, sometimes unseen. The choice Smith presents to us in this poem is not only a choice of language, although the language serves both to actuate the necessity for choice in the first place and also figures as a metonym for that choice more generally. As is imaged by his choice of surnames, Smith/Mac a' Ghobhainn is faced with a choice of identities, a choice of selves. In 'For Poets...', he lets us know that he is aware of this and that there are no easy options.

Despite the language of the poem's medium, 'For Poets...' is in many ways a 'Gaelic poem' in its sensibilities, which can partly be read in its topic and setting, and which is very much manifested in its imagery and lexis. In an article about Smith's English poetry, Colin Milton sees this poem as a clue to understanding why the English poetry is so effective. Milton writes: 'Smith's work in English owes much of its distinctiveness and power to the influence of his Gaelic inheritance' (Milton, 1997, p. 220). In 'For Poets...', Smith shows his understanding that this is the case and that it is also true of these other poets who write only in English. It has always been known, for instance, that Yeats consciously and carefully plundered the Gaelic background in the process of developing his own distinctive voice. Thus, the writers Smith observes at the poetry gathering in Ireland have, potentially (depending on their linguistic competence), a choice of two possible languages. But, as we realise on reading the poem, this is actually a three-way choice, because they could also choose, like Smith himself, to write bilingually. But, further, these writers cannot escape from the situation that has created the choice: regardless of the language they write in, they exist in a bicultural setting, and this is where hybridity begins to seep in, sometimes unnoticed.

Smith/Mac a' Ghobhainn visited Ireland several times and was a popular attraction on the Scottish/Irish poets' tours and festivals. In this poem, he, as Smith, invokes the atmosphere of an event like Turas na bhFilí/Cuairt nam Bàrd, the annual reciprocal visits of Irish and Scottish Gaelic poets, or the Galway poetry festival, with the heady trilingualism and polite tension. The irony in the poem consists in the fact that Smith finds a haven of familiarity among the Anglophone poets from Ireland, alienated as he is by the strangeness of the Irish language which is the cognate of his own mother tongue: and, of course, it is partly the closeness of the two Gaelic languages and cultures that led to his being invited to Ireland on so many occasions. The poem directly alludes to great Anglophone poets Yeats, Larkin and Dunn, two of them Irish and one Scottish, and it is easy to feel as if there are hints of other poets in there, such as Heaney. But it also mentions what it calls an 'Irish' poem, by which Smith meant that it was written in the Irish language. It appears that he was reading a translation of Muireadhach Albanach Ó Dálaigh's 'M'Anam do Sgar Riomsa A-Raoir', albeit rather a free one.[3] Significantly, the recently-widowed poet in question was, as we know, one of the most famous members of the bardic tradition to operate in Scotland, an Irishman who earned the epithet 'Alban(n)ach'

(Simms, 2006), and who therefore symbolises another, older iteration of the kind of hybridity Smith sees in the contemporary world. Milton contends that 'the idea of synthesis, of integration, is of central importance to Smith' (Milton, 1997, p. 219), so perhaps it is no accident that the elegy his eye has alighted on happens to belong to a poet who also straddled two worlds.

The use of the word 'leth' to mean 'one of' anything is, of course, a typically Gaelic idiom. Smith uses the word 'half' throughout his poem in a conscious echo of what he calls the 'Irish' poem. It also appears in the lines he has lifted from the translation he has been reading when inspired to write this one. In the magnificent anthology, *Duanaire na Sracaire* (2007), Meg Bateman has translated some instances of 'leth' in this poem as 'one of', conveying the idiomatic usage. But Smith has been reading an older translation that has been more literal in some ways and more liberal in others[4] and it has inspired him to think about the idea of 'halfness'. This is an idea he has mentioned often and it underpinned a good deal of imagery in his writing, throughout his career, in both languages. He extends the image here, telling us that, when surrounded by people speaking Irish, he feels 'half-deaf, half-blind'. This is a familiarly frustrating experience to those who have spent time with speakers of the other Gaelic language, regardless of which one the 'other' one happens to be. But Colin Milton can see an extension to the metaphor going beyond this poem and its context, because he realises that Smith feels strongly about the way his Hebridean background is generally perceived by others. Milton picks up on the frustration and, sometimes, anger expressed by Smith in his book of essays, *Towards the Human* (1986). The first essay, in particular, 'Real People in a Real Place', assumes a defiant tone as it challenges the patronising attitudes of those who look at the Gaelic community from an external perspective. In a similar (but other) context, Declan Kiberd has written about 'an imperial strategy of infantilising native culture' (Kiberd, 1995; 1996, p. 103); Murray Pittock elsewhere sees this infantilising as having been applied to Scotland in general and then the Gaelic community on a twofold basis, both from outside of Scotland and also from Lowland Scotland (Pittock, 1999, p. 27): and, while Pittock does not use this terminology, I think I am right in suggesting he sees the Gaelic experience as being a kind of double internal colonialism, to re-borrow an idea Douglas Mack borrows from Katie Trumpener (Mack, 2006, p. 7). A discussion of these issues appears in Mack's book *Scottish Fiction and the British Empire*, in which Mack goes even further and suggests that the Highlanders are dehumanised in centrist perceptions of their society (Mack, 2006, pp. 90-1). The titles of Smith's essay, and of the book itself, tend to support the view that he is vexed by the dehumanising effects of this double internal colonialism.

Observing how Smith reacts to the obscuring of the humanity of his background, Milton writes: 'Much of Smith's English poetry is concerned with making his own culture and its values and traditions visible to the non-Gael' (Milton, 1997, p. 193). Milton's idea of making Gaelic culture, values and traditions 'visible' seems to refer directly to the phrase 'half of my seeing'. It seems to me, in fact, that the phrase has two, almost diametrically opposite, meanings in Smith's poem, because it still represents inextricable integration as it does in the poem that served as its inspiration in the first place, but it also stands for the exclusion that comes about as a result of being a stranger to a language and its culture.

2 Riddled with guilt

Smith/Mac a' Ghobhainn's work is particularly relevant and topical in the context of some of the current literary criticism that is being done, both in Aberdeen and elsewhere. Smith/Mac a' Ghobhainn's work epitomises and, in some ways, problematises, issues relating to much of my current research. I am taking a broad view of the notion of the 'Gaelic literature', especially in the modern period, and trying to develop classifications and typologies that may start to allow us to define a theoretical framework for studying modern Gaelic literature in a modern way. This has been inspired by William Gillies's comments at an earlier Rannsachadh na Gàidhlig conference, also picked up on by Thomas Clancy, among others, at subsequent manifestations of Rannsachadh na Gàidhlig (Clancy, 2010). Gillies argued that it is high time we gave serious and methodical thought to how we conduct our study of Gaelic literature (Gillies, 2002). Extended criticism of Gaelic literature has been attracting more and more attention in recent years, especially since Gillies made those remarks. Critics have experimented with applying a reasonably wide range of techniques and strategies to their work in recent years. With all of this in mind, the scholarly community needs to take Gillies's advice without delay and start to have a more in-depth conversation about how we go about this business. Specifically, my instinct is that, while there are useful tools and techniques in many modern approaches to literature, there are none that entirely suit the Gaelic situation and this is because these methods have themselves arisen out of a need to explain and empower other literatures that share only some features with Gaelic. My argument is that, much as Gillies suggested, we need to ensure that we build our modern Gaelic literary criticism around a sound knowledge and understanding of what has gone before. And, while we may cherry-pick some of the most applicable methods from elsewhere, we must always move forward with the awareness and appreciation of the work of generations of scholars working within a Gaelic context.

Before we can even come to that point, we must engage in debate about how we define Gaelic literature in the contemporary period. Today's bilingual Gaelic community is evolving a literature, and more generally, a cultural environment, that is notable for its diversity: the Gaelic community of 2014 is, to a large extent, diasporic, but it goes further than that. It is not just a question of the destinations of today's Gaelic speakers as they spread out into the world to seek work, their fortune, follow loved ones, and so on. We are also now beginning to see the results in the literature of greatly widened backgrounds among the members of this community. When Fionn, Iain Bàn Òg, Iain MacCormaic, Aonghas MacDhonnchaidh, Iain MacPhàidein and the others were writing a century and more ago, they were able to assume a certain degree of shared background among their readers, and this, in turn, resulted in a large degree of linguistic, cultural and aesthetic homogeneity in their work. But when we pick up a book by Alison Lang today, and then move to a book by Niall O'Gallagher, then Christopher Whyte/Crìsdean MacIlleBhàin, then Maoilios Caimbeul or Tim Armstrong, we realise that there are no longer any such assumptions.[5] So, this poem, 'For Poets Writing in English Over in Ireland' becomes an interesting waypoint: for me, it comes to represent not only the individual choice that the native Gaelic speaker – that is to say the native bilingual – has to make in deciding whether to be a Gaelic writer, an English writer or both; but it also represents what is happening for the language, as it is being chosen by non-natives, just as Conrad chose to make his literary career in what was effectively his third language.

We might consider here the Kenyan writer and scholar Ngũgĩ Wa Thiong'o and some of his remarks about his fellow African Chinua Achebe. Over his career, Ngũgĩ has come to have strong views about choice of language. As he put it himself in his book, *Decolonising the Mind: the Politics of Language in African Literature*:

> The choice of language and the use to which language is put is central to a people's definition of themselves in relation to their natural and social environment, indeed in relation to the entire universe (Ngũgĩ, 2005 [1981], p. 4).

This reflects some of Iain Crichton Smith's sentiments in his essays in *Towards the Human*, especially that long, highly reflective opening piece, 'Real People in a Real Place', which also raises the issue of the fundamental connections between people and the places they inhabit. As Smith puts it:

> The problem of language is obviously of the first importance. If the islander were to speak English and still inhabit the island which he does in fact inhabit, what would he be then but an unreal person in an

unreal place? If he were to wake one morning and look around him and see 'hill' and not '*cnoc*', would he not be an expatriate of his own land? (Smith 1986, p. 20)

At this point, the reader might be forgiven for wondering which land he means. When language starts to become linked to ethnicity in literature, issues of community and nation-ness often follow. Declan Kiberd has written about this several times, notably in his book *Inventing Ireland: The Literature of the Modern Nation*, where he engages with Benedict Anderson's analysis of writers conducting their lives through the medium of English and this becoming a kind of exile (Kiberd, 1995, 1996, p. 2). Kiberd notes that, for some writers suffering from this kind of exile, they have come to a position whereby they had no clear sense of whom they were writing for and become ashamed as a result (Kiberd, 1995, 1996, p. 115).

Ngũgĩ recalls that Achebe struggled with a similar sense of shame but that he chose to continue writing in English. As Achebe put it:

Is it right that a man should abandon his mother tongue for someone else's? It looks like a dreadful betrayal and produces a guilty feeling. But for me there is no other choice. I have been given the language and I intend to use it. (Ngũgĩ, 2005 [1981], p. 7)

This logic was not good enough for Ngũgĩ, however, and he gave up writing in English. Achebe himself eventually came back to the issue and questioned his choices. For Ngũgĩ, the English language and literature were an imposition that interfered with his own identity: 'language and literature were taking us further and further from ourselves, from our world to other worlds' (Ngũgĩ 1981 [2005], p. 12). Smith evidently experienced a similar sense of guilt. In 'Real People in a Real Place', he stated:

To write in English becomes a form of treachery and this is so because Gaelic does not have the strength to allow explorations into another language beyond itself. If Gaelic had that strength then for someone from within to write in another language would appear the most sublime form of self-confidence; to introduce new ideas, new concepts, would be a service which would be analogous to the introduction into English of foreign words, fresh philosophies (Smith, 1986, p. 21).

In his essay 'The Double Man', he admitted to being 'riddled with guilt' (Smith, 1989, p. 140). It seems that this guilt is related to the link between language and place, between community, nation-ness and belonging.

In *Imagined Communities* (2006), Anderson explores the idea of nation-ness and how this is an expanded form of the community, which is itself, to some degree, an imagined construct. In *Inventing Ireland*, Kiberd finds some points of disagreement with Anderson, but ultimately accepts at least part of this basic premise. In particular, he considers the constructed nature of Irish identity. He lays some of the blame for the construct on people like Matthew Arnold, who had no real experience of Ireland and no real knowledge of Irish texts (relying on second-hand sources). According to Kiberd, the Irish appropriated Arnold's racist descriptions of themselves and turned them into positive versions, but, by doing so, they accepted being defined in English terms and consigned their identity to stereotyping (this is his argument in the first 'interchapter' of the book). Smith, and also Pittock and others, discuss this kind of stereotyping in relation to the Gàidhealtachd. Pittock goes as far as to blame the media for emphasising certain qualities that encourage people from elsewhere to view the Gàidhealtachd in a patronising way. His conclusion chimes with Smith's own views. Pittock writes:

> A community is a place where people live diversely, not a recreational space into which to project an imaginary totality. (Pittock, 1999, p. 39)

Ngũgĩ (2005, p. 198) describes a conference he once attended. The conference focused on the question 'What is African Literature?' and this central question was framed around a number of subsidiary questions:

> Was it literature about Africa or about the African experience?
> Was it literature written by Africans?
> What about a non-African who wrote about Africa: did his work qualify as African literature?
> What if an African set his work in Greenland: did that qualify as African literature?
> Or were African languages the criteria?
> Ok, what about Arabic, was it not foreign to Africa?
> What about French and English, which had become African languages?
> What if an European wrote about Europe in an African language?
> (Ngũgĩ, 2005 [1981], pp. 5-6)

So many of these questions – substituting the words 'Gaelic' or 'Gael' for the word 'African', of course – are just under the surface for us nowadays when we read contemporary literature that comes within a broad Gaelic framework. They mirror the kinds of questions we address within the Gàidhealtachd Literature project in Aberdeen, and they also reflect some of the concerns that exercised Smith/Mac a' Ghobhainn as he tried to define himself as a writer. Smith was insistent that we must not accept that English literature was 'superior' to Gaelic literature (Smith, 1986, p. 38). But he was frustrated by what he saw as a reluctance on the part of the audience – at least some proportion of the audience – to accept that Gaelic was a language with significance beyond itself. In 'Real People in a Real Place', he complained:

> Some years ago I wrote a play in Gaelic about the Trojan War and it was felt by some that this was not a suitable topic for a Gaelic writer.
> I disagreed, and still disagree (Smith, 1986, p. 38).

He also touched on this several times in his essay 'The Double Man'. He specifically stated that there existed a 'conservative force which drives Gaelic writers towards writing on Gaelic subject matter' (Smith, 1989, p. 138). In the contemporary scene, we find that the situation has moved on to the point where Gaelic writers are absolutely confident to write about more or less anything, in more or less any setting. Further, there are more and more of them who are willing to write in languages other than Gaelic, sometimes about the Gaelic experience.[6] And there is an increasing awareness within the literary community of the hybridity of Gaelic literature. So now we encounter English-language novels like *Portrona* and *Calum Tod*, written by Gaelic writers, and poetry in Gaelic which speaks to an international literary community written by the likes of Crìsdean MacIlleBhàin[7] and Niall O'Gallagher, and short stories about computers sitting side-by-side with stories set on peat moors. And, where Smith/Mac a' Ghobhainn wrote novellas in two versions, both English and Gaelic, and then published them separately, perhaps almost coyly, we now have Aonghas Pàdraig Caimbeul publishing *An Nighean air an Aiseag* (2013) together with his English-language novel *The Girl on the Ferryboat* (2013), credited to him as Angus Peter Campbell, with the two books appearing at the same time and designed and marketed as companion volumes. As Silke Stroh (2011) has argued, 'cultural hybridity frequently appears not as a menace or as a unilateral assimilation into the mainstream, but as a process of mutual inspiration and a creative force' (Stroh, 2011, p. 110).

3 Choosing a tradition

Working on Smith's correspondence and diaries at the National Library of Scotland, I have been struck by an impression of the lack of Gaelic as a substantial component in his professional life.[8] There are folders of letters in the archive in which entire years go by with little or no reference to Smith's role as a Gaelic writer. Most files in NLS Acc. 13496 have either no Gaelic letters or, at most, one or two.[9] When I encountered an invitation from Christopher MacLachlan to Smith to take part in a literary event alongside Derick Thomson this seemed a telling moment, in many ways. MacLachlan was inviting the two poets to read from their work and discuss how their shared backgrounds had resulted in the one, Thomson, becoming a Gaelic poet and the other, Smith, becoming an English-language poet. MacLachlan made suggestions for a running order, including recommending some poems he thought might go well: there was no indication that Smith might read out any of his Gaelic works or that his status as a bilingual writer was part of the rationale behind the event. This put into words for me an impression that was forming in my mind of Smith making his living as a writer and being surrounded professionally by a network of contacts who almost all thought of him as an Anglophone writer, or at least primarily so. I have noted elsewhere that it would have been close to impossible to make a living as a Gaelic writer during Iain Mac a' Ghobhainn's career, so there is nothing surprising about the impression that comes across in his professional schedule of his basing a career on the English work. In fact, as Smith, he discussed this himself in 'The Double Man'. But when we bear in mind the sheer bulk of writing that he produced in Gaelic, it is astonishing just how scarce any mention of Gaelic is in his correspondence and itinerary. An interesting point here, and a contradiction of what I argue later in this paper, is that, despite the high degree of self-translation he did, Smith/Mac a' Ghobhainn himself might not always have been as willing to blend the two sides of his literary identity as we sometimes imagine. In the 1980s, a number of editors of primarily Anglophone magazines invited him to contribute Gaelic writing to magazines to which he was already sending English work, although they often asked him to provide English translations if he took them up on the invitation. A sequence of letters from Joy Hendry at *Chapman* pursues this line with some vigour: the impression is that, while Smith was responding to the other points in her letters, he might not have been answering that particular query. Of course, as we know, he did publish Gaelic material in some primarily Anglophone outlets from time to time, but not often, when viewed from the perspective of his entire output. We may take short stories as an example. Out of 112 Gaelic stories that Ian MacDonald[10] has identified, only nine of these appear in the *Scotsman* newspaper and one in the *Stornoway Gazette*, which, although primarily an Anglophone publication, is firmly rooted in a Gaelic cultural environment. So, while Smith was being asked to submit Gaelic materials to English-language outlets, it appears that he was, perhaps, reluctant to do so, although we may never know whether he simply felt he had no suitable Gaelic writing on hand when the requests came in. From his correspondence, it is clear that he otherwise generally responded with alacrity and enthusiasm to requests for submissions, including those from *Gairm*, Acair and the Gaelic Books Council. Thus, this was not simply a matter of his being reluctant to spend time on Gaelic writing because his career depended on the English work.

Returning to the issue of linguistic and cultural duality: we may note that Derick Thomson (who published his creative writing as Ruaraidh MacThòmais) was also keenly aware of these matters and was affected by them himself. As a scholar, he often wrote about Gaelic literature and was perfectly capable of writing, as Derick Thomson, about the poet Ruaraidh MacThòmais, without even mentioning that he was writing about himself. Thomson contributed an introduction to Smith's *Towards the Human*, which was published in 1986, nine years before MacLachlan's invitation to the two poets. In that introduction, Thomson wrote that Smith 'has written more in English than in Gaelic, and could choose to belong to an English tradition of writing more than a Gaelic one. He still has the problems of Scottish location and Gaelic primary experience to resolve' (Thomson, 1986, p. 8). It seems to me that these are two separate issues, although they are linked: a discussion of each follows.

Stroh (2011) describes the way that national identities can be expressed in something of a confused way in Gaelic poetry (Stroh phrases this much more elegantly than I have here, pp. 99-100). There exists what we might describe as a layered sense of cultural nationalism in the Gaelic literary milieu, where writers identify with, for example, specific islands or parts of islands, then with a general Highland, island or Gàidhealtachd *ethnie*, and then with Scottishness or Britishness or something else. All of this is undoubtedly also common outside of the Gaelic literary world, but the awareness of it is very much to the fore in Gaelic literature and it therefore becomes marked. According to Thomson, 'The writer in a small country has to face problems and choices that are unfamiliar to writers in a larger one, and there are further complications when the language used is a minority one, or worse, one which appears to be approaching extinction at some finite point in time' (Thomson, 1986, p. 7). These again will be issues familiar to students of Somhairle MacGill-Eain: to choose to write in a language that appears to be going out of use is an act resonant with implications. But Colin Milton suggests that, for Smith, his choice of languages may be advantageous. He suggests that:

> the writer who also has the English language and literary tradition available to him is aware of the greater scope for the individual expression they offer him, just as the wider society outside the island offers greater (if still limited) scope for other forms of individual expression (Milton, 1997, p. 210).

In 'Real People in a Real Place', Smith exhibits agitation with the way his language is perceived by outsiders, as well as with the way the place and its people are patronised. Of course, what he presents to us in the essay is, in itself, only a perception of a perception and we are always aware of a slightly unreliable narrator in that essay. As Ray Ryan (2002, p. 93) puts it, the essay has, at times, a 'shrill' tone. It is no more shrill, though, than the writings of Ngũgĩ or Frantz Fanon, whose discursive writings often become highly emotionally charged. Robert Young has explained that this somewhat traumatised reaction is a common one, which we can see as having been brought about by the subaltern nature of their background culture. In Young's words:

> When an original culture is superimposed with a colonial or dominant culture through education, it produces a nervous condition of ambivalence, uncertainty, a blurring of cultural boundaries, inside and outside, an otherness within (Young, 2003, p. 23).

Young also discusses:

> a hybridized split existence, trying to live as two different, incompatible people at once (Young, 2003, p. 23).

It is striking that Young's terminology so closely echoes Smith's words in 'For Poets...' and in his own explanation of why he chose the imagery of the jester's motley for some of his early poetry. He explained in 'The Double Man' that he alighted on the jester as an image for the bilingual. Intriguingly, though, the poem which first establishes this image in his personal symbolism is 'An t-Amadan'. These are the last lines:

> a' sruthadh an dà dhath ri chèile
> gus am falbh mi air bheag lèirsinn
> anns an aon dath a tha cho neònach
> 's nach tuig an Rìgh fhèin mo chòmhradh.
> (Watson, 2013, p. 91)

Some of this is strikingly close to the imagery in 'For Poets...' Moreover, what Mac a' Ghobhainn is describing here is not the carefully and strictly demarcated separateness or doubleness of the motley, but a costume whose two colours have run together. He is describing a hybridising process, which his essay 'The Double Man' makes it clear is a stressful, even distressing, state to be in. With his typical mixture of erudition, surreal wit and allusions to popular culture, Smith characterised the experience like this:

> I am, I suppose, indeed the double man, a kind of monster, an Incredible Hulk, that slouches somewhere to be born. But where is that somewhere? I doubt very much that it is Bethlehem. It may be in a No Man's Land between the two languages. It may be where no one has been before. It may lie somewhere between Lewis and Wittgenstein (Smith, 1989, p. 145).[11]

Throughout his Gaelic writing, as Mac a' Ghobhainn, we can discern an awareness of these pressures and opportunities: bilingualism creates tensions, the choice of language creates pressures of finance and loyalty, and all of it creates inspiration. Examples of this include the long story sequence 'Granny Anns a' Chòrnair' (*Gairm 54*, An t-Earrach 1966), which is a family saga that explores the issues of the dilution of the Gàidhealtachd and its rapid subsumption into the globally homogenous Anglo-American culture. Similarly, the poem 'Nochdadh ri Beanntan na Hearadh' (Watson, 2013, p. 71) expresses a concern with the infiltration of both the English language and the Anglo-American culture into the very heartland of Gaelic. The Gàidhealtachd appears very often as a setting for Mac a' Ghobhainn's stories and as a locus in his poetry. The story 'A' Chroit' (*Gairm* 113, An Geamhradh 1980), for instance, is concerned with the emotional attachment with the first environment and the associated linguistic culture. That emotional attachment is explored in metaphorical and literal terms in the story 'Je t'Aime' (*Sruth* 30.11.1967). There, a little girl's French lessons spark all manner of emotional reactions in her father. He is riven by guilt, partly because of his own past behaviour. But this guilt comes to be associated with the language and the fact that his daughter is no longer allowed to do Gaelic in school, even though she wants to. The father argues with his wife, who feels Gaelic is no longer of use in the modern world. He responds: 'bha Gàidhlig math gu leòr dhuinne'. The financial benefits of English over Gaelic are also brought up in the story 'Turus Dhachaidh – I', which opens the collection *Bùrn is Aran* (Mac a' Ghobhainn, 1960). Near the end of the same volume, 'Turus Dhachaidh – II' features characters gossiping about a stranger because they assume he will not understand their Gaelic. Significantly, this story takes place in the Gàidhealtachd, which means that Mac a' Ghobhainn is portraying even the Gaelic heartland as a place where people might assume a stranger would not know the language.

The link between emotion, the first environment and language is particularly strong in the poetry. In 'Chuir thu do làmhan mum amhaich', Mac a' Ghobhainn writes 'Nach iongantach mar/ a tha a' Ghàidhlig a' toirt air ais thugam/ dealt na h-òige' (Watson, 2013, p. 199). Another poem makes the claim: 'Bidh na facail ag èirigh às an talamh' (Watson, 2013, p. 209). In 'A' Cheist', the poet questions whether his second, learned environment can ever become as close to him emotionally as his first environment and he concludes that it cannot, despite its power and beauty (Watson, 2013, p. 175). This is summed up in a sequence of poems, culminating in the short:

> Bha mi eadar òrain Uilleim Rois agus dàin Mhilton,
>   'na h-iuchraichean air chall agus dall bhith gan
>   iarraidh.'

> Tha an aon chànan mar bholtrach: tha an tèile nam
> eanchainn.
>
> Tha mi nam shuidhe ann an rùm a' leughadh D. H.
> Lawrence.
> Am baile fodham: sglapaidean geala a' seòladh seachad.
> (Watson, 2013, p. 222)

All of these tensions leave the bilingual in an invidious position. It is a position discussed by Michelle Macleod (2001). She notes that Mac a' Ghobhainn expresses a 'sense of unfulfilment and lack of self-identity' in the poem 'Tha gach ainmhidh coimhlionta' (p. 117).[12]

In the extract just quoted, the speaker in the poem imagines being between the songs of William Ross and the poems of Milton. Being between is very much a concern in a good deal of Mac a' Ghobhainn's writing. Ngũgĩ uses the same metaphor of 'being between' in a short article in which he discusses his experience of coming to accept that he should write in his native language, giving us another interesting parallel and demonstrating again that experience of the Gael is, in some ways, an experience shared throughout the postcolonial (or post-colonial) world (Ngũgĩ, 2009). The word 'eadar' itself appears more than 30 times in Mac a' Ghobhainn's Gaelic poetry, an average of about once every ten poems. The most obviously relevant poem here is one titled 'Eadar a' Ghàidhealtachd 's a' Ghalltachd' (Watson, 2013, p. 50). In that work, the speaker imagines himself not only between the Gàidhealtachd and Galltachd but also between the Gàidhealtachd and the world. In 'Ochd Òrain Airson Cèilidh Ùir' (Watson, 2013, p. 66), Mac a' Ghobhainn once again considers the link between identity, language and the first environment. He thinks of the dramatic difference between urban and rural environments and admits: 'Tha mise ceangailt' ris a' Ghàidhealtachd – / seo far na dh'ionnsaich mi mo leòn.' In 'Mo Thaipwriter', he is 'eadar dà shaoghal' (Watson, 2013, p. 173). In 'Coisichidh Sinn', he is between verses, waves, languages and graves (Watson, 2013, p. 177). Often, for Mac a' Ghobhainn, being between two languages is associated with guilt.

4 Translating culture

In Gaelic, of course, the word 'eadar' is part of the word for 'translating'. This paper began with discussion of a poem in which Smith thinks about a translated poem, and translation is a crucial aspect of understanding not only Smith as a writer but also understanding why his work has been so widely appreciated. Several of the Gaelic poems mention translation, which is to say the literal process of substituting words and structures of one language for words and structures of another. But more of the poems touch on the idea of cultural translation. For instance, a young Highland girl is described as 'beò air crisps is air lemonade'. The speaker there asks William Ross if he would write a poem for her, in her denim clothes and with her ears full of pop music. In preparing the edition of Mac a' Ghobhainn's Gaelic poems, I had to decide when (and whether) to Gaelicise terms or use Gaelic spellings for borrowings. In many cases, I resisted this, because of a sense that the hybridity was an essential component of what the poems themselves were about.

In 'The Double Man', Smith wrote 'For a non-Gaelic speaker to understand my Gaelic poetry even in translation would be difficult' (Smith, 1989, p. 137). The reason for this, he argued, was that there are concepts that defy translation. He mentioned the fact that Somhairle MacGill-Eain 'achieved much of his reputation by means of his translations' and noted that 'essays are confidently written about him by those who don't know Gaelic', a point very eloquently explored by other commentators since (Smith, 1989, p. 137). It seems to me that Smith was aware of what Salman Rushdie has called 'the state of being a "translated man", that is someone who is "translated" across cultures' (Rushdie, 1991). This is reminiscent of what Colin Milton wrote about Smith's mission to make Gaelic culture visible to the non-Gaels.

Often, Smith/Mac a' Ghobhainn realises that what he really desires is a Derridan ideal of expressing his feelings without having to rely on limited languages at all. Kevin MacNeil sees this as an underlying theme in much of his writing. In relation to Smith's stories in English, MacNeil writes: 'Crichton Smith's stories often triumph by communicating to the reader that which is, to the characters at least, incommunicable. But, furthermore, some of his stories communicate something that seems to be, paradoxically, above verbal understanding' (MacNeil, 1991, p. xxvi).

'For Poets...' appears in both the Carcanet *Selected Poems* and also the 1992/1995 *Collected Poems*. Even a glance through the *Collected Poems* is fascinating when we adopt this perspective, this notion of wondering how we call Iain Crichton Smith a Gaelic writer. The volume runs to 380 pages and features work from throughout Smith's career, but the poetry is very much selected. Most notably, there are no poems in the book in Gaelic. A number of sections of the book are dedicated to Smith's translations, either from his own Gaelic poetry or from the likes of Donnchadh Bàn's 'Moladh Beinn Dòbhrain'. But the literary identity as presented in the book is very much a monolingual one. The book's blurb is fascinating in this regard:

> As a child Iain Crichton Smith spoke Gaelic in his village on the island of Lewis. At school in Stornoway he spoke English. Like many

islanders before and since, his culture is divided: two languages, two histories entailing exile, a central theme of his poetry in both tongues. His divided perspective sharply delineates the tyranny of history and religion, of the cramped life of small communities; it also gives him a tender eye for the struggle of women and men in a world defined by denials.

A little biography appears at the bottom of the back cover. Notwithstanding the obvious minor error of the year of Smith's birth, this biography makes another intriguingly wrong statement; or, the question that might more properly concern us is: is it wrong? It states:

Carcanet publish all his poetry…

Although an understandable error, this is telling. Michael Schmidt of Carcanet came to know Smith well, and Smith's relationship with Carcanet lasted for many years. There is no doubt that they knew he was also a Gaelic writer and that he had published several volumes of Gaelic poetry, as well as more than a hundred uncollected Gaelic poems, by the time this blurb appeared. It is an unapologetic demarcation, whereby somebody has made the decision to view Smith as a separate literary identity from Mac a' Ghobhainn.

Interestingly, Kevin MacNeil's edited collection of the English language stories has a blurb that makes a claim that is similar in nature:

This book is part of a two-volume collection, comprising the complete English stories, including a large number that have never previously been published in book form, as well as others that have been out of print for many years, thus making it possible to judge Crichton Smith's achievement as a writer in full.

Again, these books of the stories are effectively making the claim that Smith, or Crichton Smith, is a different writer from Mac a' Ghobhainn. Then again, there is that phrase 'the complete English stories' that undermines this and draws to our attention the fact that the books are only presenting part of the picture, while claiming to present it in full.

Of course, we can understand and sympathise with the marketing reasons behind these two statements and appreciate that neither was meant to be a definitive academic pronouncement. But it will be useful here to explore the extent to which we might agree with them. Both the *Collected Poems* and these complete English stories acknowledge Smith's Gaelic background. In the introduction to *The Red Door*, MacNeil notes the importance of the Gaelic stories, while pointing out that the bulk of Smith's writing was in English:

Iain wrote far more material in English than he did in Gaelic, but his Gaelic short stories were – and are – held in high esteem and, in contrast with critical responses to his English-language work, his Gaelic prose is generally viewed among Gaelic speakers at least as favourably as his Gaelic poetry. (MacNeil, 2001 p. xxi)

With MacNeil and also Derick Thomson, both of them very aware of the situation regarding Gaelic literature, we keep coming back to this question of number or amount. They both want to place him, as Smith, more in the English-language writing camp, and for both of them, there seems to be an arithmetic stimulus at work. Specifically, this seems to me to be an issue of proportionality, rather than pure numerousness. To appreciate this, we need simply imagine that Iain Mac a' Ghobhainn had never written in English at all, or had published no more than the occasional poem, like MacThòmais. In that case, would his Gaelic output not then have seemed very substantial? He wrote, in Gaelic, five collections of short stories and published many uncollected stories, four novellas, five collections of poetry and many uncollected poems, many plays and radio dramas, worked on television scripts, and wrote several novels for children and teenagers. He was, in fact, one of the most prolific Gaelic writers of the century. And yet there persisted, in places, a sense that he was mainly an English writer. To some degree, therefore, that sense must stem partly from the fact that, despite his great productivity in Gaelic, he wrote a very great deal more in English. That sense did not come only from the Anglophone literary community: recall that these statements were made by figures who are intimately aware of the Gaelic literary milieu, Kevin MacNeil and Derick Thomson. In fact, as I have suggested already, some elements of the non-Gaelic literati tried to welcome more blending of his two writerly identities.

5 Conclusion: Thoughts of Murchadh

A key to unravelling Smith/Mac a' Ghobhainn's sense of his linguistic identity as a writer might lie in the Murdo/Murchadh alter-ego who was his tragicomic shadow for decades and who struggled with his own alternative literary career. On the English side of things, Murdo is more zany, more purely comedic, whereas Murchadh has a darker or more bleak side to his nonsense. Murdo is also the more likely to write macaronic outputs, such as his ice cream poem.

Thoir dhomh do lamh, my dearest friend,
is theid sinn a null gu town,
if you'll to me a *sgilling* lend,
neo's math dh'fhaodte a half crown.

Agus ceannaichidh sinn da ice cream,
slider dhut-sa 's dhomh-sa cone,

> *is ithidh sinn iad ann an* dream,
>
> *is* 'Ta' *airson* an loan. (Smith, 1993, p. 14)

I have tried to reproduce the poem as it appears in the book, with the italics where they are in the actual typesetting and with the missing grave accents, because I feel that even the typesetting is a comment on the process, regardless of whether it was deliberate or not (and I suspect it was not). In one of his own analytical notes, Murdo writes:

> Except for someone who speaks English exclusively, the poem is perfectly clear as to meaning (Smith, 1993, p. 15).

He adds:

> NB In his poetry readings Murdo was to use his bilingualism as a stylistic device (c.f. Pound and Eliot et Al*).
>
> The only drawback to this was that international audiences on the whole didn't understand Gaelic (Smith, 1993, p. 15).

This poem contains the line 'thoir dhomh do làmh', which occurs in no fewer than six of Mac a' Ghobhainn's more serious Gaelic poems – several times in one of them, and is representative of a tendency in some of his writing to use popular songs and other popular allusions to invoke a mood. The same thing happens in Smith's English writing, but most of the time the songs alluded to there come from the wider Anglo-American pop culture of the 1940s-1980s, rather than either a Gaelic or even Scottish background. So, although he is using a device that looks similar in the two languages, it has a different effect. In the Gaelic, the song lines and allusions to poetry or extracts from sayings serve to ground the poems to a particular place and its associated culture. When he does it in English, the song lines ground the poetry to a particular time and a particular Zeitgeist.

The ice cream poem is not the only macaronic one in Mac a' Ghobhainn's catalogue. There are also more serious examples, such as the poem that begins 'Bha mi thall ann an Germany, ars ise' (Watson, 2013, p. 232). In that poem, Mac a' Ghobhainn parodies the pidginisation that can sometimes be discerned in elements of the language, and he places the blame on the globalising modern world. His characteristic dark humour is still evident, as we see in:

> Chunna sinn concentration camp cuideachd. Tha e mar museum.
> Nothing but the best anns a' Ghearmailt. Ach tha rudan gu math dear.
> Wine, coffee, tha iad sin exorbitant (Watson, 2013, p. 232).

Exceptionally, the Burns line 'we twa hae paiddlt' occurs as the title of a Gaelic poem in which Mac a' Ghobhainn reminisces about youth and friendship, and which is therefore inspired by a similar sentiment to 'Auld Lang Syne' (Watson, 2013, pp. 188-9). Smith was a keen student of Burns and was a popular speaker at Burns Suppers, where he gave both of the main toasts on many occasions, especially the Immortal Memory. In a letter in the National Library, George Philp refers to Smith's growing interest in Scots. Philp notes that he is pleased that Smith now knows about and speaks about Scots literature. We might wonder what Philp would think about Murdo's version of the tartan noir genre.

In 'The Scottish Detective Story by Murdo', we find a detective investigating a murder scene and questioning the housekeeper:

> 'Ay,' said the hoosekeeper. 'He had a lang beard an' he faced baith weys.'
> 'Baith weys,' said the Inspector, gantin'. The draff o' last nicht was dowie in his mooth.
> 'He was ca'd Anti – something.'
> 'Aunti something?'
> 'Ay.'
> The hoosekeeper wis a drodlich. Forfochen, the Inspector picked up a caird fae the flair aside the howdumdeid.
> His chouks fell.
> Professor Anti-zygygy, it said.
> The Inspector faddomed it a' noo. It was a liteerary maitter. A' to dae wi' dialectic an' the contradeections' (Smith, 1993, p. 128).

This story underlines Smith's endlessly playful relationship with language. The howdumdeid is himself the somewhat constructed concept of Caledonian anti-syzygy, first coined by G. Gregory Smith but famously applied by Mac-Diarmid to the supposed geocultural boundary between Gaelic and Scots. So here, again, Smith shows an awareness of the boundaries, imagined and otherwise, between the different aspects of his own sense of himself as a writer in Scotland.

This kind of imagined boundary is what leads Silke Stroh to make a compelling argument in favour of the use of postcolonial theory in analysing Gaelic literature:

> The particularly high degree of hybridity and complexity which characterise the Scottish case make it an interesting object of postcolonial study, and an even more appropriate test case for the Celtic fringe postcolonial question than the Irish example. The distinction between Lowlands and Highlands is a crucial factor: Several texts which deny the applicability of post/colonial concepts in a Scottish framework on the grounds of its closeness to the British centre are largely based on Lowland evidence and fail to take sufficient account of Scotland's

internal Gaelic margin, which has been much more 'Other' to Britain's mainstream(s) and has often been conceptualised in ways which correspond more closely to Irish, and sometimes even overseas, experiences of colonialism and postcolonialism. However, even the Lowland experience includes marginalisation and othering by the British mainstream, and thus offers rewarding subjects for postcolonial scrutiny – especially with regard to hybridity (Stroh, 2011, p. 36).

Very usefully, Stroh casts her gaze over Mac a' Ghobhainn in the last section of her book, and she discusses there his own instinct that there is a 'danger of importing too much of an English worldview into Gaelic literature and culture' (Stroh, 2011, p. 290). This is true, but we must also be wary of drifting too far in either direction. To commit ourselves to treating Gaelic as if it were an entirely unique phenomenon is as much a mistake is it would be to commit ourselves to treating it as entirely analysable along pre-existing paradigms. As Smith might have put it, Gaelic literature is a real literature in a real culture. And, as he might also have put it, part of that cultural context extends far beyond the imagined boundaries of the Gàidhealtachd. Part of that extended cultural context is the Anglophone Highlands and part of it is the rest of Scotland. It is common knowledge that there are scholars who would have us believe that they can discuss Scottish literature meaningfully without even mentioning Gaelic or with a token acknowledgement that it exists (Watson, 2011, pp. 1-11). But, if we are dealing with a bilingual/bicultural literary community, we should be aware of the hybridity and the range of influences and be able to engage with all of it, Gaelic and non-Gaelic, in a holistic manner. As Gaelic literary critics, we should be able to apply a Gaelocentric reading of literature and general cultural studies, not only to what we see as directly Gaelic literature – notwithstanding how problematic it is becoming to define such a thing – but also to any literature that has a bearing on the Gaelic cultural awareness. We must keep in mind, as we move forward in our thinking, that our mindset and our outlook are affective as well as reflective, and that they have a bearing on the kind of literature that is produced and the way it is received both within and also outwith the Gaelic cultural milieu.

A letter in the National Library's archive discusses details for an essay that Smith is to write for an Irish magazine. The writer wants to know whether Smith will write the essay in English or in Gaelic and he discusses whether the choice of language of the essay will therefore shape the argument itself. Regardless of what Smith chooses, the writer admits he will have to translate it into Irish for publication anyway. We must continue to engage with the work of earlier Gaelic scholars, and we must continue to write criticism, both cultural and literary, in the medium of the most relevant language, which is Gaelic itself. But we must also continue to engage with theoreticians from elsewhere, and we must continue to make our academic arguments for the importance and relevance of Gaelic in other linguistic media, especially English. If Gaelic literature is both suffering, and benefitting from, hybridity, so must its criticism.

Endnotes

1 I wish to convey my thanks to the Carnegie Trust for the Universities of Scotland, whose financial support allowed me to spend time working at the National Library of Scotland. I would also like to thank the staff at the National Library of Scotland for their help in tracking down the materials I needed. I am grateful to the Research Institute of Irish and Scottish Studies for various kinds of help and support, including financial, and to my colleagues in the Gaelic Department at the University of Aberdeen.
2 I suspect the writer himself would have been amused to see his names treated in this way. For the sake of absolute clarity, it is worth mentioning that the writer was also referred to as Iain Crichton Mac a' Ghobhainn occasionally.
3 Scholars, of course, might take issue with calling this an 'Irish' poem, but Smith was not looking at it as a Celtic linguist.
4 Patrick Crotty suggested to me (personal communication) that it was probably the Robin Flower translation.
5 These writers were named at random, and without any intention to imply anything about their work. It is indicative of how the literature has moved on in recent years that it was easy to point to such diversity with so little effort.
6 We also see other languages finding their way confidently into the dialogue or even narrative in Gaelic fiction now: see, for instance, Iain F. MacLeòid's *Na Klondykers* (2005) or Màrtainn Mac an t-Saoir's *Cala Bendita 's a Bheannachdan* (2014).
7 MacIlleBhàin, in common with some of the other writers, publishes his Gaelic poetry under the Gaelic version of his name, but also writes criticism, scholarship and fiction, which he publishes under the name Christopher Whyte.
8 There are two main archives relevant to this paper in the National Library: NLS Acc. 12600 and NLS Acc. 13496. In my more recent research, I have primarily worked with archive 13496.
9 I use the term 'Gaelic letters' loosely to mean 'Gaelic-related' – when it comes to letters actually written in Gaelic, or even having some phrases in the language, then the numbers are further reduced.
10 MacDonald and I are editing Mac a' Ghobhainn's short stories, with a view to publishing them for the Scottish Gaelic Texts Society.
11 Note here the popular television allusion to 'Star Trek', the comic (or television) allusion to the 'Incredible Hulk', alongside references to Yeats and Wittgenstein and the First World War.
12 The second line of that poem is 'ach tha an dà-chànanach briste'.

Bibliography

Anderson, Benedict (2006 [1983]). *Imagined Communities*. London and New York: Verso.

Clancy, Thomas Owen (2010). 'A Fond Farewell to Last Night's Literary Criticism: Reading Niall Mór MacMhuirich', in Gillian Munro and R. A. V. Cox (eds), *Cànan & Cultar/Language & Culture: Rannsachadh na Gàidhlig 4*, 109-26. Edinburgh: Dunedin Academic Press.

Gillies, William (2002). 'On the Study of Gaelic Literature' in Michel Byrne, Thomas Owen Clancy and Sheila Kidd. (eds), *Litreachas & Eachdraidh/Literature & History: Papers from the Second Conference of Scottish Gaelic Studies, Glasgow 2002*, pp. 1–32. Glasgow: Department of Celtic, University of Glasgow.

Kiberd, Declan (1996 [1995]). *Inventing Ireland: The Literature of the Modern Nation*. London: Vintage.

Mac a' Ghobhainn, Iain (1960 [2nd edn 1974, excluding verse; 3rd edn 1987]). *Bùrn is Aran*. Glasgow: Gairm.

Mack, Douglas S. (2006). *Scottish Fiction and the British Empire*. Edinburgh: EUP.

Macleod, Michelle (2001). 'Language and bilingualism in the Gaelic Poetry of Iain Crichton Smith'. *Scottish Studies Review*, Vol. 2, No. 2, pp. 105-113.

Macleod, Michelle (2009). 'Language and Identity in Modern Gaelic Verse', in Ian Brown and Alan Riach (eds), *The Edinburgh Companion to Twentieth-Century Scottish Literature*, pp. 167-80. Edinburgh: EUP.

McLeod, Wilson, and Bateman, Meg, eds, Bateman, Meg, trans. (2007). *Duanaire na Sracaire / Songbook of the Pillagers: Anthology of Scotland's Gaelic Verse to 1600*. Edinburgh: Birlinn.

MacNeil, Kevin (2001). Introduction to Smith, Iain Crichton (2001) *The Red Door: The Complete English Stories 1949-76*. Edinburgh: Birlinn.

Milton, Colin (1997). '"Half of My Seeing": The English Poetry of Iain Crichton Smith', in Gary Day and Brian Docherty (eds), *British Poetry from the 1950s to the 1990s*, pp. 193-220. Basingstoke: Macmillan.

Ngũgĩ Wa Thiong'o (2005 [1981]). *Decolonising the Mind: The Politics of Language in African Literature*. Portsmouth: Heinemann.

Ngũgĩ Wa Thiong'o (2009). 'Translated by the Author: My life in between languages'. *Translation Studies*, Vol. 2, No. 1, pp. 17-20.

Pittock, Murray G. H. (1999). *Celtic Identity and the British Image*. Manchester: Manchester University Press.

Ryan, Ray (2002). *Ireland and Scotland: Literature and Culture, State and Nation, 1966-2000*. Oxford: Clarendon Press.

Simms, Katharine (2006). 'Muireadhach Albanach Ó Dálaigh and the Classical Revolution', in Thomas Owen Clancy and Murray Pittock (eds), *The Edinburgh History of Scottish Literature, Volume 1: From Columba to the Union (until 1707)*, 83-90. Edinburgh: Edinburgh University Press.

Smith, Iain Crichton (1986). *Towards the Human*. Edinburgh: Lines Review Editions, MacDonald.

Smith, Iain Crichton (1989). 'The Double Man', in R. P. Draper (ed.), *The Literature of Region and Nation*, pp. 136-46. Basingstoke: Macmillan.

Smith, Iain Crichton (1993). *Thoughts of Murdo*. Nairn: Balnain Books.

Smith, Iain Crichton (1995 [1992]). *Collected Poems*. Manchester: Carcanet.

Smith, Iain Crichton (2001). *The Red Door: The Complete English Stories 1949-76*. Edinburgh: Birlinn.

Stroh, Silke (2011). *Uneasy Subjects: Postcolonialism and Scottish Gaelic Poetry.* Amsterdam: Rodopi.
Thomson, Derick S. (1986). 'Introduction' to Smith, Iain Crichton (1986) *Towards the Human.* Edinburgh: Lines Review Editions, MacDonald.
Watson, Moray (2011). *An Introduction to Gaelic Fiction.* Edinburgh: EUP.
Watson, Moray (ed.) (2013). *Iain Mac a' Ghobhainn: A' Bhàrdachd Ghàidhlig.* Stornoway: Acair.
Young, Robert J. C. (2003). *Postcolonialism: A Very Short Introduction.* Oxford: OUP.

9

The massacre of Eigg in 1577

Ross Crawford

University of Glasgow

The stereotypical portrayal of Scottish Highlanders as violent and rebellious has roots at least as far back as the thirteenth century (MacGregor, 2009, pp. 7–15), but of all the epochs, the sixteenth century is typically regarded as when this belligerent nature was most fully indulged. The traditional view holds that a power vacuum emerged in the aftermath of the forfeiture of the Lordship of the Isles in 1493 by King James IV and for at least a century the West Highlands and Islands were riven by mutual dissensions and unrestrained feuding between clans.[1] Punctuating the relentless conflicts of this 'Age of Forays' (*Linn nan Creach*) were massacres committed against military personnel and civilians alike. Arguably the most infamous of these atrocities is the mass-suffocation of nearly four hundred men, women and children of the Clanranald by a MacLeod raiding party in Uamh Fhraing on the Isle of Eigg in 1577.

This event was first reported in a sole source from the late sixteenth century, before disappearing from the historical record almost entirely. Kept on life-support largely by local tradition, the story was further developed and embellished for some two hundred years.[2] By the mid-eighteenth century, the story of the massacre was firmly enmeshed within the local culture, but still largely unknown in Scotland at large. This was all to change with the dramatic increase in tourism to the Western Isles during the eighteenth and nineteenth centuries, when the massacre site became a ghoulish and highly popular attraction for visitors. Since then, the story of the cave on Eigg has been retold many times, with each successive account attempting to outdo the last for macabre detail.[3] Rarely was the veracity of the massacre thrown into question; the large amount of decomposed human remains found within the cave was often deemed 'proof enough' (Miller, 1862, p. 44).[4] The massacre of the Clanranald by their enemies, the MacLeods of Harris, became a shorthand symbol of the 'savage Highlander' and was considered by some as 'truly characteristic of the state of society in those parts at that period', a notion that has persisted into modern times (MacLean, 1846, p. 146; Smout, 1998, p. 96). Many famous names visited the cave, including Sir Walter Scott and Hugh Miller, and during his tour of the Highlands and Islands in 1773 with James Boswell, Samuel Johnson said of Eigg: 'I have heard of nothing curious in it, but the cave in which a former generation of Islanders were smothered by MacLeod' (Johnson, 1775, p. 295). The cave and the massacre story soon came to define the island for external visitors, but perhaps a more positive legacy was its regular appearance in Gaelic newspapers and periodicals from Nova Scotia and Australia during the nineteenth century. This suggests the story had become a core part of the tradition and folklore retold by émigrés, helping to maintain important links with Gaelic Scotland.[5]

Through close analysis of the surviving evidence, this paper will investigate the complex political background of the purported massacre in 1577, focusing on a possible origin for the incident: a contemporary feud between the MacLeods and the MacDonalds. Following this, the overall evidence for the massacre itself will be discussed with reference to other contemporary incidents. Without advocating a total whitewash of Gaelic conduct in war, there remains scope for questioning this event, as it remains emblematic of the perceived barbarity of the sixteenth-century West Highlands and Islands. This study has not set out to prove or disprove, condemn or exonerate, but instead untangle the knotted history of the massacre of Eigg.

The earliest known source describing the massacre is 'The Description of the Isles of Scotland', dubbed a 'military census' by Martin MacGregor (MacGregor, 2012, p. 220). It was written *c*. 1595 and was later printed by Skene in *Celtic Scotland* (1876-80).[6] The report is anonymous and its authorship is debated,[7] but the most likely candidate remains Dioness Campbell, the Dean of Limerick. 'The Description' heavily concentrates on the economic and military capabilities of the Isles, estimating their value and potential mustering of 'gude men to the weiris' (Skene, 1880, p. 431). After a brief description of the 'verie fertile and commodious' land of Eigg, the source states that

> ... in March, anno 1577, weiris and inmitie betwixt the said Clan Renald and McCloyd Herreik, the people with ane callit Angus John McMudzartsonne, their capitane, fled to ane of the saidis coves, taking with thame thair wives, bairnis, and geir, quhairof McCloyd Herreik being advertisit landit with ane great armie in the said Ile, and came to the cove and pat fire thairto, and smorit the hail people thairin to the number of 395 persones, men, wife, and bairnis (Skene, 1880, p. 433).

Unique in its mention of this massacre, 'The Description' is nevertheless just one of a series of similar reports made for the English and Scottish governments in the late sixteenth century by the Dean of Limerick. In April 1596, Campbell made a diplomatic and reconnaissance mission to Scotland with the goal of convincing his cousin, Gilleasbuig Campbell, the seventh earl of Argyll (d. 1638) to enter the war in Ireland on behalf of Queen Elizabeth (Giuseppi, 1952, pp. 181, 188, 246-8; Atkinson, 1893, p. 40). During his stay, Campbell completed a report entitled the 'Account of the West Isles of Scotland and the Descent, Connexions, etc., of the Islanders' (Robertson, 1847, pp. 41-57; Giuseppi, 1952, pp. 201-11). Similar in content and style to 'The Description', the 'Account' was written for the English authorities and focuses on the 'discention of the Illanders' to facilitate political manoeuvres in the Western Isles.[8] It principally details the feud between the MacLeans and the MacDonalds in the 1580s but does state:

> There is also controversie betwene McClod Harryes [MacLeod of Harris] and the Clanranells [Clanranald] of those islands, whearof greate murthers have ensued, but old McCloyd had always the upper hand (Robertson, 1847, p. 49).

Later in the 'Account', Campbell admits he 'never toke speciall regard' of his 'slender observations' and pledges to correct any errors or omissions when he is 'more certenlie and fullie instructed in the same' (Robertson, 1847, p. 50). Through internal evidence in the sources, it can be verified that the 'Account' was composed after 'The Description', and therefore, this later report of the MacLeod-Clanranald feud – noticeably silent regarding Eigg – may constitute the correction of a previous error. By his own admission, Campbell's knowledge of the Western Isles was limited, and his visit to Scotland in 1596 may have offered a more reliable informant in the earl of Argyll. Indeed, Argyll, would have been relatively well placed as a source due to his father Cailean's arbitration of a genuine dispute between the MacLeods and the Clanranald in the 1570s.

This feud was ignited in 1574 when the Regent Morton granted the escheat of Glenelg in the lordship of Lochaber to the Clanranald. Morton and Cailean, the sixth earl of Argyll, (d. 1584) were locked in a heated political dispute over the 'retaining' of the Crown Jewels by Argyll's wife (Hewitt, 1982, pp. 41-2; Campbell, 2002, pp. 79-80), and according to the Campbell chief the grant to the Clanranald was intended to stir up trouble for him in the Isles. The Clanranald – denounced as 'commond murtheris and oppresoris' by Argyll – allegedly used their commission to harry Glenelg 'nocht sparing the cruell slaughter of man wyiff and bairne' (Argyll Transcripts, V, p. 224). Glenelg was a longstanding possession of the MacLeods of Harris, but importantly, one-third of the lands had also been contested by the Clan Fraser since at least 1527 (MacLeod, 1938, pp. 66-8). Following their decisive defeat of the Clan Fraser at Blàr na Léine in 1544, the Clanranald was ascendant in the West Highlands and Islands, and famously partook in a raid on Urquhart Castle at Inverness in 1545 (Cathcart, 2006, p. 138; Fraser, 1883, pp. 112-3). It seems that they took full advantage of their victory by occupying Glenelg, where they eventually became the tenants of the Frasers (who essentially made the best of a bad situation). For more than a decade, the MacLeods were seemingly powerless to prevent this arrangement due to internecine strife caused by the death of their chief Uilleam in 1551, whose sole heir was his daughter, Màiri (MacLeod, 1938, pp. 72, 90-8; Thomson, 1886, pp. 547-8). The chiefship of the MacLeods was eventually obtained by Uilleam's younger brother Tormod, and he may have attempted to gain control of Glenelg around 1573, just before it was subsequently granted to the Clanranald (MacLeod, 1938, pp. 43-4, 72-5, 96; Iona Club, 1847, pp. 136-51).[9]

Two years after the feud's outbreak, on 14 September 1576, a bond of manrent was made between Cailean Campbell, the sixth earl of Argyll, and Iain Mùideartach, the venerable captain of Clanranald (also known as John Moydartach). In this bond, Iain and his son Ailean agreed to

> ... demit the lands of Glenelg in favour of Tormoud McLoyd, bind themselvis to join with the McLanes and to refer all matters regarding all slaughters and hairscheepis debates betwixt the said McCloyd of Harra to the said Earl, the Earl is held bound to maintain and defend the said Iain and Allan, and others, and to do diligence on McCloyd of Harra (Argyll Transcripts, VII, p. 19).

A provision was put in place that if the Clanranald failed to abide by this bond Lachlann MacLean of Duart would 'pursue and invade' their lands. A gift to Tómas Fraser on 16 February 1577 confirms that the lands of Glenelg still officially belonged to the Clan Fraser, and the Clanranald's tenancy presumably continued (Donaldson, 1966, pp. 131-2). Five months later, on 11 July 1577, a contract was made between Tormod MacLeod of Harris and Ailean, the son of Iain Mùideartach and new captain of Clanranald,[10] with Argyll and Lachlann MacLean of Duart acting as guarantors. Tormod and Ailean agreed to cease hostilities consisting of...

> ... debaitis, contraverseis, slauchtaris, hairschippis and all uthir injuries commitit and done be alther of thame agains utheris preceeding the dait heiroff ... (Argyll Transcripts, VII, p. 26)

The contract singled out the Clanranald as the main aggressors, and they were ordered to stop harrying the land of Glenelg. Later that year, on the

Feast of All Saints (1 November), Argyll was to judge this case at Inveraray. The contract also stated that the Clanranald had now renounced its claim to Glenelg, confirming that a land dispute was the principal cause of the discord. The two parties were to continue to 'stand amicablie ... in gude concorde and nychtbourhed' according to the terms outlined in the earlier bond of manrent made in 1576 (Argyll Transcripts, VII, pp. 19, 26). It seems that the intervening nine-month period between September 1576 and July 1577 was peaceful, contradicting the dating of the massacre to March 1577 as offered by 'The Description'.

Further consultation of the 1577 contract between MacLeod and the captain of Clanranald reveals another fascinating dimension to this quarrel. It states that Ailean's son, Ailean Òg, and Ailean's brother, Aonghas, had both committed 'offensis and injuries' against their own friends and kin 'in support of the said tormoid', Ailean Òg's grandfather (Argyll Transcripts, VII, p. 26). What began as a wrangle over land between separate clans had spiralled into a family feud within the Clanranald, internal strife instigated – or at least enflamed – by the MacLeods. According to the 'Red Book of Clanranald', the late-seventeenth century clan history by Niall MacMhuirich, Ailean's chiefship was a period of calm and tranquillity, defined by his 'good family' and many male offspring (Kennedy & MacBain, 1894, pp. 171-3). The above contract presents a markedly different picture of a chief under threat from the ambitions of his closest male relatives. Despite excising this discord, the 'Red Book' implicitly provides a possible explanation for the rift in familial relations. The mother of Ailean's first-born son, Ailean Òg, was the daughter of MacLeod of Harris, yet 'after her he took unto him the daughter of Maclean of Duart', and had a 'good family' by her, including a son, John (Iain) of Strome (Kennedy & MacBain, 1894, p. 173).[11] The wording of 'after her' is ambiguous. While it could suggest that she had died, MacDonald & MacDonald have plausibly argued that Ailean spurned MacLeod's daughter while she still lived (MacDonald & MacDonald, 1900, p. 293). We cannot know for certain if Ailean did indeed reject his current wife in favour of the daughter of MacLean of Duart (presumably Eachann Òg), but regardless his new marriage threatened the inheritance of his first-born son, Ailean Òg. After the death (or retirement) of his father Iain between September 1576 and July 1577, Ailean may have sought to sever his marital link with the MacLeods, (MacLeods, with whom his clans' relations seem strained at best, and politically realign with the Campbell/MacLean powerhouse. Upon his succession, he seems to have named his son Dòmhnall, born of his second marriage to MacLean's daughter, as his heir, supplanting his first-born son, Ailean Òg. This was a serious insult to the MacLeods and would have undoubtedly exacerbated his dispute with them, while providing clear justification for Ailean Òg to turn against his father and Clanranald kin. With help or encouragement from Tormod, Ailean Òg's grandfather, this had the makings of an attempted coup.

The 1577 contract, and judicial hearing at Inveraray that presumably followed, seems to have resolved the dispute between the MacLeods and the Clanranald, and healed the internal rift within the latter clan. Ailean's son and newly named heir, Dòmhnall, was sent to the earl of Argyll as a pledge for the future good behaviour of the clan, and he eventually succeeded his father as captain of the Clanranald (Argyll Transcripts, VII, p. 19). Meanwhile, Ailean Òg and Aonghas pledged to keep the peace, with Tormod MacLeod acting as their pledge (Argyll Transcripts, VII, p. 26). It was not until 4 February 1579 that Tormod was officially invested by the crown in the lands held by his niece Màiri since 1551 (Thomson, 1886, p. 814; Donaldson, 1966, p. 366). Members of the Clanranald continued to reside in Glenelg as late as 1610, when Lord Lovat pledged to provide them with land of equal value should he be evicted (MacLeod, 1938, pp. 68, 75). In 1611, the dispute was finally resolved in the MacLeods' favour, when Glenelg was judged to belong to them providing they pay the Clan Fraser 12,000 merks (MacLeod, 1938, pp. 68, 216).

This new information sheds light on the contemporary period, yet it cannot be denied that on the actual topic of the massacre all of these documents are almost entirely silent. In the *Red Book of Clanranald*, Eigg is only mentioned in the description of the final 'godly' years of Iain Mùideartach, who allegedly founded the church of Kildonnan on the island (Kennedy & MacBain, 1894, p. 171). In the documents from 1576 and 1577, the massacre is not cited directly, but there are references to mutual 'slauchtaris' and 'hairschippis' (armed incursions aimed at carrying off plunder) committed by each clan against the other. It may be significant that Argyll's testimony from February 1574 accuses the Clanranald with the 'cruell slauchter of man wyiff and bairne' (Argyll Transcripts, V, p. 224), as a retaliatory attack by the MacLeods on Eigg seems well within the realms of possibility. An alternative (and very speculative) explanation is that the MacLeod-sponsored attacks avowedly perpetrated by Ailean Òg and Aonghas included a raid on their own kin on Eigg. The primary aggressors on both sides of the feud came from the Clanranald, as only they were required to provide hostages to guarantee their future behaviour (Argyll Transcripts, V, p. 26).[12]

This was clearly a tumultuous period for the MacLeods and the Clanranald, and their relations must have been at an all-time low upon the succession of

Ailean, son of Iain Mùideartach. Nevertheless, when investigated in isolation, the contemporary evidence for a mass-killing of Clanranald civilians on Eigg is limited, at least to the extent suggested in 'The Description'. Arguably only hindsight distinguishes this quarrel from numerous other small-scale feuds in the sixteenth century. The above documents validate the existence of a MacLeod-Clanranald feud, but leave 'The Description' as the earliest known source that specifically mentions a massacre of Eigg. Close investigation of this source and later events on the island provides further reason to cast a reasonable degree of doubt over the reality of the incident. The report maintains a relatively sober, systematic format throughout, apart from two detours into a more anecdotal style. One of these deviations is the account of the massacre of Eigg in 1577, while the other is a description of the 'Pygmies Kirk', a cave 'in forme of ane kirk' found on a small island near the Butt of Lewis that is 'sa little, that ane mann may scairslie stand uprichtlie in it'. Once inside the cave, one could observe that some of the 'Pygmies' bones remain, which 'measurit ... not fullie twa inches lang' (Skene, 1880, p. 429). The similarity of the two stories runs deeper than their shared mention of bones in a cave. Later belief in the massacre at Eigg was predicated almost entirely upon the survival of human remains within the cave – they were regarded as irrefutable proof that the event occurred. However, when Eigg is placed alongside the more overtly fantastical story of the 'Pygmies Kirk', the bones seem less the memorial of a massacre, and more the material inspiration of folk tradition. Furthermore, the story of an ancient massacre was firmly entrenched within the cultural backdrop of the island. In 617, a priest named Donnán was martyred on Eigg, along with a number (50-150) of his monks (Anderson, 1922, pp. 142-4). In the accounts of both the Annals of Tigernach and Ulster, Donnán and 150 of his monks were burned alive, and the trace legacy of this incident may have influenced later traditions (Anderson, 1922, pp. 142-4; Bambury and Beechinor, 2000, p. 109, AU617.1).

According to 'The Description', the 'haill people' of Eigg were murdered, yet the island could still 'raise 60 men to the weiris' at the time of writing (Skene, 1880, p. 429). The loss of such a huge swathe of the island's inhabitants twenty years earlier (at most) makes this estimate extremely surprising. The buoyancy of Eigg's population in the years following the massacre is apparent in evidence originating from the first half of the seventeenth century. In 1615, following his escape from Edinburgh Castle, Sir Seumas MacDonald of Dunivaig visited various heartlands of the Clan Donald to drum up support for a raid on Dunivaig Castle in Islay. On Eigg he 'mett Coill and his companyee, togidder with his base sone, and a sone of Sir James Maksorle of the Route ... [and] they ar in nomber, as I lerne, tuelfue or thretteinth score' (Pitcairn, 1833, p. 19). Clearly, Eigg was regarded as a significant enclave of Clan Donald, and it must have recovered significantly since 1577 if the inhabitants were able to support such a substantial force of soldiers, even if it was simply a point of rendezvous. Secondly, as noted by Noel Banks (1977, p. 57), a Catholic mission came to Eigg in 1625 and 'converted' 198 of the inhabitants, but this fell well short of the total population of the island as the mission 'clearly expected to reconcile more'. Most notably, there is no mention of the massacre in the mission reports (MacDonald, 2006, p. 78). Furthermore, it is not referenced in a letter by the Clanranald chief Iain Mùideartach to Pope Urban VIII in 1626 (Campbell, 1954, pp. 110-6).

Indeed, there is no reference to the massacre in any other documents from the immediate time period, including government sources like the Privy Council of Scotland. The sheer scale of the massacre of Eigg far outstrips any other single act of bloodshed in sixteenth-century Scotland. Redress and vengeance for such unprecedented mass slaughter would surely have been pursued vigorously in court by the Clanranald as other less serious acts of violence (at least in terms of scale) were consistently reported to the Privy Council throughout the sixteenth century.[13] This silence is conspicuous and perhaps the single most telling indication of the massacre's uncertain provenance, although the possibility that attacks were perpetrated by Clanranald kin, Ailean Òg and Aonghas, at the behest of the MacLeods, may explain the absence of any complaints.

Only eleven years after the mooted massacre in 1577, lightning struck twice when Lachlann Mór MacLean of Duart raided the lands of Canna, Rum, Eigg and the 'Isle of Elennole' (Muck?) in October 1588. The provenance of this raid is on somewhat surer footing, as it was reported to the Privy Council:

> ... Lauchlane McClayne of Dowart, accompanyed with a grite nowmer of thevis, brokin men, and sornaris of Clannis, besydis the nowmer of ane hundredth Spanyeartis, come, bodin in feir of weir, to his Majesteis propir ilis of Canna Rum, Eg, and the Ile of Elennole, and, eftir thay had soirned, wracked, and spoilled the saidis haill Illis, thay tressonablie rased fyre, and in maist barbarous, shamefull and cruell maner, brynt the same Illis, with the haill men, wemen and childrene being thairintill, not spairing the pupillis and infantis ...
> (Masson, 1881, pp. 341-2).

Complaints of this nature could be exaggerated to garner attention and obtain reparations, but this raid does seem notable in its brutality and inclusion of civilians. The complaint goes on to claim such 'barbarous and shamefull crueltie hes sendle bene hard of amangis Christeanis in ony kingdome or age'. In 1589,

King James VI granted a remission for the 'treasonable burning and destruction' of the islands, and the 'cruel slaughter' of the 'inhabitants of those islands' (Innes, 1855, p. 614). Recently, writers like Noel Banks and Camille Dressler have highlighted Lachlann's raid, noting the improbability of two brutal raids on Eigg within ten years (Banks, 1977, p. 57; Dressler, 1998, pp. 16-8). To take this point further, the temporal proximity and authenticity of this raid could render it the true origin of the Eigg massacre, with a confusion, conflation, or deliberate transference of perpetrator from MacLean to MacLeod. In the 'Account', Dioness Campbell, the Dean of Limerick, describes Lachlann Mór MacLean as his 'derest kinsemen, beinge my cosen germaen', whom he had known for 'sixe and twentye yeres' (Robertson, 1847, p. 50). Their close relationship perhaps encouraged Dioness to blame the MacLeods, who had a known history of conflict with the Clanranald, for an attack on Eigg. The essence of this theory was first raised over a hundred years ago at a social event in Glasgow attended by Alexander Mackenzie, historian and editor of *The Celtic Magazine*. Mackenzie claims that Reverend MacLeod of the Small Isles parish 'raised a perfect storm by a statement that the brutal massacre in Eigg was perpetrated by the Macleans, and not by the Macleods' (Mackenzie, 1881, p. 194). Given his surname, the Reverend was presumably heckled for attempting to exonerate his ancestors, but his explanation should still be taken seriously.

The goal of this investigation was never to presume to 'prove' the massacre one way or the other, but using the event as an entry point has revealed much of value about the contemporary period, including case studies of succession crises and land disputes involving the Clanranald and the MacLeods of Harris. The topic provides fertile ground for future research into the literary afterlife of the massacre, which would provide valuable insight into the evolution of Gaelic tradition, and interactions between travellers and the local islanders in the eighteenth and nineteenth century.[14]

Even in the present day, this obscure event from the sixteenth century remains absolutely central to the external identity of the island. In 1995, the last private landlord of Eigg, 'Professor' Maruma, was prompted to purchase the island after visiting the cave:

> When I went to the cave, I knew this was the right place to be.
> The cave is the island's soul because this is where it has been hurt
> (McIntosh, 2002, p. 264).

Ultimately, the 'truth' of the massacre remains elusive, and its enduring mystery is probably essential to the popularity of the lurid story across the centuries. This 'mystery' was encapsulated in a laconic quip by the Free Church Minister of the Small Isles in 1844. The Reverend John Swanson stated:

The less I inquired into its history on the spot, the more was I likely to feel satisfied that I knew something about it (Miller, 1862, p. 42).

Despite the still persistent ambiguity, we may now feel satisfied that we know at least 'something' about the massacre of Eigg.

Endnotes

1   For some examples of modern works perpetuating this view, see Stevenson, 1994, p. 21; Macinnes, 2009, p. 128.
2   A massacre of this type is a common story-telling trope found in the traditions of many clans across the Western Isles and Highlands, with mass-burnings in churches an especially recurrent motif. Nevertheless, this trope may have been based on real repeated actions in contemporary warfare.
3   Several modern writers have discussed the Eigg massacre, with some still accepting the event as 'fact'. See Stewart, 1982, pp. 42-3; Urquhart, 1987, pp. 36-40; Kiernan, 2007, pp. 13-14. Others have shown some scepticism towards the event. See Banks, 1977, p. 57; Dressler, 1998, pp. 16-18; Rixson, 2001, pp. 114-18.
4   Following a campaign by Sir Walter Scott, the skeletons in the cave were apparently buried in the nearby churchyard of Kildonnan. In 1979, a human skull was reportedly found in the cave by a boy on holiday. It was conveyed to the Birmingham Museum, where the coroner assessed the skull was 'of some antiquity and belonged to a child (unsexed) of 5-6 years of age'. I have been unable to expand upon this information after correspondence with Birmingham Museum and the Birmingham coroner's office. See http://canmore.rcahms.gov.uk/en/site/22183/details/eigg+uamh+fhraing/ [accessed 08/12/2014]
5   For examples, see *Mac-Talla,* Vol. 1, no. 29 (December 10, 1892), p. 4; *An Teachdaire Gaidhealach,* Tasmania, No. 4 (May 1, 1857), p. 6-7. My thanks to Dr Sheila Kidd for these references.
6   John Stewart of Appin is mentioned as being alive at the time 'The Description' was written, but he died at some point between March 1593 and 8 January 1596. See Skene, 1880, p. 440; Bannerman & Black, 1978, p. 61.
7   David Caldwell has recently suggested that it was composed by John Cunningham, an Edinburgh merchant who visited Lachlann Mór MacLean of Duart in 1595/6. See Caldwell, 2013, pp. 3-11.
8   A precursor and probable template for both the *Account* and *The Description* was composed in 1593, again possibly by Dioness Campbell. 'The note of the Weste Isles of Scotland' reads almost like a condensed mixture of the later documents, featuring both muster estimations and advice on inter-clan politics. 'The note' does not record a feud between the MacLeods of Harris and the Clanranald at all, yet interestingly, it notes that Ruairidh MacLeod of Lewis, 'an ould man', is 'famous for the massacring of his awen kinsemen'. Furthermore, it alludes to the 'barbarous wars' fought between the clans in the 1580s. These feuds are more verifiable than that relating to Eigg, and it is revealing that the massacre is not mentioned. See Cameron, 1936, pp. 253-5.
9   On 18 February 1571/2, the non-entry payments for the lands of Glenelg were granted to Ùisdean Fraser of Lovat. See Donaldson, 1963, p. 286; Thomson, 1886, p. 814.
10 According to the *Red Book of Clanranald,* Iain Mùideartach died in 1574, yet the

above contracts confirm he was alive until at least September 1576. Although he is not recorded as 'umquhile' in the contract from July 1577, it seems probable that he had died, or had at the very least given control of the clan to his son, Ailean. See Kennedy & MacBain, 1894, pp. 170-1; Argyll Transcripts, VII, pp. 19, 26.
11 This marriage is confirmed by the 1576 contract, which states that Ailean's son Dòmhnall was 'gottin upone Janait MakClayne'. See Argyll Transcripts, VII, p. 19.
12 The ambiguous dating of 'March, anno 1577' offered by 'The Description' allows for yet another possibility. Until 1600, the New Year in Scotland began on 25 March, and therefore, 'March, anno 1577' could mean (by modern reckoning) 1577 if the day fell on or after 25 March, or 1578 if it fell between 1 and 24 March. 'The Description' claims that the Clanranald 'capitane' Angus John McMudzartsonne was one of the victims killed in the cave by the MacLeods, which could be Ailean's brother Aonghas, son of Iain (or John) Mùideartach. Considering his alliance with Tormod, it may seem unlikely that Aonghas would be targeted by the MacLeods, yet if the attack took place in March 1578 (not 1577) it is at least possible that he was killed for abandoning the cause of his nephew, Ailean Òg.
13 For just one example of this, consider the alleged response of the Colquhouns to the raid of Glenfinlas by the MacGregors in December 1602. See Fraser, 1869, pp. 188-9.
14 Andrew Wiseman has already contributed important work on this theme as part of the Calum MacLean Project at the University of Edinburgh. A dedicated archaeological study would offer our best chance at verifying the provenance of the (now buried) bones in the cave, assuming they can be precisely located. Many of the travellers removed artefacts from the cave, which may now remain in private collections. See Wiseman, 2014; Miller, 1842, pp. 40-1; Wilson, 1842, pp. 236-7.

Bibliography

Anderson, A. O. (1922). *Early Sources of Scottish History A.D. 500 to 1286,* Vol. 1. Edinburgh: Oliver and Boyd.
Argyll Transcripts (Transcriptions of various charters relating to Clan Campbell and their lands, made by Niall, 10th Duke of Argyll). 7 vols. Photocopy held in Glasgow University, Department of History.
Atkinson, E. G. (ed.) (1893). *Calendar of State Papers Relating to Ireland, of the Reign of Elizabeth, 1596, July-1597, December*. London: HMSO.
Bambury, Pádraig, and Beechinor, Stephen (eds) (2000). *The Annals of Ulster*. Cork: CELT,University College Cork. Available from URL: http://www.ucc.ie/celt/online/ T100001A/ [accessed 20 January 2014]
Banks, Noel (1977). *Six Inner Hebrides*. Newton Abbot: David & Charles.
Bannerman, John, and Black, Ronald (1978) 'A Sixteenth-Century Gaelic Letter'. *Scottish Gaelic Studies,* Vol. 13, Part 1, pp. 56-65.
Brown, Keith (1986). *Bloodfeud in Scotland 1573-1625: Violence, Justice and Politics in an Early Modern Society*. Edinburgh: EUP.
Caldwell, David (2013). 'An Intelligence Report on the Hebrides, 1595/6'. *West Highland Notes & Queries,* Series 3, No. 23, pp. 3-11.
Cameron, Annie I. (ed.) (1936). *Calendar of the State Papers Relating to Scotland and Mary Queen of Scots 1547-1603*, Vol. 11 (1593-5). Edinburgh: HMSO.
Campbell, Alastair, of Airds (2002). *A History of Clan Campbell,* Vol. II. Edinburgh: Polygon.

Campbell, John Lorne (1953). 'The Letter Sent to Iain Muideartach, Twelfth Chief of Clanranald, to Pope Urban VIII, in 1626'. *Innes Review,* Vol. 4, pp. 110-16.

Cathcart, Alison (2006). *Kinship and Clientage: Highland Clanship 1451-1609.* Leiden: Brill.

Donaldson, Gordon (ed.) (1963). *Registrum Secreti Sigilli Regum Scotorum,* Vol. VI (1567-1574). Edinburgh: HMSO.

Donaldson, Gordon (ed.) (1966). *Registrum Secreti Sigilli Regum Scotorum,* Vol. VII (1575-1580). Edinburgh: HMSO.

Dressler, Camille (1998). *Eigg: The Story of an Island.* Edinburgh: Polygon.

'Eigg, Uamh Fhraing', Available from URL: http://canmore.rcahms.gov.uk/en/site/22183/details/eigg+uamh+fhraing/ [accessed 8 December 2014]

Fraser, William (1869). *The Chiefs of Colquhoun and Their Country,* Vol. 1. Edinburgh.

Fraser, William (1883). *The Chiefs of Grant,* Vol. 1. Edinburgh.

Giuseppi, M. S. (ed.) (1952). *Calendar of the State Papers Relating to Scotland and Mary Queen of Scots 1547-1603, Vol. XII (1595-7).* Edinburgh: HMSO.

Hewitt, George R. (1982). *Scotland Under Morton 1572-80.* Edinburgh: John Donald.

Innes, Cosmo (ed.) (1855). *Origines Parochiales Scotiae,* Vol. 2, Part 1. Edinburgh: The Bannatyne Club.

Iona Club (ed.) (1847). *Collectanea de Rebus Albanicis.* Edinburgh: Iona Club.

Johnson, Samuel (1775). *A Journey to the Western Islands of Scotland.* London: J. Pope.

Kennedy, John, and MacBain, Alexander (eds) (1894). *Reliquiae Celticae: Texts, Papers, and Studies in Gaelic Literature and Philology Left by the Late Rev. Alexander Cameron, LL. D.*, Vol. 2. Inverness: Northern Counties Newspaper and Printing and Publishing Co.

Kiernan, Ben (2007). *Blood and Soil: A World History of Genocide and Extermination from Sparta to Darfur.* London*:* Yale University Press.

MacDonald, A. and MacDonald, A. (1900). *The Clan Donald,* Vol. 2. Inverness: Northern Counties Publishing Co.

MacDonald, Fiona A. (2006). *Mission to the Gaels: Reformation and Counter-Reformation in Ulster and the Highlands and Islands of Scotland, 1560–1760.* Edinburgh: Birlinn.

MacGregor, Martin (2009). 'Gaelic Barbarity and Scottish Identity in the Later Middle Ages' in Dauvit Broun and Martin MacGregor (eds), *Mìorun Mòr nan Gall, 'The Great Ill-Will of the Lowlander'? Lowland Perceptions of the Highlands, Medieval and Modern.* Glasgow: University of Glasgow.

MacGregor, Martin (2012). 'Warfare in the Later Middle Ages', in Jeremy Crang, Edward M. Spiers and Matthew Strickland (eds), *A Military History of Scotland*, pp. 209-31. Edinburgh: EUP.

Macinnes, Allan I. (2009). 'Slaughter Under Trust: Clan Massacres and British State Formation', in Mark Levene and Penny Roberts (eds), *The Massacre in History,* pp. 127-48. Oxford: Berghahn Books.

McIntosh, Alastair (2002). *Soil and Soul: People Versus Corporate Power.* London: Aurum Press.

Mackenzie, Alexander (1881). 'Massacre of the Macdonalds in the Cave of Eigg'. *The Celtic Magazine,* Vol. 6, p. 194.

MacLean, Rev. Donald (1846). 'Parish of Small Isles', in *The New Statistical Account of Scotland*, vol. 14 (Inverness, Ross and Cromarty), pp. 145-54. Edinburgh and London: William Blackwood and Sons.

Maclean-Bristol, Nicholas (1998). *Murder Under Trust: The Crimes and Death of Sir Lachlan Mor Maclean of Duart, 1558-1598*. East Linton: Tuckwell Press.

MacLeod, R. C. (ed.) (1938). *The Book of Dunvegan*, Vol. 1 (1340-1700). Aberdeen: Spalding Club.

Masson, David, and Burton, John Hill (eds) (1877-98). *The Register of the Privy Council of Scotland, A.D. 1545-1625*, 14 vols. Edinburgh: H.M. General Register House.

Miller, Hugh (1862). *The Cruise of the Betsey*. Boston, MA: Gould and Lincoln.

Pitcairn, Robert (1833). *Criminal Trials in Scotland*, Vol. 3. Edinburgh: Maitland Club.

Rixson, Denis (2001). *The Small Isles: Canna, Rum, Eigg and Muck*. Edinburgh: Birlinn.

Rixson, Denis (2004). *The Hebridean Traveller*. Edinburgh: Birlinn.

Robertson, Joseph (ed.) (1847) *Miscellany of the Maitland Club,* Vol. IV, Part I. Glasgow: Maitland Club.

Skene, W. F. (ed.) (1880). *Celtic Scotland: A History of Ancient Alban*, Vol. 3. Edinburgh: Edmonston and Douglas.

Smout, T. C. (1998). *The History of the Scottish People 1560-1830*. London: Fontana Press.

Stevenson, David (1994). *Highland Warrior: Alasdair MacColla and the Civil Wars*. Edinburgh: John Donald.

Stewart, James A., Jr. (1982). 'The Clan Ranald: History of a Highland Kindred'. Unpublished PhD thesis, University of Edinburgh.

Thomson, J. M. (ed.) (1886). *Registrum Magni Sigilli Regum Scotorum (1546-1580)*. Edinburgh: HMSO.

Urquhart, Judy, and Ellington, Eric (1987). *Eigg*. Edinburgh: Canongate.

Wilson, James (1842). *A Voyage Round the Coasts of Scotland and the Isles,* Vol. 1. Edinburgh: Longman.

Wiseman, Andrew (2014). 'The Eigg Massacre of 1577'. Available from URL: http://calumimaclean.blogspot.co.uk/2014/05/the-eigg-massacre-of-1577.html [accessed 10 December 2014]

10

Haggis agus: Gaelic Scotland through the minibus window

Coinneach Maclean

University of Glasgow

Professor David Crystal stated in his book *Language Death* that 'tourism is a good example of a service industry which can bring considerable benefits to an endangered language' (Crystal, 2000, pp. 132–3). A study of the popular one-day minibus tour of the Scottish Highlands formed part of a doctoral thesis that sought to consider whether the 'endangered language' and culture of Gaelic Scotland benefits from the mass tourism industry (Maclean, 2014).

It has been recognised by successive policymakers, in seeking to encourage growth in visitor numbers (Kerr, 2003), that one of the key niche markets of considerable potential is heritage or cultural tourism. Although Kalyan Bhandari has recently completed his thesis on the specifically political nationalism of aspects of Scottish cultural tourism (2012), it remains an area of limited study. Jonathan Wynn shows in *The Tour Guide* (2011) that the role of the tour guide has been little researched. Gearóid Denvir (2002), in considering the linguistic implications of mass tourism in the Irish Gaeltacht, has been forced to admit that the language impact of tourism is almost universally ignored in the literature. His view is that it was as if 'in an Anglophone world, no language exists other than English' (Denvir, 2002, p. 23).

The growth of one-day minibus tours into Highland areas is a relatively recent phenomenon of this market. According to Malcolm Roughhead, CEO of VisitScotland, in 2013 'a quarter of a million British holiday makers enjoyed an organized coach tour of Scotland, generating £67 million [...] and coach tours are popular among people of all ages' (Clark, 2014, p. 10). Many people receive their first glimpse of Highland Scotland through the window of a tour coach or minibus.

My study supplemented an autoethnographic study undertaken as a tourist guide providing services to visitors. In contrast, I instead placed myself in the position of a visitor and consumer of the narrative provided by the minibus driver/guides on the Highland landscape. It records findings from six trips taken on minibuses operated by four of the more prominent companies offering day-long tours to Loch Ness. Two trips were taken from Glasgow to Loch Ness and the same two companies were used for trips to Inverness from Edinburgh. The fifth and sixth trips were from Edinburgh using two other companies. The tour to Loch Ness-side was specifically chosen since it represents what might be described as the 'milk round' – a circuit from either Glasgow or Edinburgh visiting Glen Coe, Loch Ness and Inverness and returning down the central spine of Scotland on the A9.

These tours are the longest day trips in the United Kingdom, each covering 350 kilometres and lasting up to 12 hours. The resulting records were collected during 45 hours driving time and include personal observations and verbatim statements made by drivers/guides. The speech output quoted is drawn from an estimated ten hours narrative since each journey contained a general music to speech ratio of 75:25.

The paper makes some general observations on how the surveyed companies operated their services to Loch Ness, and their broader representation of Scotland, before moving on to describe the manner in which the Gaelic Highlands are re/presented to this segment of Scotland's mass tourism industry. All Gaelic-related themes covered by the driver/guides are noted in the paper: there was no additional narrative beyond the instances cited.

The research was conducted and successfully defended under the anthropological guidelines in part drawn from the Council of the American Anthropological Association's set of principles to guide ethnographers. These Principles of Professional Responsibility cover the need to consider informants first, to safeguard informants' rights, interests, and sensitivities, to communicate research objectives, to protect the privacy of informants, to avoid the exploitation of informants and to make reports available to informants. Each of the following quotes, which are completely anonymised, is a commonplace and not unique to any one guide or company. They illuminate a widespread and general narrative on Highland Scotland. No single guide can be identified or self-identify from what has been quoted.

In the newspaper article cited above, Roughhead was also quoted as saying: 'There is an increasing demand among visitors to Scotland for an authentic experience, one in which they can hear stories about the history and the people behind the places. Tour companies [offer] bespoke itineraries [...]

that focus on everything from wildlife, ancestry to locations associated with famous films or books' (Clark, 2014, p. 11). Accompanying this statement, one tour company director said that:

> Many people are looking for something a bit different, off the beaten track. Unlike coach drivers who have to follow certain routes our drivers have free rein and can make their own decisions. For instance, they could make a stop in Glencoe to take passengers on a waterfall walk. It's their call (Clark, 2014, p. 11).

This image of an authentic, tailored and consumer-centred approach was echoed on the same page with another tour company representative observing, 'By getting off the beaten track […] we get to where only the smaller tours can go – closer to the real people and local lives. We pride ourselves on getting out there among the locals for a truly authentic experience' (Clark, 2014, p. 12).

The tour to Loch Ness-side is offered by practically every coach company catering for mass tourism in Scotland. Had time and resources been available an identical tour could have been replicated many times over. The visitor, therefore, joins a procession of coaches heading northwards and almost all use the same locations *en route*. Thus for the standard maximum thirty-minute comfort and refreshment stop at Kilmahog, for example, there are six coaches in the car park, three belonging to one company and others to three additional companies. This places pressure on facilities and the visitor is constantly checking the time.

Many of these companies use websites to promote this 'truly authentic experience' to prospective travellers. Thus the visitor is offered the chance to 'enjoy a loch cruise' and the 'services of an experienced tour host'. In making an online booking for a journey from Glasgow to Loch Ness the tourist can be assured of a journey that will take him to the 'Bonnie, Bonnie Banks of Loch Lomond', through 'Rob Roy MacGregor country' into 'desolate Rannoch Moor' and 'haunting Glen Coe, otherwise known as the Glen of Weeping'. An alternative tour could be to 'majestic Glencoe, one of Scotland's most haunting glens'. The tour continues to Loch Ness, 'most famous for its sightings of the Loch Ness Monster, affectionately known as "Nessie."' Other company websites emphasise that 'the services of a professional driver/guide really does make a big difference to your trip'. In their tour from Edinburgh the traveller will also 'pause in Glencoe, to soak up the atmosphere in this haunting glen' and may choose to take 'a wonderful 5 star Jacobite loch cruise' on Loch Ness.

A tour from Edinburgh could take the visitor to 'famous Glen Coe where the notorious massacre of the MacDonald Clan was carried out amidst this beautiful and dramatic scenery'. 'On the banks of legendary Loch Ness', 'the world's most mysterious stretch of water', there is time to 'monster hunt'.

From Edinburgh, the minibus takes the traveller to 'infamous Loch Ness where you can go monster spotting!' The journey is through 'eerie Glencoe, the "Weeping Glen."'

Significantly, all the tours treat practically the whole of the landscape between Inverness and Blair Atholl as a wilderness lacking in narrative. Of this return leg one driver/guide, leaving Inverness, said, 'There is not much to see on the road south'.

The client's companions are multi-national. On journey 1, the minibus contained a group of seven Indians, three Americans and two Australians The oldest tourist is perhaps around fifty years of age. A full 28-seater on Journey 2 had around a dozen Germans, a group of five Canadians and an Icelandic couple. On journey 3 the group comprised seven Americans, two Indians, two Swedes, two Lebanese and a Frenchman. On journey 4 I joined a group of 33 comprising Indians, Italians, Germans, Brazilians, Americans, Norwegians and Chinese. Chinese, Swedes, Germans, Australians, Mexicans and Canadians were among the 28 present on Journey 5. On journey 6 a 44-seater coach was full: by far the largest group I encountered. Most of the travellers were in their early twenties and about a third could be described as being from East Asia.

The first general observation is that all the tours ran to rigid timetables. The driver/guide must take his passengers through a Health and Safety drill reminding them that the wearing of seatbelts is mandatory in the UK. Bob on Journey 2, lectured on punctuality and time keeping, focusing on the grave consequences of turning up late – 'You'll be making your own way back to Glasgow because I will not be waiting for you' – and so forgot to do the seat belts drill. Bob's fierce focus on time-keeping infected his clients with a dread of being late and he returned to Glasgow ahead of schedule. Because of the need for adherence to a strict schedule, the driver/guides did not deviate from the route.

On all six journeys the accuracy of general information about Scotland was at times questionable. Amanda on Journey 1, for example, explained that the Highlands 'have a better air quality which leads to whiter sheep'. The claimed summer population of sheep was between 11 to 12 million [in truth approximately 4 million]. She advised that 'most of Inverness was destroyed by the last Jacobite rising'. On Journey 2 at the viewpoint above Loch Tulla Bob explained that 'we are now at 3,000 feet above sea level' [actually *c.*1000 feet]. At Fort Augustus, pointing out the two mid-nineteenth century towers of the Benedictine monastery, he stated that it 'it is still possible to see the two towers that are all that remains of the old Fort'. He maintained that Fort William was 'named because William of Orange was based there when he was in Scotland' and that Fort Augustus 'was named after the first German leader of Scotland who came up here and renamed it' [neither actually visited]. At the flight of locks leading into Loch Ness he stated that 'Thomas Telford invented the canal lock'.

On Journey 4 Dave estimated that 'of Scotland's 6 million people [actually 5.2 million] only 10% live in the Highlands [actually 300,000]'. He claimed that *Buachaille Eite Mòr* was 'so dangerous a mountain that it kills between 15 and 30 people per year' [annualised average is two]. At Fort William he said that 'the town had mediaeval walls but they were destroyed 260 years ago so they could not be used' but did not divulge by whom these non-existent walls were used or destroyed. According to Eric, 'Loch Ness has salt water at the bottom separated from the freshwater above by a geothermal layer'.

Much of the narrative was conveyed in a slightly folksy, mythic style. Examples include Amanda's statement that 'the railways brought change in the relationship between the Highlands and the Lowlands in the nineteenth century because before then there was no intercommunication'. Her narrative on Rannoch Moor explained that 'we are seeing heather which was used to thatch houses as the walls of the houses were not strong enough to bear the weight of slate'. Later she gave a classification of water spirits which were graded by altitude, with 'the bulls being higher up and horses lower down'. Bob's commentary at Inveruglas explained the presence there of the hydroelectric generating hall: 'at this point the road used to flood with water from the hill which problem was cured by channelling it down in pipes and then they decided that they could generate electricity from the power of the water flow'. Reference made by three guides to pistol-making at Doune drew a spurious connection to the American War of Independence, in that 'a Doune pistol was used to fire the first shots of that engagement' [the likely weapon was a British army musket]. Fred, like Eric, explained that 'the Lake of Menteith was named as a badge of the Earl of Menteith's betrayal of William Wallace and to keep the memory fresh'. At Loch Lochy Chris gave a detailed description of *Blàr na Lèine* – the c.1544 battle between the Frasers and the MacDonalds – with the detail that 'because it was such a hot July day in the early 1600s the combatants stopped the battle halfway through to throw off their plaids and have a dip in the loch'.

At Linlithgow Palace Dave claimed that 'it was burnt after being used as a barracks by the English following the Battle of Culloden in 1746 where the English massacred the Scots'. He claimed that 'the Romans built fortifications on Edinburgh and Stirling Castle Rocks'. At the burial spot of the 'Wolf of Badenoch' in Dunkeld, Fred relayed the undocumented information that 'The Wolf was father to seven hundred children'. They also learned from him that 'the Stone of Destiny was taken to London and cut into shape to fit into the throne'. About the Jacobite Risings we learned that 'Bonnie Prince Charlie captured

Edinburgh Castle in September 1745 and then went to Linlithgow Palace where the fountain flowed with wine'. [While Charles did visit Linlithgow, the other statements are incorrect]. At Lix Toll Fred explained this name as the Roman numerals for 59, which is either because the visitor is 59 miles away from Glasgow [which distance is the case but the meaning is incorrect] or 'the more mythic, magical one' is that it 'was where the Roman Ninth Legion that was scouting around the territory was caught, killed and eaten by the Picts, who were quite cannibalistic'.

Following these general observations, this article now describes the manner in which Gaelic and Highland Scotland is re/presented to this segment of Scotland's mass tourism industry. It suggests that the re/presentation of the Highlands is regularly distorted and that Gaelic culture is rendered practically invisible to the 'tourist gaze'.

Gaelic Scotland is consistently portrayed as being physically separated from the rest of the country by a hard 'Highland Line' geology, with the Highlands described as beginning at the Highland Boundary Fault (HBF). The HBF is the line where three continents collided 420 million years ago on a line running from Arran in the southwest to Arbroath in the northeast (Gillen, 2003, p. 73). Because all the guides described the Highlands as beginning beyond the Fault, they project the notion of a cultural and linguistic division based on primordial geology, creating an environmentally determined Highlands with differing history, culture and language confined beyond that boundary. Amanda's statement that there was no intercommunication before the nineteenth century means that there is no narrative of Gaelic Scotland before reaching the HBF at Balloch or any point south of Blair Atholl. It is particularly poignant that Amanda translated Blair Atholl as the Gaelic for 'the plain of New Ireland' but then stated that 'the Gaelic speakers were only in the Highlands and none existed beyond this point'. Eric explains that 'there are many Highland lines but it's just when the land gets high and there were different ways of life. In the Lowlands there were towns and in the Highlands there was the clan system'. He explained that it was 'not strictly speaking a family system and, although it's not fair to use the word, it was tribal. The two areas did not like each other'. Eric deals with the essentialist characterisations in jokey fashion: 'the Highlanders were warlike, hairy, ginger-haired and wore skirts. The Lowlanders by contrast were a bit puny and not much good at fighting'. There is no mention of Gaelic.

On the journey from Edinburgh, Chris points across towards the mountains north of Loch Katrine and says 'we are heading for the Highlands – a turbulent place'. When the coach enters the narrow defile at the end of Strathyre he, Dave and Fred each informed us in almost identical language that 'we have now reached the Highlands because the land has become much higher'. Almost inadvertently, some of the guides' unguarded comments extend this intractable division between Highland and Lowland Scotland. Fred equated the division to the situation in Roman Britain, suggesting that the fact that the Romans were unable to take control of Scotland was reminiscent of the television series *Game of Thrones*, in which the barbarian people exist beyond the wall. 'Some would argue', he said, 'that it is like that today – barbarian people beyond the wall'.

Re/presentation of that Gaelic society starts axiomatically with a consideration of the nature of the clan system. Amanda explained that 'the clans were always fighting each other, with the MacGregors and the MacFarlanes always fighting the Colquhouns. They made money from raising cattle and stealing them from other people as well'. Rob Roy is used as a cynosure or focal point for this society. Fred stated that Rob Roy [died 1734] was 'a famous cattle thief in the nineteenth century' but that 'his cattle raids were more of a game than anything else. He developed the concept of blackmail, the name which means a "black rent" and the term "black" comes from the black colour of the cattle'. In seeking to identify recognisable comparative characters, the guides compound the problem of essentialism. Dave compared Rob Roy to Ned Kelly or Jesse James. He also stated that:

> Before 1707 our biggest enemy was the English. The second was the clan system. Then the landowners changed the landholding system to leasehold to prevent their heirs selling the land and they brought in the sheep and shepherds.

Chris explained the clan system by mentioning in particular the MacGregors and explains that 'Robert the Bruce was the first to ban the name of MacGregor so that they became known as the *Children of the Mist* and specialised in cattle reiving' [the MacGregors were proscribed after the battle of Glen Fruin in 1603]. He went on 'one of the principal characters, Rob Roy MacGregor, died of blood poisoning following a duel with a novice swordsman in which he allowed his arm to be pricked by his opponent's dirty blade. They deliberately kept them dirty'. Battle techniques are also treated anachronistically. Thus Chris mentions the Battle of Mulroy (1688), which he correctly describes as the last clan battle, but then says that 'it was the last battle fought with bow and arrow', bringing the use forward by almost half a century.

At Killiecrankie, Chris describes the 1689 battle and 'The Soldier's Leap', which he tells us is 23 feet wide [actually 18 feet]. Although expressing some doubts about it himself, it is credible because 'if I was being chased by 300 ginger-haired hairy Highlanders brandishing claymores, I would make that jump'. Such essentialism results in historical events being stereotyped and means that there is little space in the narrative for anything beyond the trope of the 'Highland Warrior'. Bob, however, highlighted another trope by explaining that the minister who required the cutting of the Pulpit Rock on Loch Lomond-side 'was Reverend Proudfoot, but he had problems with part of his congregation who spent the bulk of the service behind the Rock and his back drinking whisky'.

Because one of the promised tour highlights is the Massacre of Glencoe, all the guides are required to give an account of the events. Amanda claimed that 'the Highlanders rebelled in 1689 because they were Catholic' [predominantly Episcopalian] and that 'the Massacre led directly to the loss of Scottish independence in 1707 and also led to the Jacobite Rebellions'. With Bob, the Massacre tale involves the religion of James VII and sectarianism:

> James the Sixth, his father and Charles, his grandfather, were executed for the way they ran the country. So William and James fought at Killiecrankie and William lost and that made him have a grudge against the Catholic Highlanders who won the battle for James. But in 1690 at the Boyne the Dutchman was jubilant.

Bob continued, 'William made everyone sign an Oath of Allegiance and MacDonald's late signing was an excuse for William to get his revenge for Killiecrankie'.

Chris informed travellers that 'William of Orange promoted Protestant expansionism against the Catholics' and that Dalrymple, the Earl of Stair. 'hated the Highland clans because they were a block on progress'. The result of the Massacre was that 'the other clans were prepared to sign the Oath of Allegiance' [practically all the others had signed before the Massacre]. The deed was 'particularly abhorrent because it was deemed as "Murder under Trust" and King William of Orange himself had signed the order'.

Eric commenced a detailed explanation of the Massacre by saying that 'it is all to do with Scottish history – lots of killing'. He continued, 'when Campbell of Glen Lyon turns up with his troops MacIain admits them and puts them up in lieu of unpaid taxes'. Eric attributed a particularly murderous streak to Glen Lyon, since he 'personally kills MacIain, his wife and his children'. Eric assured the visitors that the punishment for this violation of Highland hospitality and Killing under Trust 'was hanging, drawing and quartering'.

Fred also introduced the Massacre with a reference to Catholicism:

> There was a Hanoverian King ruling England following the exile of Catholic James VII to France. The Jacobites were mainly Highlanders. William goes berserk and decides to make an example of the

MacDonalds. There is a saying 'As long as there is one tree standing in the Glen, the MacDonalds will not forgive the Campbells'. So every year the MacDonalds plant trees in the Glen.

Amanda was the only guide to deal directly with the 'invention' of the kilt in 1822. She explained that 'prior to 1822 the kilt had no bright colours. Sir Walter Scott invented it in 1822 when he had George IV dressed up in a toga. The kilt therefore is a relatively modern invention'. Chris provided a different version:

Sir Walter Scott discovered the Scottish regalia hidden since the 1600s [1707] and his invitation to George IV, who liked dressing up, started the tourist industry. Scott is the main reason that we have tartan all over the Royal Mile. He set up a huge pipe band. Bagpipes were used as a war cry and tartan had been made illegal. Scott turned it into a 'purple heather' story.

For other guides discussion of the accuracy of the film *Braveheart* provides the cue for mention of the kilt. The traveller learnt about the Wars of Independence and Bannockburn via a narrative derived largely from *Braveheart*. According to Bob, the only major inaccuracy in the film was the face painting and the fact that 'tartan only came around in the days of the clans'.

I was struck by the extent to which the landscape is presented to the 'tourist gaze' and given 'voice' by reference to motion pictures. Travel through the village of Doune invariably drew references from all the guides to the film *Monty Python and the Holy Grail*. At Loch Tulla Bob referenced the latest James Bond film *Skyfall*, a section of which was filmed on the road just before Kingshouse. Despite the need for a Massacre narrative in Glencoe, there was still space to reference the *Harry Potter* movies. Fred lamented the fact that Hagrid's Hut in Glencoe had to be removed because of planning constraints. *Harry Potter* associations are enlisted where none exist. There was a flurry of interest in taking photographs of the viaduct in Glen Ogle, initially jokingly described by Fred as the Hogwarts School bridge. He then admitted that the viaduct in question is actually in Glenfinnan.

The guides, in one way or another, render Gaelic largely invisible to the 'tourist gaze'. Pronunciation of the names shifts them from Gaelic. Bob and Dave pronounced Buachaille Èite Mòr as 'The Boocle' while Fred pronounced it as 'Bickle'. Nor does the process of explaining the meaning of the names necessarily lead to any comprehension that these are Gaelic words. Bob explained erroneously that brae meant 'field', auch 'river', and Trossachs 'jagged land'. None of these names were explained as being derived from Gaelic. Fred, for example, mentioned the name Alba but did not explain that it is Gaelic for 'Scotland'.

Gaelic landscape descriptors were linguistically appropriated. 'We use Scots words to describe the land', explained Eric and lakes are 'lochs', 'mountains are 'bens' and "we call our hills 'braes'. Dave stated that 'loch is the Scots word for a body of water' and went on to say that 'ben is the Scots word for "a mountain"; glen is a Scots word for "a valley."' Only two of the guides referred to the bilingual road signs but neither explained the relevance of the names. Indeed Chris said 'the bilingual road signs have no relation to where Gaelic is spoken'. The reason for their presence is that 'somebody took a decision that does not reflect where the Gaelic speaking areas are'. He did not tell his clients where these areas were.

The effort to explain Gaelic place names was clearly a challenge. Amanda claimed that 'the name "Glasgow" means "the dear green place" due to the number of trees originally in the area'. The 'firth' word in the name 'Firth of Clyde' was explained as being one of the many words for 'the mouth of the river'. Just south of the Black Mount, Loch Bà was explained as the noise the sheep make [the name probably refers to 'cattle']. Amanda further explained that 'Loch Lochy means "deep loch" as it is the third deepest after Loch Ness and Loch Morar'. In fact, Watson (1986, p. 50) suggests it may refer to a 'black Goddess'.

Dave stated that 'the whisky distillery names Glenfiddich, Glenmorangie, and Glen Grant all come from the rivers flowing through the valleys'. Approaching Tyndrum, we are advised that the name means either 'the ridge over the house' or 'the hill behind the house'. Passing by Loch Lochy, he explained that 'it was so beautiful that they decided to name it twice – Loch Loch'. The Moray Firth means 'the mouth of the River Moray'.

Chris was apologetic for the poverty of the original namers of Loch Lochy by explaining that 'the name does not do it justice. It must have been one of the last to be named'. Fred agreed with Bob and Eric that Ben Nevis means either 'hill with its head in the clouds' or 'the venomous mountain' [it is more likely named for a venomous river spirit] and claimed that these two nicknames were still in use. 'The second meaning is dying out and it was called that because it is not very high and people wanted to climb it. It killed a lot of people'. Fred revealed that Edinburgh also had a Gaelic name, Dunedin, and that 'the name means the fort of *Edin*, who was a gorgeous Scottish princess'. But for him Loch Lochy is called that 'due to the name meaning either "the dark loch" or "Loch of the Dark Goddess,"' but then says 'this is due to the discolouration by peat as it is not possible to see 10 yards in front of your hand. This is why the lochs are mysterious'. Fred is more lyrical than most in his explanations; 'the name Glencoe means "the weeping valley" because of the many waterfalls and in memory of what happened on the 13th of February 1692'. Finally, in Glen Ogle the name of the valley was translated as '"the valley of death" because of the number of rock falls' [a recent phenomenon].

Gaelic songs included in the on-board music compilations offered little elucidation to the visitor. Capercaillie's Karen Matheson singing 'Ceud Soraidh Bhuam' featured within Amanda's compilation without reference to the fact that the song was in Gaelic. Chris's musical selection commenced with traditional fiddling followed by *puirt à beul* by Julie Fowlis. The traveller was advised that 'you are not going to understand her because she is singing in Gaelic'. Of the elegy 'Ailein Duinn, o hi, shiùbhlainn leat', Dave said 'this is the girl singing the Gaelic. Don't worry if you don't understand it, neither do I. In the Lowlands we didn't have the Gaelic'.

When there was mention of the language, the guides offered a view on its nature. Amanda stated that 'it is a very inflexible language and cannot mint new words. However, the government supports it by funding the BBC'. According to Chris, 'it is largely a rural language and does not lend itself to commerce. It is not an easy language to learn as it has a different structure'. Fred mentioned Gaelic as the language from which the word 'whisky' comes. He told us that 'the Gaelic is the ancient language of Scotland now spoken by only 52,000 people but it is a very difficult language. Indeed Gaelic is a very complicated language to talk, far less to write'.

Chris believed that 'there are more Gaelic speakers in Nova Scotia than in Scotland', which is perhaps not surprising since the visitor was told that 'following Culloden there was forced conversion of the Catholics and anyone speaking Gaelic had their tongue cut out' (Amanda), 'the Government attempted to ban the speaking of Gaelic for thirty years after Culloden' (Chris) and the Disarming Act (1747) 'banned the speaking of Gaelic – it was ethnic cleansing – you couldn't be a Highlander' (Fred). Eric tells us that Gaelic was 'the language the Highlanders used to speak but it was banned by the King and nearly died out'.

There was evidence of a wider invention of landscape traditions associated with mountains when at the 'Three Sisters' viewpoint in Glencoe Amanda explained that this late twentieth-century century coining was named 'for three MacDonald girls who lost their lives in the hills after the Massacre'. The guides were disarmingly honest about their own abilities. At the Three Sisters viewpoint Eric was the only driver/guide to admit that this name is simply a modern grouping term for different hills. He then went on to say that 'the names are in Gaelic but I have a real difficulty here; there's no way I can pronounce them'. This was his first mention of Gaelic after three and a half hours of travel within a Gaelic-named landscape.

The effect of this erasure of the language was illustrated by the following exchange at the National Trust for Scotland Glencoe Visitor Centre. Standing beside me and also looking at one of the bilingual interpretation boards, an Indian man pointed to the Gaelic text and asked me 'What language is that?' I explained to him that it was Scottish Gaelic but given his look of complete incomprehension it was clear that he had not grasped Eric's throw-away comment at the Three Sisters viewpoint as to the language's existence. For this visitor and perhaps for many of our six companies' passengers it was perfectly possible to take such a twelve-hour tour through a largely Gaelic-named area and return unaware of the existence of another language in the landscape that they have traversed.

This study suggests that minibus companies either ignore the language or, when they do refer to its existence, treat it in a distorted manner. Taken along with the generally erroneous and essentialised treatment of the history and culture of Gaelic Scotland, the Scottish tourist minibus sector does not realise Crystal's claim that tourism 'can bring considerable benefits to an endangered language'. Indeed, it might be argued that their combined efforts have a detrimental impact upon visitors' understanding of Gaelic Scotland and diminishes the language's profile and status.

Bibliography

Crystal, David (2000). *Language Death*. Cambridge: CUP.
Bhandari, Kalyan (2012). 'The Role of Tourism in the Expression of Nationalism in Scotland'. Unpublished PhD thesis, University of Glasgow.
Clark, Ron (2014). 'On the Road'. *The Business Herald*, August, pp. 10-11.
Denvir, Gearóid (2002). 'The Linguistic Implications of Mass Tourism in Gaeltacht Areas'. *New Hibernia Review/Iris Éireannach Nua*, Iml. 6, tdd. 23–43.
Gillen, Cornelius (2003). *Geology and Landscapes of Scotland*. Sausalito, CA: Terra Press.
Kerr, William Revill (2003). *Tourism Public Policy, and the Strategic Management of Failure*. Oxford: Pergamon.
Maclean, Coinneach (2014). '"The Tourist Gaze" on Gaelic Scotland'. Unpublished PhD thesis, University of Glasgow.
Watson, W. J. (1986 [1926]). *The Celtic Place Names of Scotland*. Edinburgh: Birlinn.
Wynn, Jonathan R. (2011). *The Tour Guide: Walking and Talking*. Chicago, IL: University of Chicago Press.

11

Nàisean cultarach nan Gàidheal: Ath-chruthachadh tìr-dhùthchasaich ann an Albainn Nuaidh

Seumas Watson agus Marlene Ivey
Baile nan Gàidheal / Nova Scotia College of Art & Design

Ro-ràdh

Tha coimhearsnachd na Gàidhlig an Albainn Nuaidh stèidhichte air dualchas is mothachaidhean a nì cairt-iùil dhan rathad air n-adhart do luchd-ionnsachaidh a bhios ga shiubhal. San dàrna deichead dhen treas mìle-bliadhna, tha Alba Nuadh a' fiosrachadh ath-nuadhachadh cànain is cultair nach eil fhathast air cnàmh às gu buileach am measg dhaoine a dh'àraicheadh nan Gàidheil anns na crìochan far na thuinich an sinnsearan cho fad air n-ais ri còrr is dà cheud bliadhna.

A dh'aindeoin cion sgoiltean a bhith gan cumail tro mheadhan na Gàidhlig, agus gainnead air taic an riaghaltais gus, co-dhiù, bho chionn gu math ghoirid, tha dualchas nan Gàidheal air a bhith leanailteach gu ìre is gu bheil e ri sheall-tainn fhathast an cruthan fàsanta mar a tha danns is ceòl, fèill air froileagan luaidh agus, iongnadh dhe na h-iongnaidhean, nach ann a chluinnear nas trice a' Ghàidhlig fhèin ga bruidhinn aig òigridh agus coltas oirre bho chionn ùine gum biodh i balbh, na tosd, sa Mhòr-roinn an ceann beagan bhliadhnaichean. Mas fhìor sin, ma-thà, ciamar a tha atharrachadh cùrsa a' tighinn air dol-fodha Gàidheil na h-Albann Nuaidh agus dè an taobh a tha an cùrsa seo a' gabhail?

Mus till sinn dhan chuspair sin, bheirear sùil air cor na Gàidhlig sa Mhòr-roinn. Tha Cunntas-sluaigh Chanada a chaidh a chumail ann an 2011 (Statistics Canada, 2011) ag aithris gu robh ann san àm 1,275 daoine an Albainn Nuaidh ag agairt gu robh aca comas-bruidhinn na Gàidhlig. Ged nach eil ann tomhas air ìre an fhileantais aig luchd-tagraidh air a' Ghàidhlig a chur an cleachdadh, tha fhios gu bheil e na chùis shuimeil gu bheil an uimhir dhiubh shuas seachad air 490 do luchd-bruidhinn na Gàidhlig a bha air an àireamh ann an Cunntas-sluaigh

Chanada ann an 2001 (Nova Scotia Department of Finance, 2001) – àrdachadh aig ìre mheudachaidh a-null mu dhà uiread gu leth. Mas e is gu bheil an àireamh seo na samhla air adhartas a bhith dèante air ath-nuadhachadh na Gàidhlig an Albainn Nuaidh, feumar faighneachd gu dè is tobar dhan ath-nuadhachadh seo, bhon 's e luchd-ionnsachaidh a tha sa mhòr-chuid a tha ag àrdachdadh àireamh luchd-bruidhinn na Gàidhlig ann an Cunntas-sluaigh Chanada 2011. Agus ceist a bharrachd, mas ann siùbhlach a tha gin nan cainnt, dè an dòigh-ionnsachaidh as buadhaiche a chur gu piseach an cuid fhoghlaim? Gun teagamh, tha mòran a bharrachd rannsachaidh ri dhèanamh air na h-àireamhan sa Chunntas-sluaigh agus na tha ag adhbhrachadh an àrdachaidh (agus fiù 's co-dhiù a bheil àrdachadh a' gabhail àite ann an da-rìreabh), agus ceistean eile, a bharrachd air na modhan-ionnsachaidh aca, leithid: cò iad an luchd-labhairt seo? carson a tha iad ag ionnsachadh na Gàidhlig? dè cho fileanta is a tha iad? agus, dè cho tric is a tha iad ga cleachdadh?

Nuair a sgrùdar sampall de mhuinntir na h-Albann Nuaidh, daoine inbheach a fhuair buaidh air togail cànain an lùib cultair, theagamh gum faigh sinn fuasgladh do chuid dhe na ceistean seo shuas ann an seagh conaltrach. Anns an aiste seo, bheirear sùil air aon dhiubh sin, Sèidheag NicIlleMhaoil (n'in Aonghais Iain Pheadair Aonghais, às a' Mhaoirea Mhòir, Ceap Breatainn), a tha am measg an luchd-ionnsachaidh as soirbheachaile a th' againn ann an Albainn Nuaidh a thaobh a cuid fileantais agus a cuid dìlseachd dhan chànain air an do chuir sinn fhìn eòlas (agus tha aon dhe na h-ùghdairean air a bhith an sàs gu domhainn ann an iomairtean leasachadh na Gàidhlig sa Mhòr-roinn fad barrachd is dà fhichead bliadhna). Bhon eachdraidh ionnsachaidh aice, chithear gun robh an co-theagsa comannach, far a bheil iomlaid air fiosrachadh dùthchasach ga toirt seachad gu co-obrachail an cuideachd a chèile, na shuidheachadh ionnsachaidh as torraiche dhi-se, agus le sin, math dh'fhaodte gu bheil comas anns a' cho-theagsa seo buaidh a thoirt air luchd-togail na Gàidhlig eile ann an Albainn Nuaidh.

Anns a' Ghiblean 2014, 's i a' measadh air ceum a h-ionnsachaidh fhèin gu fileantas, bheachdnaich Sèidheag mar seo:

> *I am drawn to be in a live experience with a higher register of Gaelic: especially in the context of Stòras* ['Stòras a' Bhaile', faic gu h-ìosal, agus Highland Village Museum, 2013] *with its social experience and native speakers ... working on traditional skills with native speakers. Living culture, sharing your stories or songs and having people who care about them listen. If the only thing you want to do is language, then you're not really in the culture ... I hope I mentioned at some point how important visiting is.*

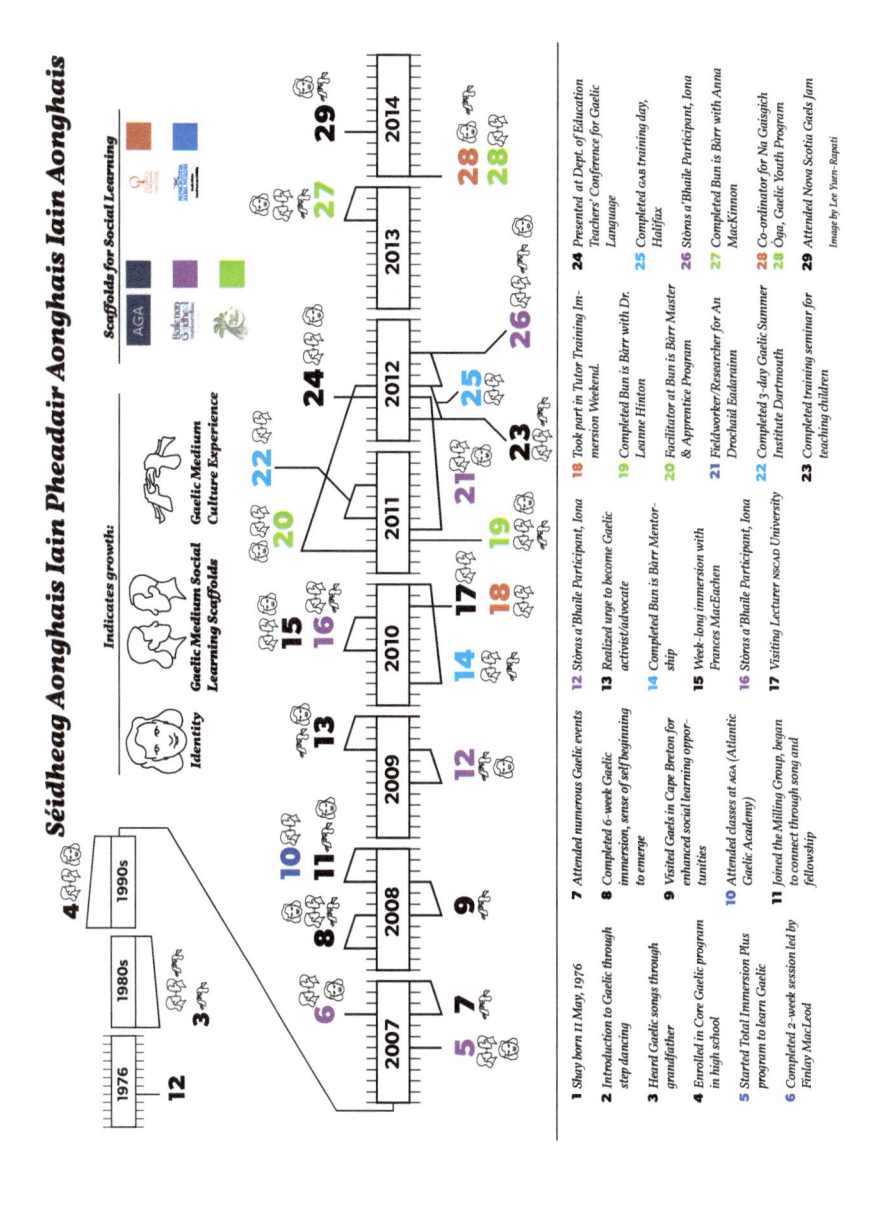

Ath-chruthachadh tìr-dhùthchasaich ann an Albainn Nuaidh   *Watson agus Ivey*

Séidheag Aonghais Iain Pheadair Aonghais Iain Aonghais

Indicates growth:
- Identity
- Gaelic Medium Social Learning Scaffolds
- Gaelic Medium Culture Experience

Scaffolds for Social Learning:
AGA, Baile Gaidhil

1. Shay born 11 May, 1976
2. Introduction to Gaelic through step dancing
3. Heard Gaelic songs through grandfather
4. Enrolled in Core Gaelic program in high school
5. Started Total Immersion Plus program to learn Gaelic
6. Completed 2-week session led by Finlay MacLeod
7. Attended numerous Gaelic events
8. Completed 6-week Gaelic immersion, sense of self beginning to emerge
9. Visited Gaels in Cape Breton for enhanced social learning opportunities
10. Attended classes at AGA (Atlantic Gaelic Academy)
11. Joined the Milling Group, began to connect through song and fellowship
12. Stòras a'Bhaile Participant, Iona
13. Realized urge to become Gaelic activist/advocate
14. Completed Bun is Bàrr Mentorship
15. Week-long immersion with Frances MacEachen
16. Stòras a'Bhaile Participant, Iona
17. Visiting Lecturer NSCAD University
18. Took part in Tutor Training Immersion Weekend.
19. Completed Bun is Bàrr with Dr. Leanne Hinton
20. Facilitator at Bun is Bàrr Master & Apprentice Program
21. Fieldworker/Researcher for An Drochaid Eadarainn
22. Completed 3-day Gaelic Summer Institute Dartmouth
23. Completed training seminar for teaching children
24. Presented at Dept. of Education Teachers' Conference for Gaelic Language
25. Completed GAS training day, Halifax
26. Stòras a'Bhaile Participant, Iona
27. Completed Bun is Bàrr with Anna MacKinnon
28. Co-ordinator for Na Gaisgich Òga, Gaelic Youth Program
29. Attended Nova Scotia Gaels Jam

Image by Lee Yuen-Rapati

185

Cùl-eòlais

Tillidh sinn air n-ais dhan àm nuair a bha e coltach nach biodh am fianais do Ghàidheil na h-Albann Nuaidh tuillidh, ach làrach fhann air an dùthaich dhan do thriall sluagh Gàidhealach gu h-eachdraidheil. A roghainn is gum biodh dha, tha a' Ghàidhlig air a bhith an làthair aig baile fad còrr `s còig glùintean san taobh an ear dhan Mhòr-roinn. An cois cànain, tha oideas cultarach air a bhith ga thoirt a-nuas gu beulach fhathast.

Gu ro-fhortanach, cha b' e is gun robh cuspair nòs nan Gàidheal ga fhàgail air dhearmad aig sgoilearan rannsachaidh anns na deicheadan a chaidh seachad: eòlaichean Ceilteach, cànanaichean, sgoilearan beul-aithris is an leithid. Tha luach an cuid oidhirpean ra fhiosrachadh anns an toradh aig rannsachadh, air a chlàradh is air a thasgadh, a thòisich anns na tritheadan dhen cheud s' a chaidh. Bhon àm sin air n-adhart, tha roinn do sgoilearan an deaghaidh a dhol an sàs san tional ann an crìochan Gàidhealtachd na h-Albann Nuaidh, gu h-àraid an Eilean Cheap Breatainn. Am measg na feadhnach comharraichte sin, bha Iain Latharna Caimbeul, Kenneth Jackson, Gordan MacGill-Fhinnein, Ralph Rinzler, Helen Creighton, MacEdward Leach, a' bhana-chràbhaiche Mairead Pheutan, Seosamh Watson agus Iain Seathach. 'S e a bu bhuil dhen t-saothair phroifeiseanta a rinneadh leotha, cruinneachaidhean a bhonntachadh a tha nan teisteanas dearbhte air susbaint dualchas na tìre. A thuilleadh, chan eil còir againn a leigeil às ar cuimhne an iomadh thabhartasan fiachail a thugadh seachad aig muinntir na coimhearsnachd is iad fhèin a' cur gu mòr ri ceòl, beul-aithris agus gabhail nan òran a tha san tasglann.

Am measg a' chunntais seo, theagamh nach eil e na iongantas gun cluinnear gur e taigh-sgoile na Beurla, barailean ceann-sios air gnàthsan dùthchasach agus droch bharail air beò-shlàinte an tuathanais a bha aig bun an adhbhair gun do chuir na Gàidheil cùl rin cuid dualchais agus cànain an àite-teine (Kennedy, 2001, tdd. 39-63). Tuigear, a rèir an rannsachaidh a rinneadh le Ealasaid Mertz (Mertz, 1989) air beachdan muinntir Mhàbu (Caitleagaich) agus muinntir a' Chladaich a Tuath (Pròstanaich), gur ann sna ficheadan dhen cheud s' a chaidh a shìn a' Ghàidhlig ri crìonadh mar a' chainnt a b' fheàrr le teaghlaichean Gàidhealach an Eilean Cheap Breatainn. Ge-tà, agus a dh'aindeoin coimhearsnachd eaconomach gun mhòran tròcair, tha e air a bhith duilich a chur às do dhùthchas Gàidheil Albann Nuaidh.

Tha nòs air chuimhne na bhunait do chultar Gàidhealach Albann Nuaidh chun an là an-diugh. 'S e an co-phàirt as cudromaiche do chumail dualchas beò, daoine a thighinn còmhla is iad a' seanchas is a' còmhradh ann an cuideachd a chèile. Anns na seachdadan dhen fhicheadamh linn, bha fianais air Ghàidhealtachd Eilean Cheap Breatainn a bu shoilleire ra faicinn aig a' ghinealach a rugadh anns na ficheadan dhen cheud ud: Gàidheil a bha sgapte an siud is an seo ann an nàbachdan tìreil air feadh an Eilein is an taobh an ear dhan Mhòr-roinn.

Eadar na bliadhnaichean 1978 is 1983, agus le taic airgid a fhuaireadh aig Rùnaire na Stàite Chanada, thug an Dr Iain Seathach gu saod trusadh mòr, brìoghmhor de bheul-aithris a chlàr e fhèin air Gàidhealtachd na h-Albann Nuaidh. Tha an co-chruinneachadh cudromach seo ga thasgadh ann aig Oilthigh Fhransaidh Xavier, ann an Antigonish, is e air ainmeachadh mar Chruinneachadh Beul-aithris Gàidhlig Cheap Breatainn (Gaelstream). Lomalàn de dhualchas a thugadh a-nuas an Albainn Nuaidh o bheul gu beul, tha clàraidhean a' cho-chruinneachaidh seo a' brodadh còmhraidh air ciamar a dh'èireas ionnsachadh air cuspairean mar a tha litreachas, cleachdaidhean, nòs agus sinnsearachd ann an àrainneachd shòisealta às aonais – san fharsaingeachd – leughadh is sgrìobhadh a bhith ann aig daoine. Gheibhear ann an co-chruinneachadh an t-Seathaich pàirt dhan t-seanchas a mhìnicheas an àrainneachd ud, mar an tuairisgeul air gnàths a' chèilidh a thug Eòs Nill Bhig (Cloinn Nìll), nach maireann, à Ceap Leitheach, air dhealbh dhuinn (Shaw, 1987, td. 17):

> Bha feadhainn ann a bha math gu seinn òrain agus feadhainn ann a bha math gu aithris dhuan agus feadhainn a bha fìor mhath gu sgeulachdan. Agus bha cuid dhiubh a bha math gu cluich ceòl agus bha cuid dhiubh math gu dannsa. Agus bha fearas-chuideachd a bha cho math 's a ghabhadh a bhith ann, tha mi 'n dùil.

Ann an Albainn fhèin cuideachd, tha luchd-rannsachaidh a' toirt iomraidh air an dòigh oideachaidh a dh'èireadh am measg Ghàidheal air a' Ghàidhealtachd sna linntean a dh'aom. Mar a sgrìobh Raghnall MacilleDhuibh (Black, 2001, tdd. xiii-xiv):

> *It is conventional to say that until ... 1709 there were virtually no schools in the Highlands. Technically that is true. What is overlooked however is that the ceilidh-house was an educational institution ... The fundamental feature of the ceilidh-house was however one which set it apart from schools both ancient and modern. The means of imparting knowledge was not reading and writing backed up by printed books, but oral transmission based on the power of recollection.*

Air leth nam measg, bha beulaichean a leithid do dhaoine mar a bha Colaidh Angain Dhòmhnaill a' Chùbair, Ceataidh Mairead ni' n Aonghais Dhòmhnaill, na bràthairean Seumas is Ailig Frans mic Aonghais 'ic Iain 'ic Mhurchaidh, Migi mac bean Nìlleig, Ruairidh Eòin a' Phlant, Peadar mac Jack Pheadair agus Eòs Theàrlaich Eòis – gus beagan aca a thoirt air ainmeachadh dhe na ceudan dhiubh air fhàgail dhe na mìltean a bh' ann aig deireadh an naoidheimh linn deug.

San t-suidheachadh seo, ma-thà, theann cùisean ri tighinn am follais gu feumadh co-aonadh a bhith ann eadar luchd-seanchais beò, an tasglann agus an luchd-ionnsachaidh a tha ri spàirn a dhèanadh gus an dùthchas ath-bhuannachadh – dilleachdan às aonais dùthchais, mar gum b' eadh.

Leasachaidhean

Anns a' bhliadhna 2004, air fhiathachadh aig a' Chlachan Ghàidhealach (an-diugh air ainmeachadh mar Bhaile nan Gàidheal), rinn Fionnlagh MacLeòid, a bha na fhear-stiùiridh air Comhairle nan Sgoiltean Àraich (CNSA) aig an àm, cèilidh air Albainn Nuaidh gus am modh teagaisg TIP (Total Immersion Plus) a chur an aithne do choimhearsnachd na Gàidhlig. Thuirt e san àm: 'It won't be the children of Gaelic speakers who do something for Gaelic, but their grand-children' (taisbeanadh a rinneadh aig a' Chlachan). Air ath-neartachadh aig a' chuid mu dheireadh dhan t-seann stoc, clàraidhean gan tasgadh gu didseatach (Sruth nan Gàidheal) agus prògraman oideachaidh anns a' choimhearsnachd, tha nòs is dualchas gu cinnteach aig cridhe ath-nuadhachaidh dearbh-aithne nan Gàidheal a tha ag èirigh às ùr an Albainn Nuaidh. 'S ann anns an t-saoghal chaidreamhach seo a bhios barrachd do luchd-ionnsachaidh a' tighinn gu ìre agus a' toirt air sealbh turas a-rithist dìleab an seana-phàrantan. Gu dearbha, cha mhòr nach eil na prògraman-teagaisg uile a chaidh a stèidheachadh bho àm turas MhicLeòid gan togail air conaltradh eadar luchd-ionnsachaidh agus Gàidheil aig an robh a' chànain bhon ghlùin, agus tha na clàraidhean beul-aithriseach gan cur gu feum anns gach modh-teagaisg a chaidh a chruthachadh. Le sin, tha luchd-ionnsachaidh a' faighinn oideachaidh nach eil stèidhichte air a' chànain a-mhàin, ach cuideachd air beairteas gnàthasan-cainnte nan daoine fhèin agus beairteas cultarach Gàidheil Albann Nuaidh a tha ga thaisbeanadh anns a' chòmhradh àbhaisteach làitheil agus anns a' bheul-aithris a bha, mar a chunnacas roimhe san aiste seo, na phàirt de bheatha làitheil nan Gàidheal an Albainn Nuaidh.

'S iad 'Gàidhlig aig Baile', 'Bun is Bàrr', agus 'Stòras a' Bhaile' na prìomh phrògraman-ionnsachaidh a chaidh a stèidheachadh anns na bliadhnaichean mu dheireadh, gach aon le taic bho Oifis nan Iomairtean Gàidhlig – oifis a chaidh a chruthachadh le Riaghaltas na Mòr-roinn (https://gaelic.novascotia.ca/) san Dùbhlachd 2006. Tha 'Gàidhlig aig Baile' na mhodh-teagaisg TIP a thug Fionnlagh MacLeòid dhan Mhòr-roinn ann an 2004. Thèid na clasaichean a chumail ann an dachaighean. Mar as trice, bidh dithis nan ceann, aon neach le Gàidhlig bhon ghlùin agus neach eile a dh'ionnsaich a' Ghàidhlig agus a phiobraicheas còmhraidh. 'S ann stèidhichte air còmhradh seach ionnsachadh bho leasanan sgrìobhte a tha na clasaichean seo (MacEachen, 2008). Tha 'Bun is Bàrr' a' leantail air na pròpraman 'Master and Apprentice' a chaidh a chruthachadh leis an Ollamh Leanne Hinton (Hinton, 2001; Hinton, 2002). Leasaichte air samhail ionnsachaidh sòisealta, bidh na pròpraman seo a' cur luchd-ionnsachaidh cuide ri luchd-bruidhinn fileanta a bhios a' cur Gàidhlig gu feum a h-uile là ann an suidheachaidhean sòisealta, cultarach. Bidh iad ag amas air luchd-bruidhinn na Gàidhlig oideachadh a chleachdas an dàrna cuid: moladh agus àrdachadh na Gàidhlig agus a dualchais ann an Albainn Nuaidh (https://gaelic.novascotia.ca/gd/d%C3%A8anadh). Mu dheireadh, 's e sgoil shamhraidh bheul-aithris a tha ann an 'Stòras a' Bhaile', anns a bheil luchd-ionnsachaidh ag obair le Gàidheil bhon choimhearsnachd air òrain, sgeulachdan agus gnèithean beul-aithris eile a gheibhear ann an dualchas Gàidheil Albann Nuaidh, an dà chuid 'beò' air bilean nan Gàidheal a ghabhas pàirt sa phròpram agus air a bheil clàran (Highland Village Museum, 2013). Tha e cudromach cuideachd, iomradh a thoirt air An Drochaid Eadarainn (http://www.androchaid.ca/), làrach-lìn air a leasachadh mar thobar taiceil do luchd-ionnsachaidh a chruthaicheadh an cois Stòras a' Bhaile. Gheobhar na broinn clàr de fhiosrachadh a chuireas air thaisbeanadh nòsan a tha fhathast an cleachdadh ann an sgìreachdan Gàidhealach mu seach sa Mhòr-roinn.

Ann am briathran Sèidheig NicIlleMhaoil, a' bruidhinn mun rathad-ionnsachaidh a chleachd i fhèin gu fileantas,

> Culturally I had no awareness of my being Gaelic until I was an adult ... I thought we all grew up the same, but eventually I came to realize that we hadn't. A sense of identity began to emerge. I didn't have a name for it. I first started with long immersions in summer and continued to be reinforced through learning something more than vocabulary. Little by little, this is us, this is me.

Ann am faclan eile, tha Sèidheag a' tarraing air a' mheadhan-ionnsachaidh ris an abrar *'social learning theory'*.

Togail an cuideachd a chèile: ag ionnsachadh na Gàidhlig gu comannach

'S e a b' athair dhan bhun-bheachd 'social development theory' an t-eòlaiche-inntinn Ruiseanach Lev Vygotsky. Chaidh Vygostsky a bhreith anns a' Bhalaruis sa bhliadhna 1896. Fhuair e am bàs leis a' chaitheamh aig aois 37, sa bhliadhna 1934. 'S ann stèidhichte air rannsachadh eòlas-inntinn mun fhàs (*developmental psychology*) a bha a' mhòr-chuid dhe shaothair. 'S e a bu bheachd aig Vygostsky gu robh ionnsachadh na cloinne an earbsa ri conaltradh sòisealta am measg dhaoine agus eadar-gnìomhachas le culaidhean a ghabhas faighinn gu cumanta san àrainneachd chorparra m' ar timcheall. 'S ann thairis air sia tuim do leabhraichean, a chaidh a sgrìobhadh eadar 1925–1934, a gheibhear am prìomh chridhe dhen tabhartas aige dhan raon anns an robh e an sàs. Theagamh gura h-e a leabhar *Thought and Language* am fear as cudromaiche dhiubh sin dhar tuigse air buannachd is leasachadh cànain. Na bhroinn, chuir Vygotsky an cèill a cho-dhùnadh gu bheil comas smaoin a' chinne-daonna ga fhàs gu conaltrach.

Ged a b' ann fada air thoiseach a bha rannsachadh an fhoghlaim aig Vygotsky ra linn, cha do chuir sgoilearan na h-Àird an Iar mòran feairt na obair air sàilleabh na beàirn san dà ideòlas phoileatagach a bh' ann san àm: calpachas an aghaidh co-mhaoineachais. Bha sgoilearan nan dùthchannan calpach suidhichte, sa mhòr-chuid, air leasachadh cànanachais-inntinn (*psycholinguistics*). Air a shon sin, bu bheag an t-suim a chuireadh ann an rannsachadh Vygostsky gus na seachadan dhen cheud sa chaidh.

A' leantail air Vygostsky, bha sgoilearan adhartach a' tòiseachadh anns na seachdadan air creideas a thoirt do rannsachadh an Ruiseanaich, gu sònraichte an t-Ollamh Albert Bandura, Canàideanach aig Oilthigh Stanford, a leudaich air obair Vygotsky le foillseachadh a leabhair *Social Learning Theory* anns a' bhliadhna 1977. 'S e is bunait do beachdan Bhandura, gur ann air trì rathaidean a bhios an cinne daonna a' fàs san inntinn agus a' togail: mothachadh, atharrais agus cumadh (modelling).

A' coimhead air mar a ghabhas teòiridh-ionnsachaidh shòisealta (air neo social learning theory) cur an gnìomh a chuideachadh le cànan a thogail, is gu h-àraid mion-chànan beulach, tha e feumail sùil a thoirt air samhlaidhean dhe na h-iomairtean a tha air a bhith dèante mu ghlèidheadh chànanan Tùsanach an Amaireaga a Tuath. Ann a bhith a' dèanadh coimeas eadar na raointean do rannsachadh cànain, sòisio-chànanachas is cànanachas-inntinn, chithear gu bheil an dà bheachd-smuain eadar-dhealaichte gus modhannan ionnsachaidh a chruthachadh agus a chur an cleachdadh. Tha an t-Ollamh Mark Warford (Warford, 2011, td. 76), air comharrachdh mhodhanan teagaisg gam bonntachadh air cànanachas-inntinn:

> *Psycholinguistic pedagogies, rooted in Western Rationalist thought, have served as a tool in this process by abstracting and decontextualizing the way we view language teaching and learning to the point that its inherently cultural nature has been minimized, if not excised.*

Le bhith a' cur cuideam mòr air oideachadh a thoirt gu ìre ann an suidheachadh comannach, tha Warford air riochdachadh a mhodh-teagaisg fhèin, air an tug e an tiotal 'Narrative Language Pedagogy':

> *Learning a language for its abstract linguistic properties (grammar) to the exclusion of the social contextual particularities of its meaning and usage only exacerbates the devastating work of linguistic conquest and colonization* (Warford, 2011, td. 76).

Ann a bhith ag àrdachadh a' bheachd aig bun 'Narrative Language Pedagogy', tha Warford ag aideachadh buaidh Vygotsky air a chuid obrach fhèin – 'the philosophical notion of conversation' – agus a' toirt creideas do dh'obair Leanne Hinton. Thug Warford (Warford, 2011, td. 81) fos-near:

> *While the focus is always on ongoing conversations between teachers and learners, the central mission for both parties is sort of an anthropological adventure, one of exploring and appropriating linguistic and cultural practices.*

Eu-coltach ri seòmar-ionnsachaidh taigh-sgoile na stàite, tha inbhe a' mhodh-teagaisg chomannaich a' crochadh air dà phuing. 'S e a' cheud tè, tha e air leth cudromach gum bi àrainneachd an oideachais ga h-eagrachadh air dòigh is gu bheil an conaltradh siùbhlach, nàdarra eadar an tàilleabhach agus an neach a tha fileanta anns a' chànain a tha ra togail. 'S e an dàrna puing gu bheil e buileach iomchaidh fìor stuthan a bhith gan cleachdadh a bhuineas dhan chuspair air làimh agus a chumas taic ris gun a bhith breugach (Warford, 2011, td. 81).

An turas a bha an cànanaiche an t-Ollamh Leanne Hinton a' bruidhinn ann an Antigonish, thug i iomradh air daoine a bhith air an tarraing a dhol an sàs ann an cultaran beò. Thuirt i: 'Lots of people feel it by seeing it in action ... we can intellectualize it, but it is only when people feel the connection that they are motivated to learn' (Hinton, 2011). Tha an rannsachadh seo a' cumail a-mach gu bheil neart cultar Gàidhealach na h-Albann Nuaidh an earbsa ri dearbh-aithne a bhios fallain. Bidh dearbh-aithne an urra ri tighinn beò am measg cuideachd a cleachdas nòs is dualchas ann.

Tha a' chliath air a bheil dearbh-aithne chultarach ga snìomh agus air a grunndachadh le coimhearsnachd ga cumadh le caochladh raointean sòisealta air an co-naisgead tro eadar-gnìomhachas dhaoine (Office of Gaelic Affairs, 2008). 'S ann air a' bhonn seo a tha an co-mhothachadh, agus am fiosrachadh, a cheanglas sliochd Gàidheil na h-Albann Nuaidh ri saoghal-inntinne an sinnsire. Do rèir, tha toradh an rannsachaidh, gu ruige seo, gar comhairleachadh, los co-cheangal a dhèanadh turas a-rithist ri dualchas agus dearbh-aithne cultar beò Gàidhealtachd na h-Albann Nuaidh, tog fianais, fairich agus gabh an sàs.

A' toirt air lèirsinn ionnsachadh stèidhichte air dualchas na coimhearsnachd

B' e is gun robh amas ar rannsachaidh a thoirt gu saod cunntas-ùine lèirsinneach a dhèanadh dealbh air mar a tha dearbh-aithne air a leasachadh tro chaochladh shuidheachaidhean sòisealta, an cois ionnsachadh na Gàidhlig. Mar shamhla air sin, tha an neach-bratha seo, Sèidheag NicIlleMhaoil, air fileantas a ruigsinn tro thaic a fhuaireadh am measg cuideachd anns a' choimhearsnachd, gu h-àraid bho na prògraman 'Bun is Bàrr' agus 'Stòras a' Bhaile' anns an do ghabh i pàirt. Aig bun a' ghnothaich, b' e rathad ionnsachaidh a bh' ann togte air nòs is cànain air an toirt seachad gu conaltrach. Tha tuilleadh luchd-ionnsachaidh ann mar phàirt dhen rannsachadh seo a chuireas an cuibhreann fhèin ris san ùine ri tighinn. Tha àireamh dhaoine ann aig ìre fileantais a ruigsinn a thàinig air rathad eile, cuid dhiubh nan oileanaich aig Oilthigh Naomh Fransaidh Xavier a thug seachad mòran ùine anns a' choimhearsnachd mun cuairt far an cluinnear Gàidhlig ga bruidhinn. Fhad 's a thèid am pròiseact seo air n-adhart, nìthear rannsachadh fhathast air a' mhodh phearsanta a chleachd taghadh dhiubh seo.

'S ann a bha an cunntas-ùine seo shuas na cho-lorg a thàinig à fiosrachadh pearsanta agus tùsan faicsinneach air an toirt seachad aig Sèidheag, còmhla ri agallamh. 'S e gu bhith a' tional na forfhais, agus ga sgrùdadh, a dh'fhiosraich na còmhraidhean a lean leatha. Air an t-seòl sin, bha comas ann air aithneachadh dà phrìomh ghoireas san ionnsachadh aice: scafallachd ionnsachaidh tro mheadhan na Gàidhlig agus fiosrachaidhean sòisealta tro mheadhan na Gàidhlig. Rinn iad bunait le chèile gus tuigsinn a thoirt às an dòigh a bha iad feumail dhi dearbh-aithne a bhunachadh.

Chaidh tùs-samhail air a' chunntas-ùine a chur air bhonn le rùn seo-aomadh. A bharrachd, thèid an tùs-samhail a chleachdadh gus tuilleadh cunntasan luchd-ionnsachaidh a thàrmachadh san àm ri teachd. Ann a bhith a' tionsgail cunntas-ùine mu seach, bidh comas ann air sgrùdadh a dhèanamh gus mìneachadh a thoirt gu aithris a dh'fhaodadh a bhith duilich ann an rian eile. 'S e is amas na h-iomairte a chur air thaisbeanadh nan sochairean a thig an lùib ionnsachaidh conaltraich a nì feum do thogail na Gàidhlig gu fileantas tro dhualchas is nòs.

An deaghaidh do Shèidheag an treas aithris air a' chunntas-ùine fhaicinn, thuirt i (An Cèitean, 2014):

> *Once I have language and cultural knowledge I have self. My identity is established, I know who I am. I have awareness of my cultural identity and so does everyone else ... so cultural experience is an everyday event. I am just living it and passing it on.*

Nàisean cultarach Gàidheil na h-Albann Nuaidh: co-dhùnadh

Ann a bhith sgrùdadh rathad-ionnsachaidh gus cànan is dearbh-aithne a thogail air nòs is dualchas, tha e nar rùn a chomharrachadh chleachdaidhean de chultar gnàthasach a gabhas a-steach ceòl is dannsa, sloinntearachd, na h-ealain chruthachail is eile. Molaidh toradh an rannsachaidh, gu ruige seo ma-tà, gu bheil turas an ionnsachaidh seo as brìoghmhoire nuair a bhios e suidhichte, air neo mar phàirt de *'situated learning approach'*, mar a theirear.

'S e a bu rùn dhan mhodh-ghabhail seo cultar dùthchasach a bhith ga shònrachadh mar thobar air leth cothromach gus fileantas cànain is dearbh-aithne nan Gàidheal a leasachadh an lùib a chèile. A dh'aindeoin dearmad ùghdarrasan oifigeil, dì-luachadh san taigh-sgoil agus am barail san fharsaingeachd gu robh cànan nan Gàidheal na thruaghan ri taobh na Beurla, tha dualchas nan Gàidheal fhathast gu math follaiseach am beatha shòisealta na Mòr-roinn.

Eadar uiread do luchd-bruidhinn a' dol am meud fo bhuaidh nòsan tradaiseanta, a bhios a' tighinn còmhla cruinn san taigh-chèilidh agus Oifis Iomairtean na Gàidhlig air a sònrachadh aig ìre riaghaltas na Mòr-roinn, theagamh gu faodamaid a ràdh gu bheil inbhe nan Gàidheal air impis a bhith na nàisean comannach, ga thogail air dualchas beò a b' aithne do dh'Albainn Nuaidh mar a dhachaigh bho chionn treis mhath a dh'ùine.

Tùsan

Black, Ronald (deas.) (2001). *An Lasair: Anthology of 18th Century Gaelic Verse*. Dùn Èideann: Birlinn.

Fettes, Mark (1997). 'Stabilizing What? An Ecological Approach to Language Renewal', ann an Jon Reyhner (deas.), *Teaching Indigenous Languages*, tdd. 301-18. Flagstaff, AZ: Northern Arizona University).

Gaelstream: gaelstream.stfx.ca/greenstone/cgibin/library. cgi?site=localhost&a=p&p=about&c=capebret&l=en&w=utf-8

Highland Village Museum (2013). *Stòras a' Bhaile 2013: Highland Village Gaelic Folklife School and Celebration, Report to Office of Gaelic Affairs*. Iona, NS: Highland Village Museum (ri fhaighinn bhon URL: http://highlandvillage. novascotia.ca/sites/default/files/inline/documents/storas_report_2013.pdf (air a ruigsinn 20.11.2015)

Hinton, Leanne (2001). 'The Master-Apprentice language learning program', ann an Leanne Hinton agus Kenneth Hale (deas.), *The Green Book of Language Revitalization in Practice*, tdd. 217-35. San Diego: Academic Press.

Hinton, Leanne (2011). Òraid leis an Ollamh Leanne Hinton, Antigonish, 10.5.11.

Hinton, Leanne, Vera, Matt, agus Steele, Nancy (2002). *How to Keep Your Language Alive: A Commonsense Approach to One-On-One Language Learning*. Berkeley: Heyday Books.

MacEachen, Frances (2008). *Am Blas Againn-fhìn: Community Gaelic Immersion Classes in Nova Scotia–An evaluation of activities in 2006–2007*. Antigonish, NS:

Oifis nan Iomairtean Gàidhlig) (ri fhaighinn bhon URL: https://gaelic.novascotia. ca/sites/default/files/inline/documents/am_blas_againn_fhin.pdf [air a ruigsinn 20.11.2015])

McLeod, S. A. (2011). 'Bandura – Social Learning Theory' (ri fhaighinn bhon URL: www.simplypsychology.org/bandura.html [air a ruigsinn air 7.2.2015]).

Mertz, Elizabeth (1989). 'Sociolinguistic creativity: Cape Breton Gaelic's linguistic tip', ann an Nancy Dorian (deas.), *Investigating Obsolescence: Studies in Language Contraction and Death*, tdd. 103-16. Cambridge: CUP.

Nova Scotia Department of Finance (2002). *2001 Census of Canada: Nova Scotia Perspective, Release no. 4: Language, Mobility and Migration*. Halifax: Department of Finance) (ri fhaighinn bhon URL: https://www.novascotia.ca/ finance/publish/CENSUS/Release4.pdf. [air a ruigsinn air 20.11.2015])

Shaw, John (deas.) (1987). *Sgeul gu Latha/Tales Until Dawn: The World of a Cape Breton Gaelic Story-Teller*. (Kingston agus Montreal: McGill-Queen's Press.

Smith, M. K. (2003, 2009) 'Jean Lave, Etienne Wenger and communities of practice', ann an *the encyclopedia of informal information* (ri fhaighinn bhon URL: www. infed.org/biblio/communities_of_practice.htm [air a ruigsinn air 7.2.2015])

Statistics Canada (2011). *National Household Survey (NHS)* (ri fhaighinn bhon URL: http://www12.statcan.gc.ca/nhs-enm/2011/dp-pd/prof/index.cfm?Lang=E [air a ruigsinn air 7.2.2015])

Vygotsky, L. S (deas. leasaichte 1986) 'Thought and Language' (Cambridge, MA: MIT, revised edition) (ri fhaighinn bhon URL: http://s-f-walker.org.uk/pubsebooks/pdfs/ Vygotsky_Thought_and_Language.pdf [air a ruigsinn air 7.2.2015])

Warford, Mark (2011). 'Narrative Pedagogy and the Stabilization of Indigenous Languages'. *The Reading Matrix*, Iml. 11, Àir. 1 (ri fhaighinn bhon URL: www. readingmatrix.com/articles/january_2011/warford.pdf [air a ruigsinn air 7.2.2015])

12

Celtic Colours: cultural sustainability

Jean S. Forward

University of Massachusetts

How does a culture and community maintain its values, language, culture and identity through time, especially through socio-economic domination and forced cultural change? In the last several centuries, commercial expansion, Christian missionising, the development of the world capitalist system and industrial development have been major sources of cultural change. 'Centuries of papal bulls posited the supremacy of Christendom over all other beliefs, sanctified manifest destiny, and authorized even the most brutal practices of colonialism' (LaDuke, 2005, p. 12).

The question for cultural persistence and sustainability, then, is how cultures and communities can survive? In Nova Scotia, multiple processes of cultural change took place. There is the cultural domination of the Indigenous Algonquian language peoples of Nova Scotia and New Brunswick by the French Acadians, which was based on trade and kinship relationships (Faragher, 2006). There is the cultural dominance of the Indigenous Algonquian language peoples and the French Acadians by the British based on policies of removal, reservations and boarding schools (Calloway, 2008; Faragher, 2006; Newton, 2001).

Scottish immigrants to Nova Scotia were often forced to leave their homelands, mostly in the Highlands and Islands of Scotland. Communities in the Highlands and Islands were dominated by Anglo-Saxon political, economic, and cultural forces as early as the eleventh century. By 1746, England dominated Scotland, economically and politically, having secured control of access to key resources and many of those of higher status, including Highland chiefs, had been assimilated to Anglo-British norms. In the process, the English language came to dominate the political, economic and cultural landscape.

In order to understand the cultural context of today and the persistence of Gaelic language and culture in Nova Scotia, we need to understand the practices in the past that perpetuated Gaelic language, history, culture and identity throughout waves of cultural change. We also need to explore the definitions of community. 'The exact definition and boundaries of a culture are not rigid and may be quite difficult to quantify with any precision' (Newton, 2000, p. 17). This definition also applies to communities. Fredrik Barth (1969) articulates quite clearly that the boundaries of community and culture are constantly in flux, fluid. Further, 'community ... [is] ... where one learns and continues to practice how to "be social" ... where one acquires "culture"' (Cohen, 1985, p. 15). This would, of course, include the use of language. 'One of the most important channels for the encapsulation and dissemination of culture is language' (Cohen, 1985, p. 21). A small number of Gaelic language speakers persist in Nova Scotia even though it is a province in Anglo-dominated Canada. Language, song, and dance in Nova Scotia, as in Scotland, have benefitted from the recent re-assertion of Gaelic cultural identity. Today, for example, road signs in Cape Breton Island are in English and Gaelic. On the Reserves, they are in Mi'kmaq.

The first Celtic Colours festival took place in 1997, as significant political changes were on the horizon in Scotland. In 1995, Joella Foulds and Max MacDonald created an organization to promote Celtic culture and music in Cape Breton. It took two years to organize this decentralized festival, working closely with communities to develop events and performances. In 1997, Celtic Colours held 27 concerts and some 20 additional events. Music, song, dance, fiddling and stepdancing are deeply rooted in the communities on both sides of the Atlantic although less oppressed historically in Cape Breton. These cultural links between Nova Scotia and Scotland have been and continue to be strengthened by the persistence and expansion of the Celtic Colours festival with performers from both sides of the Atlantic every year.

Key questions posed by these developments are how communities and cultures survive and thrive in such circumstances. How does Celtic Colours contribute to the sustainability of Gaelic language and culture? From 27 concerts in 1997, Celtic Colours is now nine days and nights of small-scale community-based tourism. The stated aims of the festival are 'to promote, celebrate and develop Cape Breton's living Celtic culture and hospitality by producing an international festival during the fall colours that builds relationships across Cape Breton Island and beyond' (www.celtic-colours.com/about/, accessed 17.8.2015). This mission is creatively pursued and fulfilled every year.

For example, in 2012, the festival included 46 performances and over 200 community cultural events, including exhibits, learning opportunities, participatory events, community meals and outdoor events. Exhibits covered topics such as 'Dhachaidh –The Geography of Home'; Cape Breton history ('Every Island Has a Story – Ours is Handmade'); geography/topography ('Sea and Sky'); and arts and crafts. Learning opportunities included language and song classes; flute, harp, fiddle, tin whistle, guitar and banjo lessons, iron works/ forging demonstrations as well as demonstrations and lessons in weaving, mask-making, rug-hooking and knitting.

In Mabou, on the west side of the island, Féis Mhàbu (the Mabou Festival) happens at the same time as Celtic Colours. It includes 'Féis Mhàbu Cultural Workshops for Youth' with language classes which include drama and storytelling. This event brings together culture, language and music for twenty children in each class. This creates a community base for culture and language persistence.

In 2012, participatory events ranged from a 'Gaelic Song Circle' to an 'All Ages Square Dance', 'Kitchen Racket and Jam Session', 'Celtic Jam Session', 'Open Stage', 'John Allan Cameron Song Session' and several other jam sessions. In addition, the 'Festival Club' was held every night after the other performances (usually starting around 10 or 11pm) at the Gaelic College in St Ann's on the east side of the island. Many of these sessions, were, in effect, ceilidhs. The ceilidh is a container of language, history, community, identity and culture which focuses on the oral tradition of poetry, song, history, and language for Gaels and their culture. It is a gathering of kin and friends to pass on language, culture and identity that has persisted for hundreds of years, possibly millennia.

Community meals were often arranged to precede or follow performances or community cultural events. Many included local foods such as locally grown root crops, i.e. potatoes, turnips, carrots, and parsnips. Meals were hosted by community groups such as churches, senior centres, the Gaelic College and others. Some were also ceilidhs such as the lunchtime ceilidh at the Celtic Music Interpretive Center (CMIC) in Judique, on the west side of the island. Outdoor events included guided walks and hikes at Big Pond or other established trails, historical walks, 'Celtic Hospitality Whale Tour' and 'Hike the Coxheath Colours and Ceilidh'.

It is relevant to add a fuller description of a few events to emphasise the inclusion of educational opportunities that integrate the Gaelic language and culture within Celtic Colours. Approximately one-third of Celtic Colours events include a significant Gaelic-language element. I attended Celtic Colours in 2012 and 2013. Obviously I had to pick and choose events to attend. One event, 'Our Gaelic Kids: Ar Clann Ghàidhealach', the Gaelic children performance at Christmas Island, was particularly memorable. Many children participated, but two families in particular, one with five young girls and one with four young boys (ages ranging from 3-11) stood out. Each family group came on stage and performed several songs in Gaelic, some of them composed by older extended family members. These children are part of a school language programme that teaches in Gaelic, French, and/or English and members of families who are continuing the Gaelic language tradition at home as well as in school. At one point, 23 children were singing Gaelic milling songs around the milling table with four elders. It is hard to accurately portray the atmosphere, but these children were evidently very proud of their abilities to perform in the Gaelic language. The introductions of each group of children made it clear that their performances increased the children's social status in the community. Language and culture are dependent in large part on young people engaging in the language and culture. Celtic Colours provides opportunities for youth to learn and perform Gaelic language, song and dance and be proud of it.

One larger performance event took place at Whycocomagh Education Center, with about a thousand people attending. Outside the performance hall was a 'Wanted Poster Wall', where students had filled out 'Wanted' Posters for the Celtic Colours performers. Individual students researched and wrote biographies on the individual performers including their homeland, profession, experience, kin relationships, etc. on each poster. It is clear that this is an integrated learning opportunity which permeates the fabric of the whole community through education/enculturation in support of the Celtic Colours festival. And, again, it emphasises young folk learning and owning their Gaelic identity.

Celtic Colours is supported by a large cadre of volunteers. In 2007, 900 people volunteered to transport performers, set up and take down seating, etc. at performances, and generally do a vast amount of legwork without which Celtic Colours would not be as sustainable as it is. By 2012, the number of volunteers had grown to over 2000.

The assertion here is that Celtic Colours is culturally sustainable and community-based and as such promotes and perpetuates Gaelic language and culture throughout Cape Breton. It is also an example of community-based and -controlled cultural tourism, making it very economically viable. According to Dalby and Mackenzie, 'the past is a resource which may be selectively mined in the creation of new boundaries of a community whose social or geographical boundaries are threatened' (Dalby and Mackenzie, 1997, p. 102). English domination has threatened Gaelic language and identity for hundreds of years. Cape Breton Gaels in Nova Scotia have a deep sense of history, language and identity. Songs in Celtic Colours including both traditional works brought over from Scotland and more recent compositions from Cape Breton, Scotland, Ireland and other communities in the Gaelic language diaspora. The songs 'mine' the past to preserve the future.

Another example of the sustainability of this cultural tourism and the Gaelic language culture it supports is the Celtic Music Interpretive Centre (CMIC) in Judique. In 2000, the Judique community created a major fundraising event, the Celtic Music Golf Tournament. This event provided the major source of capital to start the construction of the Celtic Music Interpretive Centre (CMIC) in 2005, and it remains the major fundraiser for CMIC (Rankin, 2014). The CMIC website states that the mandate is to 'to collect, preserve and promote the traditional Celtic music of Cape Breton through Education, Research and Performance' (http://www.celticmusiccentre.com/, accessed 17.8.15). The centre offers year-round ceilidhs with live traditional music, educational workshops in fiddle, piano and dance, Gaelic language immersion classes, an archive and library, a recording studio and an interactive exhibit room.

Celtic Colours provided the opportunity for Gaelic speaking/Celtic heritage folk to work together and develop the funding to create the CMIC. The CMIC continues to be integrated into the larger programme of Celtic Colours, but it now also offers year-round opportunities for the local community to continue to reproduce, sustain, and perpetuate Gaelic language, culture, song, history, etc. Both Celtic Colours and CMIC are culturally acceptable and economically viable, necessary variables for cultural sustainability. For example, the 2009 Celtic Colours festival was estimated as bringing $15.5 million into the Cape Breton economy (Scott and Pelley, 2010, p. 13). The local aspects support ecological viability. More local participation could enhance the ecological viability, e.g. with the use of more locally grown foods.

It is also clear from the list and description of events that ceilidhs are an inherent part of Celtic Colours. Ceilidhs are an inherent part of the process of perpetuation of Gaelic language and culture. Look back into Gaelic language history or pre-history. Knowledge of prehistory mainly comes from oral histories, often later written down, and found in language research and archaeology. Many of the stories contain frequent accounts of gatherings, in homes of kings, chiefs, lords and other local leaders. These gatherings included food, song/poetry/history, dance and affirmations of identity.

According to Michael Newton,
> the typical context for the exchanging of songs, poems, tales, legends, anecdotes, dances, and news of all sorts was the *cèilidh* (house-visit). This institution was crucial in disseminating the lore

and values of society from the oldest generations to the younger ones of both genders. It demanded active minds, excellent memories, faithfulness to the original version of the 'text', respect for the elder tradition-bearers and the honoured guest of the house, and participation by all (Newton, 2001, p. 101).

In conclusion, the description of these few examples supports the statement that Celtic Colours, a cultural tourism event, is community-based and reproduces and sustains Gaelic culture and language in Cape Breton, Nova Scotia in the face of the ongoing threat of political and economic domination and development. The thorough integration of ceilidhs throughout the nine days and nights utilizes this traditional venue of cultural perpetuation for Gaelic language, culture and identity to survive and thrive. Cultural sustainability requires cultural acceptance, economic and ecological viability. Celtic Colours has all three. For many more examples with extensive descriptions, see the Celtic Colours website, www.celtic-colours.com.

Bibliography

Barthel-Bouchier, Diane (2013). *Cultural Heritage and the Challenge of Sustainability*. Walnut Creek, CA: Left Coast Press.
Barth, Fredrik (1969. 'Introduction', in *Ethnic Groups and Boundaries: The Social Organization of Culture Difference*, pp. 9-38. London: George Allen & Unwin.
Calloway, Colin G. (2008). *White People, Indians and Highlanders*. Oxford: OUP.
Cohen, Anthony P. (1985). *The Symbolic Construction of Community*. London and New York: Routledge.
Dalby, Simon, and Mackenzie, Fiona (1997). 'Reconceptualizing local community: environment, identity and threat'. *Area*, Vol. 29, No. 2, pp. 99-108.
Faragher, Jack Mack (2006). *A Great and Noble Scheme*. New York: W. W. Norton.
Jones, Carleton (2004). *The Burren and the Aran Islands*. Cork: Collins Press.
Kennedy, Michael (2002). *Gaelic Nova Scotia: An Economic, Cultural and Social Impact Study*. Halifax, NS: Nova Scotia Museum.
LaDuke, Winona (2005). *Recovering the Sacred: The Power of Naming and Claiming*. Cambridge, MA: South End Press.
MacCormick, John R. (1998). *Highland Heritage and Freedom's Quest: Three Centuries of MacCormaics in Ireland, Scotland, Prince Edward Island and West Lake Ainslie, Nova Scotia*. Halifax, NS: Kinloch Books.
Newton, Michael (2000). *A Handbook of the Scottish Gaelic World*. Dublin: Four Courts Press.
Newton, Michael (2001). *We're Indians Sure Enough: The Legacy of the Scottish Highlanders in the United States*. Cambridge, MA: Saorsa Media.
Radding, Cynthia (1997). *Wandering Peoples: Colonialism, Ethnic Spaces, and Ecological Frontiers in Northwestern Mexico, 1700-1850*. Durham, NC: Duke University Press.
Rankin, Jerry (2014). Personal communication with the author.
Scott, Jacquelyn Thayer, and Pelley, Bob (2010). 'Cape Breton's Celtic Colours

International Festival: Building Social and Economic Capital Island-Wide Through a Cultural Social Enterprise Initiative'. Paper available from URL: http://www.creativemuskoka.ca/uploads/8/1/4/1/8141704/scott__pelley_cape_breton_celtic_festival_presented_at_moneison_centre_nov_19_2010.pdf (accessed 31.8.14).

13

Selling a language to save it? The business-oriented promotion of Gaelic and Irish

Sara C. Brennan, Michael Danson and Bernadette O'Rourke
Heriot-Watt University

Introduction

In this paper we will be discussing current efforts to promote the use of Gaelic and Irish within the private business sectors of Scotland and the Republic of Ireland. Business-oriented promotional initiatives represent a developing advocacy direction for both languages, though in differing respects. Declared the national language of an independent Ireland in 1922, Irish has been the object of State-led language policy and planning efforts comprising two objectives since the 1920s: maintenance in the Gaeltacht, the Government-defined, geographically delimited Irish-speaking regions of Ireland; and restoration in the rest of the country (see Ó Riagáin, 1997; Ó Laoire, 2005; Mac Giolla Chríost, 2005; Ó hIfearnáin, 2010; O'Rourke, 2011). Whilst the Official Languages Act 2003 established regulations concerning the use of Irish in public bodies throughout the Republic, initiatives targeting the private sector have been primarily devoted to supporting economic growth in the industrially underdeveloped Gaeltacht areas (see Walsh, 2011). In Scotland, on the other hand, Gaelic has historically rarely been the object of explicit state language policy or coordinated language planning efforts (Dunbar, 2010, pp. 152–3; see also McLeod, 2001). The passage of the Gaelic Language (Scotland) Act 2005 then constituted a major milestone by officially recognising Gaelic as an official language of Scotland and outlining language policy and planning objectives designed to promote the use of Gaelic within public bodies (see McLeod, 2001, 2006a; Dunbar, 2010).

Comparative research by Walsh and McLeod (2008) has looked at the implications of the Gaelic Language Act of 2005 and the Official Languages Act 2003 for language revitalisation by examining the measures which public bodies were expected to implement in order to increase their bilingual service provision. They argued that, for this legislation to have a significant linguistic impact, careful strategies were needed to equip speakers of Gaelic and Irish to use their languages in relation to public services, given the dominance of English in these domains. They suggested that strategies were needed to effectively deploy bilingual staff and warned that, without careful planning, there would be a risk that these enactments would not lead to any meaningful changes in terms of language practice. In the case of Irish in particular, Walsh (2012) has argued that the dominance of the ideology of the 'few words' (*cúpla focal*) underlying Irish language policy has influenced the extent to which symbolic aspects are prioritised over the more far-reaching and costly provisions, with the consequence of policy having only limited impact on increased language use.

By focusing specifically on private business, the present paper will examine a sector which is not compelled to adhere to state policies concerning the incorporation of Gaelic or Irish language services, including the Gaelic Language Act of 2005 and the Official Languages Act 2003. Falling outside the scope of such legislation, the integration and use of Gaelic and Irish in the private sector is instead encouraged by bottom-up initiatives put in place by language advocates, such as the Irish-language promotion organisation that will be studied here. This case study will focus on the efforts of a community language advocacy organisation to promote the use of Irish in business in its local urban area located outside the Gaeltacht. As we will discuss, such business-focused initiatives often foreground the commodifiable authenticity of these minority Celtic languages, particularly as a way of attracting increased tourism and investment. In examining the dynamics of a business-oriented approach to the promotion of Gaelic and Irish, we will seek to address the following questions: what do such initiatives achieve in terms of contributing in any meaningful way to the process of language revitalisation? Can they foster real changes in language practice, or – as it has seemed to be the case in the context of public sector legislation – do they prioritise symbolic usage of the languages over more costly service provision?

In order to address these questions, we will first briefly review the concept of a business-oriented approach to language advocacy, with the evolving relationship between economic development policy and minority language in Scotland serving as an example. We will also review the notion of Celtic authenticity, as this elusive (and valuable) quality is frequently presented to Scottish and Irish business communities as the key to reaping economic benefits through the use of minority languages, particularly through tourism. We will then turn to our examination of specific business-focused initiatives in these two countries, with a focus on new government-commissioned research in Scotland and local language promotion efforts in Ireland.

Business-oriented promotion of minority languages

Before looking at the specifics of the Gaelic and Irish initiatives studied here, it would be useful to briefly outline what we mean by business-oriented approaches and how these have developed in minority language contexts. The evolution of attitudes to minority languages and economic development policy can be illustrated by reference to the Scottish example. For a long period, even with the establishment in 1965 of the Highlands and Islands Development Board – the regional development agency for the region (now replaced by Highlands and Islands Enterprise) – there was no recognition, real appreciation nor promotion of Gaelic as an economic asset (Chalmers and Danson, 2011). Indeed, there was a continuing belief that the language was an anachronism, irrelevant to the modern economy (McLeod, 2006b). The uneven development within the Highlands and Islands was especially noticeable in the decline of the Hebrides and western seaboard – the Gaelic heartland – and the lack of modernity associated with the persistence of the language was often seen as contributing to its lagging performance. Of the different and competing rationales used to explain these beliefs as well as the official attitudes to addressing the potential of minority languages in social and economic development expressed by policymakers and practitioners, Walsh (2009) contrasts two in particular:

> The *Socio-cultural Development Approach*: embedding support within wider human development, making the connection to empowerment, self-confidence, social cohesion, initiative and participation.

And the competing and contrary rationale:

> *The Economic Growth and Modernisation Approach*: though this is seen as negative, with only global languages to be encouraged (Walsh, 2009).

Within the general context of the 1980s' transition towards endogenous growth, based on local indigenous firms and skills, there was a move towards the former approach across many regions and communities (McLeod, 2001). The Scottish 'Business Birth Rate Strategy' led in the strategic analysis of seeking to raise the rate of new firm formation, especially amongst women, the young, council house residents and other groups with apparent low levels of entrepreneurship (Lloyd and Danson, 2013). The theoretical and empirical rationales underpinning this approach were consistent with Walsh's emphasis on building confidence and empowering the poor to become enterprising (Walsh, 2009), as this quote captures:

There was also some recognition that the low levels of economic development, despite above average financial and other incentives, stemmed partly from a lack of self-confidence in the Gaelic-speaking communities, based on the low status of the Gaelic language and culture which had resulted in a 'powerful debilitating effect on community self-confidence' ... it was 'no coincidence that the Gaelic speaking areas have been among the most difficult in which to stimulate entrepreneurship and development' (Chalmers, 2010, p. 62, quoting Bòrd Leasachaidh na Gàidhealtachd is nan Eilean, 1989).

In this environment, the language economist François Grin has similarly presented contrasting paradigms to explore the reasons to promote language and economic development jointly. In particular these include: raising productivity through applying bilingual/minority language skills (firm, market and management paradigm); protecting sustainability through language diversity (development paradigm); realising economic impact benefits (language sector and multiplier paradigm); and applying the public good argument (welfare paradigm) (Grin, 2009). Deindustrialisation and the replacement of top-down regional and industrial policies with endogenous, internal strategies therefore were intensifying the pressures to consider a more positive official attitude to the potential role of minority languages in economic development. So, by the late 1980s, there were the first suggestions that an alternative to the depressing scenario of minority languages dying in failing local economies might be possible, with a linking of enterprise, confidence and Gaelic offered as key. This justified a change to policy and practice and a need to identify 'development of the Gaelic language and culture as a means of raising self-confidence and stimulating economic and social development' (Lingard et al., 1993: p. 1).

As Willie Roe, the former Chair of Highland and Islands Enterprise (HIE), argued in 2005 at the launch of the Gaelic Arts Strategy:

Placing more value on, and investing in, the native language and cultural traditions of the region will result in fortifying cultural identity and sense of place, increasing confidence and self-esteem. This in turn can lead to population retention, inward migration, greater entrepreneurial activity, business creation and ultimately higher GDP. Quite simply, at HIE we believe that there is a direct link between levels of confidence and levels of economic activity and economic growth (reported by Chalmers, 2010, p. 64).

These recommendations of the late 1980s and early 1990s have recently been explored in the report published by Highlands and Islands Enterprise on the

Economic and Social Value of Gaelic as an Asset (which will be discussed in more detail later on).

As seen in other minority language situations (Grin, 2009), there has thus been a notable policy-level shift in Scotland in discourse on the relationship between Gaelic and the economy, and with business in particular. Whereas Gaelic was once viewed as irrelevant or even detrimental to the modern Scottish economy, there is now recognition of how beneficial investing in Scotland's Gaelic language and culture can be to economic development.

Language, tourism, and Celtic authenticity

As much recent sociolinguistic literature attests, one of the most prominent ways in which language and culture are mobilised to stimulate economic development and growth within the contemporary globalised economy is through tourism (see the special issue of the *Journal of Sociolinguistics* edited by Heller et al. (Vol. 18, No. 4), 2014, for a comprehensive review). Ranking amongst the world's largest industries, tourism 'mobilize[s] modernist markers of social difference as resources for generating the kind of 'authenticity' which guarantees the value of distinctive products' – and one of those markers is often language, and 'local' or minority languages in particular (Heller, Jaworski and Thurlow, 2014, pp. 430–31; see also, e.g., Coupland & Coupland, 2014; Moriarty, 2014; Duchêne and Heller, 2011; Pietikäinen and Kelly-Holmes, 2011; Pujolar, 2006; Coupland et al., 2005).

In line with such analyses, Gaelic and Irish are both frequently mobilised in the generation and marketisation of an authentic 'Celticity'. Scotland and particularly Ireland effectively constitute the centres of the Celtic periphery that also includes Wales, Cornwall, and Brittany (Kneafsey, 2002, p. 133), and the notion of a 'homogenous Celticity' has long emerged from 'the historical relationship between the peripheral Celtic lands and a hegemonic, non-Celtic core' (Harvey et al., 2002, p. 10; see also Lilley, 2002; Brown, 2006). This dichotomy can be succinctly distinguished as follows:

> Saxon culture [...] is predicated on order, rigour, rationality, rectitude, reasoning, pragmatism, utilitarianism, materialism and industrialization. Celtic culture, by contrast, is wild, free, tempestuous, imaginative, spiritual, spontaneous, irrational, whimsical, mystical and agrarian (Brown, 2006, p. 7).

Whilst this dichotomy may originally have been mobilised in justifying British territorial claims (see Lilley, 2002), the traits it ascribed to the Celts are now fundamental to the market appeal of 'authentic' Celticity. Harvey et al. (2002) assert that a Celtic renaissance has developed over the past few decades as a form of 'place-based reaction' to the processes of globalisation and modernity (Harvey et al., 2002, p. 8), with Celticity valued as a counterpoint to 'a world of urbanization, industrialization, bureaucratization, secularization, cosmopolitanization and supposed civilization, a mechanized world that had lost touch with nature, spirituality, authenticity and tradition' (Brown, 2006, p. 5). The romanticised traits of the Celts that had once marked them as 'anything but business-like' (Brown, 2006, p. 7) are thus exactly the characteristics that currently make Celticity so good for business. Amongst the signs used to evoke this now highly marketable 'spatial, temporal and cultural peripherality' are the Celtic languages, which are often used to evoke the 'otherness' of the Celtic lands and their inhabitants (Kneafsey, 2002, pp. 132, 135).

Language promotion and economic development in Scotland and Ireland

In the following two sections, we will finally turn to a discussion of the business-oriented promotion of Gaelic and Irish in Scotland and Ireland. First addressing the Scottish context, we will focus on the findings of a comprehensive report entitled *Ar Stòras Gàidhlig: Economic and Social Value of Gaelic as an Asset* that was commissioned by Highlands and Islands Enterprise in partnership with Bòrd na Gàidhlig, Creative Scotland, Scottish Natural Heritage, Highland Council, Argyll and Bute Council, and Comhairle nan Eilean Siar and published by Highlands and Islands Enterprise in 2014. In looking at this text, we will present some of the current arguments linking support for the Gaelic language in the private sector with increased economic development. We will then examine the business-oriented promotional initiative of a local Irish language advocacy organisation in Ireland, thereby exploring how discourses concerning the relationship between minority Celtic languages and economic growth are translated into practical measures and implemented on the ground.

Business-oriented promotion of Gaelic
As signalled in the earlier quote from Willie Roe, Scotland's Highlands and Islands Enterprise has increasingly recognised the need to generate economic development in order to create new jobs and business in these regions, and that the growth of the cultural and creative industries would be most beneficial for the circumstances of the Gàidhealtachd. Whilst the low levels of economic development in the Highlands and Islands were at least partially attributed to the lack of confidence stemming from the low esteem and status of the Gaelic language, there have been many recent reports on the potential role of Gaelic arts and culture in recognising and addressing this negativity (see Gaelic

Review Group, 1982; Sproull and Ashcroft, 1993; Pedersen, 1993; Chalmers, 2003; Chalmers, 2010; Westbrook et al., 2010; Chalmers and Danson, 2011). These have demonstrated that the arts and culture – including the language – can instead help reverse the decline of the economy, potentially rendering business development in these sectors (as well as in leisure and education) a key element of sustainable growth. The aim of this research was to consider, evaluate and evidence the current and potential use of Gaelic as an asset to the economy and society of the Highlands and Islands and Scotland. As prefaced by the former Chair of HIE a decade ago:

> Our investment in Gaelic language and Gaelic arts and culture not only brings about the direct creation of employment in the Gaelic sector, jobs which are largely based in the Highlands and Islands, but represents an investment in the seedbed of the cultural and creative sector ... Increased cultural vibrancy and nurturing a 'creative cluster' make the area more attractive as a location, helping drive economic growth. Gaelic not only plays an essential and crucial part in this, but it also helps reinforce the culture of sustainable development across the region, which is at the heart of everything we do at HIE (Willie Roe, speaking at the launch of the Gaelic Arts Project, reported by Chalmers, 2010, p. 64).

The report commissioned by HIE and partners thus concluded that:

> The problems facing Gaelic as a minority language within a context of majority English use are not limited to Gaelic alone, but are encountered by other minority languages such as Welsh and Irish. Despite this, a positive framework can be developed around a 'linguistic political economy of development' where language, culture and development can co-exist positively and work with each other (DC Research, 2014, p. 2).

Overall, the study by DC Research revealed that Gaelic was most often found to be critically important to enterprises in the creative industries sectors (e.g. music, art, design, performance, theatre, media, publishing, digital/ICT), as well as to those in the heritage and learning sectors. A range of advantages were found to accrue to enterprises that actively used Gaelic in the market place; these included 'enhancing *distinctiveness/uniqueness* of products and services, enhancing perceptions of *authenticity and provenance*, and *increasing appeal* of products/services to *target markets*' (DC Research, 2014, pp. 52–3).

Given the context of a declining economy and demographic challenges in the Gàidhealtachd, there has been a growing acknowledgement that employment and enterprise are crucial in the drive to develop Gaelic, more than the use of Gaelic on its own can help to drive the economy (DC Research, 2014; Chalmers and Danson, 2011). This has been driven by the importance of the normalisation of the language, including the use of Gaelic by businesses, but also more generally in the media, education (especially through Gaelic-medium education), and in wider society (DC Research, 2014, p. 5). These studies have generated evidence to support the contention that there would be feedback from firms and organisations using Gaelic into the local population and entrepreneurs, thereby positively reinforcing the impacts of confidence, self-esteem and local demand and multiplier effects within Gaelic-speaking communities.

Thus the argument from Williams (1988, p. 279) in Ireland that there is a clear and demonstrable link between the survival of a minority language and the economy – 'no jobs, no people; no people, no Gaeltacht' – seems to be borne out through the identification of positive synergies between economic development and language development. This is not a simple association, however, but rather a complex and nuanced relationship as suggested a decade ago: 'culture could play a critical role in human development through its effect on identity and confidence, and even its job creation aspects and marketability' (Chalmers, 2003, p. 23).

Nevertheless, and partly reflecting the long-established negativity towards the language amongst some local and incoming entrepreneurs, there remains much potential for exploiting Gaelic in the marketplace. In the traditional Gàidhealtachd of the Hebrides and North-West Highlands, where the population has been declining and ageing and living standards have remained persistently well below the Scottish and UK averages (Chalmers and Danson, 2011), the promise of economic expansion would be especially welcome. The estimated potential economic value to the Scottish economy of Gaelic as an asset in the three growth sectors of creative industries, food & drink and sustainable tourism could be in the region of between £81.6 million and £148.5 million (DC Research, 2014, p. 10). As these are the main sectors in which private businesses are located in the Gàidhealtachd regions, the opportunities to nurture and grow the economy and community appear obvious.

Notable in confirming the reappraisal and appreciation of the economic and private business role now afforded to the language, Highlands and Islands Enterprise has been presenting a 'Gaelic as an Economic Asset Award' in a national annual awards ceremony 'to recognise progress made by a business or social enterprise in realising the economic value of Gaelic' (Scottish Gaelic Awards, 2014). This is scored in terms of measured added value which can be attributed to the use of Gaelic as an asset, and is expected to be associated with creative industries, food and drink, tourism, commercial provision of language acquisition or any other innovative use of Gaelic. As these awards receive widespread coverage in both the Gaelic and business world, the profile of the language is raised and reinforced within both spheres of Scottish life.

Nevertheless, this situation highlights the continuing implicit tension between the dual objectives of economic development and minority language maintenance (Macleod, 2009; MacKinnon, 1992, 1997; Fishman, 1990), with strong debate still surrounding whether commodification of the language is a price worth paying and a feasible means to regenerate its use in everyday life. A parallel objective of the recent studies has been to explore the implications of these competing forms of economic and business development for Gaelic in the community and home. While there have been some partisan positions taken, especially within academia, the general support from communities, government agencies and non-departmental public bodies (NDPBs) (as evidenced in DC Research, 2014) and in the approval of their recommendations from these organisations for more investment and promotion of use of the language in business (see the endorsement in Highlands and Islands Enterprise, 2014) suggests the dominant approach is for further business-oriented promotion of Gaelic.

Indeed, it is explicitly highlighted in the current operating plan (HIE, 2015), where there are strategic efforts to integrate policies proactively across culture, enterprise and community development, thereby bringing together 'sectoral work on creative industries, food and drink, and tourism, with ... work to enhance the use of Gaelic as an asset, support for crofting community development, as well as other community-led cultural activities' (HIE, 2015, p. 10). In partnership with communities, local authorities and other business and social development agencies, the focus of HIE – 'Building the capacity of communities and in support of community asset ownership which often underpins sustainability and growth aspirations, including support for Gaelic' (HIE, 2015, p. 16) – is consistent then with the *Socio-cultural Development Approach* (Walsh, 2009). Embedding this further, a Gaelic resource development officer for HIE in the Hebrides has been appointed 'to develop an action plan for proactive activities to support clients to grow the use and value of Gaelic in their organisations, adding value to their business and local economy',[1] while there is a commitment in the HIE Gaelic Language Plan (Highlands and Islands Enterprise 2012) with an emphasis on realising the potential commercial and business elements of the language and a focus on fragile areas and crofting communities.

Business-oriented promotion of Irish

Our Irish case study focuses on language advocates in Ballyroe (*Baile Rua* in Irish),[2] a small town situated in the west of the Republic of Ireland, and how they have adopted business-oriented approaches as part of a broader revitalisation agenda for the language. The business-oriented promotion initiative that is the object of our study is run by Baile Rua le Gaeilge ('Ballyroe with Irish'), a community language-development partnership based in Ballyroe, which lies outside the Gaeltacht – at least as currently defined. Based on interviews with members of this organisation, the overarching goal of Baile Rua le Gaeilge is to promote and support the use of Irish in Ballyroe and its surrounding county in view of achieving the Irish Language Network status proposed by the Gaeltacht Act 2012. This Act, which represented the first significant piece of legislation in which the concept of Gaeltacht was broadened to explicitly include Irish speakers beyond the geopolitically-delimited territorial space of the Gaeltacht, included provisions for currently non-Gaeltacht areas to be recognised as Irish-speaking communities participating in cross-country language networks.

As part of their overall promotion of Irish within their local community, Baile Rua le Gaeilge launched a specifically business-oriented initiative in the early 2010s. Describing how the initiative came about, Eoin (the development officer of the organisation) explained that the mandate of Baile Rua le Gaeilge was to promote Irish, and that the organisation had been happy with their results in terms of education and culture through organising festivals and helping with language classes. Having an impact on business, however, had proved much harder; as he put it, they 'needed to come up with a strategy that would cajole, convince, in Irish *plámás*, 'to convince with charm', people to be part of this'. Further detailing their strategy, Mícheál (the chief architect behind the initiative) described how the members of Baile Rua le Gaeilge recognised from the start that 'when you're approaching business people, you have to approach them from a business point of view,' so the initiative had to be 'business-driven.' 'There was no use in the worldwide,' he added, 'in [...] saying to business people that we wanted to do this because of language promotion'. The initiative was thus designed to highlight the marketing advantages of Irish as its driving argument. Moreover, the initiative was specifically represented as a strategy for using the Irish language to contribute to their local urban area's economic regeneration in the wake of the 2008 financial crisis in Ireland. In line with this strategy, the use of Irish in business was portrayed as a 'value for money exercise,' in the words of Mícheál, where 'despite the fact that there was no investment or subscription required,' a shop or business would 'see a return on it'.

In order to then substantiate the promoted marketing advantages and the economic return of using Irish in business in this non-Gaeltacht area, Baile Rua le Gaeilge tapped into contemporary discourses on the value of language as a source of cultural authenticity. More specifically, their initiative linked commercial Irish to increased numbers of visitors and shoppers being attracted to the town: Irish was represented as enhancing Ballyroe's existing tourism image as a bastion of traditional, timeless Ireland known for its traditional music, old narrow streets and locally owned shops. As Baile Rua le Gaeilge explained on their website, the use of Irish in business would strengthen this image: commercial Irish would 'raise the local and national profile of [Ballyroe] as a centre of excellence in [the] promotion of traditional culture including music, dance and language, making it a more attractive visitor destination.' Thus rather than framing this initiative as a matter of language promotion, the organisation transforms the commercial use of Irish into a question of tourism, place branding, and increased revenue flowing into the town – which constitutes a strategically convincing argument in favour of Irish in a post-crisis Ireland where tourism is one of the main drivers of economic activity.

This initiative does not, however, advocate just any use of Irish in business. Based on interviews with members of Baile Rua le Gaeilge and local business owners affiliated with them, this business-oriented initiative has effectively adopted an almost exclusively visual orientation to the commercial use of Irish, and has done so for a number of reasons. In terms of making the initiative 'business-driven', visual Irish-English bilingualism is more easily made cost-effective: becoming a 'bilingual business' becomes a matter of hanging the free bilingual signs provided by the organisation or including some Irish on menus when reprinting them, rather than being a question of providing language training for staff or hiring an Irish-speaking worker. Commercial bilingualism in this visual form thus becomes 'low-cost' or even 'no-cost' and potentially renders Irish accessible to all members of the business community. Indeed, as Baile Rua le Gaeilge's informational booklet proclaims, 'we strongly believe that the Irish language can be a great advantage to every type of business in various ways, even if you don't have fluent Irish!' Thus with the support system offered by the organisation, business owners with very little Irish, or possibly even no Irish, are enabled to run a 'bilingual business' at minimal cost, in terms of either money or time.

Beyond calculations of cost and benefit, the visual orientation espoused by the initiative also seems to address the linguistic insecurities, social anxieties, and bad memories that are still often attached to speaking Irish. Eoin and Mícheál both characterised the initiative's approach as 'softly, softly' and emphasised the fun, voluntary, and low-demand nature of participation in it, thereby distancing the initiative from the compulsory Irish of the education system that left so many students of previous generations scarred by their forced encounter with the language. Other subjects were of course compulsory in school, but we would suggest that the negative associations attached to Irish in particular reflect the argument that anxieties about language are in fact often an expression of other sorts of anxiety relating to social difference, social order, social change, and (unequal) access to job markets (see Cameron, 1995, 2000).

Similarly, several business owners affiliated with the initiative emphasised the complex relationship between spoken Irish and questions of customer comfort and even fear. They did not want to make their customers uncomfortable by imposing the language upon them and touching on bad memories from school or insecurities surrounding linguistic proficiency. As put by one business owner in particular, members of the business community did not want to risk instilling 'the fear' in customers by addressing them in Irish and putting them in the position of responding. The emphasis on visual commercial bilingualism thus enabled business owners to integrate Irish whilst avoiding the complex sociolinguistic dynamics of speaking the language.

Spoken Irish is of course not entirely left out of the initiative, but it is seemingly marginalised. Currently, the primary spoken-language strategy aimed at business owners is the provision of little cards or flyers with Irish greetings and phrases accompanied by their phonetic transcriptions. This material, however, is more oriented towards helping both business owners and visitors with little to no Irish try the language out and have fun with it rather than towards supporting a full conversation or commercial interaction through Irish. The oral use of the language is thus portrayed as a relatively less integral element of commercial bilingualism. Whilst representing something of a departure from the long history of State-led Irish-language policy and planning, which has (at least officially) sought to maintain or revitalise Irish as a community language, this strategy seeks to render Irish as accessible – and affordable – as possible for the business community of Ballyroe.

The members of Baile Rua le Gaeilge did indeed express a desire to more fully integrate spoken Irish into the business-oriented initiative, but acknowledged that incorporating Irish as a communicative means for business interactions would be more costly both in terms of promotion and support on the part of the organisation, and implementation on the part of the businesses. For the time being, the emphasis thus remains on a largely visual bilingualism with symbolic or tokenistic spoken aspects.

Concluding remarks

Whilst such business-oriented approaches can be seen to draw on discourses concerning the added value and market differentiation of a minority language, this approach often tends to favour the foregrounding of commercial bilingualism, rather than the use of the language on its own. The promoted form of bilingualism is largely visual, with oral language mostly restricted to tokenistic or symbolic phrases and greetings. Bilingualism in this form is in contrast with active bilingualism, which involves increased use of the spoken language, be this on an individual or societal level.

This commercial bilingualism, however, allows businesses to minimise the costs of integrating the minority language (by printing bilingual signage rather than paying for language lessons, for example) whilst maximising its benefits (i.e. visually capitalising on the language's Celtic authenticity whilst maintaining tourist- and investor-friendly Anglophone practices). As such, promoting the minority language can become a cost-effective and non-loss-making venture, thus encouraging buy-in from the business community.

Whilst it could be said that the tokenistic approach of bilingualism in business contexts does not lead to any perceived increase in active use of the language (or may indeed generate cynicism towards the language and its use; see, for example, Kelly-Holmes (2005)), the status-enhancing effect of the visibility provided by similar initiatives – particularly those directed towards tourists – is well-documented in minority language research (e.g. Kallen, 2009; Pujolar and Jones, 2011).[3] Indeed, many other language planning initiatives for Gaelic and Irish – including Gaelic or Irish-medium television – could also be seen to have limited effect in terms of increasing an active Gaelic- or Irish-speaking population. Nevertheless, the presence of Gaelic and Irish in these new spaces (from which the languages previously had been absent) changes how the language is perceived. Linguistic landscape studies in minority language contexts have also shown the positive effect of the visibility of these languages in public spaces, albeit through official bilingual signage etc., which – whilst again potentially can be seen as tokenistic – can have an effect on the value and perceived status of such languages. It should be pointed out that the business initiative promoted through Baile Rua le Gaeilge's project is just one component in a larger language planning initiative on the part of this Irish language movement that includes more explicit efforts to increase active use of the language. These include support for local Gaelscoileanna, summer colleges for teenagers to learn Irish, support for pre-school initiatives to encourage parents to use Irish with their children, and conversation classes for adults.

In asking the question regarding whether or not business-oriented approaches contribute in any meaningful way to the revitalisation of minority languages, we also of course need to re-think what is actually meant by revitalisation in the first place and to move away from previous interpretations, which have tended to emphasise returning to a previous situation of generalised linguistic usage or to a linguistic form that has ideally remained unchanged (see King, 2001; Romaine, 2006; Jaffe, 2011). The seemingly insignificant tokenistic forms of revitalisation such as those promoted through business initiatives have brought minority languages into new spaces and to new types of users and – perhaps most importantly – to a group of users such as the business community which was often antagonistic towards or at best indifferent to the use of minority languages.

Endnotes

1   www.scotgrad.co.uk/companies/h/highlands-and-islands-enterprise-hie/placements/gaelic-resource-development-officer-aytndxmdpl (accessed 13.8.2015)
2   In adherence with the ethical requirements of the ongoing fieldwork that these analyses draw upon, the names of all organizations, people, and places in the Irish case study have been rendered anonymous.
3   As described by Heller (2003, 2010), minority languages are frequently invested with new – though not always unproblematic – value through their integration into the globalised contemporary economy by virtue of their ability to authenticate, and thus differentiate, products or services on saturated markets and to aid in the construction of niche markets.

Bibliography

Bòrd Leasachaidh na Gaidhealtachd is nan Eilean (1989). 'Public infrastructure and entrepreneurship – The case of the Scottish Highlands and Islands'. Paper presented at OECD Conference on Enterprise and Employment Creation in Rural Areas, Paris.

Brown, Stephen (2006). 'Tiocfaidh ár lá: introduction to the special issue'. *Journal of Strategic Marketing*, Vol. 14, No. 1, pp. 1–9.

Cameron, Deborah (1995). *Verbal Hygiene*. London and New York: Routledge.

Cameron, Deborah (2000). *Good To Talk? Living and Working in a Communication Culture*. London: Sage.

Chalmers, Douglas (2003) The Economic Impact of Gaelic Arts and Culture. Unpublished PhD thesis, Glasgow Caledonian University.

Chalmers, Douglas (2010). 'The need to integrate policy and good practice – a decade of empirical evidence', in Gillian Munro and Iain Mac an Tàilleir (eds.), Coimhearsnachdan Gàidhlig An-diugh/Gaelic Communities Today, pp. 61–72. Edinburgh: Dunedin Academic Press.

Chalmers, Douglas, and Danson, Mike (2011). 'The economic impact of Gaelic arts and culture within Glasgow: minority languages and post-industrial cities', in Anne Lorentzen and Bas van Heur (eds) (2011) *Cultural Political Economy of Small Cities*, pp. 95–110. Abingdon: Routledge.

Coupland, Bethan, and Coupland, Nikolas (2014). 'The authenticating discourses of mining heritage tourism in Cornwall and Wales'. *Journal of Sociolinguistics*, Vol. 18, No. 4, pp. 495–517.

Coupland, Nikolas, Garrett, Peter, and Bishop, Hywel (2005). 'Wales underground: discursive frames and authenticities in Welsh mining heritage tourism events', in Adam Jaworski and Anne Pritchard (eds.), *Discourse, Communication and Tourism*, pp. 199–222. Clevedon: Channel View,

DC Research (2014). *Ar Stòras Gàidhlig: Economic and Social Value of Gaelic as an Asset (Final Report May 2014)*. Inverness: Highlands and Islands Enterprise.

Duchêne, Alexandre, and Heller, Monica (eds) (2012). *Language in Late Capitalism: Pride and Profit*. London and New York: Routledge.

Dunbar, Robert (2010). 'Language Planning', in Watson and Macleod (eds), pp. 146–71.

Fishman, Joshua A. (1990). 'What is reversing language shift (RLS) and how can it succeed?' *Journal of Multilingual and Multicultural Development*, Vol. 11, pp. 5–35.

Gaelic Review Group (1982). Cor na Gàidhlig: Language, Community and Development: The Gaelic Situation, Inverness: Highlands and Islands Development Board.

Grin, François (2009). 'Promoting language through the economy: competing paradigms', in Kirk and Ó Baoill (eds) (2009), pp. 1–12.

Harvey, David C., et al. (eds) (2002a). *Celtic Geographies: Old Culture, New Times*. London & New York: Routledge.

Harvey, David C. (2002b). 'Timing and spacing Celtic geographies', in Harvey et al. (2002a), pp. 1–17.

Heller, Monica (2003). 'Globalization, the New Economy, and the Commodification of Language and Identity'. *Journal of Sociolinguistics*, Vol. 7, pp. 473–92.

Heller, Monica (2010). 'The Commodification of Language'. *Annual Review of Anthropology*, Vol. 39, pp. 101–14.

Heller, Monica, Jaworski, Adam and Thurlow, Crispin (2014). 'Introduction: Sociolinguistics and tourism – mobilities, markets, multilingualism'. *Journal of Sociolinguistics*, Vol. 18, No. 4, pp. 425–58.

Highlands and Islands Enterprise (2012). *Ar Plana Gàidhlig: Iomairt na Gàidhealtachd 's nan Eilean 2012-15/Our Gaelic Plan: Highlands and Islands Enterprise 2012-15*. Inverness: Highlands and Islands Enterprise,

Highlands and Islands Enterprise (2014). 'Research reveals value of Gaelic to businesses and communities in Scotland'. Available from URL: www.hie.co.uk/about-hie/news-and-media/archive/research-reveals-value-of-gaelic-to-businesses-and-communities-in-scotland.html#sthash.MfnmzoOq.dpuf (accessed 14.5.2015)

Highlands and Islands Enterprise (2015). *Building Our Future – Operating Plan 2015-2018*. Inverness: Highland and Islands Enterprise.

Jaffe, Alexandra (2011). 'Critical perspectives on language-in-education policy: The Corsican example', in Teresa McCarty (ed.), *Ethnography and Language Policy*, pp. 205-30. London: Routledge.

Kallen, Jeffrey L. (2009). 'Tourism and representation in the Irish linguistic landscape', in Elan Shohamy and Durk Gorter (eds.), *Linguistic Landscape: Expanding the Scenery*, pp. 270–83. London: Routledge.

Kelly-Holmes, Helen (2005). *Advertising as Multilingual Communication*. Basingstoke & New York: Palgrave MacMillan.

King, Kendall A. (2001). *Language Revitalization Processes and Prospects: Quichua in the Ecuadorian Andes*. Clevedon: Multilingual Matters.

Kirk, John M., and Ó Baoill, Dónall P. (eds) (2009). *Language and Economic Development: Northern Ireland, the Republic of Ireland, and Scotland*. Belfast: Cló Ollscoil na Banríona.

Kneafsey, Moya (2002). 'Tourism images and the construction of Celticity in Ireland and Brittany', in Harvey et al. (eds.) (2002a), pp. 123–38.

Lilley, Keith D. (2002). 'Imagined geographies of the "Celtic fringe" and the cultural construction of the "Other" in medieval Wales and Ireland', in Harvey et al. (eds.) (2002a), pp. 21–36.

Lingard, R. A., Pedersen, Roy N., and Shaw, John W. (1993). *Iomairt na Gàidhlig: A Strategy for Gaelic Development in the Highlands and Islands of Scotland*. Inverness: Highlands and Islands Enterprise.

Lloyd, Greg, and Danson, Mike (2013). 'Beyond devolution: roads to coherent autonomies?' *Environment & Planning C*, Vol. 30, No. 1, pp. 78–94.

Mac Giolla Chríost, Diarmait (2005). *The Irish Language in Ireland: From Goídel to Globalisation*. London & New York: Routledge.

MacKinnon, Kenneth (2010). 'The Gaelic language-group: Demography, language-usage, transmission and shift', in Watson and Macleod (eds) (2010), pp. 128–45.

MacKinnon, Kenneth (1997). 'Gaelic as an endangered language – Problems and prospects'. Paper presented at Workshop on Endangered Languages: Steps in Language Rescue, University of York.

Macleod, Michelle (2009). 'Gaelic language skills in the workplace', in Kirk and Ó Baoill (2009), pp. 134–52.

McLeod, Wilson (2006a). 'Gaelic in contemporary Scotland: Contradictions, challenges and strategies'. Available from URL: www.poileasaidh.celtscot.ed.ac.uk/MCLEODCATALAN2.pdf (accessed 14.5.2015)

McLeod, Wilson (2006b). 'Securing the Status of Gaelic: Implementing the Gaelic Language Act 2005'. *Scottish Affairs*, No. 57, pp. 19–38.

McLeod, Wilson (2001). 'Gaelic in the New Scotland: Politics, Rhetoric and Public Discourse'. *Journal on Ethnopolitics and Minority Issues in Europe*, pp. 1–33.

Moriarty, Máiréad (2014). 'Contesting language ideologies in the linguistic landscape of an Irish tourist town'. *International Journal of Bilingualism*, Vol. 18, pp. 464–77.

Ó hIfearnáin, Tadhg (2010). 'Irish-speaking Society and the State', in Martin J. Ball and Nicole Müller (eds) (2nd edn 2010), *The Celtic Languages*, pp. 539–86. London & New York: Routledge.

Ó Laoire, Muiris (2005). 'The language planning situation in Ireland'. *Current Issues in Language Planning*, Vol. 6, No. 3, pp. 251–314.

Ó Riagáin, Pádraig (1997). *Language Policy and Social Reproduction: Ireland 1893-1993*. Oxford: Clarendon Press.

O'Rourke, Bernadette (2011). *Galician and Irish in the European Context: Attitudes towards Weak and Strong Minority Languages*. Basingstoke: Palgrave MacMillan.

Pedersen, Roy N. (1993). *The Dynamics of Gaelic Development*. Inverness: Highlands and Islands Enterprise.

Pietikäinen, Sari, and Kelly-Holmes, Helen (2011). 'The local political economy of languages in a Sámi tourism destination: Authenticity and mobility in the labelling of souvenirs'. *Journal of Sociolinguistics*, Vol. 15, pp. 323–46.

Pujolar, Joan (2006). *Language, Culture and Tourism: Perspectives in Barcelona and Catalonia*. Barcelona: Turisme de Barcelona.

Pujolar, Joan, and Jones, Kathryn (2011). 'Literary tourism: new appropriations of landscape and territory in Catalonia', in Duchêne and Heller (2011), pp. 93–115.

Romaine, Suzanne (2006). 'Planning for the survival of linguistic diversity'. *Language Policy*, Vol. 5, pp. 441–7.

Scottish Gaelic Awards (2014). 'Award categories' (online). Available from URL: www.scottishgaelicawards.co.uk/categories.html (accessed 14.5.2015).

Sproull, Alan, and Ashcroft, Brian (1993). *The Economics of Gaelic Language Development*. Glasgow: Glasgow Caledonian University.

Walsh, John (2009). 'Ireland's socio-economic development and the Irish language: Theoretical and empirical perspectives', in Kirk and Ó Baoill (2009), pp. 70–81.

Walsh, John (2011). *Contests and Contexts: The Irish Language and Ireland's Socio-Economic Development*. Bern: Peter Lang.

Walsh, John (2012). 'Language policy and language governance: A case-study of Irish language legislation'. *Language Policy*, Vol. 11, pp. 323–41.

Walsh, John, and McLeod, Wilson (2008). 'An overcoat wrapped around an invisible man? Language legislation and language revitalisation in Ireland and Scotland'. *Language Policy*, Vol. 7, pp. 21–46.

Watson, Moray, and Macleod, Michelle (eds) (2010). *The Edinburgh Companion to the Gaelic Language*. Edinburgh: Edinburgh University Press.

Westbrook, Steve, et al. (2010). *The Economic and Social Impacts of the Fèisean*. Inverness: Highlands and Islands Enterprise.

Williams, Colin (1988). 'Language planning and regional development: Lessons from the Irish Gaeltacht', in Colin Williams (ed.), *Language in Geographic Context*, pp. 267–302. Clevedon: Multilingual Matters.

14

Camanachd – fada bharrachd na dìreach gèam

Grant Jarvie agus Ùisdean MacIllInnein
Oilthigh Dhùn Èideann

Ro-ràdh

Chan eil ach camanachd fhèin far am faodar a ràdh le ùghdarras no cinnt sam bith gu bheil an spòrs tùsanach do dh'Alba, agus le eachdraidh is dreach cultarail a tha fìor shònraichte tron cheangal leis a' Ghàidhlig. Tha camanachd air a bhith aig cridhe choimhearsnachdan an Alba bho Hiort agus na h-Eileanan Siar gu Taobh Siar Rois, sìos gu Cinn Tìre agus gu Obar Dheathain, agus an uair sin gu na bailtean mòra leithid Glaschu agus Dùn Èideann, Manchester agus Lunnainn. Tha e air a dhol bàs ge-tà air feadh a' chòrr dhen t-saoghal.

Tha luach mòr ga chur air dualchas agus cleachdaidhean na camanachd agus air na tha e a' cur ri saoghal sòisealta, eaconamach agus foghlaim na dùthcha anns an latha an-diugh. Tha am pàipear seo ag amas air dà phrìomh cheist: (i) dè an tomhas eachdraidheil agus cultarail a bu chòir a dhèanamh air camanachd an Alba agus an lùib saoghal nan eilthireach?; agus (ii) dè cho cudromach 's a tha an gèam anns an latha an-diugh, seach a bhith air a mheas dìreach mar spòrs? Carson a bu chòir dhan stàit maoin is stòras a chur ri camanachd?

Buaidh eachdraidheil agus chultarail na camanachd

Tha deagh argamaid ann airson grunn spòrs fa-leth a mheas no a thomhais 'Albannach' – cròladh, camanachd, goilf agus bòbhladh – agus tha prìomhachas gu cinnteach aig a' chiad thrì (Jarvie agus Burnett, 2000). Gan gabhail còmhla, faodar beachd a dhaingneachadh mar spòrs a tha tùsanach do dh'Alba agus thall thairis mar phàirt de stòras cultarail na dùthcha (Burnett, 1995).

Bha iad uile gu math stèidhichte mus cualas riamh mun ghluasad Shasannach 'luth-chleasachd' (*athleticism*). Ann an 1800, cha robh spòrs eile ann a bha cho follaiseach no cumanta ri cròladh air feadh na dùthcha. Cha robh goilf agus bòbhladh rim faicinn cho tric, ach tha dualchas Albannach gu math follaiseach fhathast nan lùib le faclan co-cheangailte ris an spòrs aithnichte ann am briathrachas cumanta.

Nuair a thàinig goilf gu bhith san fhasan ann an Sasainn, bhathas ag ràdh gum biodh cluicheadair proifeiseanta ann an Surrey (nach robh idir ann) a' bòstadh mun dòigh anns am biodh e a' làimhseachadh an luchd-chleachdaidh, ag ràdh:

> *I just humour them by talking like a Guild Street carter who's having a bit of backchat with an Aberdeen fishwife. It makes the profits something extraordinary* (Jarvie agus Burnett, 2000, td. 16).

Bha camanachd ga cluich, aig amannan eadar-dhealaichte, tro Bhreatainn gu lèir, ach a-mhàin, cleas na Gàidhlig, ann an Arcaibh agus Sealtainn (MacLennan, 1997, 1999). Anns an naoidheamh linn deug, bha camanachd ga cleachdadh leis na Gàidheil (cleas na Gàidhlig) mar tè de na prìomh cheanglan agus suaicheantasan cultarail a bha iad a' giùlan air feadh an t-saoghail. 'S e pàirt dhen dualchas a tha sin a th' againn fhathast tro stòras airgid, duaisean, cupannan, buinn eireachdail, phrìseil agus shònraichte, agus iad air beag luach aig a' chòrr de dh'Alba mar stòras nàiseanta. A bharrachd air a bhith nan duaisean cudromach, tha na cupannan is eile cudromach airson an cuid eachdraidh agus dualchais fhèin, na ceanglan fa leth ri buidhnean a stèidhich iad, agus an luchd-ciùird a chruthaich iad le sàr-sgilean, innleachdan agus eòlas (sportscotland, 2015).

Am measg an fheadhainn as luachmhoire agus as inntinniche tha Bhàs Littlejohn aig Oilthigh Obar Dheathain, cupa airgid, stèidhichte air samhla Ròmanach bhon cheathramh linn RC a tha air a chumail ann an Tasglann Bhurrell ann an Glaschu, le leabhran is làmh-sgrìobhainn inntinneach còmhla ris ga mhìneachadh agus a' luaidh eachdraidh na camanachd.[1]

'S e an dealbh *A Highland Landscape with a Game of Shinty* an dealbh as ainmeile agus as prìseile a th' ann gu h-eachdraidheil a' mìneachadh saoghal na camanachd. Bha an dealbh air a dhol à follais bho 1962 ach nuair a bhathas a' rannsachadh fad thrì bliadhna airson taisbeanadh aig Gailearaidh Dhealbhan Nàiseanta na h-Alba *Playing for Scotland*, lorg tè de dh'àrd-oifigearan a' Ghailearaidh an dealbh fo chùram an teaghlaich a bha air a cheannach ann an 1923 agus fhuaras cead a thaisbeanadh anns an Fhaoilleach 2015.

Tha e do-dhèanta dealbh buileach coileanta a dhèanamh air buaidh agus inbhe na camanachd tro eachdraidh an seo, ach tha grunn aithrisean ann a tha cuideachail agus cudromach (faic MacLennan 1996, 1998). Mar bhunait air clàr-ama na camanachd a dhealbh faodar ceum is tachartas no dhà a chomharrachadh a tha fìor chudromach. Tha a' chiad aithris sgrìobhte againn, far am faic sinn am facal 'shinty' an toiseach, ann an 1549 (MacLennan 1993, 1998) far

A Highland Landscape with a Game of Shinty, air ainmeachadh air David Cunliffe and A. Smith, Mauchline. Le cead Gailearaidh Nàiseanta na h-Alba.

a bheil camanachd ga chasg ann an cladh eaglaise an Glaschu; ann an 1698 rinn Màrtainn Màrtainn luaidh air muinntir Hiort ga chluich; tha dealbh cudromach againn de chamanachd ann an Sydney, Astràlia ann an 1841; chaidh a' chiad bhuidheann a stèidheachadh gu foirmeil le bun-reachd an 1851 aig Oilthigh Obar Dheathain; ann an 1893 chaidh Comann na Camanachd, buidheann-riaghlaidh an spòrs, a stèidheachadh; ann an 1924 chaidh a' chiad ghèam a chluich aig ìre eadar-nàiseanta eadar Alba agus Èirinn aig Gèamaichean Thailteann am Baile Àtha Cliath; ann an 1993 chomharraich Comann na Camanachd a' chiad ceud bliadhna aca mar bhuidhinn agus ro 2005 bha an spòrs air cruinn-leum a ghabhail gu bhith ga chluich as t-samhradh agus air a riaghladh le Bòrd-stiùiridh mar chompanaidh fo bharantas (MacLennan, 1993, td. 22; MacLennan, 1998, td. 612; Camanachd Association, 2005). Tha e cudromach dhan spòrs cuideachd a thaobh ìomhaigh agus inbhe (gun tighinn air teachd-a-steach) gu bheileas air a bhith ga chraoladh air telebhisein gu math nas trice na tha iomadach spòrs 'dualchasach' eile leis a' BhBC agus BBC Alba.

Camanachd ann an saoghal mòr na h-Alba

Cuiridh stàit sam bith stòras mu choinneamh spòrs airson iomadach adhbhar: slàinte, an eaconamaidh, neartachadh sòisealta, foghlam, adhbharan cultarail, aithne nàiseanta no eadar-nàiseanta agus turasachd. Tha uibhir de chothroman ann a bhith a' lìbhrigeadh phoileasaidhean riaghaltais tro spòrs thar raointean-obrach mhinistearan gu bheil mì-chinnt ga adhbhrachadh nuair a tha siostaman caibineit riaghaltasan a' deasbad càite am bu chòir a bhith ga làimhseachadh. Ann an Alba, tha spòrs aig a' cheart àm taobh a-staigh uallaichean slàinte agus deagh bhith-beò, agus anns an Rìoghachd Aonaichte tha e stèidhichte fo uallach Cultair, nam Meadhanan agus Spòrs. Tha na Cainèidianaich ag aithneachadh luach spòrs mar eachdraidh le bhith ga làimhseachadh ann an Roinn Dualchais Chanada, air a bhonntachadh air lagh ùr – Achd Ghnìomhan Corporra agus Spòrs, 2003.[2] Ann an deasbad ann an Taigh nam Morairean air riaghladh spòrs anns an Dùbhlachd 2014 chaidh aontachadh:

> *In summary, nothing short of a tapestry of government and political objectives became woven into the world of sport, while sport and recreation has now become an important contributor to virtually every department of state.*[3]

Tha buaidh is freumhan na camanachd a' sìneadh a-mach bho ghèam agus spòrs a-mhàin, ge-tà, agus air adhbharan dualchais agus traidiseanan, tha e fhathast na phàirt cudromach de shaoghal culturail agus sòisealta iomadach coimhearsnachd ann an Alba.

Tha ceanglan làidir gan cumail eadar cluicheadairean agus grunn aithrisean spòrs (a thaobh meud agus tomhaisean leithid àireamh), a' cumail taic ris a' phrionnsabal poileasaidh gu bheil airgead-seilbh spòrs agus poileasaidh inntinneach an co-cheangal ri spòrs coimhearsnachd, a bhith a' gabhail pàirt, ag obair gu saor-thoileach, agus co-cheanglan catharra a' togail air calpa sòisealta. Cho-dhùin measadh spòrs agus calpa sòisealta Delaney agus Keaney (2005) gu robh ceangal buadhmhor eadar a bhith an sàs ann an spòrs agus a bhith a' dèanamh rudan eile. Tha sin ri ràdh, chan ann a-mhàin an calpa cheanglan ach anns a' mheur de chalpa sòisealta a tha a' togail nan ceanglan sin mar dhrochaidean.

Cho-dhùin Delaney agus Keaney cuideachd gu robh buill ann am buidhnean spòrs nas dualtaiche a bhith a' bhòtadh, a bhith an coluadar le luchd-poileataigs, a' cur an ainmean ri athchuingean agus a bhith le tomhas nas àirde de dh'earbsa sòisealta. Tha seo a cheart cho fìor mu chamanachd 's a tha e mu spòrs eile.

Thuirt Daniel Tarschys, a bha na Rùnaire Coitcheann airson Comhairle na h-Eòrpa:

> *The hidden face of sport is also the tens of thousands of enthusiasts who find in their football, rowing, athletics and rock climbing clubs a place for meeting and exchange but above all the training ground for community life* (Jarvie le Thornton, 2012, td. 172).

Thuirt Louise Frechette, an riochdaire dioplòmasach Canèidianach a bha na Leas-Rùnaire Coitcheann air an UN airson ochd bliadhna, gu robh tòrr a bharrachd cumhachd aig spòrs na dìreach sàmhlachas. Tha spòrs a' cur air adhart conaltradh, a' slànachadh briseadh eadar dhaoine, coimhearsnachdan agus dùthchannan agus a' cuideachadh le fàs anns an eaconamaidh.[4]

Tha na tha a' gabhail pàirt ann an spòrs na naidheachd air sgàth a cheangail le slàinte ach tha na h-argamaidean mu ùrachadh sìobhalta co-cheangailte ri gluasadan agus ro-innleachdan sòisealta a cheart cho làidir. Tha e na amas aig a' bhuidheann nàiseanta spòrs sportscotland 165 ionad spòrs coimhearsnachd (*hubs*) a chruthachadh ro 2016. Tha buidhnean camanachd, gu sònraichte ann an sgìrean dùthchail agus iomallach, air a bhith a' frithealadh leithid de ghoireasan agus innleachdan ann an tòrr àiteachan (gu cudromach far a bheil Gàidhlig fhathast ga bruidhinn gu cunbhalach) airson còrr math is ceud bliadhna.

Ach bheireadh cothrom a bhith a-staigh air lìonradh na b' fharsainge neart dhan bheachd gum biodh barrachd stòrais air a chur ri camanachd a' cuideachadh le ceanglan sòisealta. Cha bhiodh ionmhas mar sin a' cumail taic ri spòrs a-mhàin ach a' caomhnadh chosgaisean eile ro-làimh, le dearbhadh gu bheil an t-ionmhas gu camanachd ag obair an co-bhuinn ri seirbheisean poblach eile mar phàirt dhen ghlaodh sòisealta a tha a' buinnig seasmhachd do chuid de choimhearsnachdan.

Tha camanachd a' tairgse meadhan do mhòran dhaoine air saoghal tarraingeach agus siùbhlach le toileachas agus modhan-labhairt a bhuinnig. Tha luchd-poileataigs agus luchd-aithris a' cleachdadh samhlaidheachd, sluagh agus beachdan-smuain a' ghèaim a shoilleireachadh mì-chinnt agus dùbhlain eile an t-saoghail. Tha daoine gu math ainmeil ann an saoghal nan ealan, leithid Billy Connolly, air a ràdh gum bu chòir camanachd aithneachadh mar spòrs nàiseanta na h-Alba, seach gu robh cùisean aig ìre cho ìosal le sgioba ball-coise na dùthcha.[5]

Tha grunn chluicheadairean ball-coise proifeiseanta leithid Dòmhnall Park agus Donnchadh Shearer bhon Ghearasdan gu math moiteil à saoghal na camanachd agus an ceangal fhèin ris. Gu dearbh, thuirt Shearer aig cuirm anns a' Ghearasdan beagan bhliadhnaichean air ais gur e nach do chluich e ann an cuairt dheireannach Cupa na Camanachd an rud a bu thàmailtiche na shaoghal mar neach-spòrs.[6]

Tha ceanglan làidir eadar ceòl, saoghal nan ealan agus camanachd – air a chleachdadh leis a' chòmhlan Runrig; ann an cuirmean a' luaidh gaisgich anns a' Chiad Chogadh, agus tha luchd-ciùil ainmeil leithid Julie Fowlis agus Gary Innes ga chur gu feum air an àrd-ùrlar gu math tric. Tha prògraman telebhisein leithid *Hamish MacBeth* air a chleachdadh agus cuideachd tha fiolmaichean eadar-nàiseanta leithid *Brave* agus *Outlander* ga chur air adhart ann an sgeulachdan no dealbhan mar shamhla air Alba no cùisean cultarail Gàidhealach.

Tha neart spòrs nas treasa na samhlachas. Tha barrachd an lùib eachdraidh na camanachd na duaisean, tachartasan agus cinn-latha nuair a thachair gnothaichean ainmeil no àraid. Tha deagh eisimpleir eile againn aig a' cheart àm is camanachd ga cleachdadh ann am pròiseact slàinte airson a bhith a' cuideachadh dhaoine le trioblaidean inntinn a tha nan tàire an iomadach coimhearsnachd. Ann an 2014, chaidh compàirteachas a stèidheachadh eadar buidheann-riaghlaidh na camanachd agus Alzheimer Scotland far a bheil co-chruinneachadh tasglainn na camanachd ga chur gu feum mar stòras airson goireasan a chruthachadh a tha gan cur an sàs le daoine a tha a' fulang le diofar ìrean de sheargadh-inntinn no dementia. Chaidh sgioba camanachd eadar-lìn a chruthachadh fon ainm 'Shinty Memories Club' fo stiùir na buidhne Alzheimer Scotland agus tha sin a-nis ga thoirt a-staigh fo bhratach nas fharsainge agus nas làidire, Lìonradh Dualchas Spòrs na h-Alba, stèidhichte aig ionad nàiseanta a' bhuill-coise aig Hampden an Glaschu, a bhios a' stiùireadh chùisean ann an diofar raointean slàinte. Bhon chiad dol-a-mach, chaidh camanachd gu math fada air thoiseach air gach spòrs eile a bha anns a' phròiseact air Facebook a thaobh bualadh air an làrach agus tadhal air an làrach-lìn.

Chaidh seataichean de 100 Cairt-Cuimhne a dheisealachadh ann an Gàidhlig agus am Beurla le maoin a fhuaras bho neach le ùidh sa ghnothach (neach gun Ghàidhlig) a bha mothachail air a' bhuaidh a bh' aca a thaobh goireas slàinte agus a bha a' tuigsinn an fheuma a bh' ann an dèanamh gu dà-chànanach.7

Cha robh e fada gus an deach dearbhadh an co-cheangal ri suidheachadh na camanachd nach robh cus theaghlaichean no sgiobaidhean ann nach robh eòlach air neach no daoine a bha fo ìmpidh a' dèiligeadh ri seargadh-inntinn. Tha mòran aig spòrs ri chur ri taic airson faothachadh do dhaoine anns an t-suidheachadh seo, agus tha camanachd air a bhith aig toiseach na h-iomairt a bhith a' dol an sàs ann an leithid de thrioblaidean inntinn ann an sluagh a tha aig mòr-aois sa chumantas. Tha an ceangal eadar camanachd agus saoghal ball-coise air a neartachadh tron phròiseact seo is taisbeanadh mu chamanachd gu bhith a' dol air adhart aig stadium nàiseanta a' Bhuill-coise, Hampden ann an Glaschu airson sia mìosan bhon Fhoghar 2015.

Tro leithid de dh'iomairtean, coluadar agus ceanglan, tha inbhe na camanachd ga h-àrdachadh agus le taic an SFA (Comann Ball-coise na h-Alba), tha na h-uibhir de bhuannachd agus de mhisneachadh ann dhan Ghàidhlig cuideachd.

Risorgimento: camanachd, ceanglan cultarail agus saorsa

Ann an seadh cumhachd 'bog', agus gu sònraichte ceanglan cultarail, tha camanachd air a bhith na drochaid agus na meadhan air coluadar eadar daoine le ceanglan ris an t-seann dhùthaich, agus cuideachd Èirinn is Alba, a dhaingneachadh. Chaidh geamaichean iomain agus camanachd a chumail air bonn-stèidh eadar-nàiseanta aig diofar ìrean bho 1924. Tha e cudromach gun tuigear carson a ghabh dà spòrs bho na h-aon freumhan slighe gu math eadar-dhealaichte tro eachdraidh, agus gu h-àraidh anns an 20mh linn, gan toirt gu far a bheil iad an-diugh.

A dh'aindeoin eachdraidh is sloinneadh nan geamaichean air a bheil *camanachd* no *iomain* againn an-diugh (biodh an eachdraidh sin fìor no fuadain), chan eil an ceangal foirmeil eadar an dà chòd ach mu 125 bliadhna a dh'aois. 'S ann nuair a bhathas a' cur gach gèam air bun-stèidh agus fo rianachd is structaran ùra aig deireadh na 19mh linn a thàinig an sgaradh. Thàinig leasachadh air an spòrs an Èirinn aig astar nach fhacas an Alba, le ìmpidh ga cur ris tro structaran na h-Eaglaise agus nam paraistean.

Stèidhicheadh Cumann Lúthchleas Gael (Gaelic Athletic Association) an Èirinn le uallach an spòrs (agus gu leòr eile a bharrachd air, gu h-àraidh peil no ball-coise Gàidhealach) ann an 1884 agus Comann na Camanachd ann an Alba an 1893. Feumar coimhead air mar a thachair sin ann an co-theacs gach suidheachaidh fa-leth, suidheachaidhean gu math eadar-dhealaichte.

Bha an Ciaradh Ceilteach, no 'Celtic Twilight', air laighe air an dà thaobh dhen chuan. Nuair a bha Seumas Mac a' Phearsain a' lorg 'Ossian' ann 1760, cha robh ann ach toiseach-tòiseachaidh air slighe nas doimhne agus nas maireannaiche. Mus do thòisich Sir Walter Scott a' snìomh a chuid fhèin de dh' 'eachdraidh' na h-Alba, bha an gnothach dèanta. Bha fèill air na h-Èireannaich a bharrachd air na h-Albannaich tron Roinn Eòrpa air fad mar *Kulturvolk* (Trevor-Roper, 1983; MacLennan, 1998, td. 137).

An Alba, bha 'Turas an Rìgh' (the 'King's Jaunt') air tachairt an 1822, mu fhichead bliadhna ro ghaiseadh a' bhuntata agus imrich mhòr gu taobh thall an t-saoghail. Chaidh an dà spòrs a chur air bun-stèidh ùr agus an ath-nuathachadh aig fìor àirde an Dùsgaidh Cheiltich, gluasad a sgaoil feadh na Roinn Eòrpa. Bha iad, air a' cheann thall, a' dol a ghabhail slighe gu math eadar-dhealaichte, ge-tà.

Aig aon ìre an Alba, ach gu ìre gu math nas treasa an Èireann, mhisnich-eadh tuinn de dh'fhaireachdainnean nàiseantach. Cha robh aithne mhòr sam bith aig Èirinn Phròstanach air a cuid nàiseantachd; 's ann a bha i an taobh eile, moiteil às a' cheangal le Mòr-Bhreatainn mòr. Ach ro dheireadh na naoidheamh linn deug bha smuaintean is fèin-aithne na h-Èireann fìor gheur agus air a dhearbhadh ann an gluasadan agus gnìomhan poilitigeach (Dewey, 1974, td. 42).

Ged a bha co-ionnanachd ann agus ged a bha suidheachaidhean an ìre mhath nan sgàthan de chèile a thaobh mì-thoileachas an lùib an fhearainn, fearg an aghaidh uachdarain, sgoilearachd àrd-ìre Cheilteach agus sàr-spòrs, 's ann air na beàrnan a bha ann a thaobh cheanglan stèidh foirmeil agus fìor phoileataigs a chaidh bàta leasachaidh eachdraidh agus an saoghal eadar-dhealaichte a bha tighinn air na creagan.

Feumar na thachair ann an camanachd Alba agus Èirinn a mheasadh an coimeas ri na thachair anns a' ghluasad ris an canar Crìosdaidheachd fhèitheach ('*muscular Christianity*') – fìorghlaine bodhaige, neart bhall, astar smuain is gnìomh – beachd uachdarachd innleachdail agus bodhaige a thug buaidh gun tomhas air raon farsaing de spòrs a' tighinn suas gu deireadh na naoidheamh linn deug.

Thachair tòrr de na chaidh air adhart anns an dà chamanachd ann an rugbaidh, ball-coise, bocsadh agus lùth-chleasachd. Ach bha ceanglan gu math eadar-dhealaichte aig Alba agus Èirinn ris a' chòrr de Bhreatainn a thug buaidh air a' cheann thall air mar a ròghnaich iad nàiseantachd, agus an ìre an uair sin a thug sin buaidh air gach spòrs fa-leth mar a bha iad ag atharrachadh agus a' leasachadh mar bhuidhnean.

Thachair an t-atharrachadh gu smachd is riaghailtean an saoghal spòrs aig an dearbh àm far an robh geamaichean air imrich bho shuidheachaidhean dùthchail gu na bailtean, bho bhith a' gabhail pàirt gu bhith an suidheachadh amhairc, agus bho chur-seachad gu farpais. Tha Kevin Whelan, mar eisimpleir, dhen bharail gun do lìon an GAA bho 1884 nàdar de tholl no 'vacuum dòrainneach' a chaidh fhàgail leis a' Ghoirt ann am meadhan na linne agus a dh'adhbhraich gun deach gnothaichean agus tachartasan cultarail a sgrios (Whelan, 1994). Bha an GAA cuideachd mar einnsean cumhachdach an lùib a bhith a' cur an cèill an nàiseantachd ùr 'Risorgimento' a bha an uair sin a' sgaoileadh air feadh na Roinn Eòrpa. Chruthaich an nàiseantachd chultarail seo an dùthaich mar sheòrsa de choimhearsnachd shàmhlachail an inntinnean dhaoine (Whelan, 1994). Bha fèin-aithne na dùthcha ri sàbhaladh à eabar de dh'eachdraidh, cànan agus dualchas.

'S dòcha nach eil eisimpleir nas fheàrr ann na an GAA nuair a thig e gu bhith ag ath-chruthachadh traidiseanan. Ma tha sinn a' gabhail ri sin, tha neart nas treasa buileach aig an dearbh argamaid a thaobh na h-Alba, gum bu chòir dhan dearbh rud a bhith air tachairt an Alba air sgàth 's na rinneadh le Comann na Camanachd agus iad a' toirt beò a' ghèam an sin. Air a h-uile coltas is taobh, chanamaid gu robh na suidheachaidhean cho coltach is gun fheumadh na h-aon ghluasadan agus teachd-a-mach a bhith ann aig an aon àm. Ach cha b' ann mar sin a bha.

Feumar coimhead gu dlùth air an dòigh anns a bheil sinn a' faicinn an dà shuidheachadh co-ionann agus air an làimh eile eadar-dhealaichte rè agus thar ùine, àite agus suidheachaidhean anns an dà dhùthaich. Feumar cuideachd measadh cruaidh agus mionaideach a dhèanamh air na bha air cùl agus a' misneachadh nam prìomh dhaoine a bha an sàs anns na h-iomairtean seo.

Ann an Èirinn bha an sluagh an ìre mhath briste an dèidh bliadhnaichean de làmhachas làidir agus an Gort Mòr anns na 1840an. Chaidh an Dr Dubhghlas de hÍde (Douglas Hyde), ceannard Chonradh na Gaeilge (Gaelic League) agus a' chiad cheann-suidhe a bh' air Saorstát Éireann an dèidh 1922, do Ghàidhealtachd Alba ann an 1886. Thuirt esan:

> *The Famine destroyed everything. Poetry, music and dancing stopped. Sport and pastimes disappeared. And when times improved, those things never returned as they were* (*Irish Post*, 1895; faic cuideachd Jarvie, 1998).

Seo far a bheil an diofar a tha cho bunaiteach eadar Comann na Camanachd agus an GAA, agus far an lorg sin freumhan an sgaraidh eadar an dà bhuidhinn. Cha tàinig Comann na Camanachd riamh air adhart le beachdan cho fìor dhìoghrasach agus cho nàiseantach is follaiseach ri òraidean an Àrd-Easbuig Croke a bha cho cudromach ann a bhith a' dealbh agus agus a' stèidheachadh an GAA. Agus cha mhò a bha buidheann-riaghlaidh na camanachd coltach ris an GAA, mar a mhìnich Pádraig Ó Fainin mar a chaidh a chruthachadh ann an 1904:

> *In its origins and aims the child of its time, a party to the reawakening of a national consciousness, a mass movement whose sweep and surge would like and intertwine the promotion of the games with the trend of national thought and action through the final design of the nineteenth century, and to the present day* (MacLennan, 1998, td. 139).

Cha bu chòir iongnadh a bhith ann gu robh an GAA a' taobhadh cho làidir ri beachdan nàiseantach agus gu robh e na shamhla air na gluasadan a bha a' dol aig an àm. Cha robh a' chòrr ceann-ùidhe gu bhith aig a' chùis.

Dh'fhairtlich e air Comann na Camanachd a bhith a-staigh air saoghal mòr poileataigs is cumhachd dìreach a chionn 's nach b'urrainn dha, no nach robh e deònach a dhol an sàs anns an t-sruth luaisgeanach mun cuairt. Sin ged a bha làn chothrom aca le na bha de dhaoine ceangailte ris a' ghèam an sàs ann am poileataigs leithid MacShimidh, Sir Uilleam Sutharlan am Ball Pàrlamaid, agus Am Morair Strathcona, Seumas Iain Mac a' Phearsain à Bàideanach, a bha na Mhinistear Cogaidh aig aon àm.

Seach gun deach Comann na Camanachd a chruthachadh an dèidh, seach ro, nan tachartasan bunaiteach a bhuineas do na 1880an agus strì an fhearainn air a' Ghàidhealtachd, bha e do-dhèanta gum biodh an aon teachd a-mach aig an dà bhuidhinn. Bha ceannbhairean saoghal na camanachd buileach-glèidhteachail agus cha robh sannd sam bith aca a dhol an sàs ann an gnothaichean mòra an t-saoghail an lùib an spòrs. Bha nàiseantachd sam bith a bha nan sealladh, leis an fhìrinn, cumhang, Gàidhealach, agus gu math ainneamh, Ceilteach.

Cha b' e turchairt a bh' ann nas mò gur e an GAA a' bhuidheann spòrs agus cultarail a bu treasa a bh' anns an dùthaich, le dlùth-cheangal ris na riaghladairean ùra ged a bha gu leòr de na buill aca dhen bharail gu robh Aonta Angla-Èireannach 1921 gann de na bha cuid de na nàiseantaich a' sùileachadh. Cha do sguab Camanachd riamh an dùthaich mar a thachair leis an reabhlaid shòisealta a bha Mícheál Ó Cíosóg (Michael Cusack) ag ràdh a bh' anns an GAA nuair a stèidhich e a' bhuidheann (de Búrca, 1980; King, 1996).

Air an làimh eile, nam biodh barrachd air èirigh còmhla ri Iain Murdoch nuair a dh'iarr e air Alba (ann an 1886) 'èirigh fo shàil uachdarain Anglo-Norman agus iad fhèin a dhearbhadh coltach ri na croitearan bochda' (Hunter, 1986, td. 200) no air a bhith a' gabhail feairt den bhrosnachadh a bha a' tighinn bho leithid Màiri Mhòr nan Òran, Iain G. MacAoidh agus feadhainn eile anns an Eilean Sgitheanach, bhiodh eachdraidh na camanachd agus na Gàidhealtachd gu math eadar-dhealaichte.

Camanachd an Alba gun a saoradh

Chan eil raon nas cumhachdaiche no nas cudromaiche far am faigh sinn dearbhadh gur e barrachd na dìreach gèam a th' anns a' chamanachd na fianais a lorgar an lùib raointean cogaidh.

Bha camanachd na meadhan aig MacShimidh aig àm Chogadh nam Boers air saighdearan a mhisneachadh agus a thoirt còmhla. Bhathas a' cluich camanachd anns a' Chogadh Mhòr agus anns an Dàrna Cogadh agus ann an campaichean nam prìosanach (le POWs). Dìreach mar a bha na h-eilthirich bhochda air an acairean cultarail fhèin a thoirt leotha anns na 1840an agus an dèidh sin, bha na saighdearan a' cleachdadh an cuid spòrs agus cultair airson an ceanglan leis an dachaigh a chumail suas, bho Afraga a Deas chun na Roinn Eòrpa agus fiù 's am Montevideo.[8]

Thraogh camanachd air ais chun na Gàidhealtachd ron naoidheamh linn deug. Chaidh a sgaoileadh a-mach a-rithist bhon sin gu meadhan na dùthcha le sluagh a b' fheudar, no a bha deònach, gluasad gu deas.

Cha mhò tha e an-còmhnaidh air aithneachadh gu cothromach gu bheil eachdraidh leantainneach ann do chamanachd deas air a' Ghàidhealtachd suas chun dàrna leth dhen naoidheamh linn deug. Tha dearbhadh ann gu robh clann ri camanachd am meadhan na h-Alba agus gu sònraichte ann an Dun Èideann agus mun cuairt air a' bhaile mu 1850 (Burnett, 2000a, tdd. 93, 116, 208, 210; Burnett, 2000b). Ann an 1816 ghearain buill Chomann Goilf Burgess gu robh a' chluich aca air machraichean Bruntsfield cunnartach air sgàth cunnart bho chluicheadairean camanachd (Robbie, 1936, td. 44). Gheibhear cuideachd dearbhadh gu math follaiseach air camanachd anns a' phrìomh-bhaile aig ceann an iar Ghàrraidhean nam Prionnsaichean, tro dhealbhan leithid 'A View of Edinburgh from the North of Castle Rock' le David Octavius Hill.[9] Rinn Charles Altamount Doyle dealbh eile, 'Winter Sports on Duddingston Loch', ann an 1876, far a bheil camanachd a-rithist gu math follaiseach.[10]

'S ann an suidheachaidhean mar seo, tha fhios, a bu dualtaiche an lagh a chleachdadh an aghaidh na camanachd, cleas mar a thachair gu ìre leis a' Ghàidhlig – fo ìmpidh le reachdan rìoghail agus laghan an aghaidh 'geamaichean mì-rianail'. A thuilleadh air sin thàinig an spòrs fo bhuaidh luchd na Sàbaid a thàinig ri linn an Ath-leasachaidh agus a chuir casg air spòrs air latha fois agus a bha an lùib atharrachaidhean aithghearr air dòigh-beatha na Gàidhealtachd. Gu math tric bha na poilis an sàs, leithid mar seo an Siorrachd Dhùn Èideann an 1842:

> *Many complaints having been made of boys playing at shinty or football upon the public roads, the Constable is directed to put an immediate stop to it.*[11]

Chaidh an lagh cuideachd a chur an sàs ann an sgìrean Gàidhealach, leithid anns an Òban an 1843:

> *And be it Enacted, That every person shall be liable to a penalty of not more than forty shillings who on any road, bridge, or quay within the limits of this Act shall commit any of the following offences (that is to say,) Every person who shall fly any kite, or play at shinty, football, or other game, to the annoyance of passengers.*[12]

'S e an luach as motha a th' ann an gnothaichean leithid an lagh gu bheil iad fìrinneach agus dearbhte. Air an làimh eile, tha seòrsa eile de dh' 'fhianais' againn nach eil ach fuadain, mar eisimpleir *Leabhar Comann nam Fìor Ghàidheal*, a chaidh fhoillseachadh ann an 1881 (McIntyre-North, 1881). Tha luchd-rannsachaidh air an tarraing chun an leabhair seo gu math tric, ach bu chòir a bhith cùramach mu chuid dhen stuth a tha air fhoillseachadh ann – leithid gur e Noah a' chiad chamanaiche.

Chan urrainnear an aon chasaid fhàgail air leabhar mòr eile – Album Littlejohn – a tha a' cur gu mòr ris an tuigse a th' againn air saoghal na camanachd – an 'intriguing web with wayward strands', mar a bh' aig an Ollamh

Peadar English nach maireann à Gleann Urchadain air camanachd ann anns an ro-ràdh de chruinneachadh dualchais a dh'fhoillsich e mun Ghleann (English, 1985).

Nas cudromaiche buileach na gin dhiubh sin, chan eil mòran air tighinn thugainn no chaidh fhoillseachadh a thaobh mìneachadh air eachdraidh na camanachd, co-theacs agus briathrachas na chaidh a sgrìobhadh leis an sgoilear ainmeil Alasdair MacBheathain (Alexander Macbain). 'S e Alexander Littlejohn a thug leabhar mòr do dh'Oilthigh Obar Dheathain mar thìodhlaig, còmhla ri cupa eireachdail a bha airson farpais eadar oilthighean na h-Alba.[13]

Thug sreath de gheamaichean sònraichte far an deach riaghailtean agus dòighean-cluiche a thaisbeanadh agus a dheasbad, Comann na Camanachd, a' bhuidheann-riaghlaidh, gu bith ann an 1893. Tha faisg air trì fichead buidheann uile-gu-lèir a-nis a' cluich aig diofar ìrean, mu 2,500 neach gu h-iomlan, le 2,700 ball clàraichte den Chomann. Tha an Comann an dùil an àireamh sin a leudachadh 20% ro 2017 gu barrachd air 3,000. Bha ruith an airgid anns a' bhliadhna 2013 faisg air £600,000.[14] Ann an Èirinn tha an GAA a' cosg nam milleanan mòra agus a' frithealadh tè de na h-ionadan spòrs as fheàrr anns an Roinn Eòrpa, Pàirc an Chrócaigh (Croke Park) ann am Baile Àtha Cliath, agus ga lìonadh gu cunbhalach. Tha còrr is 200,000 cluicheadair fo a sgèith – mu thimcheall ceud neach a' cluich an Èirinn mu choinneamh gach cluicheadair an Alba. A dh'aindeoin sin, tha Alba air a bhith gu math soirbheachail anns na geamaichean eadar-nàiseanta bho chaidh an cur air bonn-stèidh as ùr anns na 1990an.

Co-dhùnaidhean

Tha slighe gu math fada agus riaslach air a bhith aig camanachd mar spòrs stèidhichte bhon bha an gèam a' stri ri tighinn-beò anns na glinn agus air na monaidhean is cladaichean feadh na Gàidhealtachd agus nas fhaide air falbh na sin. Bha fuaim nan caman ri cluinntinn fad is farsaing bho Wimbledon, gu Manchester, agus fiù 's air taobh an ear na h-Alba an Obar Dheathain, far an do choinnich buidheann air na machraichean air Là na Bliadhn' Ùire, 1849, 'for conducting the long established Celtic game'.[15]

Chaidh an gèam a shlaodadh, an aghaidh a toil gu math tric, tron fhicheadamh linn, a-steach dhan ath thè, tro Chogaidhean Mòra an t-saoghail agus tro iomadach sàrachadh leis an eaconamaidh agus àireamhan-sluaigh. Gu math calg-dhìreach an aghaidh struthan a bha a' cuartachadh na Gàidhlig cuideachd.

Agus a dh'aindeoin gach nì agus le fàs air fàire anns na bailtean mòra, agus ann an cuid de dh'àiteachan far an robh an gèam a' tighinn-beò còrr is 100 bliadhna air ais.

'S e barail nan cluicheadair fhèin agus luchd-riaghlaidh an spòrs gu bheil camanachd am measg nan geamaichean as fheàrr air an t-saoghal. Tha sinne dhen aon bharail, ma tha camanachd gu bhith a' tighinn-beò agus a' soirbheachadh, gum feum a h-uile duine a tha an sàs ann a bhith misneachail agus lèirsinneach, ag amas air na h-ìrean as àirde. Tha camanachd na stòras prìseil nàiseanta – agus le taobh eadar-nàiseanta nach deach aithneachadh gu cothromach gu ruige seo. Le taic bhon riaghaltas, oilthighean, ùghdarrasan ionadail agus sgoiltean, chan eil adhbhar mòr sam bith ann carson nach atharraicheadh sin gu maith na dùthcha agus sluagh na h-Alba.

Tha barrachd air gèam far comhair an seo, barrachd air aithne. Ged a tha e furasta gu leòr ceangal a dhèanamh ri slàinte agus dualchas feumar cuideachd coimhead air co-cheanglan sòisealta, ìrean agus soirbheachadh foghlaim is eile a tha a' cheart cho cudromach a thaobh na camanachd nuair a thig e gu cuibhreann de stòras poblach na stàite iarraidh. Tha an argamaid gu bheil camanachd a' cur ri daoine, coimhearsnachdan agus sgìrean cudromach agus bunaiteach, a cheart cho math is gun urrainnear dearbhadh gu bheil an gèam a' cur ri na roinnean dhen stàite a tha fo uallach an Riaghaltais.

Feumar còraichean na camanachd a bhuinnig ach an seas i air a casan fhèin. Chan eil còraichean spòrs air an aithneachadh leis an UN mar tè de choraichean a' chinne-daonna. Gun teagamh, tha riaghaltasan air barrachd taic a thoirt seachad, gu dìreach bho stòras no ionmhas stàite, no barantas do thachartasan, no tro airgead Crannchuir, ach dìreach mar a tha sin na chaomhnadh gu math cudromach dhaibh aig amannan, feumar coimhead air a' bhuaidh mhaireannach a tha gu bhith aig seo. Agus gu ìre tha camanachd air dèiligeadh ri seo ann an dòighean gu math soirbheachail, seach gu bheil taobhan air an spòrs a tha gu math nas fharsainge na dìreach an gèam fhèin.

Nòtaichean

1 Tha an leabhran (*album*) fo chùram an oilthigh agus farpais airson a' chupa fhathast ga cluich. MS 800/1, Invercharron Challenge Cup Deed of Gift, fo chùram an Tasglainn Shònraichte, Oilthigh Obar Dheathain.
2 *Physical Activity and Sport Act* (S.C. 2003, c. 2).
3 House of Lords Debates, 4 Dùbhlachd 2014, Colbh 1456 (Lord Moynihan).
4 Louise Frechette, Forum Spòrs na Cruinne, UN, Òraid an Leas Rùnaire Coitcheann, Màrt 17 (ri fhaighinn bho URL: http:www.un.org.press/en/2000/20000317.dsgsm88. doc.html) (air a ruigsinn 6.10.15).
5 Bha Connolly a' bruidhinn aig cuirm ann an Talla Usher an Dùn Èideann (faic *Daily Record*, 18 Sultain 2009).
6 Chaidh a' chuirm 'Lochaber Gold' a chumail an toiseach anns a' Ghearasdan anns an t-Sultain 2011.
7 Tha an stuth Camanachd stèidhichte gu mòr air stuth a bhuineas do cho-chruinneachadh a tha air a chaomhnadh ann an Tasglann Comhairle na

Gàidhealtachd an Inbhir Nis.
8   Faic, mar eisimpleir, *Inverness Courier*, 13 Iuchar 1842.
9   Tha an dealbh a' nochdadh anns an leabhar *A Picture of Edinburgh* (1995), tdd. 50-51, agus 's ann le Banca Rìoghail na h-Alba a tha an dealbh.
10 Tha an deabh a' sealltainn an locha bhon taobh deas le suas gu trì ceud neach ri spòrs air, eadar siubhal air an deigh, cròladh agus camanachd.
11 1814: Dùn Èideann, Regulation of Police, April 12 : XXIV (No Snow-Balls or Squibs shall be thrown nor Foot-Ball, Shinty, or any other game be played on any of the Streets, Squares, Lanes or Passages under the like Penalty as aforesaid) (penalty not exceeding 20 shillings). Taing do Iain Burnett, Taigh-Tasgaidh Nàiseanta na h-Alba, a thug seo gu ar n-aire.
12 1822: Oban Town Council Bye-Laws, adopted 27 December 1822 (shinty playing on the streets under a penalty respectively not exceeding five shillings). Taing do Mhurchadh Dòmhnallach ann an tasglann Chomhairle Earra-Ghàidheal airson seo a tharraing gu air n-aire.
13 Faic nòta 1.
14 Fiosrachadh mu chamanachd bho Àrd-Oifigear Chomann na Camanachd, an t-Sultain 2015; fiosrachadh mun GAA bho làrach-lìn an GAA, https://www.gaa.ie
15 *Inverness Courier*, 11 Faoilleach 1849 (a-mach air an North of Spey Shinty Club).

Tùsan

Burnett John (1995). *Sporting Scotland*. Dùn Èideann: National Museums *Scotland* Enterprises.
Burnett, John (2000a). *Riot, Revelry and Rout: Sport in Lowland Scotland before 1860*. East Linton: Tuckwell Press.
Burnett, John (2000b). 'Sport, Scotland and the Scots: An Introduction', ann an Jarvie agus Burnett (2000), tdd. 1-18.
The Camanachd Association (2005). Memorandum of Association of the Camanachd Association. Ri fhaighinn bhon URL: http://www.shinty.com/wp-content/uploads/2010/03/Memorandum-of-Association-for-web.pdf (air a ruigsinn air 28.10.2015).
de Búrca, Marcus (1980). *The GAA: A History of the Gaelic Athletic Association*. Baile Àtha Cliath: Wolfhound Press.
Delaney, Liam, agus Keaney, Emily (2005). *Sport and Social Capital in the United Kingdom: Statistical Evidence from National and International Survey Data*. Lunnainn: Department of Media, Culture and Sport.
Dewey, Clive (1974). 'Celtic Agrarian Legislation and the Celtic Revival: Historicist Implications of Gladstone's Irish and Scottish Land Acts, 1870-1886'. *Past & Present*, 64, tdd. 30-70.
English, Peter R. (1985). *Glen Urquhart: Its Places, People, Neighbours and its Shinty in The Last 100 Years and More*. Obar Dheathain: Sgioba Chamanachd Ghlinn Urchadain.
Hunter, James, deas. (1986). *For the People's Cause: From the Writings of John Murdoch, Highland and Irish Land Reformer*. Dùn Èideann: Crofters Commission.
Jarvie, Grant (1998). *Sport in the Making of Celtic Cultures*. Lunnainn: Cassells Academic.
Jarvie, Grant, agus Burnett, John, deas. (2000). *Sport, Scotland and the Scots*. Dùn Èideann: Tuckwell Press.

Jarvie, Grant, le Thornton, James (2a deas. 2012). *Sport, Culture and Society: An Introduction.* Lunnainn: Routledge.

King, Seamus J. (1996). *A History of Hurling.* Baile Àtha Cliath: Gill and Macmillan.

North, C. N. McIntyre (1881). *Leabhar Comunn nam Fior Ghaël/The Book of the Club of True Highlanders.* Lunnainn: Richard Smythson.

MacLennan, Hugh D. (1993). *Shinty!* Inbhir Narann: Balnain Books.

MacLennan, Hugh D. (1996). 'Shinty: Some Fact and Fiction in the Nineteenth Century'. *TGSI*, Iml. 59, tdd. 148-274.

MacLennan, Hugh D. (1997). 'Shinty's Place and Space in World Sport' (ri fhaighinn bho URL: http://www.electricscotland.com/history/sport/shinty1.htm) (air a ruigsinn air 6.8.2015).

MacLennan, Hugh D. (1998). 'Shinty Dies Hard: "Scotland's national game" – a re-assessment and re-definition, with particular reference to its survival and development in the nineteenth century in Australia, Canada, England and Ireland'. Tràchdas PhD, gun fhoillseachadh, Oilthigh Obar Dheathain.

A Picture of Edinburgh (1995). Dùn Èideann: City of Edinburgh Museums and Art Galleries.

Robbie, J. Cameron (1936). *Chronicle of the Royal Burgess Golfing Society of Edinburgh 1735-1935.* Edinburgh: Morrison & Gibb.

Trevor-Roper, Hugh (1983). 'The Invention of Tradition: The Highland Tradition of Scotland', ann an *The Invention of Tradition*, deas. le Eric Hobsbawm and Terence Ranger, tdd. 15-41. Cambridge: CUP.

Whelan, Kevin (1994). Tribune Essay. *Tribune Magazine,* 16 October.

15

Syntactic innovation in Manx and Sutherland Gaelic

Christopher Lewin

University of Edinburgh

1. Introduction

It is widely recognised that the use of literary Common Gaelic in Scotland obscures the details of the early development of Scottish Gaelic to a large extent, and the rise of a distinct standard Scottish Gaelic in the eighteenth century obscures regional variation and features which might be considered sub-standard. This is most noticeable in relation to the most 'divergent' of the 'peripheral' dialects, in which progressive features may be unattested, or barely attested, until the dialect monographs of the twentieth century. Manx provides a valuable point of comparison, since in certain respects it shows similar developments to Scottish peripheral dialects, but has a far greater body of texts dating from the seventeenth century onwards which are largely unaffected by the pre-existing literary standards of wider Gaeldom.

To illustrate this, this paper will examine the use of object personal pronouns with the verbal noun instead of possessives, a feature which becomes increasingly dominant in Manx during the period of attestation (Broderick, 2009, pp. 345–6),[1] and which is found in East Sutherland Gaelic (Dorian, 1978) and other dialects (MacInnes, 2006, p. 124). The following is an example from East Sutherland (1a), with its equivalent in standard Scottish Gaelic (1b) and conservative (1c) and progressive forms (1d, 1e) of Manx.

(1a)   An d' robh a' ghrian dalladh iad?
       INTERROG PAST was the sun blinding them
       'Was the sun blinding them?'
       (East Sutherland Gaelic) (after Dorian, 1978, p. 99)

(1b)   An robh a' ghrian gan dalladh?
       INTERROG was the sun at-their blinding
       (standard Scottish Gaelic)

237

(1c)   Row yn ghrian dyn noalley?
       was the sun at-their blinding
       (Manx, conservative pattern, common until early 18th century)

(1d)   Row yn ghrian dyn noalley ad / dy ghoalley ad?
       was the sun at-their blinding / at-his blinding them
       (Manx, mixed pattern, common in 18th century)

(1e)   Row yn ghrian doalley ad?
       was the sun blinding them
       (Manx, progressive pattern, common in 18th century, almost universal in 19th century and last native speakers)

2. Manx

Manx does not show simply a two-way variation between use of possessives and of personal pronouns. There are additional complexities owing to the following facts:

1. The possessives and personal pronouns can be used simultaneously.
2. The third person singular masculine possessive can be generalised and used with the pronouns in the plural and in the first and second person singular.
3. In the first and second person singular, the possessives *my* and *dty* can never be accompanied by the personal pronouns *mee* and *oo* (although combination with the generalised third person possessive is possible);[2] in the third person singular, on the other hand, it appears that the possessive cannot appear without the pronoun; in the plural the plural possessive can occur on its own or with the pronoun.

The consequence of this variation, coupled with the fact that in Manx simple inflected tenses remained in common use alongside periphrastic equivalents formed with *jannoo* 'do', and that, as in Irish, non-emphatic personal pronouns can be inverted in the infinitival construction, is that in some cases up to six synonymous and interchangeable variations of verbal forms with pronominal objects can be found. For example, 'I lost them' can be expressed as follows (with literal equivalents in Scottish Gaelic) (2):

(2)   Chaill mee ad (inflected verb, object personal pronoun)
      lost I them
      Chaill mi iad

Ren mee nyn goayl (periphrastic, plural possessive)
did I their losing
Rinn mi an call

Ren mee nyn goayl ad (periphrastic, plural possessive and pronoun)
did I their losing them
*Rinn mi an call iad

Ren mee y choayl ad (periphrastic, singular possessive and plural pronoun)
did I his losing them
*Rinn mi a chall iad

Ren mee coayl ad (periphrastic, personal pronoun only)
did I losing them
*Rinn mi call iad

Ren mee ad y choayl (periphrastic, inverted pronoun)
did I them PTCL losing
*Rinn mi iad a chall

The greatest variability is in the eighteenth century, the period of the translation of the Bible and other religious texts into Manx, known as 'Classical Manx'. Prior to this period, in the attested Early Manx of Bishop Phillips' Prayer Book translation (c.1610), there is less variation and more use of the conservative forms with the possessives (Thomson, 1953, pp. 62–3); in the nineteenth century use of the pronouns alone becomes dominant (cf. Broderick, 2009, pp. 345–6). It would seem then, that the eighteenth century was a period of variation and shift in the manner of expressing personal pronominal objects of non-finites in spoken Manx, and this would seem to be reflected in the written language, which did not have the model of a well-established prescriptive and archaic standard to obscure contemporaneous developments, although the possible significance of register variation here cannot be altogether excluded.

The complexity noted above suggests that the shift to using object personal pronouns does not represent a simple replacement of the native construction by one modelled on English syntax (since the mixed constructions have no parallel in English), and points to some of the internal structural pressures which may have contributed to the change. There are good grounds for thinking that it is predominantly an internal development, although the influence of language contact as an additional factor in the rise of the pronoun-only construction cannot be ruled out.

3. Pressures leading to a shift from possessives to personal pronouns as objects of the verbal noun in Manx

In all varieties of Modern Goidelic the historical preposition *ag* in the progressive construction is pronounced differently from when it is followed by an ordinary noun. In Irish *ag* followed by a noun phrase is pronounced [egʲ], i.e. a generalisation of the third person singular masculine inflected form (O'Brien, 1956), but with a verbal noun it is generally pronounced [ə] [əg] [əgʲ] (De Bhaldraithe, 1953, p. 224), representing a continuation of the original simple preposition *oc*, *ag*, with assimilation to the phonetic environment. In Scottish Gaelic this is reflected in the spelling *a' bualadh* 'hitting' v. *aig fear* 'at a man'; in Manx the historical preposition has entirely disappeared except before vowels, where only the consonant remains. It seems likely that *ag* with the verbal noun is now to be analysed as a progressive particle rather than a preposition (McCloskey, 1983, p. 27). This divergence would have meant that the progressive construction could no longer be transparently analysed as a preposition + noun phrase.

Similarly, the inverting infinitival construction with *do* 'to' (see (3) below) could originally be analysed syntactically in terms of the verbal noun being a noun, case governed by preceding elements and followed by a prepositional phrase. However, later the *do* is weakened to *a* (Manx *y*), or elided completely, making its identity with the preposition non-transparent, and the noun phrase which is the semantic object of the verbal noun ceases to be marked for case by what precedes it. The resulting 'indivisible unit' (O'Rahilly, 1975, p. 266) can only be analysed as a non-finite verb phrase, since nouns in Gaelic do not allow complements which precede them (3) (cf. also Lash, 2010).

(3) [tar éis [an dorais [do bhualadh]]] >   [tar éis [[an doras] a bhualadh]]
     after the door-GEN to hitting   after the door-NOM PTCL hitting
     'after striking the door' (after O'Rahilly, 1975, p. 266)

The rise of constructions where the nominal character of the verbal noun was no longer transparent would have led acquirers to analyse it, in all its semantically verbal uses, as being in fact a verb (cf. Lightfoot's [1979] 'transparency principle' and Roberts' [2007, p. 131] 'simplicity preference'). Of course, signals of the older interpretation of the verbal noun as a noun remained, including its governing of the genitive case and its homophony with the verbal noun used in unambiguously nominal use, such as after the definite article and when itself in the genitive case. However, these would be analysed as marked features of the non-finite verb, i.e. the situation would be interpreted as follows:

> 'non-finite verbs (anomalously for verbs) license genitive case on their object'

rather than,

> 'verbal nouns license genitive case because they are nouns'.

For the fossilisation, rather than immediate loss, of features after their historical motivation has been removed by syntactic change, see Simpson (2004). After the reanalysis has taken place, there is gradual actualisation (cf. Timberlake, 1977, Harris and Campbell, 1995, pp. 79–81) of the change whereby the signals of the non-finite verb's former nominal character gradually disappear.

With the logic of the genitive marking lost sight of, it is not surprising that its loss tends to be especially common in verbal noun objects. In Manx, the loss of genitive marking seems to be more prevalent after verbal nouns than elsewhere, resulting in its near total abandonment by the eighteenth century except in a few fixed expressions.[3] The decline of the genitive after verbal nouns may have been accentuated by the loss of distinct genitive inflections for most nouns (Thomson, 1992. p. 119).

The possessives with verbal nouns fared better than the genitive of nouns, remaining common in the eighteenth century, probably because the change from a possessive clitic before the non-finite to a pronoun placed after it was more salient – involving as it did a change in position and not only in form (4a) – than the relatively small, and in many cases undetectable, change from genitive to nominative-accusative inflection in noun objects (4b).

(4a)   my woalley   >   bwoalley mee
       my hitting   hitting me
       '(to) hit me'

(4b)   T'eh troggal yn voght   >   T'eh troggal yn boght
       is he raising the poor-SG-GEN   is he raising the poor-SG-NOM/ACC
       'He lifts the poor' (after Psalm 113:6, Phillips' translation)

Nevertheless, it is not surprising that the change from using possessives to using the nominative-accusative personal pronouns in time occurred, given the anomaly of using possessives (or prefixed clitic object pronouns homophonous with the possessives as they perhaps ought synchronically to be analysed) to express a direct object,[4] and the ever-present analogical pressure of the example of finite verbs, and perhaps also the analogy of the English construction.

Another structural pressure which may have contributed to the emergence of object pronouns with verbal nouns is the ambiguity of some of the possessives. In Manx all of the plural possessives have the same form, *nyn*,[5] which causes nasalisation. The addition of the personal pronouns would have provided clarification. The existence of forms with both possessives and pronouns, and the scarcity of pronoun-only forms in the early language, suggest that these were originally reinforcing pronouns such as found in Welsh. The fact that pronouns and possessives cannot be used together in the first and second person singular, with the most unambiguous and phonetically salient of the possessives, suggests that the reinforcing pronouns appeared first in the plural, subsequently spreading to all persons (cf. Broderick, 2009, p. 345). In time the pronouns come to be interpreted as the primary manifestation of the object, and the possessives, being redundant, gradually drop out of use.

Speakers were faced with the problem of the ambiguity of the plural possessive also in ordinary noun phrases and in complex possessives. However, here, unlike in Welsh, the possessives are not reinforced or replaced by personal pronouns but by the forms of the preposition *ec* 'at'. The following illustrations (5) are given with literal Scottish Gaelic equivalents:

(5a) *nyn dhie* > *yn thie ain*
 ar taigh > an taigh againn
 'our house'

(5b) *er nyn son* > *er nyn son ain* / *er y hon ain* / *(er) son ain*
 air ar son > *air ar son againn / *air a shon againn / *(air) son againn
 'for us'

That personal pronouns were selected to supplement the possessives with verbal nouns, and nowhere else (and only with verbal nouns in verbal use), provides further support for the view that these constructions were considered to be verb phrases and subject to analogical pressure from the construction with finite verbs.

Further factors in the process may include the role of emphatic and reflexive pronouns, which seem to have been accepted as objects of verbal nouns earlier than non-emphatic pronouns (cf. Scottish Gaelic *mise fhaicinn* but not *mi fhaicinn*), and the pressure to remove ambiguity between the periphrastic passive and perfect constructions (e.g. in Early Manx *t'eh er ny varroo*, Scottish Gaelic *tha e air a mharbhadh*, might be interpreted as 'he is killed' or 'he has killed him' (Thomson, 1986, p. 13; Broderick, 2009, p. 346)). In any case, it is clear that a number of plausible internal motivations for the rise of personal pronouns as objects of verbal nouns can be demonstrated, without having to resort to the influence of English. It should also be noted that grammaticalisation of verbal nouns into various kinds of non-finite verbs is a very widespread process cross-linguistically (Haspelmath, 1989, p. 292), and such processes seem to have occurred in all branches of Indo-European (Disterheft, 1980); the Celtic languages are peculiar in this regard only in that the process is still underway or else happened relatively recently.

A final peculiarity of the Manx verbal noun, which should be mentioned since it has a bearing on the comparison with Sutherland Gaelic, is the generalisation of the progressive prevocalic *g* (the remnant of the preposition / particle *ag*) to non-progressive constructions. For example *ren mee gee* 'I ate' and *foddym gee* 'I can eat'; a comparison with the same structures rendered into Scottish Gaelic–**rinn mi ag ithe* and **faodaidh mi ag ithe*–makes clear why they are nonsensical in terms of their historical analysis. Nevertheless, these forms are attested in Early Manx, and practically universal in eighteenth-century Manx, to the extent that the historically 'correct' forms are probably to be regarded as ungrammatical. As mentioned above, the reanalysis of the preposition *ag* as a progressive particle appears to have taken place in all the Goidelic dialects. In Manx, a second reanalysis has taken place, whereby the *g-* came to be regarded as a general marker of a non-finite verb, whether progressive, infinitival or gerundive. It is noteworthy that the non-finite *g-* never appears on verbal nouns still used clearly as a noun; so one finds *ren yn ghrian girree* ('the sun rose'), but *irree ny greiney* ('sunrise'); *oardagh yn leigh nee adsyn gynsagh dhyt* ('the sentence of the law which they shall teach thee', Deuteronomy 17:11), but *mychione yn ynsagh echey* ('of his doctrine', John 18:19).

4. Sutherland

In the Gaelic of the East Sutherland fisher communities studied by Dorian, '[m]ost speakers prefer the construction with the personal pronoun as object' (Dorian, 1978, p. 99). She notes that '[i]t was possible only with great difficulty to elicit a full paradigm of possessives with the verbal noun' and states that she heard only one used spontaneously. Robertson, in his 1902 study of Sutherland dialects, notes the same feature as being usual in his time, having heard it 'far and wide from young and old both in Sutherland and in the Reay Country' (Robertson, 1902, pp. 119–20). He also notes an example heard in Kiltarlity in East Inverness-shire.

Robertson, like Dorian, notes that the older construction is sometimes used, but suggests that this is 'perhaps rather in stereotyped phrases than in extempore combinations' (Robertson, 1902, p. 119). He notes the example *Tha mi ag ionndrain bhi 'g ur cumraigeadh* ('I am sorry to trouble you'). The same likely applies to Dorian's solitary spontaneous example, /ha šĩn´ ši:č kə tʰ ɛKən/ (*tha sinn sìthichte gad fhaicinn*)[6] 'We're pleased to see you'.

Sutherland Gaelic, like other Goidelic dialects (including Manx), has a tendency to delay pronoun objects of finite verbs towards the end of the clause. In contrast, according to Dorian (1978, p. 96–7) 'with the verbal noun... the pronoun object tends to stay in close proximity'. This is contradicted by several examples both from Robertson and from Dorian's own sample texts, which show the pronoun shifted rightwards after verbal nouns as with finites (6a–6d):

(6a) bha sinn fhaighinn cruinn e
were we getting collected it
'we were getting it in a lump [lit. 'collected, gathered']' (Dorian, 1978, p. 187)

(6b) 'S tarrg an àrd an aghaidh an cnonc iad
and pulling up against the hill them
'And dragging them up against the hill' (Dorian, 1978, p. 187)

(6c) 's fàgail air cnoncan a' sin e
and leaving on hillock there it
'and leaving it on a wee hill there' (Dorian, 1978, p. 191)

(6d) Bha mi a' togail an aird i
was I PROG lifting up her
'I was lifting her up' (Robertson, 1902, p. 120)

In Manx, too, pronoun objects of both finite verbs and verbal nouns are shifted rightwards (6e), and in both Manx and East Sutherland Gaelic this may be taken as further evidence of the verbal analysis of the 'verbal noun' in these constructions and the influence of the analogy of the finite verb.

(6e) Ta'n gheay-niar sheebey lesh ersooyl eh
is the wind east sweeping with-it away him
'the east wind sweeps him away' (Job 27:21)

A further peculiarity of East Sutherland Gaelic is what Dorian (1978, pp. 132–3) calls the 'complementary infinitive'. This infinitival construction is used after a variety of nominal, verbal and adjectival structures such as *feumaidh* 'must', *bu chòir* 'should', *is caomh leis* 'like to', *tha e duilich* 'it is difficult', and largely replaces the bare verbal noun (when intransitive) and the inversion infinitive (when transitive) of other Scottish and Irish dialects. The construction consists of a leniting particle /ə/, often elided, the lenited verbal noun, and any object following (7).

(7a) [ch]a bu chaomh leam a dh'fhaicinn an seòrst' ibir
 not would-be dear with-me PTCL seeing the sort work
 'I wouldn't like to see that sort of work' (Dorian, 1978, p. 187)

(7b) Bha 'g iarraidh chreic bó
 was PROG wanting [PTCL] selling cow
 'Was wanting to sell a cow' (Dorian, 1978, p. 183)

(7c) /bə xə: l′ɛtʰ urax šɔ/
 bu chaomh leat fhuireach seo?
 would-be dear with-you [PTCL] staying here
 'Would you like to stay here?' (Dorian, 1978, p. 133)

This would appear to be the same construction as found in a couple of examples in the hymns of Donald Matheson of Kildonan parish (around Helmsdale) published in the early nineteenth century (2nd edn 1825) and cited by Robertson, where the particle *do* is used where it is not historically expected (8). (Note that in (8a), the first *do* is the privative prefix, i.e. *do-àireamh* 'innumerable', whereas the second is the particle in question.)

(8a) Bha do bhuaidhean-s' do aireamh, / Cor nach fhar mi do 'n innseadh
 were your virtues uncountable so not can I PTCL their telling
 'Your virtues were countless, so that I cannot ennumerate them'[7]

(8b) Cha 'n urra...do dh'ainmeachadh
 not can... PTCL naming
 'it is not possible to name it' (Robertson, 1902, p. 119)

Manx practice is similar in that it frequently has the noun object follow an infinitival verbal noun rather than being inverted, and in Early Manx examples with a leniting particle *y* (sometimes elided) are common (9). However, it is unclear whether this particle is identical with the preposition *do* (it may rather be a proleptic possessive), and the later language shows no propensity to extend the particle *dy* to modals such as *foddee* 'can' and *lhisagh* 'should', which continue to take the bare verbal noun.[8]

(9) gy jeaninsh y phrechéel masky ny hangristiin berchys kriist
     that would-do-1SG-EMPH PTCL preaching among the unchristians riches Christ-GEN
     'that I should preach among the Gentiles the…riches of Christ' (Phillips, Romans 12:8)

Dorian ascribes the use of object pronouns with the verbal noun in East Sutherland, along with certain other features such as the use of *faighinn* instead of *fàs* to mean 'get' in the sense of 'become', use of plural pronoun *iad* to refer to *aodach* 'clothes', and use of *gloineachan* '(drinking) glasses' to mean 'spectacles', to 'interference' from English (Dorian, 1978, p. 174). O'Rahilly (1972, p. 136) makes the same connection: 'the nominal character of the verbal noun has been so far forgotten (probably owing to the influence of English) …' As in Manx, however, internal motivations for this innovation exist in the form of analogy with finite verbs and increasing opacity of the historical analysis of verbal noun constructions. The role of English cannot be excluded, but it is probably not the whole story. O'Rahilly is perspicacious in his summary of the shift which has taken place in the analysis of the verbal noun, but overlooks important potential motivations for it. His use of the word 'forgotten' also introduces an undertone of prescriptive judgement which linguists today would disavow, as does Robertson's contrasting of Sutherland usage with 'the right idiom' (Robertson, 1902, p. 119).

Nonetheless, the likelihood of contact phenomena should be taken seriously, given the long history of bilingualism in nearby Caithness, the influence of the local power centres of Dunrobin Castle and Dornoch Cathedral, and contact between Sutherlanders and English-speakers in the military (cf. Gunn and MacKay, 1897; Dorian, 1978, pp. 6ff.). On the other hand, if the use of pronouns in place of possessives was already well-established in the mid-nineteenth century, as implied by Robertson's comment about 'young and old', when presumably the majority of the population in many areas was still largely monolingual, and if it is found over a wide area of the northern Highlands (Sutherland proper, the Reay Country, East Inverness-shire and probably Easter Ross, and parts of Lewis according to MacInnes (2006, p.

124)), it may be felt that the case is strong for treating it as a native development and a dialect feature of the region. Dorian (1978, p. 173) herself notes that widespread influence of English on Gaelic is a relatively recent phenomenon in the East Sutherland communities she studies: 'Gunn (1888–9, p. 177) makes a special exception of the Embo and Brora fishing communities when condemning the adulterated Gaelic of East Sutherland in the late nineteenth century'.

The use of *do* in Matheson's hymns suggest that this non-standard feature of verbal noun syntax at least was already established in East Sutherland at the turn of the nineteenth century, to the extent that it creeps into the Gaelic of someone presumably aiming to use the literary standard register. This construction seems to be similar to the generalisation of *g-* in Manx, as both represent a levelling of different constructions and a generalisation of a certain element as a general infinitival particle. It should be noted that both seem to be internal developments and do not correspond to English constructions; in English neither *I can to go nor *I can going are grammatical.

Unlike Manx, Sutherland Gaelic does not show intermediate stages[9] and mixed constructions in the emergence of pronoun objects of non-finites; speakers choose either the standard construction with possessives or else just use the pronouns. However, given the paucity and lateness of the available data, the possibility cannot be excluded that constructions corresponding to those in Manx existed in earlier stages of the dialect. Nor need we expect such forms: the pressure of the analogy of the construction with finite verbs may be sufficient to effect a direct change to the new construction, which would first be used only sporadically, and later become usual. Unlike Manx, East Sutherland Gaelic partially maintains a distinction in form between the plural possessives,[10] so there is less of an ambiguity here to be resolved by reinforcing pronouns. The pressures in East Sutherland Gaelic, therefore, may be somewhat different from those which acted on Manx, though the result is similar.

I should stress that I am not positively arguing that the Sutherland construction is not modelled on English syntax, only that this is not the only, or even necessarily the most likely, explanation, and scholars of Gaelic should be wary of ascribing any innovation which happens to resemble an English form to influence from that language without considering all the evidence. I hope I have demonstrated, too, the potential value of Manx as a point of comparison in studies of Scottish Gaelic (and Irish). Finally, it is also to be hoped that more work will be done on syntactic variation in Gaelic dialects in future.

Endnotes

1 The Manx verbal noun constructions outlined in this paper are described and discussed in greater depth in Lewin, 2016.
2 I am assuming for present purposes that the particles *dy* and *y* used with the verbal noun represent the third person masculine possessive (cf. Scottish Gaelic *ga* and *a*, Irish *(d(h))á* and *a*), although there are certain problems with this analysis (cf. Thomson, 1952, p. 273).
3 Such as *geddyn vaaish* 'dying', *caigney cheeilley* 'chewing the cud', *shooyl ny dhieyn* 'begging', lit, 'walking the houses'.
4 There is some orthographic evidence to suggest that the possessive before ordinary nouns, and the possessive as direct object of a verbal noun, were perceived as distinct. Thomson (1986, p. 14) notes that the spelling *m'y* by the Bible translators suggests that they interpreted it as an abbreviation of *mee y*, rather than necessarily perceiving it as identical to the possessive. We may also note the spelling *e* 'his, her, its' before ordinary nouns, but *y* as the third person singular object before verbal nouns, and often in complex preposition (e.g. *er y hon* or *er e hon* 'for him, for it').
5 Apart from sporadic examples of *nar* in the first and second person plural in Early Manx, which, however, is not attested before verbal nouns or in complex prepositions (Thomson, 1953, p. 39).
6 Dorian uses phonetic transcription throughout the body of her book (including for this example) but Gaelic orthography in the texts in the appendix (Dorian 1978: 179-191). I render examples in phonetic transcription into the orthography in the present paper.
7 According to Dwelly, *far* or *fàr* is a Sutherland form of *tàir* 'get, obtain'. He quotes the present example (Clyne and Thomson, 1991, s.v. *cor*) and translates *nach fhar* as 'cannot'. Presumably the sense is something like English 'get to do something', cf. Welsh *cael gwneud*. Dwelly states that *cor* is a reduction of *air chor 's gun* 'so that', and is '[u]sed negatively in Sutherland locally'. Dorian (1978, p. 158) records *fàr ás* [faːr ɛs] as a Brora and Golspie form with the meaning 'run away', whereas Embo has *tàr ás* [tʰaːr ɛs]. She does not record the senses 'get' or 'be able'.
8 There is some extension of the use of *dy* to constructions where it might not be expected historically (e.g. *cur er peiagh jannoo / dy yannoo red ennagh* 'make someone do something'), but it does not seem to have become a general infinitival marker as in East Sutherland Gaelic.
9 Unless the lenition in the following example from Dorian's sample texts is a remnant of an elided possessive: *bha sinn fhaighinn cruinn e* 'we were getting it in a lump' (lit. 'we were getting it round, gathered') (Dorian, 1978, p. 181), cf. Manx *dy gheddyn eh*.
10 Though it conflates the first and second person plural, as other Scottish Gaelic dialects do in pronunciation (Borgstrøm, 1940, p. 100; 1941, p. 52; Oftedal, 1956, p. 211).

Bibliography

Borgstrøm, Carl H. (1940). *The Dialects of the Outer Hebrides*. Oslo: Oslo University Press.

Borgstrøm, Carl H. (1941). *The Dialects of Skye and Ross-shire*. Oslo: Oslo University Press.

Broderick, George (2009). 'Manx', in Martin J. Ball and Nicole Müller (eds), *The*

Celtic Languages, pp. 305–56. London: Routledge.
Clyne, Douglas, and Thomson, Derick (eds) (1991). *Appendix to Dwelly's Gaelic–English Dictionary*. Glasgow: Gairm.
Disterheft, Dorothy (1980). *The Syntactic Development of the Infinitive in Indo-European*. Columbus, OH: Slavica.
Dorian, Nancy (1978). *East Sutherland Gaelic*, Dublin: DIAS.
Dwelly, Edward. *Illustrated Gaelic–English Dictionary*. Available from URL: www.cairnwater.co.uk/gaelicdictionary (accessed 12 August 2015).
Gunn, Adam, and MacKay, John (eds) (1897). *Sutherland and the Reay Country*. Glasgow: MacKay.
Harris, Alice C., and Campbell, Lyle (1995). *Historical Syntax in Cross-Linguistic Perspective*. Cambridge: CUP.
Haspelmath, Martin (1989). 'From purposive to infinitive – a universal path of grammaticalization'. *Folia Linguistica Historica*, Vol. 10, pp. 287–310.
Lash, Elliott (2010). 'The rise of OV word order in Irish verbal-noun clauses', in Anne Breitbarth et al. (eds), *Continuity and Change in Grammar*, pp. 225–48. Amsterdam: John Benjamins.
Lewin, Christopher (forthcoming). 'The syntax of the verbal noun in Manx Gaelic'. *Journal of Celtic Linguistics*, Vol. 17, 147–239.
Lightfoot, David (1979). *Principles of Diachronic Syntax*. Cambridge: CUP.
MacInnes, John (2006). 'Cainnt is Cànan', in Michael Newton (ed.), *Dùthchas nan Gàidheal: Collected Essays of John MacInnes*, pp. 120–30. Edinburgh: Birlinn.
McCloskey, James (1983). 'A VP in a VSO language?', in Gerald Gazdar, Ewan Klein and Geoffrey K. Pullum (eds), *Order, Concord and Constituency*, pp. 9–55. Dordrecht: Foris.
O'Brien, M. A. (1956). 'Etymologies and Notes'. *Celtica*, Vol. 3, pp. 168–84.
Oftedal, Magne (1956). *The Gaelic of Leurbost, Isle of Lewis*. Oslo: Norwegian Universities Press.
O'Rahilly, T. F. (1972 [1932]). *Irish Dialects Past and Present*. Dublin: DIAS.
O'Rahilly, T. F. (ed.) (1975 [1941]). *Desiderius: otherwise called Sgáthán an Chrábhaidh, by Flaithrí Ó Maolchonaire*. Dublin: DIAS.
Roberts, Ian (2007). *Diachronic Syntax*. Oxford: OUP.
Robertson, Charles M. (1902). 'Sutherland Gaelic'. *TGSI*, Vol. 25, pp. 84–125.
Thomson, R. L. (1952). 'The syntax of the verb in Manx Gaelic'. *Études Celtiques*, Vol. 5, pp. 260–92.
Thomson, R. L. (1953). 'Early Manx. A Contribution to the Historical Study of Manx Gaelic arranged as a supplementary volume to the Moore-Rhys edition of the Phillips Prayer Book (1610)'. Unpublished BLitt thesis, University of Glasgow.
Thomson, R. L. (1986). 'Ned Maddrell Memorial Lecture, 1986: Change or Decay?' Unpublished typescript.
Thomson, R. L. (1992). 'The Manx language', in Donald MacAulay (ed.), *The Celtic Languages*, pp. 100–36. Cambridge: CUP.
Timberlake, Alan (1977). 'Reanalysis and Actualization in Syntactic Change', in Charles N. Li (ed.), *Mechanisms of Syntactic Change*, pp. 141–77. Austin, TX: University of Texas Press.
Simpson, Andrew (2004). 'The EPP, fossilized movement and reanalysis', in Eric Fuß and Carola Tripps (eds), *Diachronic Clues to Synchronic Grammar*, pp. 161–89. Amsterdam: John Benjamins.

16

A' suathadh ri iomadh rud: Comas is cothrom faclaireachd a leudachadh tro bhriathrachas a' chultair dhùthchasaich

Hugh Cheape

Sabhal Mòr Ostaig

Tha ana-ceartas ga dhèanamh an seo air gnàthas-cainnt a chleachd Aonghas Caimbeul, 'Am Puilean', à Nis ann an Leòdhas mar tiotal an fhèin-eachdraidh a dh'fhoillsich ann an 1973. B' e sin 'suathadh ri iomadh rubha', agus tha mi a' togail na h-abairte mar tiotal a' phàipeir seo le lùths a thig às airson briathrachas a' chultair dhùthchasaich (*material culture*). Tha stòiridh beatha Aonghais cho annasach, tarraingeach agus bu chòir an leabhar a bhith aig gach neach a leughas an cànan, gus sealladh air leth sònraichte fhaighinn air saoghal Gàidhealach, eadar saoghal inntinn a' Ghàidheil agus saoghal ann an da-rìribh anns am biodh a' Ghàidhlig fhileanta shiùbhlach air bilean an t-sluaigh (Caimbeul, 1973) .

Tron t-sreath de cho-labhairtean Rannsachadh na Gàidhlig, tha luchd-labhairt a' togail chuspairean sgoilearach aig àrd ìre thairis air na bliadhnaichean bho chaidh an sreath a stèidheachadh anns a' bhliadhna 2000. Tha na sgoilearan sùil a thoirt air a' chànan, gu h-àraidh air a' chànan fhèin ann an litreachas agus ann am beul-aithris, eadar rosg is bàrdachd, air gràmar agus cànanachas eachdraidheil, le bhith a' togail eòlas fogharachd (*phonetics*) agus a bhith a' sgrùdadh gu mionaideach a' mhorf-eòlais (*morphology*). Tha sgoilearan eile air naidheachdan ùra a tharraing à eachdraidh is airceòlas, eadar eachdraidh cinneadais (*clanship*) is eachdraidh shòisealta agus eaconamach, agus seallaidhean air atharrachaidhean tro ro-eachdraidh na h-Alba. Nam bheachd-sa, bha sgaradh ann an còmhnaidh eadar an cànan is eachdraidh, le cànanachas air a chur an dàrna taobh agus mac an duine air a chur an taobh eile. Rinneadh adhartas le dearbhachd o chionn greis mhath anns na diofar raointean sgoileireil agus cuspairean anns an fharsaingeachd. A thaobh tarraing ùr air an eachdraidh, feumar aithneachadh a thoirt do shaothair sgoilearan mar an Dr

Aonghas MacCoinnich air Clann Choinnich agus na Sìophortaich, agus an Dr Màrtainn MacGriogair, le seallaidhean ùra air Reachdan Eilean Ì, sgaraidhean eadar Chlann Griogair agus na Caimbeulaich, agus tuigse nas doimhne air eachdraidh na Gàidhealtachd anns an fharsaingeachd. Aig cridhe na cùise, 's e comas ionmholta agus eòlas sònraichte a tha aca, le bhith a' cur sgilean cànanach ri eachdraidh na h-Alba. Tha seallaidhean agus bun-bheachdan ùra a' tighinn an-àirde agus bu chòir buidheachas a thoirt dhaibh air an son (faic, mar eisimpleir, MacGregor, 2002, tdd. 196-239; MacCoinnich, 2006, tdd. 137-52). Tha iad a' leudachadh nan seallaidhean againn gu mòr, agus a' toirt misneachadh dhuinn ath-sgrùdadh thar-chuspaireil a leasachadh air eachdraidh na Gàidhealtachd, le sùil, ma dh'fhaodte, air cultar dùthchasach am measg cuspairean eile.

Rinneadh rannsachadh luachmhor air cànan is cànanachas na Gàidhlig cuideachd tro na bliadhnaichean, a thug dhuinn soilleireachadh agus leudachadh air modh, cruth is eachdraidh a' chànain. Tha sgoilearan mar an t-Ollamh Domhnall MacAmhlaigh a' toirt dealbh dhuinn air atharrachaidhean a thàinig air a' chànan, gu h-àraid fo bhuaidh suidheachadh caochlaideach dà-chànanach, suidheachadh a tha cha mhòr gu tur uile-làthaireach. A rèir an deilbh a thug e dhuinn, tha beachd aige gu bheil seòrsa de chànan ùr againn, 'Gàidhlig Ùr'. Bha MacAmhlaigh a' sgrìobhadh air mar a tha an cànan a' togail a-steach faclan is structaran bhon Bheurla agus gu bheil a' Bheurla Shasannach agus a' Bheurla Ghallda a' gabhail gnothaich ris a' Ghàidhlig le cailcean (*calques*), agus am beachd MhicAmhlaigh b' e seo '*a productive phenomenon of English interference*' (Macaulay, 1986, td. 121).

Ged a tha seallaidhean sgoilearach a' sìor ghluasad agus a' sìor atharrachadh, tha sgoilearan cànanach a' riaghladh fhathast ann an raon-rannsachaidh na Gàidhlig – suidheachadh a tha ceart is iomchaidh – agus tha iad air cudrom a chur air fòn-eòlas (*phonology*) agus obair sgrùdaidh air dualchainntean air taobh iosaglosan fhuaimneachaidh. Gu deimhinne, tha na slighean rannsachaidh seo an dà chuid freagarrach agus luachmhor. A rèir còmhraidhean pearsanta le coimhearsnachdan eadar Ceann a Tuath agus Ceann a Deas an Eilein Sgitheanaich, mhothaich mi gun robh luchd na Gàidhlig buailteach a bhith mothachail air sgaraidhean eadar na dualchainntean a thaobh briathran is briathrachas, gun a bhith a' cur cuideam no aithne air sgaraidhean a thaobh fuaimneachadh. Gu tric, tha iad a' toirt iomradh air na faclan sònraichte no abairtean dualchasach agus gnàthach a bhuineas don dùthaich aca fhèin. Tha na Gàidheil eòlach air na *shibboleths* a bhios a' comharrachadh nan dualchainntean. Ann an coimhearsnachd an t-Sabhail Mhòir, tha Niall MacFhionghain, air no 'Niall Heast' mar a chanas iad ris, air sgrìobhadh mu fhaclan agus abairtean Ceann a Deas an Eilein Sgitheanaich le cudrom air briathrachas bhon sgìre seo (MacFhionghain, 2002). Thòisich e le bhith a' toirt sùil air fuaimneachadh fhaclan ann an cleachdaidhean mar 'dorasd' an àite 'doras', 'creic' an àite 'reic', 'trog' an àite 'tog', 'seitheach' an àite 'soitheach', 'faithnich' an àite 'aithnich', am measg eisimpleirean a tha aithnichte, ged nach eil eadar-dhealachaidhean eadar aon dualchainnt is dualchainnt eile cho follaiseach san latha an-diugh. Dh'innis Niall Heast dhuinn gum biodh beachd ri cluinntinn gum faodar 'truailleadh sa' chanan' a chantail mu dheidhinn phàirt den fhuaimneachadh fhaclan a bha e a' toirt dhuinn (MacFhionghain, 2002, td. 284). Rinn e liosta de dh'fhaclan is briathrachas bhon sgìre le mìneachadh sònraichte orra le feadhainn nach d'fhuair e anns an Fhaclair Ghàidhlig aig Dwelly, nam measg innealan obrach, eich is uidheam, ainmhidhean is eòin, a' mhuir agus an t-iasgach, bàtaichean agus saidhbhreas de dh'fhaclan eile, a' mhòr-chuid dhiubh a' tighinn bho bhith-beò agus obair làitheil. Chithte facal no dhà a bha àbhaisteach ann an obair an fhearainn ach a tha ainneamh san latha an-diugh ri linn mar a tha cleachdaidhean àiteachais ag atharrachadh, faclan mar 'bota', 'culadh', 'fuaidreag', 'clisneach', 'faic', 'foidearachd', 'gailleanach', 'gniomhadh', 'geathalaich', 'plocan', 'pollag', 'reap', 'rongais' agus na h-uimhir de dh'fhaclan eile (MacFhionghain, 2002).

A dh'aindeoin nam mìneachaidhean a thug Niall Heast dhuinn, chan eil sealladh glan againn an-còmhnaidh air a' bhriathrachas seo no air ìomhaigh is tuigse mu chruth is cleachdadh (*form and function*) an uidheim seo. Tha an uireasbhaidh seo ri faicinn ann an sgrùdaidhean eile le sgoilearan a' chànain aig an ìre as àirde (faic, mar eisimpleir, Thomson, 1978, tdd. 174-8). Feumar aithneachadh gu bheil an comas is an t-eòlas seo a' fàs gann; chan eil an t-uidheam fhèin, no ìomhaighean dheth, ri fhaicinn gu tric taobh a-muigh thaighean-tasgaidh. Anns an dàrna leth dhen fhicheadamh linn, gheibheadh luchd-obrach nan taighean-tasgaidh ann an Alba trèanadh ann am faclaireachd (*lexicography*). Lean iad ris a' mhodh-obrach aig an Ollamh Alexander ('Sandy') Fenton nach maireann, a bha a' togail cheanglaichean eadar am facal agus an cleachdadh (Fenton, 1985, tdd. 43–59; Cheape, 2012, tdd. 2–3). Le obair-chruinneachaidh an Taigh-tasgaidh Nàiseanta air feadh na dùthcha, bhathas a' togail briathrachas bhon dà chuid a' Ghàidhlig agus a' Bheurla Ghallda, a' dèanamh cinnteach gu dè a bha gach facal agus abairt a' ciallachadh agus a bhith gan clàradh le iomradh bho bheul-aithris nam biodh am fiosrachadh seo fhathast ri làimh.

Lean Sandy Fenton air le modh obrach agus raon sgoilearachd an Eitneòlais (*Ethnology*) mar phàirt de shaidheans mhic-an-duine. Bho thùs, bha sgoilearan Eitneòlais a' trusadh bhriathran airson faclairean nan dualchainntean, gu h-àraidh anns na dùthchanan Lochlannach. Ann an Alba, is dòcha gum faodar a ràdh gun robh troimhe-cheile ann air taobh nan cànan tro na linntean, ach bha an suidheachadh fada na bu mhiosa anns an Eilbheis. Is ann anns an Eilbheis a thòisich sgoilearan Eitneòlais a bhith a' trusadh fiosrachadh air cultar dùthchasach le faclan is abairtean co-cheangailte ris, agus a bhith ga chlàradh air mapaichean. Thàinig modh sgoilearachd an-àirde fon ainm *Wörter und Sachen* (*'Words and Realities'* no *'words and things'*), agus dh'fhoillsicheadh a' chiad atlas cànanach ann an 1928 airson *Rätoromanischen Schweiz* (Steensberg, 1993, tdd. 16-18). Gu ìre, bha sgioba 'Faclair an t-Seann Chanain Albannaich' no *Dictionary of the Older Scottish Tongue* agus 'Faclair Nàiseanta na h-Alba' no *Scottish National Dictionary* – daoine mar Jack Aitken agus David Murison còmhla ris an oileanach aca, Sandy Fenton – a' tarraing air modh obrach sgoilearan na Roinn Eòrpa le sùil air *Wörter und Sachen*. Ann am bliadhnaichean tràtha Sgoil Eòlais na h-Alba, mar eisimpleir, bha sgrùdadh ga dhèanamh air an dà chuid cultar dùthchasach agus dualchainntean, le iomairt airson an tarraing ri chèile. Sgrìobh an t-Ollamh Aonghas Mac an Tòisich ann an 1952:

> *This whole field is a fascinating example of the close interconnection of a linguistic and a non-linguistic subject. On the one hand there is the problem of the distribution and provenance of a series of material objects; on the other there is the problem of the distribution and provenance of a series of names for material objects. Neither can be studied without the other* (McIntosh, 1952, td. 26).

Chaidh obair deasachaidh a dhèanamh airson atlas cànanach ann an Alba agus ann an Èirinn agus thàinig buaidh air an obair seo bho sgoilearan na Roinn Eòrpa agus bho leabhar a sgrìobh an t-Ollamh Tomás Ó Rathaille ann an 1932, *Irish Dialects Past and Present*, le caibideilean air Gàidhlig na h-Alba agus Gàidhlig Eilean Mhanainn. Bha Ó Rathaille a' leantainn air le eòlas fogharachd, gun chudrom air gràmar no briathrachas, ged a bha e ag aideachadh gun robh raon eadar-dhealachaidhean ann an dualchainntean; ach mar a sgrìobh e: '... *individually these differences are of small importance, but taken collectively their number makes them important enough*' (O' Rahilly, 1932, td. 240). Anns na lethcheudan, bha atlas cànanach na h-Alba, *The Linguistic Atlas of Scotland*, a' leantainn an aon slighe le bhith a' cur eadar-dhealachadh briathrachais (*lexical differentiation*) aig ìre innleachd na b' ìsle. Chaidh sgrùdadh a thòiseachadh anns na 1930an air dualchainntean Gàidhlig fo làimh sgoilearan Lochlannach, mar Nils Holmer, Carl Borgstrøm, Carl Marstrander, Alf Sommerfelt agus Magne Oftedal, cuideachd ionnsaichte a thug sùil mhionaideach air am fuaimneachadh agus am morf-eòlas, gun bheachdan air faclaireachd (faic, mar eisimpleir, Oftedal, 1956). A' togail air saothair sgoilearan a chruthaich mapaichean an lùib shuirbhidhean air cànanan eile, agus air saothair nan sgoilearan Lochlannach, bhathas a' cruinneachadh bhriathran bho bhile an t-sluaigh eadar Hiort is Peairt, ach gun ghuth air acfhainn, àirneis, obair chiùird, cleachdaidhean àiteachais no teicneòlas.

Air taobh thall Shruth na Maoile, lean an t-Ollamh Heinrich Wagner slighe eile le atlas cànanach na h-Eireann, *Linguistic Atlas and Survey of Irish Dialects*, agus thog e fhèin an dòigh-obrach a bha air chùlaibh atlas *Rätoromanischen Schweiz*, a' suathachadh ri abairtean agus briathrachas mar chomharrachadh air dualchainntean. Fhad 's a bha Wagner a' trusadh agus a' clàradh eadar 1949 agus 1956, chleachd e ceisteachan a bha stèidhichte air cuspairean co-cheangailte ris a' bheatha làitheil agus teachd-an-tìr cho math ri gnèithean gràmair. Bha earrannan anns a' cheisteachan air obair taobh a-muigh agus am broinn an taighe, eadar àirneis is obair taighe, air obair fearainn agus air iasgach. Bha beachd ann gun robh e tòrr na b' fhasa còmhradh socrach no deasbad fhaighinn le muinntir na dùthcha mun bheatha aca agus air cuspairean a bhuineadh don sgìre fhèin (Wagner, 1981, td. x). Anns an obair-trusaidh aige, fhuair Wagner taic agus comhairle bhon Dr Caoimhín Ó Danachair, a bha ag obair aig an àm ud airson Coimisiún Béaloideas Éireann. Choisinn Ó Danachair mòr-chliù mar sgoilear eitneòlas na Roinn Eòrpa air fad agus bha buaidh mhòr aige air modhan-obrach nan taighean-tasgaidh (Gailey agus Ó hOgain, 1982). B' àbhaist dha a bhith an còmhnaidh a' tarraing ri chèile uidheam is ainm tron obair-rannsachaidh aige fhèin. Anns an t-seagh seo lean e gu dlùth ri dòighean-obrach eitneòlasach an atlas chànanaich agus chuir e fhèin air chois cùrsa ceuma ann an 'Cultar Dùthchasach' ann an Coláiste Ollscoil na hÉireann, Baile Átha Cliath.

Tha sinn air a bhith a' gluasad air adhart an-dràsta le clàradh dhualchainntean agus togail fhaclairean – le iomradh air *Survey of the Gaelic Dialects of Scotland* (1997) agus 'Faclair na Gàidhlig' – agus sgrùdadh theacsaichean is làimh-sgrìobhainnean a bharrachd air cànanachas (faicibh Macleod agus McClure, 2012). Gun fhacal air oideachadh no trèanadh, tha sinn deiseil is deònach a bhith a' gabhail a-steach briathrachas bho gach taobh. Is dòcha gu bheil beàrn ann fhathast ann an saoghal sgoilearachd far nach eil ach grèim caran lag air cultar dùthchasach agus far nach b' urrainn do sgoilearan a' chànain a bhith a' suathadh ri iomadh rud mar a bu chòir dhaibh. Bha Ó Rathaille ag obair taobh a-muigh faclaireachd ach b' urrainn dha aithneachadh gun robh beàrn ann. Sgrìobh e aig deireadh an leabhair aige air dualchainntean mu bhriathrachas agus cleachdaidhean ach le fios gun robh bacadh ann:

> ... *it is easy enough to say that a particular word is in use today in a particular area; but to say that such and such a word is not in use in a particular district may well be risky, in view of the fact that the vocabulary of most districts has as yet been imperfectly explored* (O' Rahilly, 1932, td. 244).

Agus e a' toirt sùil air briathran is abairtean, bha an t-Ollamh Domhnall MacAmhlaigh a' sgrìobhadh air ùr-ghnàthachadh ann an dòighean-labhairt, mar a tha an cànan air tarraing a-steach faclan is briathrachas a tha feumail ann a bhith a' làimhseachadh saoghal ùr sòisealta is eaconamach. Cha robh an uair sin – agus ma dh'fhaodte nach eil fhathast – buidheann sam bith a tha ri cleachdadh briathrachas ùr teicneòlais, le comas air a fhreagarrachd a mheasadh, m.e. iris a tha ag amas air cuspairean teicneòlais. Mar a tha fios againn, cha d'fhuair briathrachas teicneòlais an aon urram bho sgoilearan 's a th' aig air cànan litreachais. A thaobh briathrachas teicnigeach, sgrìobh Domhnall MacAmhlaigh ann an 1986:

> ... *usage is irregular and inconsistent and there is strong evidence of poor control of technical vocabulary in a majority of written documents ... There is still a genuine impoverishment of technical vocabulary and the highest priorities for Gaelic dictionary makers are in this field* (Macaulay, 1986, td. 123).

Carson a bha coltas bochdainn air taobh a' chànain no carson a tha an cànan a dhìth anns an raon a tha fa-near dhuinn? Le foghlam oifigeil tro mheadhan na Beurla agus foghlam fo sgàil achdan Pàrlamaid Lunnainn, thòisich feadhainn a' dèanamh sabaid an aghaidh a' mhì-rùin agus dìth suime dhan Ghàidhlig a bha cumanta aig an àm. Nochd beachdan, mar eisimpleir, ann an duilleagan iris a' Chomuinn Ghàidhealaich, *An Gàidheal*, a dheasaich an t-Urr. Tòmas MacCalmain eadar 1946 agus 1958, a ghabh an cothrom a bhith ag iomairt às leth a' chànain agus ag eagrachadh bheachdan na thaic. Sgrìobh Iain N. MacLeòid ann an 1947 mu 'Dhìmeas na Gàidhlige':

> ... Ciod am feum do mhinistear seirbhis Ghàidhlig a chumail mur tig an sluagh ga eisdeachd? Chan e am ministear idir as coireach ach dìreach nach eil ar Gàidheal ag iarraidh aoradh a dheanamh nan cainnt fhèin – chan eil i fasanta gu leòr! ... Tha an aon seòrsa dìmeas air a dheanamh air a' Ghàidhlig aig cruinneachaidhean de gach seòrsa anns a' Ghàidhealtachd. Ma bhios ministear no banaltrum no maighstir-sgoile no dotair a' faighinn tiodhlaic o'n t-sluagh an uair a bhios iad a' fàgail na sgìre, feumaidh gach moladh is deagh-chliù a tha orra a bhith air a chur an cèill le muinntir na sgìre am Beurla chruaidh Shasainn. Tha sin air a mheas nas urramaiche do'n neach a

tha a' fàgail na bhith a' deanamh luaidh air a bhuadhan an Gàidhlig, eadhon ged bhiodh làn a chinn de chanan a mhàthar aige (MacLeòid, 1947, tdd. 86-7).

Bha seo agus gu leòr a bharrachd aig an Leòdach, a bha na b' ainmeile mar 'Alasdair Mòr', Sgitheanach a b' àbhaist a bhith a' sgrìobhadh ann an *Gasaet Steòrnabhaigh* le 'Litir a Beàrnaraigh'. Bha làn fhios aige fhèin dè a bha ceàrr agus sgrìobh e mu fhoghlam tro mheadhan na Beurla gun dùil aige gun tigeadh latha eile. Chuir e beachd air adhart, ge-tà: 'Nach ann air Beurla Shasainn a thogadh [Gàidheil] anns an sgoil, agus nach e sin a' cheart mhodh fhoghlaim a tha air clann na Gàidhlige an diugh, agus is ann nas miosa a bhios an iomairt sin a' dol gus am bi teagasg na Gàidhlige co-ionnan ri foghlam Beurla Shasainn ann ar sgoilean Gàidhealach' (MacLeòid, 1947, td. 87). Bha cuibhle an fhortain a' tionndadh mean air mhean ach dè chanadh a' mhòr-chuid no am mòr-shluagh? Thàinig beachd eile an clò a bha gu math cumanta fhathast ann an 1954: 'Tha a' Ghàidhlig math gu leòir 'na h-àite fhéin – 's e sin ri ràdh, air là fainge, no air a' chroit, no aig an iasgach. Math gu leòir air céilidh, cuideachd, no air "concert", gu h-àraidh ma tha cùis-bhùird de ridire no de dh'uasal ga moladh am Beurla Shasuinn. Ach cùm 'na h-àite fhéin i.' Cò sgrìobh na briathran seo ach Ruaraidh MacThómais agus Fionnlagh Domhnallach, mar fhir-deasachaidh *Gairm* (MacThómais agus Domhnallach, 1954, td. 303). Nach eil fhios againn gun robh iad a' sgrìobhadh le ìoranas, ach faodar a ràdh gur ann anns an dearbh shaoghal seo a bha (is a tha) saidh-bhreas de dh'fhaclan, briathrachas is gnàthas-cainnte ri fhaotainn.

Bha MacThómais a' moladh gum bu chòir urram a thoirt don chànan agus a bhith 'dol an ceann ar dleasdanais a thaobh na Gàidhlige' (MacThómais agus Domhnallach, 1954, td. 303). Chuireadh briathrachas, gu h-àraidh ainmean, bho thasglannan an Taigh-tasgaidh Nàiseanta gu Oilthigh Ghlaschu airson iomairt faclair Roinn na Ceiltis, 'Faclair Eachdraidheil Gàidhlig na h-Alba', a chaidh a stèidheachadh ann an 1966, fo stiùir MhicThómais, a bha an Cathair na Ceiltis anns an Oilthigh. Bha feadhainn eile a' cur bhriathran air adhart chun an Fhaclair agus dh'fhoillsicheadh co-chruinnichidhean bho na Nisich agus 'Am Bard Bochd' air cuspair an 'Taigh Ghàidhealaich', agus bho Mhurchadh MacLeòid à Crabhlasta ann an *Gairm* ann an 1968 mar fhreagairtean ri ceisteachan a sgaoil 'Am Faclair Mòr' (MacLeòid, M., 1968; [MacLeòid, T.], 1968, tdd. 339-41). Air a mhisneachadh leis na faclan annasach a thàinig thuige, chuir Coinneach Dòmhnallach clachan eile ri càrn an Fhaclair bho chuspair sònraichte, obair na mònach, fo sgeul 'Trusadh dhan an Fhaclair' (MacDhòmhnaill, 1976, td. 338-40; MacDhòmhnaill 1977, td. 74-7). A bharrachd air na bha ri fhaighinn fhathast bho shluagh na Gàidhealtachd, bha luach

Fig. 177.

Wecht of skin.

Guit no dallanach – air neo criathar gun tuill tron chraiceann – mar ainmean ri *blind sieve* no *wecht* anns a' Bheurla Ghallda. Dealbh bho Stephens, 1871, p. 314.

Inneal-làimhe airson ropaichean a dhèanamh, no 'corra-shùgain' a rèir Eòghan Dòmhnallach, Cille Mhoire, an t-Eilean Sgitheanach (2012). Dealbh le Seònaid NicLeòid, Fearann Dòmhnaill.

ri lorg anns an fhiosrachadh a bha ann an tasglannan is co-chruinnichidhean nan taighean-tasgaidh, le sùil air taobhan eile a' chànain agus na tha fa-near dhuinn anns a' phàipear seo.

Bha measgachadh de fhiosrachadh ann an tasglannan nan taighean-tasgaidh le cnag na cùise gun robh ceangal dlùth teann eadar an cànan agus rudan cinnteach ann an da-rìribh. Thug an t-Urr. Dòmhnall Mac an Tòisich, fear nan seanfhaclan, 'Cròcan' sònraichte à Srath Spè dhan Taigh-tasgaidh Nàiseanta ann an 1783, le ainm dha anns a' Ghàidhlig. 'S e seòrsa de shlabhraidh os cionn an teine a bh' ann, le dubhan air an crochte a' phrais no an coire, air a snaidheadh de fhiodh giuthais. Bha sgoilearan a' dèanamh mhion-sgrùdaidhean tron naoidheamh linn deug às leth an Taigh-tasgaidh Nàiseanta air airceòlas agus eachdraidh na Gàidhealtachd. Gu tric bha an obair seo mar chur-seachad nan saor-làithean, le nòtaichean a rinn iad mu làrach no tobhta no uidheam a rachadh fon amharc aca. Chuireadh iad na nòtaichean fo chòmhdach ionnsaichte an irisean sgoilearail mar *Proceedings of the Society of Antiquaries of Scotland*. Chuir iad am follais uaireannan fiosrachadh a tha air leth inntinneach a thaobh eachdraidh ionadail shònraichte no a thaobh a' chànain. Chithear, mar eisimpleir, aithisg bheag, ann an imleabhar 16 de ghnìomharran a' Chomainn, 'Notice of a Knocking Stone or Barley Mortar of Granite from Ballachulish', le naidheachd air clach mhòr a bha na phronnadair, 's e sin, mortair no clach-chnotainn a bha aig fear Iain MacCoinnich is a theaghlach ann am Bail' a' Chaolais. Ged nach robh comas sa Ghàidhlig aig an ùghdar, sgrìobh e sìos anns an aithisg gur e 'cnotag' a bha ann, gun cante 'eòrnachan' ris anns na h-eileanan agus gun do chuir an teaghlach a' chnotag seo gu feum fad cha mhòr dà cheud bliadhna le bhith a' pronnadh an eòrna airson biadh (Christison, 1882, tdd. 25-6). Ann an aithisg eile, 'Jottings from Mid-Lochaber' (Duns, 1882), bha iomradh air clach mhòr eile far an tug ùghdar air choreigin mion-chunntas air làraichean agus air acfhainn a chunnaic e. Chunnaic John Duns a' chlach seo agus chuala e mu deidhinn, le comhairle air a' chànan a tha cho fìor an-diugh is a bha e aig an àm ud:

> *It was my intention to say something about ... the huge boulder in Glen Nevis, known as 'The Stone of Council' ... But I soon found that a knowledge of Gaelic is indispensable to one who would gather up the threads of tradition and weave them into an historical narrative, with the help of Gaelic names for natural objects and the Gaelic names of places. Enough, however, was ascertained to show that in this, as in other out-of-the-way districts of our land, there are fields of rich promise in this department waiting for investigation by capable workers. The aged, in whose memory local traditions are as clear and definite as the facts of written history, are passing away, and, even in these remote localities, a new generation is rising far too busy with positive knowledge to care much for traditional lore* (Duns, 1882, td. 55).

Anns an latha an-diugh thathar a' tòiseachadh air rannsachadh eadar-chuspaireil agus co-obrachail airson toradh na h-obrach seo a chur gu feum. Tha saothair a' tighinn an àirde à obair rannsachaidh air cultar dùthchasach an dà chuid aig sgoilearan nan oilthighean agus aig luchd-obrach nan taighean-tasgaidh. Tha ceangal ann cuideachd le saoghal glèidhteachais (*conservation*) agus raon rannsachaidh saidheans agus teicneòlais air a' Ghàidhealtachd (faic Cox, 2009). Chuir Sabhal Mor Ostaig OGE cùrsa MA 'Cultar Dùthchasach agus an Àrainneachd' air dòigh ann an 2005 agus thàinig e gu ìre ùr ann an 2012 mar MSc 'Cultar Dùthchasach agus Eachdraidh na Gàidhealtachd'. Tha an cùrsa a' coimhead air dòighean-beatha, dòighean-obrach, teachd-an-tìr agus càrn eòlais traidiseanta a tha ri làimh gus ar tuigse a leasachadh agus a leudachadh mu na linntean a dh'fhalbh agus mu ar latha fhèin. Tron chùrsa for-cheum seo, tha na h-oileanaich a' cur phròiseactan rannsachaidh air dòigh air cuspairean eadar muir is tìr le tràchdas MSc mar ceann-uidhe. Rè a' chùrsa gheibh iad brosnachadh a bhith ag obair còmhla ri coimhearsnachdan: cothrom a bhith a' toirt toradh na h-obrach rannsachaidh aca air ais dha na sgìrean air a bheil i stèidhichte agus cothrom a bhith a' tarraing air cleachdaidhean cànanach agus gnàthasan-cainnt sgìrean ionadail fa-leth. Seo mar a bhios iad ag ionnsachadh mu chleachdadh an fhearainn, uaireannan le cuimhne air ainmean-àite, mu fhaclan is abairtean a bhuineas ri àiteachas, ionaltradh, àireachas, mu dhòighean airson sprèidh is beathaichean a chumail agus fhasgadh, agus a bhith ag ionnsachadh mu stòrasan eile mar mhuilnean, eadar beag is mòr, agus clachan bràthan. Thathar a' clàradh bhriathran agus abairtean air làrach-lìn 'Briathrachas Cultar Dùthchasach' fo làrach-lìn an t-Sabhail Mhòir agus tha am briathrachas ga chur gu feum ann am Faclair na Gàidhlig (http://www.smo.uhi.ac.uk/~sm00hc/briathrachas.html, air a ruigsinn air 6.8.2015).

Le bhith a' dèiligeadh ri cuspair a' chultair dhùthchasaich anns an fharsaingeachd, eadar Alba, Èirinn, Sasainn, an Roinn Eòrpa agus Ameireaga a Tuath, thathar a' toirt sùil air cultar dùthchasach is faclaireachd agus ga chur air clàr-obrach na Gàidhlig. Fo bhuaidh chuspairean mar 'Eitneòlas' no '*Folklife Studies*', tha sinn a' seachnadh eachdraidh rìghrean agus bhlàran, corra uair a bhith a' leigeil seachad nan leabhraichean bitheanta agus a' cumail cluas ri claisneachd, agus a' tarraing air seanchas agus òrain agus a' cleachdadh a' chànain fhèin mar fhianais. Le bhith a' lorg briathrachas a' chultair dhùthchasaich, a bharrachd air cànan nan coimhearsnachdan far a bheil a' Ghàidhlig làidir fhathast, tha sinn a' creachadh nan seann leabhraichean, nan irisean agus nam pàipearan-naidheachd bhon dàrna leth den naoidheamh linn deug. Tha sinn a' togail air a' chànan a tha ri fhaighinn anns na pàipearan-naidheachd a chaidh am meud tro na bliadhnaichean sin, agus gu h-airidh an dèidh cur às do Achd na Stampa ann an 1855. Aig an àm seo cuideachd, dh'fhoillsicheadh *An Gàidheal* (1871-7), *The Celtic Magazine* (1875-88), *The Celtic Monthly* (1892-1917), *An Deò-Ghrèine* (iris a' Chomuinn Ghàidhealach a thòisich ann an 1905), agus gnìomharran no leabhraichean bliadhnail a thigeadh an clò bho na buidhnean ùra, leithid Comunn Gàidhlig Inbhir Nis bho 1872, Comunn Gàidhlig Ghlaschu bho 1891 agus Comunn Gàidhlig Dhùn Dèagh (1910-18) (MacLeod, 1976, tdd. 202-3, 227, 230).

Tha e na iongnadh gun robh pailteas de luchd-leughaidh agus sgrìobhadairean ùra ann an saoghal na Gàidhlig tro na bliadhnaichean eadar mu 1870 agus 1914. Nochd seòrsa de 'choimhearsnachd chànanach' aig an àm, a' mhòrchuid dhith sgapte anns na bailtean mòra agus thall thairis, aig an robh comas leughaidh agus comas sgrìobhaidh anns a' Ghàidhlig (Cheape, ri thighinn). A thuilleadh air coltas luchd-leughaidh orra, bha cianalas orra airson na dùthcha a dh'fhàg iad agus ìomhaigh làidir dhith nan inntinn. Thog iad na sgilean aca tro Chomunn nan Sgoiltean Gàidhlig, a chaidh a steidheachadh ann an 1811, agus mus tàinig Achd an Fhoghlaim ann an 1872, chaidh mu 90,000 neach tro shiostam nan sgoiltean Gàidhlig (MacLeòid, R., 1981). Le sùil air a' chultar dhùthchasach, tha luach fhathast anns an litreachas bho dheireadh an naoidheamh linn deug, ged as dual do sgoilearan ar latha fhèin a bhith a' cur sìos air litreachais às a' ghàrradh-càil no *Kailyard*.

Ma dh'fhaodte gun robh sgàil a' ghàrradh-càil air ùghdaran na linne seo ach, bho shealladh a' chultair dhùthchasaich, tha cuid dhiubh airidh air ath-leughadh air adhbharan na faclaireachd. Tha luach sònraichte ri tharraing bho shaothair lìonmhor ùghdaran mar Eachann MacDhùghaill (1880-1954) agus an t-Urr. Iain MacRuairidh (1843-1907). Rugadh Eachann MacDhùghaill ann an Eilean Chola agus chuir e seachad a bheatha obrach le Poileas Ghlaschu. Fhuair e 'foghlam' anns an seann taigh-chèilidh agus bha eòlas mòr aige air seann chleachdaidhean (faic Pàipear-Taice A). Chuir e an t-eòlas agus an seanchas gu feum agus mar a chaidh a sgrìobhadh mu dheidhinn: 'Facail nach fhaigheadh tu am Faclair agus gnàthasan nach cluinneadh tu aig neach eile – iad sin gheibheadh tu am pailteas an Gàidhlig Eachainn' (MacCalmain, 1954, td. 364; faic MacDhùghaill, 1924, 1930). Tha na faclan a chuir Iain MacRuairidh fa-near dhuinn bhon naoidheamh linn deug airidh air ar sgrùdadh fhathast agus chithear gun do chuir am ministear na mìltean dhiubh ann an clò tro bheatha ministrealachd thrang nach robh cho maireannach (Laing, 2013). 'S fheudar saothair MhicRuairidh a bhith fon amharc againn airson adhbhar a' chultair dhùthchasaich ach, a thuilleadh air sin, a chionn 's gu robh an t-Urr. Uilleam MacMhathain den bheachd gum b' e Iain MacRuairidh an sgrìobhadair Gàidhlig a b' fheàrr a bh' ann riamh. Tha adhbhar eile againn, gun robh stoidhle sgrìobhaidh aig MacRuairidh leis an tug e dhuinn cunntas agus ìomhaigh fada na bu mhionaidiche air saoghal co-aimsireil muinntir nan sgeulachdan agus, a bharrachd air seo, chleachd e faclan, abairtean agus briathrachas a tha annasach san latha an-diugh ach a bha aithnichte fhathast don luchd-èisteachd agus luchd-leughaidh aig an àm. Ann an 1893, nochd an sgeul 'Tàillear Ghearraidh-Bo-Stig' bho bheul-aithris Bheinn na Faoghla far an do rugadh 's a thogadh am ministear fhèin. Seo an aithris fhaiceallach, mhion-fhiosrach a thug e dhuinn air àirneis an taighe, tuairisgeul a dh'aithnicheadh a luchd-leughaidh agus a bheireadh doimhneachd dhan tuigse aca:

> Cha robh de dh' earnais ann an tigh Mhicheil ach dà leabaidh – leaba mhor agus leab' ard; sreath chlach mu choinneamh an teine, agus sgrath rèisg air an uachdar gu beinge; tri sunnagan connlaich, loban gu gleidheadh shìl; ciste gu gleidheadh mhine; coidhean gu gleidheadh ime; noigean gu bleoghan bhainne, miosair shuidheachaidh no dha; crannachan is loinid is ròineachan; spal-ladhair gu fighe nam plataichean; corc-ràsair gu marbhadh agus gu gearradh na feola; da chuaich fhiodha agus da spain adhairc…. Bha 'n earnais a reir an latha agus na linn anns an robh iad beo. Ach an deigh a h-uile cùis, eadar na bha Micheal a' dèanamh a dh'aiteach agus na bha an Tàillear a' cosnadh, maille ri maruinn spreidhe, cha robh dith no deireas orra latha deug 's a' bhliadhna (MacRury, 1892, td. 32).

Còmhla ris an Urr. Iain MacRuairidh agus an dèidh 'Caraid nan Gàidheal', bha treubh beag de mhinistearan anns an naoidheamh linn deug agus anns an fhicheadamh linn a chuir tòrr a bharrachd ri cuspairean mar eachdraidh agus beul-aithris a tha a' suathadh ri prionnsapalan moralta, gus an saoileadh tu nach biodh e cho iomchaidh dha na daoine seo a bhith a' leantainn air a choltas de chuspairean saoghalta agus a bhith a' trusadh seanchais (Meek, 2002, tdd. 109-11). Nam measg bha daoine bhon chreideamh Chlèireach mar Phàdraig Dòmhnallach, Gilleasbuig Mac a' Chlèirich, Seumas MacDhùghaill, Iain MacGriogair Caimbeul, Alasdair Stiùbhart, Teàrlach Robasdan agus eile. Bha Donnchadh MacAonghais na mhinistear ann an Òban Latharna a rinn is a dheasaich co-chruinneachadh de sgeulachdan anns an t-sreath *Waifs and Strays of Celtic Tradition* (MacInnes, 1891). Chuir e cuideachd briathrachas ann an clò airson 'Clèibh' no '*Highland Panniers*' ann an aiste bheag a sgrìobh e fon tiotal 'Notes of Technical Terms' ann an 1894. Chuir e beachd cudromach air adhart an uair sin: '*The following and many other technical terms being on the eve of falling into oblivion, it is desirable that they be preserved and put upon record to prevent their being lost for ever*' (MacInnes, 1894, td. 213). Bha an t-Urr. Teàrlach Robasdan (1864-1927) air an aon ràmh leis agus lean e fhèin air a bhith a' trusadh briathrachas teicnigeach a rèir feallsanachd ùr foghlaim teicneòlais a bha a' tighinn an àirde air feadh na Roinn Eòrpa aig deireadh an naoidheamh linn deug. Bhuineadh e do Shrath Tatha, rugadh e ann an Obar Pheallaidh agus bha e na shearmonaiche anns an Eaglais Chlèireach Aonaichte – 'Robasdan Fada' mar a chanadh iad ris ann an Eilean Diùra, far an robh e steidhichte mar shearmonaiche. Chruinnich e cainnt is cànan ann an diofar sgìrean agus gu h-àraidh air tìr-mòr na Gàidhealtachd agus an sgìrean far a bheil an cànan air crìonadh bhon uair sin. Sgrìobh e na h-uimhir mu theicneòlas dùthchasach agus tha an obair trusaidh aige fhathast a' feitheamh ri sgrùdadh domhainn (faic NLS MSS 443-54 [Robertson Collection]).

Faodar na sgrìobh a' chlèir a sgrùdadh le buannachd, gu h-àraidh na sgeul-achdan aca nach eil a' coimhead ro ghealltanach. Tha pailteas dhen ghnè seo ri fhaotainn; dh'fhoillsicheadh am pàipear, 'The Religion and Mythology of the Celts', ann an iris Comunn Gàidhlig Inbhir Nis ann an 1894, pàipear a sgrìobh an t-Urr. Gilleasbuig Dòmhnallach, Cill Taraghlain. An uair a thàinig am ministear seachad air beachdan fasanta romansach nan làithean sin, thòis-ich e le seanchas aige fhèin air sìthichean, slachdanan draoidheachd, eòlas an dèididh, eòlas an t-snìomha agus an droch shùil. Bha rann no dhà annasach drùidhteach ann, mar eisimpleir, bho bheul-aithris nan Eilean Siar, far an robh e a-mach air latha a b' fheàrr imrich:

Na falbh Di-luain,
'S na gluais Di-mairt,
Tha Di-ciadain craobhach,
'S tha Diardaoin dàlach,
Dihaoine chan eil e buadhmhor,
'S cha dual dhuit falbh a-màireach.

Chithear nach biodh feum ann ghluasad idir agus b' urrainnear an gille-mam-aidh a ghleidheadh fo gheasaibh aig an taigh. Seo rann eile, a chaidh fhoill-seachadh mus do nochd *Carmina Gadelica*, a bha a' cumail ri chuimhne airson fèilltean agus làithean nan dròbh – margaidheachd an àite Crìosdaidheachd:

Diardaoin latha Ghille Chaluim chaoimh
Latha chur chaorach air seilbh
A dheilbh 's a chur bà air laogh (MacDonald, 1894, tdd. 45-6).

Mar is trice tha naidheachd mu na seann taighean-cèilidh pailt is cumanta. Seo dhuinn naidheachd a bha measail aig a' mhòr-shluagh ach faodar a ràdh gun robh sgrìobhadairean naidheachdan den t-seòrsa seo a' feuchainn ris an luchd-leughaidh aca a riarachadh agus gu robh iad buailteach a bhith fo bhuaidh romansach. Bho àm gu àm, thigeadh guth eile air ais bho Chanada far an robh seanchas a' tighinn an clò anns a' phàipear-naidheachd *Mac-Talla*. Bha car eile air an naidheachd seo fo pheann deasachaidh Eòghann G. MacFhionghain agus chuir esan tòrr bho na sgrìobh an t-Urr. Iain MacRuairidh ann an duill-eagan *Mac-Talla* (Laing, 2013, tdd. 53-79). Mar eisimpleir beag air guthan eadar-dhealaichte, bha aon sgrìobhadair, Aonghas MacFhionghain, ag aithris air na taighean-ceilidh dà fhichead bliadhna roimhe sin:

> Bha iomadh taigh-céilidh san àite; taigh an tàilleir agus a' cheàrdach; ach bha aon taigh àraid ann far am biodh a' chuid mhòr de na gillean òga a' cruinneachadh. Bhiodh an taigh làn bho ochd uairean, àm fheasgair, gus am bitheadh fada air adhart san oidhche, a-rèir 's mar a bha cùisean a' còrdadh riu.… Bhiodh ceò an tombaca cho dùmhail 's gur gann a chitheadh tu solus a' chrùisgein no aodann a chéile. 'S ann mar sud a dh'ionnsaich mise a' phìob-thombaca 'n toiseach, a' lasadh am pìoban do chàch. Tha cuimhne agam air oidhche shonraichte a tharruing mi fichead oiteag de thombaca làidir á seann phìob dhubh chrèadha, air son seann tromb. B' e sin misg a bu mhò a bh' ormsa riamh (MacFhionghain, 1902, td. 78).

Bu mhiann leinn an còmhnaidh a bhith a' leughadh mu òrain mhòra no seanchas na Fèinne ach bha Aonghas còir a' toirt dhuinn ceòl is craic a b' àbhaist a bhith aca an saoghal baile beag am meadhan an naoidheamh linn deug. Bhiodh an ceòl agus na h-òrain ann an toiseach, agus an sin na sgeul-achdan is an craic. Thug e dhuinn naidheachd air beatha an da-rìribh bho fhear a bha air an luing-fhoghlaim *Hogg* a bha thall ann an Grianaig aig an àm ud, ag innse dhaibh:

> … gu'm biodh aca ri leum thall 's a bhos o thaobh gu taobh dhe'n luing, a' nigheadh agus a' sgrìobadh clàir ùrlair agus uachdar na luinge, cas-ruisgte gun bhròig 's gun stocain, 's a' tarraing ghunnaichean mòra mach 's a stigh air na cliathaichean, a' tarruing ròpaichean 's a' togail shiùil, le Beurla bhrais troimh thrombaidean fada pràise, air ais is air aghart le am bàtaichean beaga eadar long is tìr, agus uair 's an t-seachduin ag ionnsachadh snàmhadh dlùth air an luing (MacFhionghain, 1902, td. 78).

Am measg litreachais nan làithean seo, bha teacsaichean oifigeil. Le gort a' bhuntàta, galar sgaoilte an fhiabhrais mhòir, na Fuadaichean agus èiginn mhòr anns a' Ghàidhealtachd air fad, chuireadh sgrìobhainnean an clò le comhairle don t-sluagh. Cha tàinig an iomairt seo bho Riaghaltas Bhreatainn ach bho luchd-fearainn agus uachdaran le oighreachdan anns a' Ghàidheal-tachd. Nochd a' chiad phìos susbainteach ann an 1838, fo pheann Mhic 'ic Iain – Sir Frangan MacCoinnich Gheàrrloch – le tiotal 'Beachd-chomhairlean airson feum do Thuathanaich agus Choitearan Gaidh'lach'([Mackenzie], 1838), agus ann an 1846, nochd tràchdas goirid 'An Seòl air an Glacar agus an Glèidhear an Sgadan, an Trosg, an Langa, an Traille agus an Falmair' le tionndadh gu Gàidhlig air duilleagan aghaidh ri aghaidh. Rinn an t-Urr. Alasdair MacGriogair eadar-theangachadh air a' Bheurla dheth agus sgrìobh e anns an Ro-ràdh nach robh e furasda idir dha a bhith a' togail eadar-theangachadh bho Bheurla gu Gàidhlig le briathran glan, iomchaidh, soilleir air sgàth 's gun robh a h-uimhir de bhriathrachas teicniceach anns an tràchdas agus gun robh gnàthasan-cainnte an dà chànain cho eadar-dhealaichte ('... *one of the most difficult tasks I have ever attempted... . The number of technical expressions in the excellent Treatises, and the difference in the idioms in the two languages, made it no easy matter to convey the spirit of the original into the translation, in plain, and at the same time, in almost literal terms*') (Lauder, 1846, td. 4). Dh'fhoillsich 'Comunn Dùchail na h-Alba' comhairle ann an cruth bileig shingilte fon tiotal 'Rabhadh Bliadhnail do Luchd Aiteachaidh na Gaeltachd, air Aiteachadh Chroitean agus Gharaidhean' (Comunn Dùthchail na h-Alba, 1848). Thàinig a' bhileag bhon chlò ann an 'Dunedinn, Sraid a' Phrionnsa, An Ceud-Mios 1848', a' leantainn gu dlùth ri Gort a' Bhuntàta agus a' cleachdadh na Gàidhlig nach gabhadh ach eadar-theangachadh bhon Bheurla le briathran mar 'tuathanas a' chaibe' (*spade husbandry*), 'barrachadh lìonmhor' (*frequent cropping*) no 'buntàta luatharach' (*early potatoes*) agus bun-bheachdan nach robh aithnichte aig an àm ud, ged a chaidh an cruthachadh anns a' Bheurla aig àm an t-Soilleireachaidh (Comunn Dùthchail na h-Alba, 1848; faic an dòigh-sgrìobhaidh aca anns a' Phàipear-Taice B).

Bha gnàthas-cainnt eile ann a chaidh a chleachdadh anns an dàrna leth den naoidheamh linn deug le briathrachas gu math tomadach is tàmailteach. 'S iad briathran laghail air an deachaidh riaghailtean nan oighreachdan a chur an cèill. Mar sin dheth, rinneadh eadar-theangachadh bhon Bheurla leis mar a bha Gàidhlig aig an luchd-leughaidh no an luchd-èisteachd mar chànan màthaireil. Tha eisimpleir romhainn air 'Riaghailtean agus Cumhaichean' (Articles and Conditions) a chuir oighreachd Shir Sheumais MhicMhathain ri muinntir Leòdhais ann an 1879, le briathrachas a bha an dà chuid teicnigeach agus connspaideach agus a chuir an cèill adhbharan aimhreit is ùpraid. Chuireadh a h-uile seòrsa de chnap-starra agus sgiùrsadh nam beulaibh agus bacadh eadar an tuath agus dòigh-beatha dhùthchasach, agus 'mar a chaidh am maor tro Gharrabost', bha fios aig na Leòdhasaich air na thachradh nam briseadh na riaghailtean, gum biodh iad 'buailteach bhi air fhògradh gu h-aithghearr mach as an t-seilbh' (Lews Estate, 1879, td. 13). Bha leisgeul aig na h-uachdarain anns an fheallsanachd ùr agus reachdas a thaobh slàinte an t-sluaigh a bha a' sileadh sìos bho Riaghaltas na Rìoghachd Aonaichte aig an àm. Dh'fhàs uallach ro throm, ge-tà, air muinntir nan eilean, mar eisimpleir, gu bhith a' cur suas gun dàil 'tighean comhnuidh ... le clach 'us aol ... da sheòmar an car is lugha ... siomlairean anns na cinnbhallachan (gables) ... a' bhàthaich le dorus air leth aig ceann no air culthaobh an tighcomhnuidh' (Lews Estate, 1879, td. 5).

Ann an co-dhùnadh, feumaidh sgoilearachd agus rannsachadh ann an raon a' chànain ann an Alba a bhith a' cumail ceum ri atharrachaidhean briathrachais fo bhuaidh teicneolais agus a' chultair dhùthchasaich, agus a rèir mar a sgaoil cleachdaidhean is atharrachaidhean nar latha fhèin. Feumaidh obair rannsachaidh sùil a thoirt an còmhnaidh air clàraidhean a tha ri làimh, eadar co-chruinneachaidhean nan taighean-tasgaidh agus stuth sgrìobhte nach eil fo amharc sgoilearan cànanachais. Tha eisimpleirean air leth tarraingeach againn air dòighean beatha an fhicheadamh linn far an robh dòighean labhairt agus gnàthasan-cainnt air bilean an t-sluaigh bhon naoidheamh agus ochdamh linn deug (faic [Campbell], 1957, tdd. 313–17; [MacLeod], 2005; Dòmhnallach, 1996, td. 95). Dh'fhaodadh a ràdh gu bheil dàimh nach aithnichte eadar na dòighean beatha agus an cànan, no nach eil briathran agus abairtean a thathas a' clàradh anns na taighean-tasgaidh fo phrosbaig sgoilearachd fhathast. Bha obair air leth ri làimh ann an saothair Aonghais 'Ease' MhicLeòid (1916–2002) mun bhaile aige, Calbost, agus na bailtean mu a thimcheall ann an Leòdhas. Rinn esan co-chruinneachadh mòr de dh'àirneis agus de dh'uidheam cuide ri briathrachas a bheireadh dealbh dhuinn air teachd an tìr agus atharrachaidhean a thàinig fon amharc aige mar sàr Ghàidheal (Hirst, 2005; Robson, 2004). Nach eil beàrn ann fhathast air taobh a' chultair dhùthchasaich, far a bheil feum ann airson drochaid eadar cànan is eachdraidh, agus airson drochaid mar cho-aghaidh (*interface*) de dh'obair làitheil is còmhradh air bilean an t-sluaigh, a bhith gan tarraing ri chèile le surd? Mar bu trice, 's e aon sgoilear nar measg a chuir aithne air a' chuspair seo – agus cha toirear iongnadh oirnn idir. Nuair a thug an Dr Iain MacAonghais seachad pàipear do Chomunn Gàidhlig Inbhir Nis anns a' Mhàrt 2006, rinn e iomradh air eòlas sònraichte leis na briathran a leanas:

> *All of us who have been brought up in Gaelic-speaking communities know that in addition to the songs and stories we heard from childhood onwards, there were (and no doubt still are) a great number of items of information usually just mentioned in passing, and that these are of a kind which are apt to escape the notice of students of tradition, or if they do get mentioned at all in published works, are more often than not relegated to footnotes. Yet they are frequently of great interest not only in themselves but because of their association*

and connections with other aspects of our history and culture and the immense fabric of Gaelic tradition in its entirety… . It is important to remember that there are many men and women who do not consider themselves to be tradition bearers at all and who yet can have at their command a surprisingly wide range of traditional lore. And the smallest snippet of that lore can sometimes fill a vacant space in our picture of the culture of our nation (MacInnes, 2004, tdd. 406, 418).

Pàipear-Taice A (bho MhacDhùghaill, 1924, td. 169)
A' Ghobhar

Is e 'bò an duine bhochd' a theirteadh ris a' ghobhair. Anns an t-seann aimsir an uair a bha barrachd dhaoine is na bu lugha de na fèidh anns a' Ghàidhealtachd, bha a' ghobhar ro phailt anns an dùthaich. Tha ainmean àitean, sean-fhocail is gach uile sheòrsa ranntachd, ged nach biodh eachdraidh idir orra, ga dhearbhadh sin. Chan urrainn dhomh innseadh ciamar a tha mi nam inntinn fhèin a' comh-chaigneachadh na gobhair is an èibhlidh chuachaich. Faodaidh gur e rann a bhios gu tric a' ruith air mo mheòmhair a tha aig bun an smuain:

'A' ruith nan gobhar feadh nan creag,
'S e 'n t-èibhleadh beag bu docha leam …'

Co dhiubh, tha e fior gun d' fhalbh a' ghobhar is an t-èideadh dùthchail mun aon àm, is chan eil teagamh nach toir sinn iomad uair sùil iargaineach nan dèidh le chèile. Bha e air a chunntadh gun robh bainne nan gobhar na bu bhrìoghmhoire nam bainne nam bò, is gu sònraichte gun robh e math gu càise a dhèanamh…. Mar a e air a chunntadh gun robh bainne bà ruaidh na b' fheàrr na bainne bà air bith eile, bha bainne nan gobhar geala na bu bhrìoghmhoire na bainne seòrsa eile. An Eirinn tha an aon earbsa aca à bainne nan gobhar gu leigheas na caitheamh is a tha anns an eilean againne à 'bainne gun ghaoth'.

Pàipear-Taice B (bho Chomunn Dùthchail na h-Alba, 1848)

Innear Theann. – Is còir i so a chruinneachadh gu cùramach o na beathaichibh 'us o na pòrraibh luibheanach – duilleagan seargta, criadh loisgte, lusan salach, luath, pòll, feamainn, agus gach spruilleach eile. Rachadh na stuthan sin a mheasgachadh 'an ceann a cheile, an cumail o chaitheamh, le an còdaich thairis, chum an dion, cho math agus a ghabhas deanamh, o ghaoith, o ghrèin 's o uisge, – faodar breath de thalamh tròm a chur thairis orra.

Innear Bhog. – Is còir i so a ghleidheadh, rachadh gach dreabhas air feadh an tighe, uisg a' bhàich, stuth an tighe dhìomhair a chruinneachadh ann an amar. Faodar amar a dheanamh de bharail air a cur fodha 's an talamh, no tòll a dheanamh air a chàramh suas air gach taobh le *aspalte*, clach 'us aol, no cràidh. Oibrichidh innear bhog air bàrr aig gach ceum de 'fhàs mòran na's fheàrr agus na's luaithe na innear theann ùin fhada mu'n dearg an ùir oirre chum na freumhan òga 'bheathachadh.

Tùsan

Caimbeul, Aonghas (1973). *Suathadh ri Iomadh Rubha: Eachdraidh a Bheatha le Aonghas Caimbeul (Am Puilean)*, deas. le Iain Moireach. Glaschu: Gairm.

[Campbell J. L.] 'Fear Chanaidh' (1957). 'An dòigh air an rachadh Tigh Dubh a thogail'. *Gairm*, Àir. 20, tdd. 313–17.

Cheape, Hugh (2012), 'Alexander Fenton'. *Proceedings of the Society of Antiquaries of Scotland*, Iml. 142, tdd. 1–8.

Cheape, Hugh (ri thighinn). 'Coimhearsnachd chànanach mar fhoillseachadh àraid ann an sgrìobhaidhean bho dheireadh an 19mh linn', ann an *Rannsachadh na Gàidhlig 7*, Glaschu.

Christison, Robert (1882). 'Notice of a Knocking-stone or Barley Mortar of Granite from Ballachulish'. *Proceedings of the Society of Antiquaries of Scotland*, Iml. 16, tdd. 25-6.

Comunn Dùthchail na h-Alba (1848). *An Dara Rabhadh Bliadhnail do Luchd Aiteachaidh na Gaeltachd*. Dùn Eideann: Comunn Dùchail na h-Alba.

Cox, Richard (deas.) (2009). *Dualchas agus an Àrainneachd*. Slèite: Clò Ostaig.

Dòmhnallach, Domhnall Eairdsidh (1996). 'Bàrd a' bruidhinn mu chuid bàrdachd fhèin'. *SGS*, Iml. 17 (*Fèill-Sgrìbhinn do Ruaraidh MacThomais*), tdd. 87–102.

Duns, John (1882). 'Jottings from Mid-Lochaber'. *Proceedings of the Society of Antiquaries of Scotland*, Iml. 16, tdd. 49–56.

Fenton, Alexander (1985). 'The Scope of Regional Ethnology', in *The Shape of the Past 1: Essays in Scottish Ethnology*. Dùn Èideann: John Donald, tdd. 43–54.

Fox, Adam, agus Woolf, Daniel (deas.) (2003). *The Spoken Word: Oral Culture in Britain 1500-1850*. Manchester: Manchester University Press.

Gailey, Alan, and Ó hÓgain, Dáithí (deas.) (1982). *Gold under the Furze: Studies in Folk Tradition Presented to Caoimhín Ó Danachair*. Baile Àtha Cliath: Glendale Press.

Hirst, Caroline (2005). *'Back to the wind, front to the sun': The Traditional Croft House*. Port Nis: Urras Leabhraichean nan Eilean.

Laing, Calum (2013). *An t-Urramach Iain MacRuairidh: A Bheatha agus na Sgrìobhaidhean Aige*. Inbhir Nis: Clàr.

Lauder, T. D. (1846). *Directions for Taking and Curing Herrings, and for Curing Cod, Ling, Tusk and Hake*. Dùn Èideann: T. Constable.

Lews Estate (1879). *Rules and Regulations of Lews Estate in Gaelic and English*. Steòrnabhagh: Lews Estate.

MacAulay, Donald (1986). 'New Gaelic?' *Scottish Language*, Iml. 5, tdd. 120-5.

MacCalmain, T. M. (1954). 'Eachann MacDhùghaill: Beagan mu dheighinn agus cunntas air na sgrìobh e an Gàidhlig', *Gairm*, Àir. 8, tdd. 362-8.

MacCoinnich, Aonghas (2006). 'Cleiffis of Irne: Clann Choinnich agus gnìomhachas iarainn, c. 1569-1630', ann an Wilson McLeod, James E. Fraser agus Anja Gunderloch (deas.), *Cànan & Cultar/Language & Culture: Rannsachadh na Gàidhlig 3*, tdd. 137–52. Dùn Èideann: Dunedin Academic Press.

MacDhòmhnaill, Coinneach D. (1976). 'A' trusadh dhan Fhaclair', *Gairm*, Àir. 96, tdd. 338–40.

MacDhòmhnaill, Coinneach D. (1977). 'A' trusadh dhan Fhaclair', *Gairm*, Àir. 97, tdd. 94–7.
MacDonald, Archibald (1894). 'Religion and Mythology of the Celts'. *TGSI*, Iml. 19, tdd. 37–49.
MacDhùghaill, Eachann (1924). 'Beachdachadh mu Ainmhidhean na Gàidhealtachd'. *TGSI*, Iml. 31, tdd. 135-74.
MacDhùghaill, Eachann (1930). 'Beachdachadh mu Ainmhidhean na Gàidhealtachd. Earrann II'. *TGSI*, Iml. 35, tdd. 98-144.
MacFhionghain, Aonghas (1902). 'An Tigh Cèilidh'. *Mac-Talla*, Iml. 11, td. 78.
MacFhionghain, Niall (2002). 'Faclan agus Abairtean – Ceann a Deas an Eilean Sgitheanaich'. *TGSI*, Iml. 62, tdd. 277-97.
MacGregor, Martin (2002). 'The Genealogical Histories of Gaelic Scotland', ann am Fox agus Woolf 2002, tdd. 196-239.
MacInnes, Rev. Duncan (deas.) (1890). *Folk and Hero Tales. Waifs and Strays of Celtic Tradition II – Argyllshire Series*. Lunnainn: David Nutt.
MacInnes, Rev. Duncan (1894). 'Notes on Gaelic Technical Terms'. *TGSI*, Iml. 19, tdd. 213-7.
MacInnes, John (2004). 'A Fieldwork Miscellany'. *TGSI*, Iml. 63, tdd. 406-18.
McIntosh, Angus (1952). *Introduction to a Survey of Scottish Dialects*. Dùn Èideann: Thomas Nelson.
[Mackenzie, Sir Francis] (1838). *Hints for the Use of Highland Tenants and Cottagers. By a Proprietor*. Inbhis Nis: Robert Carruthers.
Macleod, Donald John (1976). 'Gaelic Prose'. *TGSI*, Iml. 49, tdd. 198-230.
[MacLeod, George] Seòras Chaluim Sheòrais (2005). *Muir is Tìr*. Steòrnabhagh: Acair.
Macleod, Iseabail, agus McClure, J. Derrick (deas.) (2012). *Scotland in Definition: A History of Scottish Dictionaries*. Dùn Èideann: John Donald.
MacLeòid, I. N. (1947). 'Dìmeas na Gàidhlige', *An Gàidheal*, Iml. 52, tdd. 86-7.
MacLeòid, Murchadh (1968). 'A' trusadh dhan an Fhaclair', *Gairm*, Àir. 64, tdd. 339–41.
MacLeòid, Ruairidh (1981). 'Comann nan Sgoiltean Gàidhlig', *Gairm*, Àir. 114, tdd. 161-5.
[MacLeòid, Tarmod], 'Am Bàrd Bochd' (1968). 'A' trusadh dhan an Fhaclair'. *Gairm*, Àir. 63, tdd. 270-6.
MacRury, John (1893). 'Tàillear Ghearraidh-Bo-Stig'. *TGSI*, Iml. 19 (1893), tdd. 25-37.
MacThómais, Ruaraidh, agus Domhnallach, Fionnlagh (1954). 'Roimh-ràdh'. *Gairm*, Àir. 8, td. 303.
Meek, Donald E. (2002). 'The Pulpit and the Pen: Clergy, Orality and Print in the Scottish Gaelic World', ann am Fox agus Woolf, 2002, tdd. 84-118
Oftedal, Magne (1956). *The Gaelic of Leurbost, Isle of Lewis*. Oslo: Norwegian Universities Press.
O' Rahilly, T. F. (1932). *Irish Dialects Past and Present, with Chapters on Scottish and Manx*. Baile Àtha Cliath: Institiúid Ard-Léinn Bhaile Átha Cliath.
Robson, Michael (2004). *The Angus Macleod Archive. An Introduction to the Collection*. Port Nis: Urras Leabhraichean nan Eilean.
Steensberg, A. (1993). 'Wörter und Sachen / Terms and Realities', ann an Hugh Cheape (deas.), *Tools and Traditions: Studies in European Ethnology Presented to Alexander Fenton*, tdd. 16-21. Dùn Èideann: National Museums of Scotland.
Stephens, Henry (3rd edn 1871). *The Book of the Farm*, Vol. 1. Edinburgh: W Blackwood and Sons.

Thomson, Derick S. (1978). 'Words and Expressions from Lewis'. *TGSI*, Iml. 50, tdd. 173-200.
Wagner, Heinrich (1981). *Linguistic Atlas and Survey of Irish Dialects*. Baile Àtha Cliath: Institiúid Ard-Léinn Baile Átha Cliath.

17

Briathrachas an iasgaich ann an Eilean Bharraigh: faclan airson nan sgothan

Ciorstaidh NicLeòid

Oilthigh Dhùn Èideann

Tha beatha nam Barrach air a bhith an eisimeil ris an iasgach fad iomadach linn. Le crìonadh anns a' Ghàidhlig mar phrìomh chànan na coimhearsnachd agus atharrachaidhean mòra air tighinn air an iasgach fhèin, chuireadh romham na h-uiread de bhriathrachas agus de sheanfhaclan agus a b' urrainnear co-cheangailte ris an iasgach a ghleidheadh mus deigheadh an call bhon chainnt airson tràchdas Maighstearachd na Feallsanachd (MPhil) aig Oilthigh Ghlaschu (NicLeòid, 2012). A' cleachdadh agallamhan le Barraich a tha air am beòshlainte fhaighinn bhon iasgach, rinneadh clàraidhean den bhriathrachas seo. Fhuaras farsaingeachd bhriathrachais mun cuairt air ceithir prìomh roinntean: sgothan, uidheamachd, èisg agus an t-sìde. Anns a' phàipear seo, bheirear sùil air a' bhriathrachas a tha aca airson nan sgothan fhèin. A thuilleadh air a' chruinneachadh fhèin, rinneadh sgrùdadh an dà chuid a thaobh dualchainnt agus seimeantaig nam faclan a chruinnicheadh, le prìomhachas air an sgrùdadh seimeantaig. Anns na leanas, chithear am briathrachas a chaidh a thionail agus bheirear iomradh air an dà chuid dualchainnt agus seimeantaig.

Sgrùdadh air dualchainntean

Chaidh obair ionmholta a dhèanamh le Carl H. Borgstrøm a' rannsachadh agus a' sgrudadh dualchainnt Ghàidhlig Bharraigh. Chaidh a shaothair fhoillseachadh fon tiotal 'The Dialect of Barra in the Outer Hebrides' ann an 1937 (Borgstrøm, 1937). Gheibhear cuideachd fiosrachadh mu dhualchainnt Bharraigh ann an toraidhean 'Suirbhidh Dualchainntean Gàidhlig na h-Alba' (SGDS), pròiseict rannsachaidh a thòisich aig Oilthigh Dhùn Èideann ann an 1949 (Ó Dochartaigh, 1997, Iml. 1, td. vii). Chleachdadh ceathrar luchd-bhratha à Barraigh anns an rannschadh seo. Bha dithist dhiubh sin air fiosrachadh a thoirt seachad do Bhorgstrøm (Ó Dochartaigh, 1997, iml. 1, td. 84). Am measg toraidhean 'Faclair Eachdraidheil Gàidhlig na h-Alba' (HDSG), pròiseact a thòisich ann an 1966 fo stiùir an Ollaimh Ruaraidh MacThòmais, gheibhear faclan is abairtean a chaidh an tionail an measg nam Barrach mar an ceudna. Anns an rannsachadh seo chuireadh feum cuideachd air *Linguistic Atlas and Survey of the Irish Dialects* (LASID) (Wagner 1958-1969), rannsachadh a rinneadh fo stiùir Heinrich Wagner. Ged nach deach luchd-bratha à Barraigh a chleachdadh bha a rannsachadh a' gabhail a-steach Gàidhlig na h-Alba.

Am measg nam faclairean, liostaichean fhaclan agus leabhraichean a chuireadh gu feum san rannsachadh seo bha an leabhar *Gaelic Words and Expressions from South Uist and Eriskay* (Campbell, 1972). Am measg an luchd-bratha a chleachd Maighstir Ailein, bha seanchaidhean agus bàird nan sgìrean agus daoine aig an robh Gàidhlig a-mhàin. Leis gur h-ann air an sgìre as fhaisge air Barraigh a tha an cruinneachadh seo agus le faisg air trì mìle facal sa chruinneachadh fhèin, chleachdadh an leabhar mar phrìomh thùs rannsachaidh. Nochd faclan agus abairtean à Barraigh san deasachadh as ùire (1972) de chruinneachadh Mhaighstir Ailein, le faclan a chaidh a thogail bho Niall Mac na Ceàrdaich agus Anna NicIain a' nochdadh ann.

Air cuspair an iasgaich, chaidh an leabhar *Muir is Tìr* le Seòras (Calum Sheòrais) MacLeòid fhoillseachadh ann an 2005 (MacLeòid, 2005). Rugadh MacLeòid ann am Beàrnaraigh Leòdhais aig deireadh an naoidheamh linn deug. A thuilleadh air a' chruinneachadh bhrathrachais fhèin a tha a' gabhail a-steach iomadh chuspair co-cheangailte ris an iasgach, cleachdaidhean, dòighean obrach agus seann eòlas, tha dealbhan-làimhe eireachdail a' nochdadh an cois nam faclan san leabhar.

Sgrùdadh leiseachail

Bha prìomhachas air fòn-eòlas agus cruth-eòlas ann an *SGDS*, agus is ann mar seo a tha cuid rannsachadh cànanachais ann an Gàidhlig na h-Alba anns an fharsaingeachd. Is e glè bheag de rannsachadh leicseachail a tha aithnichte ann an sgoilearachd na Gàidhlig ach tha sgrùdadh sgoilearachd leicseachail air nochdadh. Rinn Alex J. MacAskill (1966) sgrùdadh leicseachail anns a' phàipear aige 'Differences in Dialect, Vocabulary and General idiom between the Islands'. Thug MacAskill sùil air obair-sgrìobhaidh sgoilearan Gàidhlig aig Acadamaidh Rìoghail Inbhir Nis far an robh e na tidsear (MacAskill, 1966, td. 64). Le sgoilearan às na h-Eileanan Siar a' frithealadh na sgoile aig an àm, rannsaich MacAskill eadar-dhealachaidhean briathrachais eadar sgoilearan às na eileanan diofrach, sgoilearan Barrach nam measg.

Chaidh sgrùdadh leicseachail air dualchainntean Gàidhlig nan Eilean Siar a dhèanamh le Seumas Grannd cuideachd (Grannd, 1987, 1995-6). Chleachdadh ceisteachain le luchd-bratha air feadh nan Eilean Siar, 'interviewing ordinary native Gaelic speakers, using a questionnaire which was designed to highlight the differences between dialects' (Grannd, 1995-6, td. 52). Rinn Grannd sgrùdadh coimeasach air Gàidhlig Ìle agus dualchainntean Earra-Ghàidheal agus Arainn (Grannd, 2000), far an tugadh iomradh cuideachd air dualchainntean eile (Grannd, 2000, td. 2). Is e an rannsachadh a rinn Roy Wentworth (2003, 2005) an rannsachadh as fharsainge a tha air nochdadh o choinn ghoirid a thaobh leicseòlais ann an Gàidhlig na h-Alba. A thuilleadh air a thràchdas PhD air fòn-eòlas dualchainnt Ghàidhlig Gheàrrloch (Wentworth, 2005), nochd cruinneachadh leicseachail fon tiotal *Faclan is Abairtean à Ros an Iar: Gaelic Words and Phrases from Wester Ross* ann an 2003.

Sgrùdadh seimeantaig

Is e glè bheag de dh'obair sgoilearail ann an Gàidhlig na h-Alba a tha air sgrùdadh a dhèanamh air seimeantaig a' chànain ann an doimhneachd. Thug an t-Ollamh Roibeard Ó Maolalaigh òraid seachad air a' chuspair aig Rannsachadh na Gàidhlig 5 ann an 2008 agus e ag ràdh: 'The meaning of lexical items (i.e. dictionary words) represent one of the most understudied aspects of Scottish Gaelic' (Ó Maolalaigh, 2008b: 7). A thuilleadh air an òraid seo, rinn Ó Maolalaigh sgrùdadh seimeantaig na alt air Gàidhlig Thiriodh (Ó Maolalaigh, 2008a) agus san alt aige air 'snowflake' (Ó Maolalaigh, 2010). Thug Meek (2006) sùil air cleachdadh an fhacail *smùid* anns a' Ghàidhlig Albannaich agus e a' ceangal *smùid* ri *bàta-mùid*.

Nochd 'Semantic Distribution in Gaelic Dialects' le Myles Dillon ann an 1953, far an tugadh sùil air caochlaideachd sheimeantach an dà chuid ann an Gàidhlig na h-Èireann agus na h-Alba. Sheall Liam Mac Mhathúna (1978) air seimeantachd na Gaeilge na aiste ach thugadh iomradh air Gàidhlig na h-Alba ann an cuid dhiubh. Rinn Colm Ó Baoill (1978) sgrùdadh coimeasach eadar Gaeilge Uladh agus Gàidhlig na h-Alba agus thog e an aire dha na sgaraidhean seimeantach a nochd, mar a rinn Grannd (2000) na chuid rannsachaidh air Gàidhlig Ìle.

Gàidhlig ann am Barraigh

Tha crìonadh dha-rìribh air a thighinn air cleachdadh agus comas na Gàidhlig am measg an t-sluaigh ann am Barraigh agus Bhàtarsaigh. Nuair a chaidh rannsachadh Borgstrøm a dhèanamh anns na tricheadan bha a' Ghàidhlig mar phrìomh cànan na coimhearsnachd, ged a bha i nas treasa anns na sgìrean iomallach na bha i ann am Bàgh a' Chaisteil fhèin. Bha cuid mhath na cloinne gun a' Bheurla ro aois na sgoile agus corra seann bhodach is chailleach gun Bheurla mar an ceudna (Borgstrøm, 1937, td. 71). Sheall toraidhean a' chunntais-sluaigh ann an 1931 gun robh tuilleadh daoine ann am Barraigh gun Bheurla agus le Gàidhlig a-mhàin na bha ann le Beurla a-mhàin (Duwe, 2005, td. 7). Gun teagamh cha b' ann mar sin a bha suidheachadh na Gàidhlig anns an eilean nuair a rinneadh obair-làraich an rannsachaidh seo ann an 2011-12. Cha do lorgadh duine sam bith gun Bheurla agus lorgadh gu leòr a bhuin don àite agus a thogadh ann gun chomas sa Ghàidhlig a leigeadh leotha a cleachdadh gu làitheil.

Tha dearbhadh a' chrìonaidh seo san sgrùdadh a rinneadh le Duwe (2005) air freagairtean ceistean na Gàidhlig anns na cunntasan-sluaigh bho 1881-2001. Thathar a' sealltainn gun do thòisich crìonadh a thighinn air a' Ghàidhlig mar chànan na coimhearsnachd anns na 1940an. Chithear anns na toraidhean on chunntas-shluaigh as ùire gu bheil comas sa Ghàidhlig fhathast a' crìonadh anns an eilean agus lùghdachadh bho 66.4% de shluagh an eilein le comas air a' Ghàidhlig a labhairt ann an 2001 agus 62% ann an 2011 (National Records of Scotland 2011). Mheas Duwe (2005, td. 1) gun e leasachaidhean ann am foghlam tro mheadhan na Gàidhlig anns an eilean ìre ro-sgoile prìomh adhbhar an lùghdachaidh ann a' chrìonadh seo am measg na h-oigridh às dèidh 1981.

Is ann mar thoradh air crìonadh na Gàidhlig anns an eilean a thàinig an cuspair rannsachaidh seo gu bith, le cunnart ann gun cailleadh an eòlais air briathrachas an iasgaich. Anns na leanas bheirear sùil air toraidhean an rannsachaidh ach an toiseach mìnichear san aithghearrachd mar a rinneadh an rannsachadh agus mar a thaghadh an luchd-bratha.

Modhan-obrach
Ceisteachain
Chuireadh ceisteachain iomchaidh leithid Faclair Eachdraidheil na Gàidhlig agus LASID gu feum ann a bhith a' cruthachadh cheisteachan dha na ceithir prìomh roinntean rannsachaidh: sgothan, uidheamachd, èisg agus sìde. Thugadh sùil air na 60 facal ann an *SGDS* co-cheangailte ris a' mhuir, a' chladach, an iasgach no an t-sìde agus 125 a nochd air an dearbh chuspair ann an LASID. Chleachdadh cuideachd an leabhar *Muir is Tìr* agus faclair Dwelly (2001) aig àm leasachadh nan ceisteachan. Rinneadh tuilleadh rannsachaidh air an iasgach ann am Barraigh agus na bhiodh bitheanta anns an eilean: na dòighean iasgaich, na ghlacadh iasgairean, agus na bhathar agus a thathar a' cur gu tìr. Chaidh paidhleat a dhèanamh air a' chiad cheisteachan le triùir den luchd-bhrata agus chaidh na ceisteachain air fad a leasachadh mar thoradh air a' phaidhleat.

Dealbhan

Thogadh dealbhan de sgothan agus uidheamachd iasgaich mun cuairt an eilein agus chleachdadh na dealbhan seo cuide ris na ceisteachain airson faclan a thrusadh agus soilleireachadh fhaighinn.

Agallamhan

Chleachdadh agallamhan airson faclan agus abairtean a thionail. Dh'fhaighnich mi dhen luchd-bratha an robh Gàidhlig aca airson facal a thugadh dhaibh sa Bheurla bhon cheisteachan no gu dè a chanadh iad ris na bha sa dhealbh sa Ghàidhlig. Gu tric thigeadh tuilleadh fhaclan bho mhìneachadh no còmhradh nàdarra air a' chuspair tron agallamh fhèin no às dèidh làimh. Dh'iarrainn faclan no abairtean air an robhar eòlach bho sgìrean eile a sheachnadh mur an robhar gan cleachdadh am Barraigh. Bha mi ag amas air faclan no abairtean a bha nàdarra ann an Gàidhlig Bharraigh. A thuilleadh air agallamhan nan dachannan fhèin, thugadh cuid den luchd-bhratha còmhla corra uair airson beachdachadh air a' chuspair. Anns na cruinneachaidhean seo, chumadh còmhradh mun chuspair leis an luchd-bhratha. Bhruidhneadh iad eadarra fhèin no mhìnicheadh iad seann chleachdaidhean agus uidheamachd dhomhsa. Chaidh na h-agallamhan agus na cruinneachaidhean uile a chlàradh le inneal-clàraidh didsiteach.

Luchd-bratha

Dh'fheumadh an luchd-bratha a bhith freagarrach airson rannsachadh cànanachais den leithid agus a bhith deònach pairt a ghabhail anns an rannsachadh far an deigheadh an clàradh agus an ainmeachadh. Thaghadh luchd-bratha a chaidh àrach agus a thogail anns an eilean le pàrantan bhon eilean mar an ceudna. A thuilleadh air seo, dh'fheumadh Gàidhlig a bhith aca mar phrìomh chànan na dachaigh nuair a bha iad òg agus gun cleachdar a' Ghàidhlig gu làitheil dhan latha an-diugh. A thaobh an iasgaich, dh'fheumadh mion-eòlas a bhith aca air an iasgach ann am Barraigh tro bhith ag obair sa ghnìomhachas agus beòshlainte fhaighinn uaireigin nam beatha obrach. Chleachdadh naoinear luchd-bratha, seachdnar fhear agus dithist bhan. Bha ochdnar dhiubh a bha air an dreuchd a leigeil seachad agus bha aona fhear fhathast gu mòr an sàs ann an obair an iasgaich air an eilean. Bha ochdnar eadar 60 is 79 bliadhna a dh'aois nuair a rinneadh an rannsachadh agus dithist còrr is 80 bliadhna a dh'aois. Chaidh a' mhòr-chuid dhiubh a thogail ann an teaghlaichean iasgaich far an robh an t-athair agus bràithrean an athar na iasgair. Dh'fhàg seo iad eòlach air faclan agus abairtean nach robh cho bitheanta nam beatha inbheach fhèin ach a chualas nan òige.

Chaidh eisimpleir Uí Churnáin (2007) a leantail agus giorrachadh ann an clò trom airson gach neach-bratha. Gheibhear trì litrichean aig toiseach nan giorrachaidhean seo a' riochdachadh ainm an neach-bhratha agus dà àireamh às dèidh sin a' riochdachadh bliadhna-bhreith an neach-bhratha (gun an 19), mar eisimpleir **CIM30,** Calum Iòsaph MacLeòid a rugadh ann an 1930. San tràchdas fhèin (NicLeòid, 2012) gheibhear fiosrachadh a bharrachd mun luchd-bratha, an teaghlach agus am beatha.

CIM30: Calum Iòsaph MacLeòid
CMN45: Calum MacNèill
CPM45: Ciorstaidh P. NicLeòid
DBM47: Dòmhnall B. MacLeòid
DUM67: Dòmhnall Uilleim MacLeòid
IDS29: Iain Mac na Ceàrdaich
MFM51: Màiri Flòraidh NicLeòid
RDU42: Roddy MacLeòid

Gheibhear fiosrachadh mu fhuaimneachadh an fhacail ann an IPA ann an clò trom anns na leanas agus cruthan san tuiseal thabhartach agus ghinideach nuair nach eilear a' leantail nan cruthan cumanta a gheibhear ann an dualchainntean eile. A thuilleadh air na faclan fhèin, gheibhear air uairean eisimpleir den chleachdadh ann an seantans. Far nach eil giorrachadh ainm a' nochdadh ri taobh facal is ann air tàillibh agus gun d' fhuaras am facal seo aig gach neach-bratha.

Sgoth agus na sgothan

An taca ri cuid a dhualchainntean, is e *sgoth* am facal coitcheann a fhuaras ann am Barraigh airson 'boat' seach *bàta*.

    1.1   *sgoth, -an* **skɔ̃** ainmear boireann, tabhartach: *sgothaidh*, ginideach: *na sgothadh*; 'boat – generic, small boat without a deck – specific'

- **CIM30:** *Chì thu na sgothan aig cidhe Bhàgh a Tuath no chì thu na sgothan aig cidhe Bhàgh a' Chaisteil.*
- **CPM45**: *Even leis na tràileirean chanadh tu ' 'eil na sgothan a-muigh an-diugh?'*
- **CIM30**: *Tha sgoth, chan eil i ach ma fhichead troigh, eadar fichead troigh agus tha bàta nas motha na tha sin ... deich troigh fichead, chan eil na h-uidhir de dhiofar ann.*

Chithear sa mhìneachadh mu dheireadh gu bheil cleachdadh sònraichte aig *sgoth* agus is e seo airson sgoth a tha nas lugha na bàta. Dh'innseadh dhomh gu bheil *a' gheòla(g)* nas lugha na tha *an sgoth* agus *am bàta* nas motha. Gheibhear am mìneachadh sònraichte seo mar an aon mhìneachadh air an fhacal *sgoth* ann an Dwelly (2001, td. 78):

Sgoth, -Skiff, (sailing-boat, sharp at stem & stern, carrying lugsail, or lugsail and jib, and measuring from about 14ft to 30ft keel. The mast is lowered a-stem, not a-stern as in other boats).

Agus a-rithist anns an leabhar *Muir is Tìr* (MacLeòid, 2005, td. 7):

Sgoth: Skiff (two-ended boat).

A thaobh morf-eòlais chithear gu bheil deireadh -(e)adh air an fhacal seo sa ghinideach. Is e feart dhualchainnt Bharraigh a tha seo far a bheil –(e)adh air deireadh ainmear boireann sa ghinideach. Nochd am feart seo feadh an rannsachaidh agus nochd e san sgrùdadh aig Borgstrøm mar an ceudna. Fhuair Ó Maolalaigh (2008a, td. 482) agus NicIlleDhuinn (2011, td. 82) fianais den ghinideach ann an Gàidhlig Thiriodh agus tha am feart seo cuideachd ri chluinntinn ann an dualchainntean Gàidhlig sgìrean eile leithid Uibhist a Deas agus Èirisgeigh. Chithear cuideachd gu bheil cruthan palataiche (palatal) rin lorg san tuiseal thabhartach. Is e an t-eisimpleir a fhuaras leis an fhacal sgoth 'leis an sgothaidh'. Bha am feart seo cuideachd nochdte feadh an rannsachaidh agus cluinnear e ann an dualchainntean eile sna h-Eilean Siar.

Chithear gu bheil cuid de na fhaclan a thathar a' cur gu feum airson nan sgothan a' mìneachadh gu dè a thathar a' glacadh leis an sgoth, na gu dè an uidheamachd no dòigh-ghlacaidh a tha aig an sgoth no cò bad san togadh an sgoth.

1.1 *sgoth, -an* **skɔ̃** ainmear boireann, tabhartach: *sgothaidh*, ginideach: *na sgothadh*; 'boat – generic, small boat without a deck – specific'

    1.1.1 *sgoth-bharailtean* 'stock boat' **CMN45**
    1.1.2 *sgoth-chlèibh* 'creel boat' **RDU42**
    1.1.3 *sgoth-chreachainn* 'scallop boat' **RDU42**
    1.1.4 *sgoth-fhosgailte* 'open boat' **CMN45**
    1.1.5 *sgoth-ghiomaich* 'lobster boat' **DBM47**
    1.1.6 *sgoth-iasgaich* 'fishing boat' **CMN45**
    1.1.7 *sgoth-Manach* 'Manx built boat' **CMN45**
    1.1.8 *sgoth-portain* 'green crab boat' **DBM47**
    1.1.9 *sgoth-seòlaidh* 'sail-boat' **CIM30**
    1.1.10 *sgoth-Suaineach* 'Swedish built boat' **CMN45**

1.2 *bàta* - ə/-ɔ -*aichean* **RDU42, DBM47, CMN45**, -*annan* **CIM30** ainmear fireann 'ship, boat with a deck'

    1.2.1 *bàt'-aiseig* **RDU42**, *bat'-eiseig* **CIM30** 'ferry boat'
    1.2.2 *bàta-bathar* 'cargo boat' **CMN45**
    1.2.3 *bàta-cargo* 'cargo boat' **CMN45**
    1.2.4 *bàta-chlèibh* 'creel boat' **RDU42**

1.2.5   *bàta-chreachainn* 'scallop boat' **RDU42**
1.2.6   *bàta-chrùbag* 'brown crab boat' **RDU42**
1.2.7   *bàta-ghiomach* 'lobster boat' **RDU42**
1.2.8   *bàta-smùide* **RDU42**, *bata-smùideadh* **DBM47** 'steamboat'
1.2.9   *bàta-seòlaidh* 'sail-boat' **RDU42**
1.2.10 *bàta-siùil* 'sail-boat' **DBM47**
1.2.11 *bàta-sàbhailidh* 'lifeboat' **DBM47, MFM51, CIM30**
1.2.12 *bàta-teasairginn* 'lifeboat' **RDU42, CPM45, CMN45**

Nochd eisimpleir de feart sònraichte ann an dualchainnt Bharraigh aig feadhainn san fhacal *bàta* agus is e sin cleachdadh [-ɔ] seach [-ə] aig deireadh fhacail gun bheum. Fhuaras dearbhadh den an seo ann an *SGDS* bho neach-bratha 28, ann am faclan leithid, *bail*e (65), *dorch*a (332), *eal*a (370) agus *tall*a (826), ach is e [-ə] a bha aig an triùir luchd-bratha eile. Mhìnich Borgstrøm seo mar:

> When this vowel stands in absolute final position before pausa, it is lowered and retracted to the position of ɔ (low-back); it is not-round, and the articulation is still rather loose, so that it is different from the ordinary ɔ; I transcribe ɔ̃. This final ɔ̃ is characteristic of the Barra dialect, and is not heard e.g. in Uist. When another word follows immediately, the sound is ə. (Borgstrom, 1937 td. 99)

Mar sin, nuair a nochd *bàta* le facal eile ga leantail mar a tha againn eadar 1.2.1 agus 1.2.12, is e /-ə/ a bhiodh aig an luchd-bratha air fad.

1.3   *eathar, -raichean* ainmear fireann 'small boat'

Tha *eathar* cumanta ann an cuid a dhualchainntean airson *sgoth* no *bàta*. Cha chualas tric *eathar* ann am Barraigh ged a thathar eòlach air ciall agus cleachdadh an fhacail ann an sgìrean eile. Feadh nan agallamhan agus nan cruinneachaidhean, cha deach a chleachdadh ach corra uair le dithist den luchd-bhratha **RDU42** agus **CMN45**, ged a nochd *sgoth* sa bhitheantas leotha.

Anns an liosta a leanas, gheibhear cuid de na faclan eile a nochd airson sgothan. Chithear gu bheil cuid dhiubh nam faclan iasaid. Tha fuaimneachadh Gàidhlig air na faclan seo, ge-tà, agus thugadh iad seachad mar fhacal Gàidhlig ach tha am freumh ann am Beurla fhathast meadhanach follaiseach. Thathar air liath a chleachdadh gus aire a thoirt dha na faclan nach eilear air lorg anns na faclairean/liostaichean fhaclan Gàidhlig.

1.4   Sgothan
1.4.1   *birlinn, -ean* 'galley'
1.4.2   *curach* **kuRɔx** 'coracle' **RDU42**
1.4.3   *dòraidh* 'dory' **RDU42**

1.4.4   *drioftair, -ean* 'drifter' **RDU42, DBM47, CMN45**
1.4.5   *druiseag* 'Loch Fyne built boat' **CMN45**
   1.4.5.1   *druiseag bheag*
   1.4.5.2   *druiseag mhòr*
1.4.6   *faighfidh* 'Fife-built boat, fifey'
1.4.7   *gheat* **jɑht** 'yacht'
1.4.8   *paidhir* 'pair (of fishing boats)'
1.4.9   *riongair, -ean* 'ring-net boat'
1.4.10 *sgaf, sgafaidh -ean,* ainmear boireann 'Scaffie'
1.4.11 *sùlaire* 'Zulu'

DBM47: 'S ann a bha 'ad gan togail aig àm nan 'Zulu' Wars.
CMN45: Bha toiseach dìreach agus deireadh cas orra.

1.4.12 *tarbh* 'very wide small Fifey'

CMN45: Sin agad sgoth a bha uabhasach cruinn, 'Fifey' ach bha i uabhasach leathann son a fad.

1.4.13 *tràileir* **trɑ:lər´**, -an 'trawler' tràileir sgadain '
   1.4.13.1   tràileir sgadain 'herring trawler'
   1.4.13.2   tràileir Sputnik 'Sputnik trawler' **RDU42**

IDS29: Bhiodh na tràileirean a' sguabadh grunnd na mara.

Bheirear sùil nas mionaidiche a-nis air ceithir faclan airson sgothan ann am Barraigh.

1.5.1   *soitheach* ainmear fireann 'ship, vessel, dish'

Is e a' chiad fhacal *soitheach*, agus is e ainmear fireann a tha ann airson 'ship' no 'vessel'. Gheibhear cuideachd *soitheach-seòlaidh* airson 'sailing ship/vessel'. Air uairean thig sgaraidhean am follais chan ann a-mhàin ann an ciall ach cuideachd ann am fòn-eòlas. Tha ciall *sgoth* air *soitheach* no 'vessel' agus cleachdar *soitheach* cuideachd airson 'vessel' anns an t-seagh 'dish' no rudeigin anns an cuireadh tu nithean, gu h-àraidh biadh. Fhuaras sgaradh ge-tà ann am fon-eòlas eadar /sɤ-əx/ 'ship, vessel' agus /sæ-əx/ 'dish, vessel'. Leis an iolra *soithichean* a' nochdadh anns an òrdugh chumanta *nigh na soithichean* 'wash the dishes', chualas gur h-e /sɛ-ixən/ a bhiodh aca ach gun e /sɤ-əx/ a bhiodh aca ann *soitheach-seòlaidh* no 'sailing-ship'.

Tha iomradh air an sgaradh seo ann am fon-eòlas a' nochdadh ann an sgrùdadh Gàidhlig an eilein anns an rannsachadh *SGDS*, far an do nochd dà fhuaimneachadh airson an fhacail aig triùir de na ceithrar luchd-bratha on eilean (Ó Dochartaigh, 2007, Iml. 5, td. 234). Mar an ceudna, gheibhear fianais den sgaradh seo ann an Gàidhlig Uibhist a Deas agus Èirisgeidh sa chruinneachadh aig Maighstir Ailein (1972, td. 225):

SOITHEACH, 253, *Saghach*, a ship [sö'ɔx]: *Saigheach* [a dish] (Uist pronunciation for *taighe*) [sæ'ɔx]. IT is considered quite a blunder to call a dish a *saghach*, and I have seen giggling enough at the expense of a Mainlander who used *saghach* in that sense.

Thogadh Borgstrøm an aire dhan sgaradh seo ann am Barraigh agus e ga shoilleireachadh: 'Note *sø'-əx* "ship, vessel" but *sæ'-əx* "dish, vessel" M. Ir. Soithech' (1937, td. 89). Tha Dillon (1953, td. 323) cuideachd a' toirt iomradh air an sgaradh seo agus e ag ràdh gu bheilear ga lorg an dà chuid ann an Barraigh agus Uibhist a Deas. Tha an rannsachadh seo a' toirt dearbhadh dhuinn gu bheil an sgaradh fon-eòlach fhathast ri chluinntinn ann an Gàidhlig Bharraigh.

1.5.2   *long* ainmear boireann 'model/toy boat', 'large sailing boat'

Is ann glè ainneamh a tha dìreach aon chiall aig aon fhacal fon-eòlach. Is e poileisimidh (*polysemy*) a tha air nuair a tha tuilleadh na aon chiall aig aon fhacal fhon-eòlach agus nuair a thathar den bheachd gu bheil dàimh eachdraidheil eadar na ciallan diofrach. Homanaimidh (*homonymy*) a tha air aon fhacal fon-eòlach le còrr is aon chiall gun dàimh eachdraidheil eadar na ciallan (Taylor, 2009, td. 103).

Dealbh 1 **Long** a rinn RDU42 le crogan 'dried milk'.

RDU42: Bhiodh iad a' dèanamh 'models' bheaga fhios agad na *luingeannan* a bhiodh sinn ag ràdh ris na *luingeannan*.

RDU42: ach nuair a thàinig na long ship 's e an aon rud a bh' aca air an uair sin.

CMN45: 'S e bàta mòr siùil a bh' ann [an long], ach bhiodh sinne a' cleachdadh *long* air an sgothan beaga a bhiodh sinn a' dèanamh, na sgothan a bhiodh sinn a' dèanamh le crogain 'dried milk' agus na sgothan a bhiodh sinn a' dèanamh a-mach à fiodh.

CPM45: Bhiodh e aig Roddy nuair a bha e beag ach cha robh aig an fheadhainn againne fhios agad aig Dòmhnall Uilleam is aca sin, tha mi smaointinn gun do dh'fhalbh e, dh'fhalbh am facal an uair sin cha bhiodh iadsan ga chleachdadh nuair a bhiodh iad a' cluich le sgothaṇ.

Mar a chithear bhon mhìneachadh a thugadh seachad, tha dà phrìomh chleachdadh den fhacal *long* ann am Barraigh. Is e am prìomh chleachdadh dèideag no modal de sgoth agus an dara ciall soitheach-seòlaidh, mar a tha aig cuid a dhualchainntean eile. Chithear san dealbh eisimpleir de *long* a rinn RDU45 a-mach à crogan *'dried milk'*. Chleachdadh *long* airson modalan de sgoth a bhiodh aig daoine nan dachannan nam measg, modalan ann an glainne. Mar sin bhiodh *long* air a chleachdadh airson dèideag a bhiodh aig clann airson cluich ach cuideachd airson nam modalan nach bhiodh freagarrach idir dhaibh.

Cha do nochd long airson dèideag no modal anns an rannsachadh aig Borgstrøm (1937, td. 86); b' e 'a sailing-ship' an aon chiall a bha aige. Ach tha fianais air a' chleachdadh seo ri lorg ann an obair Dhòmhnaill Mhic na Ceàrdaich, bàrd is sgrìobhaiche às an Leideig, Eilean Bharraigh a rugadh ann an 1885. Nochd *long* le ciall dèideag grunnd tursan anns an dealbh-chluich 'Long nan Òg' (Mac na Ceàrdaich, 2014, tdd. 286-308) agus cuideachd anns an sgeulachd ghoirid 'Lughain Lir', mar a chithear san loidhne 'cha'n e sin taobh a bhios luingeas nan òg a' dol idir' (Mac na Ceàrdaich, 2014, td. 400).

Mar a thugadh iomradh cheana, is e an dara tuigse a tha aca air an fhacal *long* soitheach-seòlaidh. Chithear anns na h-earrannan shuas gu bheilear eòlach air an tuigse seo ann am Barraigh. Nochd *long* leis an dara chiall seo cuideachd ann an saothair Mhic na Ceàrdaich anns a bhàrdachd 'Long nan Daoine' (Mac na Ceardaich, 2014, td. 90). Tha Dwelly (2001) a' leigeil fhaicinn gu bheil am facal *long* air a chleachdadh gu farsaing agus e ga mhìneachadh mar 'any kind of ship' air td. 598 ach le ciall shònraichte 'square rigged vessel with 3 and sometimes 4 masts' air td. 78.

    1.5.3   *geòla, -gan -ɔ* ainmear boireann, tuiseal tabhartach a' gheòlaidh **CMN45** 'dinghy, dory'

        1.5.3.1   *geòlag, -an* ainmear boireann 'dinghy' **CIM30** 'small geòla' **MFM51, DBM47**

Is e *geòla(g)* na tha aca air sgoth bheag a chleachdas o thìr chun na sgothadh air acaire. Is e *geòla(g)* an sgoth as lugha a chleachd an luchd-bratha. Chaidh innse dhomh le **DBM47** gum feumadh deireadh 'square' a bhith air *geòla(g)* ach bha **CIM30** den bheachd gu bheil dà dhiofar seòrsa *geòlag* ann, tè le 'deireadh square' agus tè le deireadh ann an cruth 'y'.

Nochd an dà chuid *geòla* agus *geòlag* tron rannsachadh airson 'dinghy'. Mhìnich **CIM30** gun e *geòlag* a bhiodh aige fhèin fad an t-siubhail agus gun e an t-iolra *geòlagan* a bha aige. Dh'aontaich iad uile gun e *geòlagan* a bhiodh aca mar iolra ach is e *geòla* seach *geòlag* a bha aig **CMN45**, **RDU42** agus **CPM45**. Ach chaidh an dà fhacal *geòla* agus *geòlag* a chleachdadh le **DBM47** is **MFM51** agus iad a' tuigsinn gum biodh *geòlag* na bu lugha na *geòla*. Gabhaidh seo tuigsinn tàillibh is e meanbhan (*diminutive*) boireannta a tha ann an '-ag'. Tha e na eisimpleir air mar a dh'fhaodas sgaradh nochdadh nuair a tha dà fhacal air an cleachdadh airson an dearbh rud.

1.5.4 bàta-sàbhailidh/bàta-teasairginn

Air uairean ann an cànan gheibhear an aon chiall, no faisg air an aon chiall, aig dà fhacal agus canar ann an suidheachadh den leithid gu bheil ceangal sionanaimeach (synonymous) eadar na faclan. Leis gu bheil cuid de fhaclan nas fhaisge air a chèile ann an ciall na tha cuid eile, thathar den bheachd gu bheil faclan a sgèile sionanaimeach ann (Cruse, 2011). Tha sionanaimidh iomlan (absolute synonymy) aig aon cheann den sgèile agus tha Cruse ga mìneachadh mar a leanas:'We shall define absolute synonyms as words which are mutually substitutable in all context without change of normality' (2011, td 142). Chan fhaicear sionanaimidh iomlan tric ann an cànan sam bith (Cruse, 1986, 2011; Saeed, 1999). Nuair a nochdas sionanaimidh iomlan, tha cànain buailteach aon de na faclan a chall ann an cleachdadh làitheil a' chànain no faodar sgaradh seimeantach a dhèanamh eadar na faclan.

Fhuaras an dà chuid *bàta-sàbhalaidh* agus *bàta-teasairginn* bhon luchd-bhratha ann am Barraigh airson 'lifeboat'. Chaidh dealbh de sgoth an RNLI ann am Bàgh a' Chaisteil a chleachdadh nuair a dh'fhaighnicheadh dhiubh gu dè bhiodh aca sa Ghàidhlig air a son.

Dh'fhaodte gu bheil eisimpleir again, ma-thà, de mhonanaimidh (*mononymy*), rud nach eil idir bitheanta, sin far a bheil dà fhacal ann airson an dearbh rud. Chaidh dealbh den t-soitheach RNLI *Edna Windsor*, a tha stèidhichte ann am Barraigh, a shealltainn dhan luchd-bratha. Mar sin, bha fhios gun teagamh aig an luchd-bratha gun robh mi a-mach air dearbh sgoth. Dh'innis **CIM30**, **DBM47** agus **MFM51** dhomh gun e *bàta-sàbhailidh* a chleachdadh fhèin agus ged a bhathar air *bàta-teasairginn* a chluinntinn, cha robhar den bheachd gun e *bàta-teasairginn* a bhiodh aca am Barraigh. Chleachdadh **RDU42, CPM45, CMN45** *bàta-teasairginn*, ge-tà, agus ged a chualas *bàta-sàbhailidh* air a chleachdadh air a shon, is e *bàta-teasairginn* a bhiodh acasan. Bha **RDU42** den bheachd gur h-e *bàta-teasairginn* a bha aige o thùs: '*bata-teasairginn*, 's e a chanamaid an toiseach chanainn'. Mar sin tha e doirbh a bhith cinnteach gu dè a bhiodh aca nuair a chaidh bàta RNLI a stèidheachadh am Barraigh ann an 1931. Le cinnt, tha an dà chuid bàta-sàbhailidh agus bàta-teasairginn air an cleachdadh anns an eilean an-diugh. Is e *bàta-teasairginn* a tha aca air

Radio nan Gàidheal air a shon agus ma dh'fhaodte gu bheil sin a' toirt buaidh air cleachdadh muinntir an eilein. Ach thuirt **CMN45**: 'uill *bàta-teasairginn* a chanadh 'ad rithe ach chan ann tric a bhiodh 'ad a' cleachdadh sin', agus mhìnich e gur h-e 'lifeboat' a chluinnear ann an còmhraidhean sa Ghàidhlig. Is e seacaid-sàbhalaidh a bha aca uile seach seacaid-teasairginn, a tha a' nochdadh ann am faclair Mark (2004, td. 64).

Co-dhùnadh

Anns an dealachadh, chunnacas gu bheil grunn fhaclan air an cleachdadh ann an Gàidhlig Bharraigh airson sgothan agus diofar sheòrsaichean agus meudan dhiubh. Gun teagamh is e *sgoth* am facal coitcheann a tha aca airson 'boat' seach *bàta* ach thathar a' cur feum air *sgoth* agus *bàta* le ciall nas mionaidiche. Tha feartan dualchainnt Bharraigh cuideachd follaiseach le cruth nas fhaide aig deireadh ainmearan boireann sa ghinideach *sgoth, na sgothadh* agus cuideachd cruth palataichte san tuiseal thabhartach *leis an sgothaidh*. Chithear gu bheil faclan airson nan sgothan a' dearbhadh cò às a thàinig iad, no càite an deach an togail, dè ghlacadh iad air no dè an dòigh ghlacaidh a bha aca. Tha sinn cuideachd air fhaicinn gu bheil eisimpleirean de phoiliseimidh, le *long*, agus monanaimidh, le *bàta-teasairginn/bàta-sàbhailidh*.

Buidheachas

Bu mhath leam taing chrìdheil a thoirt dhan luchd-bhratha air fad a bha cho còir, coibhneil agus a bha fialaidh len cuid tìde agus an eòlas.

Tùsan

Borgstrøm, Carl H. J. (1937). 'The Dialect of Barra in the Outer Hebrides'. *Norsk Tidsskrift for Sprogvidenskap*, Iml. 8, tdd. 71-242.

Campbell, John Lorne (deas.) (2a deas. 1972). *Gaelic Words and Expressions from South Uist and Eriskay: collected by Rev. Fr. Allan McDonald*. Oxford: OUP.

Cruse, D. A. (1986). *Lexical Semantics*. Cambridge: CUP.

Cruse, D. A. (3a deas. 2011). *Meaning in Language: An Introduction to Semantics and Pragmatics*. Oxford: OUP.

Dillon, Myles (1953). 'Semantic Distribution in Gaelic Dialects'. *Language*, Iml. 29, tdd. 322–5.

Dwelly, Edward (2001 [1901-11]). *The Illustrated Gaelic-English Dictionary*. Glaschu: Gairm Publications.

Duwe, Kurt (2005) *Gàidhlig (Scottish Gaelic) Local Studies: Vol. 02: Eilean Bharraigh (Isle of Barra)*. Available from URL: http://www.linguae-celticae.org/dateien/Gaidhlig_Local_Studies_Vol_02_Barraigh_Ed_II.pdf (air a ruigsinn 23.1.2015).

Grannd, Seumas (1995-6). 'The Lexical Geography of the Western Isles'. *Scottish Language*, Iml. 14/15, tdd. 52–65.

Grannd, Seumas (1997). 'The Lexical Geography of the Western Isles'. *SGS*, Iml. 17, tdd. 146-9.

Grannd, Seumas (2000). *The Gaelic of Islay: A Comparative Study.* Obar Dheathain: Roinn na Ceiltis, Oilthigh Obar Dheathain.

MacAskill, Alex J. (1966). 'Difference in Dialect, Vocabulary and General Idiom between the Islands'. *TGSI*, Iml. 43, tdd. 62-88.

MacLeòid, Seòras (2005). *Muir is Tìr*. Stornoway: Acair.

Mac Mathúna, Liam (1978). 'On the Expression of "Rain" and "It is Raining" in Irish'. *Ériu*, Iml. 29, tdd. 37-59.

Mac na Ceàrdaich, Dòmhnall (2014). *D.M.N.C.: Sgrìobhaidhean Dhòmhnaill Mhic na Ceàrdaich*. Inbhir Nis: Clàr.

Mark, Colin (2004). *The Gaelic-English Dictionary: Am Faclair Gàidhlig-Beurla.* Lunnainn: Routledge.

NicIlleDhuinn, Iona E. (2011). 'Sgrùdadh air Gàidhlig Thiriodh: Leicsigean, Briathrachas agus Gràmar'. Tràchdas MA neo-fhoillsichte, Oilthigh Ghlaschu.

NicLeòid, Ciorstaidh (2012). 'Briathrachas an Iasgaich ann an Eilean Bharraigh'. Tràchdas MPhil neo-fhoillsichte, Oilthigh Ghlaschu.

Ó Curnáin, Brian (2007). *The Irish of Iorras Aithneach, County Galway,* Volume 1. Baile Àtha Cliath: Institiúid Ard-Léinn Baile Átha Cliath.

Ó Dochartaigh, Cathair (deas.) (1994-7). *Survey of the Gaelic Dialects of Scotland.* Iml. 5. Baile Àtha Cliath: Institiúid Ard-Léinn Baile Átha Cliath.

Ó Maolalaigh, Roibeard (2008a) '"Bochanan modhail foghlaimte": Tiree Gaelic, Lexicology and Glasgow's Historical Dictionary of Scottish Gaelic'. *SGS*, Iml. 24, tdd. 473–523.

Ó Maolalaigh, Roibeard (2008b). 'Glasgow's Historical Dictionary of Scottish Gaelic and Preliminary Comments on Gaelic Lexical Semantics'. Pàipear neo-fhoillsichte a thugadh seachad aig Rannsachadh na Gàidhlig 5, Oilthigh St Francis Xavier, 21-4 Iuchar.

Ó Maolalaigh, Roibeard (2010). 'Caochlaideachd Leicseachail agus "Snowflakes" sa Ghàidhlig', ann an Gillian Munro agus R. A. V. Cox (deas.), *Cànan & Cultar / Language and Culture: Rannsachadh na Gàidhlig 4,* tdd. 7-21. Dùn Èideann: Dunedin Academic Press.

National Records of Scotland (2011) Scottish Census 2011: Release 2c Table KS206SC – Inhabited Islands (ri fhaighinn bho URL: http://www.scotlandscensus.gov.uk/ods-web/standard-outputs.html) (air a ruigsinn 22.1.15).

Saeed, J. I. (4mh deas. 1999). *Semantics*. Oxford: Blackwell Publishing Ltd.

Taylor, John R. (2009). *Linguistic Categorization*. Oxford: OUP.

Wagner, Heinrich (deas.) (1958-69). *Linguistic Atlas and Survey of the Irish Dialects,* Iml. 4. Baile Àtha Cliath: Institiúid Ard-Léinn Bhaile Átha Cliath.

18

Gàidheil, Goill agus coimhearsnachd na Gàidhlig: Ideòlasan cànain am measg inbhich a fhuair foghlam tro mheadhan na Gàidhlig

Stiùbhart S. Dunmore

Oilthigh Dhùn Èideann

Ro-ràdh

Ann an litreachas an t-sòisio-chànanachais, thathas a' smaoineachadh gum bi ideòlasan cànain – mar chreideamhan agus seasamhan mu dheidhinn cànain – gu tric a' cur ris na dòighean anns am bi coimhearsnachdan sònraichte a' cleachdadh nan cànanan aca ann am beatha làitheil (Silverstein, 1979, td. 193; Dauenhauer is Dauenhauer, 1998, td. 64; Kroskrity, 2004, td. 496). Gu h-àraid, tha cuid de dh'eòlaichean a' cumail a-mach gum bi ideòlasan cànain, an dà chuid ann an comann farsaing agus ann an coimhearsnachdan beaga, gu tric a' dol an aghaidh – agus a' tarraing sìos – nan cleachdaidhean labhairt dùthchasach aig coimhearsnachdan mìon-chànanach (Fishman, 1991, td. 395; Makihara, 2010, td. 45). Uime sin, thathas a' creidsinn gum faod sgrùdaidhean air ideòlasan cànain – a bheir sùil air na ceanglaichean eadar cleachdadh labhairt is seasamhan cànain – a bhith a' cur ris an tuigse a th' againn air adhbharan a th' air cùlaibh nan atharrachaidhean sòisealta a bhios a' nochdadh gu tric an lùib gluasaid cànain. Sa phàipear seo bidh mi a' tarraing aire do chuid dhe na h-ideòlasan cànain a chaidh a chur an cèill le luchd-compàirt ann an agallamhan mar phàirt dhen rannsachadh dotaireil agam. Ri linn an rannsachaidh seo thug mi sùil air na cleachdaidhean, beachdan agus ideòlasan cànain a tha aig buidheann de dh'inbhich (N=130) a thòisich ann am foghlam tro mheadhan na Gàidhlig sna bliadhnaichean bu tràithe 's a bha e ri fhaighinn ann an Alba.

A rèir a' chunntais-shluaigh mu dheireadh (2011) tha 57,602 luchd-labhairt na Gàidhlig (thairis air trì bliadhna a dh'aois) beò ann an Alba san latha an-diugh (National Records of Scotland, 2013). Tha an àireamh sin a' cunntadh dìreach beagan a bharrachd air aon às a' cheud dhen t-sluagh air fad, ged a bha buidhnean leasachaidh na Gàidhlig air am brosnachadh air sàilleabh 's gu robh an crìonadh san àireamh seo air a lùghdachadh gu mòr eadar cunntasan-sluaigh 2001 is 2011. B' e 2.2% meud a' chrìonaidh sin, an coimeas ri 11.1% eadar 1991 is 2001. A thuilleadh air a' phuing chudromach seo, bha toraidhean a' chunntais-shluaigh a' sealltainn fàs – airson a' chiad turais – san àireamh de luchd-labhairt na Gàidhlig fo aois fichead bliadhna, ged a bha am fàs sin beag, beag bìodach (0.1%; National Records of Scotland, 2013). Thug na h-àireamhan seo air ceannard Bòrd na Gàidhlig aig an àm, Iain Aonghas MacAoidh, a ràdh ann an 2014 gu robh crìonadh na Gàidhlig a-nis faisg air stad ann an Alba, mar thoradh air cho soirbheachail 's a bha siostam foghlaim tro mheadhan na Gàidhlig san deichead seo (Bòrd na Gàidhlig, 2014). A dh'aindeoin sin, ge-tà, chan eil ach glè bheag de dh'fhianais againn air mar a tha na h-àireamhean seo a' dèanamh dàimh leis an ìre 's am bi an òigridh sin a' cleachdadh na Gàidhlig sna beathannan làitheil aca.

Gu deimhinne, chan eil Gàidheil na h-Alba nan aonar idir ann a bhith a' feuchainn ri am mìon-chànan dùthchasach ath-bheòthachadh tro shiostam an fhoghlaim. Anns a' cho-theacsa eadar-nàiseanta bidh eisimpeirean aithnichte eile a' nochdadh ann an suidheachdaidhean farsaing, a' gabhail a-steach dùthchannan leithid Frìoslann, Hawai'i, a' Chuimrigh, Èirinn, Sealann Nuadh, Dùthaich nam Basgach, Catalòinia agus a' Bhreatainn Bheag, gus buidheann bheag dhe thìrean iomchaidh ainmeachadh. Anns an fharsaingeachd, ge-tà, chan eil mòran fianais idir ri faicinn bho na co-theacsaichean seo a bhios a' dearbhadh gu cinnteach gu bheil foghlam tro mheadhan a' mhìon-chànain a' cur ri amasan an ath-bheòthachaidh rè ùine fhada (ach cf. Woolard, 2011; Hodges, 2009). Gu dearbh, tha Fishman (1991, 2001, 2010, 2013) air a bhith a' cumail a-mach ann an sgrìobhaidhean teòiridheil thar còrr is fichead 's a deich bliadhna nach soirbhich le iomairt ath-bheòthachaidh sam bith a tha stèidhte air an sgoil, mas e 's nach eil an cànan fhèin air a chleachdadh ann an comann, anns a' choimhearsnachd, agus gu seach àraidh, san dachaigh.

'S e cùis iongnaidh a th' ann, mar sin, nach eil ann ach glè bheag dhe phròiseactan rannsachaidh a chaidh a dhèanamh sa cho-theacsa eadar-nàiseanta thuige seo, a dh'amaiseadh air freagairtean soilleir a thoirt air na ceistean teòiridheil bunasach seo. B' ann air mion-shampallan dhe luchd-agallaimh a thogadh sgrùdaidhean fa leth le Woolard (2011) agus Hodges (2009) air cleachdadh nam mìon-chànanan am measg inbhich a fhuair foghlam àrd-sgoile trompa, ann an sgìrean bàilteil dhe Chatalòinia agus dhen Chuimrigh. Ged as e deagh phìosan rannsachaidh càileachdail na mìon-ìre a th' annta, is dòcha nach biodh toraidhean nam pàipearan seo air an lorg am measg sampallan nas motha.

Ann an 2014 chuir mi crìoch air pròiseact rannsachaidh a bha stèidhte air sampall dhe 130 luchd-chompàirt a thòisich ann am foghlam tro mheadhan na Gàidhlig eadar 1985 is 1995. Am measg an t-sampaill seo stiùir mi agallamhan le 46 daoine, gus sùil a thoirt air na cleachdaidhean is ideòlasan cànain a rachadh a chur an cèill a thaobh na Gàidhlig. An lùib an sgrùdaidh chàileachdail seo, mar sin, tha mi air a bhith a' feuchainn ris na cleachdaidhean, na h-ideòlasan is na beachdan cànain a mheasadh am measg inbhich a thòisich ann am FMG sna h-ochdadan agus aig toiseach nan naochadan. Gu h-àraidh, thug mi sùil air cho tric 's a bhios iad a' bruidhinn a' chànain, na dòighean anns am bi iad ga bhruidhinn, agus na h-adhbharan a dh'fhaodadh a bhith air cùlaibh nam pàtranan seo (an dà chuid a thaobh ideòlais agus cul-fhiosrachaidh shòisealta).

Dh'fhàs foghlam tro mheadhan na Gàidhlig ann an Alba gu luath thar nan deich bliadhna às dèidh dha a bhith air a stèidheachadh, mar a chìthear ann an Clàr 1, gu h-ìosal:

Clàr 1 (tùs: MacFhionghuin 2005)

Bliadhna / Sgìre	1985/ 86	1986/ 87	1987/ 88	1988/ 89	1989/ 90	1990/ 91	1991/ 92	1992/ 93	1993/ 94	1994/ 95
Earra-Ghàidheal & Bòd	X	X	4	8	14	26	36	47	57	54
Eileanan an Iar	X	4	19	20	51	107	189	272	365	457
Comhairle na Gàidhealtachd	12	31	44	75	127	178	234	328	425	472
Galltachd / Eile	12	29	44	66	94	120	155	187	233	275
Iomlan	24	64	112	169	286	431	614	834	1080	1258
Aois: 30/6/2014	33-4	32+	31+	30+	29+	28+	27+	26+	25+	24+

Faodar faicinn, mar sin, gun do thòisich 24 daoine chloinne ann an dà chlas mheadhan na Gàidhlig ann an 1985. B' iad na clasaichean bun-sgoile Ghlaschu is Inbhir Nis a thòisich sa bhliadhna ud, agus thòisich aonadan a bharrachd ann an sgìrean sgapte eile gu luath thar nan deich bliadhna às a dèidh. Taobh a-staigh an deicheid ud, faodar fhaicinn gun do thòisich còrr is dà cheud deug sgoilear am broinn an t-siostaim. Ann an dòigh, is e an àireamh sin an domhan iomlan dhe luchd-chompàirt (no *informant universe*) a bhiodh comasach pàirt a ghabhail san sgrùdadh, a rèir na slat-tomhais a chaidh a chleachdadh a thaobh aoise (eadar 24 is 34 aig deireadh na h-Ògmhios 2014).

Am measg an 46 luchd-agallaimh a ghabh pàirt san rannsachadh, bha 31 nam boireannaich is 15 nam fireannaich; bha 17 luchd-compàirt à bailtean na Galltachd bho thùs, 12 às a' Ghàidhealtachd, agus 17 a bharrachd às na h-eileanan (eadar na h-Eileanan Siar, an t-Eilean Sgitheanach agus Tiriodh). A thuilleadh air sin, thagh 21 luchd-agallaimh an còmhradh againn a stiùireadh tron Ghàidhlig, ged a chaidh measgachadh-cànain a chleachdadh gu math tric leis an luchd-chompàirt fhèin. Chaidh na 46 agallamhan, a bha leth-chruthaichte (no semi-structured), uile a chlàradh agus a thar-sgrìobhadh leis an rannsaiche fhèin. Gu h-iomlan tha an corpas seo a' lìonadh bharrachd air fichead uair de chòmhradh, a rinneadh eadar an Dùbhlachd 2011 is an Dùbhlachd 2012. Ghabh na cleachdaidhean tar-sgrìobhaidh a-steach prionnsabalan a bha stèidhte air an 'ethnography of speaking', a chruthaich Dell Hymes (1974) airson sùil mhionaideach a thoirt an dà chuid air an t-seòrsa cànain a bhios luchd-labhairt a' cleachdadh, agus brìgh nam faclan fhèin. Cuiridh an dòigh-obrach seo teacsa agus co-theacsa ri chèile ann a bhith a' sgrùdadh còmhradh agus conaltradh (faic cuideachd Ochs, 1979).

B' e aon dhe na toraidhean as cudromaiche a thàinig a-mach às an rannsachadh dotaireil agam nach bi a' mhòr-chuid dhen luchd-chompàirt a' bruidhinn ach glè bheag de Ghàidhlig sna beathannan làitheil aca (Dunmore, 2015). 'S e sin ri ràdh gu bheil cleachdadh sòisealta na Gàidhlig am measg an luchd-chompàirt gu math lag san fharsaingeachd. Cha robh ach 10 a-mach às an 46 luchd-agallaimh a' cur an cuid Gàidhlig gu feum san àite obrach; am measg càch, cha robh a' Ghàidhlig air a cleachdadh ach gu ìre bhig san latha an-diugh. Fiù 's am measg daoine a chleachdas tòrr Gàidhlig ag obair, bha e follaiseach gu leòr nach robh a' mhòr-chuid a' bruidhinn mòran Gàidhlig san dachaigh, neo ann an co-theacsaichean neo-fhoirmeil an lùib nam beathannan làitheil aca.

Cha bhi mi ag ràdh cus mu dheidhinn cleachdaidhean cànain sa phàipear seo, ge-tà, air sgàth 's gu bheil mi airson aire shònraichte a tharraing chun nan còmhraidhean fhèin a chleachdas an luchd-fhreagairt airson na cleachdaidhean cànain aca a mhìneachadh. Airson an obair sin a dhèanamh, chleachd mi frèam-obrach sgrùdail ris an canar ideòlasan cànain ann an sòisio-chànanachas an là an-diugh. Tha barrachd na dìreach aon mhìneachadh air an fhrèam-obrach seo air a chleachdadh san litreachas iomchaidh, ach cha chreid mi nach e am fear a leanas am measg na feadhainn as fheàrr. Sgrìobh Boudreau agus Dubois (2007, p. 104) gur e a tha ann an ideòlas cànain:

> *a set of beliefs on language or a particular language shared by members of a community ... These beliefs come to be so well established that their origin is often forgotten by speakers, and are therefore socially reproduced and end up being 'naturalized', or perceived as natural or as common sense.*

A' togail air an tuigse seo, sgrìobh Jillian Cavanaugh (2013, td. 46) gu bheil rannsachadh air ideòlas cànain an urra ri 'an analytical unpacking of how speakers understand, view, and use language'. Is ann a rèir brìghean na h-abairte a tha seo a chleachdas mi i sa phàipear seo. Sgrìobh Makihara (2010, tdd. 44–5) gur ann tric a bhios buaidh aig ideòlasan cànain ann a bhith a' toirt air luchd-labhairt na cànanan aca a chleachdadh ann an diofar dhòighean, an dàrna cuid ann a bhith a' cur ri, neo a' dol an aghaidh gluasaid cànain ann an coimhearsnachdan sònraichte. Mar sin, thathas a' smaoineachadh – co-dhiù bho shealladh teòiridheil – gu bheil ideòlasan cànain a' dèanamh diofar mòr do chleachdadh cànain ann an co-theacsaichean farsaing.

Sgrùdadh

Sa chòrr dhen phàipear seo, bu mhath leam aire a tharraing gu cuid dhe na h-ideòlasan cànain a bhiodh an luchd-chòmpairt agam a' cur an cèill a thaobh na Gàidhlig, agus gu h-àraid chun na feadhainn sin tha a' cur ri ar tuigse mu choinneamh nan adhbharan airson cion cleachdaidh na Gàidhlig am measg an luchd-fhreagairt. Tha a' chiad fhear dhiubh sin a' cumail a-mach gu bheil 'sodalachd' (no 'snobbery') a' nochdadh ann an coimhearsnachd na Gàidhlig gu ìre mhòir, agus an darna dhiubh ag ràdh nach bu chòir dhan a' choimhearsnachd seo a bhith 'a' putadh' neo 'a' sparradh' a' chànain air a' mhòr-chuid dhen t-sluagh. Mu dheireadh, bheir mi sùil air cuid dhe na h-adhbharan nach bi luchd-fhreagairt a' smaointinn orra fhèin mar 'Ghàidheil', sna faclan aca fhèin.

'Sodalachd'

Gu h-ìoranta, tha a' chiad ideòlas air am bu mhath leam beachdachadh gu tur eadar-dhealaichte, agus an ìre mhath calg-dhìreach an aghaidh ideòlas na sodalachd a' nochd san rannsachadh ainmeil aig Nancy Dorian ann an Cataibh an Ear, bho chionn còrr is fichead 's a deich bliadhna. Sa choimhearsnachd sin bhiodh luchd-labhairt na Gàidhlig gu tric a' bruidhinn air 'sodalachd' agus 'pròis'. Mhothaich Dorian (1981, td. 103) gur e 'pròis' an rud a bu mhiosa a bhiodh luchd na Gàidhlig a' faicinn san sgìre, agus gu h-àraid, gu robh cuid a' faireachdainn gu robh cuid eile 'ro phròiseil' a bhith a' brudhinn na Gàidhlig. Thuirt Dorian (1981, td. 103): 'the bitterest accusation that one [East Sutherland Gaelic] speaker can level against another is that he is "too proud" to speak Gaelic'.

An coimeas ris a' chreideamh sin, ge-tà, bu mhath leam sealltainn cuid dhe na dòighean anns an robh luchd-chompàirt san rannsachadh agamsa a' coimhead air sodalachd taobh a-staigh coimhearsnachd na Gàidhlig. Mar a mhìnicheas Anna agus Susaidh sa chiad earrann a th' agam an seo, tha faireachdainn làidir aig cuid gu bheil sodalachd a' nochdadh mu choinneamh nan cleachdaidhean cànain a tha aig feadhainn eile:

Anna   Maybe there's a generation thing [...] we're in this sort of world with Gaelic and it's a bit controversial but you know it's very much like 'oh she speaks terribly' or 'listen to her'=
Susaidh   =Oh there's a <u>huge</u> snobbery in it [...] I think you just hit the nail on the head when you were saying that it's wrong and what you said earlier about there being a snobbery and it being=
SD   =Yeah
Susaidh   judgemental – it's like that is <u>very</u> true in Gaelic which is something that actually really, really frustrates me about Gaelic

Mar sin, chaidh an t-ideòlas a tha fo cheist agam an seo – a bhios a' dèanamh a-mach gu bheil daoine ann an coimhearsnachd na Gàidhlig sodalach a thaobh an t-seòrsa cànain a chleachdas cuid eile – a chur an cèill gu soilleir san earrann gu h-àrd. Am measg cuid eile dhen luchd-fhreagairt, ge-ta, tha an t-ideòlas air a chur air adhart ann an dòigh car diofraichte, mar a tha follaiseach san earrann a leanas, anns am bi Ross a' bruidhinn air 'breith' taobh a-staigh coimhearsnachd na Gàidhlig. A rèir an neach-chompàirt seo, bidh a' 'bhreith' seo a' nochdadh sònraichte tric am measg muinntir an t-Sabhail Mhòir:

Ross   Mura h-eil thu air a bhith gu Sabhal Mòr Ostaig cha bhi fios agad no tuigse agad dè seorsa daoine a bhios a' frithealadh an /t-/àite sin [...] fhios 'ad **the judgement look**- 'chleachdadh an tuiseal **instead of this** tuiseal **and blah blah blah**' **you know** na Gàidhlig **police- you know** na **grammar police** [...] **you know** '**it's not aspirated**' rudan eile- **you know actually** tha mise caran coma uaireannan

Tha Ross a' faicinn breith a thaobh cànain – agus gu h-àraidh a thaobh gràmar na Gàidhlig –am measg muinntir an t-Sabhail Mhòir (no na 'daoine a' bhios a' frithealadh' an àite), agus is iad na 'grammar police' sna faclan aig Ross fhèin. Dh'innis Anna do Shusaidh, san earrann roimhe, gur e sgaradh eadar na ginealaich a th' anns an t-sodalachd seo, agus tha Ross a' coimhead air a' chùis bho shealladh car coltach ri sin; 's e luchd-frithealaidh nan cùrsaichean Gàidhlig aig Sabhal Mòr Ostaig an fheadhainn as coireach. A rèir luchd-chompàirt eile, 's e an fheadhainn aig a bheil Gaidhlig bho thùs a tha sodalach ann a bhith a' diùltadh bruidhinn ri luchd-ionnsachaidh. Tha Eilidh a' mìneachadh na faireachdainn shònraichte seo gu h-ìosal:

Eilidh   Em tha beàrn mòr an-dràsta eadar (.) **you know** na seann Ghàidheil aig an robh a' Ghàidhlig o thùs agus Gàidhlig an là an-diugh [...] tha: tòrr nach eil deònach a bhith a' bruidhinn ris an luchd-ionnsachaidh [...] em (.) **you know** tha gu leòr eile ann ag ràdh 'och, dè am feum ann a bhith a' bruidhinn na Gàidhlig?' neo 'dè a' Ghàidhlig (neònach) a th' agad?' Em **so** tha **tensions** an-sin tha mi a' smaoineachadh

Chìthear, mar sin, gu bheilear a' creidsinn gu bheil sodalachd ann taobh a-staigh saoghal na Gàidhlig. Chan eil e fo cheist agamsa an-dràsta a bhith a' dearbhadh an e ideòlas stèidhte air an fhìrinn a tha seo; na tha feumail dhòmhsa, 's e bhith a' coimhead air na creideamhan a th' aig an luchd-chompàirt, agus mar a tha iad sin a' bualadh air na dòighean anns am bi na h-inbhich sin a' cleachdadh na Gàidhlig. Am measg cuid mhath dhen luchd-chompàirt, tha e coltach gu bheil an t-ideòlas seo gan cur dheth bho bhith bruidhinn na Gàidhlig, agus a' cur dì-mhisneachd orra.

'Putadh' na Gàidhlig

Air an làmh eile, thathas a' faireachdainn gu tric sna h-agallamhan nach eil còir aig coimhearsnachd na Gaidhlig an cànan aca a 'phutadh', neo a 'sparradh', air a' mhòr-chuid de dh'Alba. A rèir coltais tha an creideamh sin stèidhte air an tuigse nach eil a' Ghàidhlig freagarrach neo buntainneach do dh'Alba air fad, agus gu dearbh, gu bheil sgìrean mòra ann far nach eil an cànan iomchaidh fiù 's san eachdraidh aca, mar a tha Iain agus Fiona a' mìneachadh sna h-earrannan a leanas:

Iain [T]ha mi a' smaointinn gu bheil Gàidhlig gu math cudromach anns na: (.) sgìrean (.) far a bheil- far an robh Gàidhlig anns an eachdraidh aca [...] ach chan eil mi a' smaointinn gum bu chòir dhaibh Gàidhlig a phutadh air na h-àiteachan (.) nach eil er (.) a' faireachdainn gu bheil iad ceangailte ris a' chànan [...] chan eil sinn ag iarraidh a bhith a' putadh Gàidhlig **you know**?

Bidh cuid dhen luchd-chompàirt a' cur a' chreideimh seo an cèill ann an co-theacsa iomadachd cànain. Mar eisimpleir, tha Fiona a' cumail a-mach san ath earrann nach e an aon chànan Albannach a th' anns a' Ghaidhlig:

Fiona [T]ha mi smaointinn g' eil sgìrean ann far a bheil Albais ga bruidhinn agus far nach eil 's dòcha Gàidhlig cho cudromach [...] cha chreid mi g' eil e ciallach a bhith eh a' sparradh (.) eh a' Ghàidhlig anns na h-àiteachan sin [...] Tha mi 'smaointinn (.) gu bheil sin aig cridhe trioblaidean na Gàidhlig – mas e cànan nàiseanta a bh' ann cha /bhiodh sinn/ anns an t-suidheachadh anns a bheil sinn an-diugh

Anns an aon doigh, tha Liam ag ràdh gu h-ìosal nach bu chòir dhuinn, mar choimhearsnachd cànain, a bhith a' smaoineachadh air a' Ghàidhlig mar a' phrìomh chànan nàiseanta air sgàth na h-Albais. Gu dearbh, bidh esan fiù 's ag argamaid gum bu chòir dhan a' Ghàidhlig a bhith air a cumail beò dìreach sna h-àiteachan far an robh i air a bruidhinn gu dùthchasach. Ars esan:

Liam   [Y]ou know it would probably be good to keep Gaelic to where it was – well – where it was traditionally spoken I would say

SD   Mm hmm

Liam   I mean there's parts of the country – I mean I'm not 100% sure about Gaelic history but there's probably parts of the country where Gaelic was never spoken […] I don't think of Gaelic as being a (.) you know a kind of (.) eh you know like the Scottish national language in a way

SD   Do you not no?

Liam   You know it's <u>one</u> of our – you know – there's other kinda – there's Scots and things as well […] I'd say to kind of keep [Gaelic] to where it was traditionally spoken or where it was spoken in the past

San dòigh seo, ged nach eil Liam buileach cinnteach dìreach far an robh a' Ghàidhlig air a labhairt gu h-eachdraidheil, tha e co-dhiù dhen bheachd gum bu chòir dhi a bhith air a glèidheadh dìreach sna h-àiteachan sin a-mhàin. A-rithist, cha dèan mi dearbhadh an-seo gu bheil (no nach eil) an creideamh a tha seo fìor ann an da-rìribh; tha an sgrùdadh agam a' coimhead air na h-ideòlasan cànain a th' aig inbhich sa bhuidheann seo, is chan ann air an fhìrinn eachdraidheil shòisio-chànanach. Tha faireachdainn làidir ann am measg cuid dhen luchd-chompàirt, mar sin, nach bu chòir do choimhearsnachd na Gàidhlig a bhith ag adhbharachadh connspaid, le bhith ag iarraidh na Gàidhlig san dùthaich air fad – agus gu h-àraidh air Ghalltachd – air sgàth na h-Albais.

Gàidheil neo Goill?

Bidh Fishman (1991, 2001, 2013) a' cur cuideam trom air a' cheangal eadar mion-chànanan agus na coimhearsnachdan cinnidh anns an robh iad stèidhte bho chionn linntean. Ann an co-theacsa na Gàidhlig ann an Alba, ge-tà, chan eil e buileach soilleir aig amannan cò a' choimhearsnachd iomchaidh a tha fo cheist an lùib cultar na Gàidhlig; an e na h-Albannaich air fad a th' anns a' choimhearsnachd sin, air neo an e na Gàidheil? Thar nan linntean b' urrainnear a ràdh gu sìmplidh gur iad na Gàidheil a bh' ann, ach chaidh am prionnsabal sin a cheasnachadh beagan aig deireadh an 20mh linn (faic Macdonald, 1997; Oliver, 2002). Anns an fharsaingeachd, cha bhiodh mòran dhen luchd-chompàirt agamsa a' smaointinn gu làidir orra fhèin mar 'Ghàidheil', agus cha do nochd am facal sin às aonais mo cheiste mu dheidhinn. Air an làimh eile, cha robh faireachdainn làidir ann nach e Goill a bh' annta nas motha. Dh'fhaighnich mi do Beth:

SD   Would you call yourself a Gael?
Beth   Um wow um: (.) yeah I guess so
SD   Yeah
Beth   I – it's not something I would ever call myself but if I was asked the question I guess so yeah
SD   Yeah, but otherwise not specifically
Beth   It's not something that I really stro- I don't go around saying ((confrontational voice)) 'oh I'm a Gael' kind of thing

Gu dearbh, cha robh cuid dhen luchd-chompàirt fhèin uabhasach cinnteach dè dìreach a tha ann an 'Gàidheal'. An coimeas ris an teirm seo, bha a' mhòr-mhòr-chuid na bu chofhurtaile an cuid fhèin-aithne mar Albannaich a chur an cèill anns na h-agallamhan a stiùir mi. Dh'fhaighnich mi do Mark, mar eisimpleir, an e Gàidheal a th' ann-san:

SD   Do you consider yourself a Gael for instance?
Mark   Eh (.) ((sighs)) och I mean (4.8) well kind of yeah
SD   Mm hmm
Mark   Em you know (.) I kinda come from that kinda heritage
SD   Yeah in terms of heritage uh huh
Mark   And I kind of (.) you know I've got more kind of (island links) […] I would count myself primarily as Scottish
SD   Yeah
Mark   Em and (.) I don't know if I'd include Gaelic as part of that

San aon dòigh, tha Fionn a' mìneachadh san earrann a leanas gur e Albannach a th' ann sa chiad àite, agus a thuilleadh air sin, gur e Gall, is nach e Gàidheal a th' ann air dòigh air bith. Nuair a dh'fhaighnich mise an e Gàidheal a bh' ann, thòisich Fionn a' gàireachdainn:

Fionn: [T]ha mis' gam fhaicinn fhìn mar Albannach gun teagamh (.) dìreach – tha an teaghlach agam ann an sheo – sin far a bheil an (.) an dachaigh againn
    […]
SD: Dìreach (.) an e Gàidheal a th' annad cuideachd mar sin?
Fionn: ((gàireachdainn)) Chan e uill- ((gàireachdainn)) cha chanainns' gur e Gàidheal a th' annam idir **no** (.) 's e Gall a th' annam […] a tha air tionndadh mar gum biodh ((gàireachdainn)) em **yeah** bidh mise an-còmhnaidh ag ràdh gur ann à xxx ((Galltachd)) a tha mi

Gu dearbh, san earrann a leanas, tha e doirbh do dh'Anna creidsinn gum biodh duine fon ghrèin ag radh gur e Gàidheal a th' ann. A-rithist, bha ise fiù 's a' gàireachdainn fhad 's a bheachdaich i air brìgh an fhacail sin. Mar a mhìnich i, b' fheàrr leatha fhèin am facal Beurla Ghallda 'Teuchter':

Anna   Does anyone call themselves that- 'I'm a Gael'? [...] I don't know what constitutes that (3.1) in the Gaelic world ((gàireachdainn)) Planet Gael! [...] I quite like 'Teuchter' though

SD   You like that one?

Anna   I like that yeah – I'm a Teuchter 'yeah you're a bit teuchie' (.) I am a bit teuchie sometimes, I quite like that

SD   ((gàireachdainn))

Anna   Gael's a bit (.)

Susaidh   You do know it's a derogatory term?=

Anna   =plaid and what do you call that big sword?=

SD   [=Claymore?]=

Susaidh   [=Sword?]=

Anna   =Claymore – that's what Gael reminds me of (.) big tartan plaid in a battle

Ged a tha am facal 'Teuchtar' na 'derogatory term' a rèir a caraid Susaidh, b' fhada a b' fheàrr le Anna am facal sin an àite 'Gàidheal', agus i mì-chreidmheach fiù 's an canadh duine sam bith gum b' e Gàidheal a bh' ann. Anns an fharsaingeachd, chan eil fèin-aithne làidir aig a' mhòr-mhòr-chuid dhen luchd-chompàirt mar Ghàidheil, is chaidh am facal 'Albannach' a chleachdadh tòrr na bu trice airson iomradh a dhèanamh air an cuid fhèin-aithne chultaraich.

Co-dhùnadh

Mholainn gu bheil ceistean mòra a' nochdadh mu choinneamh ideòlasan cànain agus coimhearsnachd na Gàidhlig am broinn nan earrannan ris an do tharraing mi aire sa phàipear seo. Sa chiad àite, tha cuid mhath dhen luchd-agallaimh a' cumail a-mach gu bheil 'sodalachd' na cùis nàire taobh a-staigh na coimhearsnachd sin – ge b' e luchd-ionnsachaidh no tùsanaich as coireach air a shon ann am faclan an luchd-agallaimh fhèin. Tha an fhaireachdainn seo a' crochadh air creideamhan an luchd-chompàirt; is mathaid nach eil an t-ideòlas seo air a stèidheachadh ann am fìrinn, ach tha e fhathast a' toirt buaidh air deòin agus misneachd an luchd-chompàirt an cuid Gàidhlig a chur gu feum.

Tha beachdan diofrachte air an cur an cèill mu dheidhinn àite na Gàidhlig ann an Alba. Ged a bha cuid dhen luchd-agallaimh a' faireachdainn gu bheil a' Ghàidhlig iomchaidh air Ghàidhealtachd, bha e coltach gu robh cuid eile gu làidir dhen bheachd nach eil i a cheart cho freagarrach air Ghalltachd, agus nach bu chòir a bhith ga 'putadh' sna h-àiteachan sin. An-sin, tha ceist a' nochdadh a tha co-cheangailte ris a' Bheurla Ghallda, no ris an Albais sna faclan aig cuid dhen luchd-chompàirt fhèin. A dh'aindeoin 's gur e an fhèin-aithne Albannach an tè ris an robh a' mhòr-mhòr-chuid a' dèanamh an dàimh as treasa, cha b' ann gu dìreach a bha iad a' ceangal na Gàidhlig leis an dùthaich air sgàth na h-Albais.

Mu dheireadh, bidh tiotal a' phàipeir seo a' ceasnachadh a bheil fèin-aithne aig an luchd-chompàirt mar Ghàidheil. Anns an fharsaingeachd, chan eil ach faireachdainn lag aig cuid gu bheil, agus tha feadhainn eile a' diùltadh an fhacail gu tur. Ma tha sinn, mar choimhearsnachd cànain, ag amharc ris an t-siostam foghlaim airson dìon na Gàidhlig san àm ri teachd, mholainn gum bu chòir dhuinn faighneachd trì ceistean dhinn fhèin. Is iad sin: co às a thàinig na h-ideòlasan seo; carson a tha iad ann am measg inbhich a fhuair an cuid foghlaim tron chànan; agus dè a ghabhas dèanamh airson ìomhaigh nas fheàrr a chruthachadh airson na coimhearsnachd againn, agus airson na Gàidhlig mar chànan bheò ann an Alba.

Mìneachadh nan tar-sgrìobhaidhean

[facal]	còmhradh tar-lùbte (*overlapping speech*)
(.)	stad sa chòmhradh (<1 diog)
(2.2)	stad sa chòmhradh (>1 diog)
=facal	gun stad eadar luchd-labhairt
fac-	fèin-bhacadh
(facal)	tar-sgrìobhadh mi-chinnteach
(x)	còmhradh nach gabh tuigsinn
xxx	ainm air a leigeil a-muigh
/facal/	mearachd/cleachdadh neo-àbhaisteach
((facal))	beachdan an sgrùdaiche fhèin
[…]	còmhradh air a leigeil a-muigh
::	fuaim fada
<u>facal</u>	cuideam sònraichte air an fhacal
words	atharrachadh eadar cànain

Tùsan

Bòrd na Gàidhlig (2014). 'Gaelic education helps reverse decline of the Gaelic language'. Ri fhaighinn air loidne bho URL: www.gaidhlig.org.uk/bord/en/news/article.php?ID=474 (air a tharraing a-mach 09.7.2014)

Boudreau, Annette, agus Dubois, Lise (2007). 'Français, acadien, acadjonne: Competing discourses on language preservation along the shores of the Baie Sainte-Marie', ann an Alexandre Duchêne & Monica Heller (eds), *Discourses of Endangerment: Ideology and Interest in the Defence of Languages*, tdd. 98–120, London: Continuum,

Cavanaugh, Jillian (2013). 'Language ideologies and language attitudes', ann am Peter Auer, Javier Caro Reina & Göz Kaufmann (eds), *Language Variation: European Perspectives IV*, tdd. 45–55. Amsterdam: John Benjamins.

Dauenhauer, Nora Marks, agus Dauenhauer, Richard (1998). 'Technical, emotional, and ideological issues in reversing language shift: Examples from Southeast Alaska', ann an Lenore A. Grenoble agus Lindsay J. Whaley (eds), *Endangered Languages: Current Issues and Future Prospects*, tdd. 57-98. Cambridge: CUP.

Dorian, Nancy (1981). *Language Death: The Life Cycle of a Scottish Gaelic Dialect*. Philadelphia, PA: University of Pennsylvania Press

Dunmore, Stuart S. (2015). 'Bilingual life after school? Language use, ideologies and attitudes among Gaelic-medium educated adults'. Tràchdas PhD neo-fhoillsichte, Oilthigh Dhùn Èideann.

Fishman, Joshua A. (1991). *Reversing Language Shift: Theoretical and Empirical Foundations of Assistance to Threatened Languages*. Clevedon: Multilingual Matters.

Fishman, Joshua A. (deas.) (2001). *Can Threatened Languages Be Saved? Reversing Language Shift Revisited: A 21st Century Perspective*. Clevedon: Multilingual Matters.

Fishman, Joshua A. agus García, Ofelia (eds) (2a deas. 2010). *Handbook of Language and Ethnic Identity: Disciplinary and Regional Perspectives* Vol. I. Oxford: OUP.

Fishman, Joshua A. (2010). 'Sociolinguistics: Language and ethnic identity in context', ann am Fishman, agus García 2010, tdd. xxiii–xxxv.

Fishman, Joshua A. (2013). 'Language maintenance, language shift, and reversing language shift', ann an Tej K. Bhatia agus William C. Ritchie (2a deas.), *The Handbook of Bilingualism and Multilingualism*, tdd. 466–94.

Hodges, Rhian (2009) 'Welsh language use among young people in the Rhymney Valley'. *Contemporary Wales*, Iml. 22, tdd. 16–35.

Hymes, Dell (1974). *Foundations in Sociolinguistics: An Ethnographic Approach*. Lunnainn: Tavistock Publications.

Kroskrity, Paul V. (2004). 'Language ideologies', ann an Alessandro Duranti (deas.), *A Companion to Linguistic Anthropology*, tdd. 496–517. Oxford: Blackwell.

Macdonald, Sharon (1997). *Reimagining Culture: Histories, Identities and the Gaelic Renaissance*. Oxford: Berg.

MacFhionghuin, Coinneach (2005) 'Gaelic-medium education 1985-2007'. Ri fhaighinn air loidhne bho URL: www.cnag.org.uk/munghaidhlig/stats/ (air a tharraing a-mach 10.2.2012).

Makihara, Miki (2010). 'Anthropology', ann am Fishman agus García 2010, tdd. 32–48.

National Records of Scotland (2013) 'Statistical Bulletin Release 2A'. Ri fhaighinn air loidhne bho URL: www.scotlandscensus.gov.uk/documents/censusresults/release2a/StatsBulletin2A.pdf (air a tharraing a-mach 26.9.2013)

Ochs, Elinor (1979). ' Transcription as Theory', ann an Elinor Ochs agus Bambi B. Schiefflin, *Developmental Pragmatics*, tdd. 43–72. New York: Academic Press.

Oliver, James (2002). 'Young People and Gaelic in Scotland: Identity Dynamics in a

European Region'. Tràchdas PhD neo-fhoillsichte, Oilthigh Sheffield.

Silverstein, Michael (1979). 'Language structure and linguistic ideology', ann am Paul R. Clyne, William F. Hanks agus Carol L. Hofbauer (deas.), *The Elements: A Parasession on Linguistic Units and Levels*. Chicago: Chicago Linguistic Society, pp. 193–247.

Woolard, Katherine (2011). 'Is there linguistic life after high school? Longitudinal changes in the bilingual repertoire in metropolitan Barcelona'. *Language in Society*, Iml. 40, tdd. 617–48.

19

Cuimseachadh air cruth ann am foghlam tro mheadhan na Gàidhlig (FMG): A' leasachadh chomasan cànain le ceartachadh iomchaidh

Sìleas L. NicLeòid

Sabhal Mòr Ostaig

Ann a bhith a' coimhead air sgilean cànanach sgoilearan a gheibh an cuid foghlaim tro mheadhan na Gàidhlig agus gam measadh gu cothromach, tha e air leth cudromach a bhith a' gabhail a-steach fiosrachadh air modhan anns an tèid an teagasg is an ceartachadh sa chànain. Às aonais fios mun fhios a-steach (*input*) sin, cha ghabh sgrùdadh fìorachail cothromach den fhios a-mach, 's e sin comasan cànain na cloinne, a choileanadh.

Gu h-àraidh ann an Canada, ach, cuideachd, ann an iomadh dùthaich eile far a bheil còrr is aon chànan stèidhichte mar phrìomh mheadhan teagaisg ann an siostam an fhoghlaim (bogadh cànain), tha deasbad air a bhith a' dol air adhart ann an rannsachadh air dè na modhan teagaisg cànanach agus modhan ceartachaidh as fheàrr gus sgilean cànanach nan sgoilearan a thoirt gu ìre fìor àrd (Ellis, 2013; Goo is Mackey, 2013; Lyster is Ranta, 2013 is 1997; Ammar, 2008).

'S e ceist mhòr san deasbad seo sa chiad dol-a-mach am bu chòir am prionnsabal 'cuimseachadh air cruth' a chleachdadh, le bhith a' dèanamh cinnteach gun tèid cruth gramataigeach na cànain a thogail gu ceart aig a' mhion-ìre leis an luchd-ionnsachaidh air neo am bu chòir do luchd-teagaisg am fòcas a chumail air sgilean conaltraidh is còmhraidh ann an teagasg agus gabhail ris gun tog a' chlann cruth gramataigeach na cànain gu ceart thar ùine. A' togail air an sgaradh bhunaiteach sin, bidh luchd-rannsachaidh a' leantainn dà phrìomh bheachd a thaobh na dòigh ceartachaidh as fheàrr ann an teagasg cànain, agus 's iad sin:

(i) **fios air ais dìreach**: a' ceartachadh gràmair gu dìreach is gu fosgailte *(explicit correction)* air neo a' toirt air an neach-bhruidhinn a bhith ri fèin-cheartachadh tro fhios air ais for-chànanach (diofar sheòrsaichean de *prompts*)

(ii) **fios air ais neo-dhìreach**: a' ceartachadh gràmar gu neo-dhìreach no gu falaichte (m.e. tro *recasts*)

A rèir tràchdas (i) tha e nas èifeachdaiche a bhith a' toirt fios air ais dìreach don neach-ionnsachaidh (faic Ellis, 2013; Lyster et al., 2013; Ellis, Loewen is Erlam, 2006; Lyster, 2004; Vásquez is Harvey, 2010; Nicholas, Lightbown is Spada, 2001). Dh'fhaodadh sin tachairt le bhith a' togail – gu follaiseach – mhearachdan a nì neach-ionnsachaidh ann an labhairt gus aire an neach-bhruidhinn a tharraing don trioblaid agus gus an cruth ceart innse dhi sa bhad. Air an dòigh sin, bidh an neach-ionnsachaidh mothachail nach do chleachd i facail no rosgrann ann an cruth ceart agus, le bhith a' cluinntinn na bu chòir cleachdadh na àite, gheibh i cothrom an eileamaid ghramataigeach sin a chuimhneachadh gu ceart. A bharrachd air ceartachadh dìreach, tha modhan obrach fosgailte ann a dh'fhaodadh a bhith na b' èifeachdaiche buileach: 's iad diofar chruthan de *prompts* (fios air ais for-chànanach) don neach-bhruidhinn, a bheir dhi an cothrom fèin-cheartachadh a dhèanamh (Ellis, Loewen is Erlam, 2006; Lyster, 2004 is 2002; Lyster is Ranta, 1997).

> *Although explicit correction [...] draws attention to form, it does so in a way that does not allow for negotiation because it provides the form unilaterally and thus creates an opportunity for the learner to repeat the teacher's alternative form but not to self-repair* (Lyster, 2002, td. 247).

Tha sin a' ciallachadh ann an còmhradh sa chlas gun cuir an neach-teagaisg stad air an neach-bhruidhinn ma thèid mearachd gràmair a dhèanamh, ach, an àite a bhith ag innse a' chrutha cheirt, bheir iad *prompt* air choreigin dhi, gus an cnuasaich i a-rithist air cruth na h-eileamaid a bha ceàrr. Thathar an dùil gun tog an neach-bruidhinn an uair sin air an eòlas a th' aice mar-thà (Lyster, 2002).

Tha diofar sheòrsaichean de *prompts* ann: ceistean soilleireachaidh (ag iarraidh soilleireachd bhon neach-bhruidhinn, tro cheist no iarrtas: 'B' àill leibh?', 'Am faod thu seo a ràdh a-rithist?'), ath-aithris air na chaidh a ràdh, le cuideam ceasnachaidh làidir air a' phàirt cheàrr gus aire a tharraing don mhearachd, sanasan for-chànanach (ceistean leithid 'An ann mar sin a bhios sinn ga ràdh?', no pìosan fiosrachaidh eile a bheir beachd don neach-bruidhinn gun deach e ceàrr an àiteigin, m.e. 'Tha tràth eadar-dhealaichte a dhìth an seo') no *elicitation* ('tarraing a-mach', i.e. ag iarraidh eileamaid shònraichte bhon neach-bhruidhinn, m.e. tro ath-aithris le beàrn far a bheil an eileamaid cheart a dhìth) (faic Ellis, Loewen is Erlam, 2006; Lyster, 2004; Lyster is Ranta, 1997).

A rèir an dàrna tràchdais (ii), tha e nas cudromaiche gum faigh an luchd-ionnsachaidh cothroman a bhith a' dol air adhart le còmhradh fiù 's ma nì iad mearachdan nan labhairt, gun ceartachadh an neach-teagaisg a bhith a' cur stad orra is, math dh'fhaodte, gan dì-mhisneachadh (Goo is Mackey, 2013; Truscott, 1999). An àite a bhith gan ceartachadh gu follaiseach, thèid fios air ais neo-dhìreach a sholarachadh, tro *recasts*. Tha sin ri ràdh gun dèan an neach-teagaisg ath-aithris air a' phìos far an deach an neach-bruidhinn ceàrr, ach leis a' chruth cheart, mar a bha e a dhìth (Ellis, Loewen, is Erlam, 2006; Lyster, 2004; Nicholas, Lightbown is Spada, 2001). Thathar an dùil gum faigh an neach-ionnsachaidh an cothrom a bhith ag aithneachadh diofar eadar na thuirt i fhèin is ràdh an neach-teagaisg is gun obraich i a-mach càite an robh a' mhearachd. 'S e modh obrach fìor chumanta a tha seo ann an teagasg cànain, leis gu bheil mòran luchd-teagaisg draghail gun cailleadh an luchd-ionnsachaidh am misneachd nan rachadh an ceartachadh gu dìreach is gu follaiseach ro thric (Vásquez is Harvey, 2010; Seedhouse, 1997).

Chithear sgaradh làidir am measg an luchd-rannsachaidh a thaobh èifeachdachd tràchdas (i) vs tràchdas (ii), agus cuid a' dèanamh eadar-dhealachadh a bharrachd le bhith ag ràdh gu bheil e an crochadh air suidheachadh agus amas an teagaisg am bu chòir (i) no (ii) a chleachdadh. Airson beachd soilleir a chur an cruth air na puingean sin, tha e deatamach sa chiad dol-a-mach tilleadh do thoiseach na cùise is a' cnuasachadh carson a thòisicheadh air uiread cuideim a chur air modhan ceartachaidh is fios air ais ann an teagasg cànain bho thaobh rannsachaidh.

Gu ìre, 's e freagairt gu math sìmplidh a gheibhear an sin, agus 's e sin nach robh sgilean cànanach luchd-ionnsachaidh cho math aig a' mhion-ìre 's a shùilicheadh, a dh'aindeoin is gun robh iad air am bogadh sa chànain. Thog e ceann ann an Canada, mar eisimpleir, gur ann tric a bhios clann a thogas cànain tro bhogadh san sgoil a' togail sgilean glè mhath ann an tuigse na cànain agus gum bi iad reusanta fileanta innte cuideachd, ach nach eil iad cho math aig a' mhion-ìre chànanach, m.e. a thaobh gràmar (faic Lyster, 2002 is 2004; Swain is Lapkin, 1995).[1]

> *Over the last two decades, research has shown that second language (L2) learners in language immersion classrooms develop high levels of comprehension skills as well as considerable fluency and confidence in L2 production, but experience long-lasting difficulties in grammatical development* (Lyster, 2002, td. 237).

Tha a' phuing seo gar toirt do thaobh phragtaigeach a' phàipeir seo, oir b' e an dearbh dheargadh san rannsachadh airson a' PhD agam gun robh clann a bha air a' Ghàidhlig ionnsachadh tro bhogadh cànain san sgoil (foghlam tro mheadhan na Gàidhlig) glè mhisneachail, math air tuigsinn is air còmhradh sa Ghàidhlig a leantainn agus fileanta gu leòr airson an cuid bheachdan a chur an cèill ann an dòigh air choreigin. Ach, aig an aon àm, mhothaicheadh iomadh duilgheadas glè chunbhalach a thaobh ceartachd aig ìre ghramataigeach.

'S e an ath cheum sa phàipear seo sùil mhionaideach a thoirt air toraidhean an rannsachaidh sin a thaobh sgilean gràmair na cloinne agus a thaobh beachdan an luchd-teagaisg air modhan ceartachaidh, mus tillear do na puingean deasbaid a thogadh anns an ro-ràdh, don cheist gu dè an t-slighe as èifeachdaiche airson fios air ais do luchd-ionnsachaidh ann am bogadh cànain.

Mar bhunait a' PhD, chumadh agallamhan ann an naoi diofar sgoiltean ann an ceithir diofar sgìrean ann an Alba (eadar eileanan is bailtean mòra), le 80 sgoilear FMG eadar P4 agus S2, 32 phàrant agus 16 luchd-teagaisg, agus fhuaireadh còrr is mìle duilleag de thras-sgrìobhaidhean bho na h-agallamhan sin. Thug agallamhan nan sgoilearan eadar deich is fichead mionaid gach pàiste.

'S ann a bha am pròiseact a-mach air a' cheangal eadar cànain agus cultar ann am FMG, agus mar phàirt den togail fiosrachaidh, dh'fhaighnicheadh ceistean don chloinn timcheall air an cuid sheasamhan mu choinneimh na Gàidhlig agus mu FMG san fharsaingeachd. Bhathar a-mach air beachdan na cloinne a thaobh cànain agus, cuideachd, ann am pàirt eile, air an cuid sgilean ann an Gàidhlig. Cha b' ann aig ìre fhoirmeil no tro sgrùdadh cànanach an dàta a thogadh am fiosrachadh sin, ge-tà; na àite, bhathar airson cluinntinn bhon chloinn fhèin (is bhon luchd-teagaisg) mar a bha iad a' faireachdainn mun cuid sgilean Gàidhlig is mar a dhèanadh iad fhèin measadh orra.

Ged nach robhar ri sgrùdadh foirmeil gramataigeach, cha b' urrainnear gun a bhith mothachail air iomadh duilgheadas cànanach a thogail bh' aig a' chloinn anns an dàta sin. A dh'aindeoin 's gun robh e coltach gun robh a' mhòr-chuid de na sgoilearan a' faireachdainn gu math misneachail sa chànain is dòigheil a bhith ga bruidhinn, cha robh an cuid Gàidhlig cho math is a bhite a' sùileachadh, às dèidh eadar ceithir agus ochd bliadhnaichean de bhogadh sa chànain. 'S e seo a' chiad phàirt den trioblaid a thathar airson deasbad sa chaibideil seo.

Ged a tha e cumanta ann an sgrùdadh cànain nàdarrach gun a bhith a-mach air na tha 'ceart' no 'ceàrr' gu gramataigeach agus, na àite, a bhith a' bruidhinn air diofar chleachdaidhean cànanach, thathar a' dol leis a' bhriathrachas 'ceart vs. ceàrr' agus 'mearachdan' seach 'cleasan' anns a' phàipear seo.

Bhiodh cùisean eadar-dhealaichte nan robhar air bruidhinn ri inbhich le Gàidhlig bho thùs a-mhàin, far am bite an dùil gun cleachdadh iad a' chànain fhathast gu làitheil is gu gnàthach am measg a chèile, ann an diofar rèimean agus co-theagsaichean. Ge-tà, tha suidheachadh cànanach na h-òigridh eadar-dhealaichte a thaobh na Gàidhlig, air sgàth 's gur e an dearbh thrioblaid a th' aig a' chànain *nach* bi daoine òga ga cleachdadh rin co-aoisean ann an dòigh nàdarrach is shòisealta (cf. NicLeòid, ri nochdadh; O' Hanlon, 2013; Stiùbhart, 2011; Oliver, 2006). Don a' mhòr-chuid, tha e fìor nach bruidhinn iad i ach ri daoine à ginealaichean eile, m.e. ris an luchd-teagaisg san sgoil air neo rim pàrantan no seann-phàrantan. Agus mar sin, cha b' urrainnear dìreach gabhail ris gu bheil a' chainnt aca ag atharrachadh gu gnàthach, tro bhith ga cleachdadh am measg a chèile, mar a dhèanadh mòr-chànainean agus, far an cleachdadh iad gleus-cainnt ann an cruth neo-àbhaisteach, nach b' e 'mearachdan' a bh' ann ach atharrachadh nàdarrach no cleas cànanach ùr.

Tha diofar ga shealltainn an seo eadar atharrachadh cànain gnàthach, mar a bhios e a' tachairt gu nàdarrach anns a h-uile cànain, thairis air ùine mhòr fhada, dìreach air sgàth 's gum bi daoine ga cleachdadh gu làitheil agus a' cur bhriathran ùra, structaran ùra agus chleachdaidhean ùra a-steach, agus atharrachadh cànain air sàilleabh crìonadh cànain (faic Dorian, 1981 is 1994). Ann an co-theacsa mion-chànain, bidh atharrachaidhean cànain a' tachairt glè thric gu mì-nàdarrach, m.e. air sgàth mhearachdan a thèid a chleachdadh cho cunbhalach is gun sgaoil iad gu farsaing agus ri linn buaidh na mòr-chànain, mì-chinnt agus beàrnan eile ann an ionnsachadh, gu h-àraidh am measg nan ginealaichean òga (cf. Bell et al., 2014; Baker, 1992; Dorian, 1981). Air sgàth nan adhbharan sin, thèid gabhail ris an seo gur e mearachdan a th' ann far am bi na sgoilearan a' dol an aghaidh gleusan-cainnt gramataigeach traidiseanta,[2] seach atharrachaidhean no cleasan ùr nàdarrach.

Bha an rannsachadh a' gabhail a-steach agallamhan le luchd-teagaisg cuideachd, agus 's ann tron dàta sin a thàinig an dàrna pàirt den trioblaid am bàrr: bha mì-chinnt mhòr ga seallltainn am measg luchd-teagaisg a thaobh modhan ceartachaidh a dh'fhaodadh iad cleachdadh gus sgilean Gàidhlig na cloinne a leasachadh gun a bhith gan dì-mhisneachadh aig an aon àm.

Sa phàipear seo, bidh mi a-mach air (1) na mearachdan gramataigeach as cumanta am measg nan sgoilearan, a' sealltainn eisimpleirean à corpas nan agallamhan, agus (2) air draghan a chaidh a thogail leis an luchd-teagaisg a thaobh modhan ceartachaidh agus dìth stiùiridh dhaibh sa chùis sin.

Airson beachd fhaighinn air na trioblaidean a bu mhotha a bh' aig na sgoilearan a thaobh gràmar na Gàidhlig, chaidh sùil mhionaideach a thoirt air na h-agallamhan air fad a-rithist, agus thogadh eisimpleirean airson sia de na seòrsaichean mhearachdan a bu chumanta a mhothaicheadh gu cunbhalach san dàta.

Airson na mòr-chuid, b' e gleusan-cainnt fìor chumanta agus bunaiteach a bh' annta a bhiodh mòran cloinne a' cleachdadh gu ceàrr gu cunbhalach.

Gu h-inntinneach, mhothaicheadh na cleasan sin an dà chuid am measg luchd-ionnsachaidh FMG[3] agus sgoilearan aig an robh a' Ghàidhlig bho thùs (ged a bhiodh iad beagan na bu stèidhichte am measg luchd-ionnsachaidh).

1) Duilgheadas le *'s e* vs. *tha*

Glè thric, bhiodh na sgoilearan a' cleachdadh *tha* far am bu chòir *'s e* a chleachdadh. Gu h-iongantach, nochd an trioblaid seo fada na bu trice am measg sgoilearan aig ìre na h-àrd-sgoile.

Ìre na bun-sgoile:
- **Tha e** ... *language* math airson a bhith ag ionnsachadh.
- **Tha e cànan** math!
- **Tha iad math tidsearan.**

Ìre na h-àrd-sgoile:
- Bha am bun-sgoil, **bha e** *building* gu math beag.
- ... **Tha e cuspair** ... caran ... beag, oir tha, chan eil tòrr de daoine a' bruidhinn e.
- **Tha mise** an *only Gaelic person* air am bus agam.

2) Gun a bhith a' sèimheachadh ainmearan às dèidh riochdairean seilbheach

Thàinig e am bàrr gu bheil mì-chinnt mhòr am measg sgoilearan ceangailte ri riochdairean seilbheach agus cruth an ainmeir a bu chòir cleachdadh às an dèidh. Bhiodh cuid den chloinn gun a bhith a' cleachdadh sèimheachadh idir an sin, agus bhiodh cuid eile ga dhèanamh ceart ann an co-theacsa no dhà (m.e. nuair a thòisicheadh an t-ainmear le connrag) agus a' dol ceàrr ann an co-theacsaichean eile, air neo dìreach a' dol air ais is air adhart eadar cruthan ceart is ceàrr fad an t-siubhail, a' daingneachadh nach robh iad cinnteach idir mun ghleus-cainnt sin. A-rithist, mhothaicheadh an trioblaid seo na bu trice am measg sgoilearan aig ìre na h-àrd-sgoile na aig ìre na bun-sgoile.

Ìre na bun-sgoile:
- *[C]uin a bhios tu a' bruidhinn Beurla mar as àbhaist?*
  Ri **mo caraidean** agus ... ri **mo pàrantan**, ru d, rud beag.
- Nuair a tha mi a' bruidhinn gu **mo co-oghaichean**.
- Bha **mo seanmhair** agus mo mar ... dè 'n ... bha **mo** *grandparents*, **mo mamaidh** is dadaidh aig **mo Dadaidh** agus **mo uncailean** is antaidh air an taobh aig **mo Dadaidh**.

Ìre na h-àrd-sgoile:
- Agus chan eil fios aig **mo Dadaidh** air.

- Tha Gàidhlig aig **mo ... bràthair** agus **mo athair**.
- Dh'ionnsaich mi Gàidhlig aig **mo taigh**.

3) A' cleachdadh roimhear + riochdaire fa leth, seach riochdairean roimhearach

B' e trioblaid ghramataigeach eile a chaidh a thogail ann am freagairtean na cloinne gun robh mòran dhiubh a' cleachdadh roimhearan + riochdairean fa leth an àite riochdairean roimhearach. Mhothaicheadh sin far nach robh cuideam sònraichte air an riochdaire *(*aig i)*, ach fada na bu trice ann an co-theacsa far an robh iad airson cuideam a chur air an riochdaire *(*le iadsan)*. Nochd na mearachdan sin an dà chuid aig ìre na bun-sgoile agus aig ìre na hàrd-sgoile, le roimhearan sìmplidh agus le roimhearan fillte.

Ìre na bun-sgoile:
- Uill, tha iad a' faighinn faclan ùra. Agus faodaidh iad iad ag ràdh gu daoine eile nach eil Gàidhlig **aig iad**, agus a' tidseadh iad.
- Tha e ag ionnsachadh rud bheag **bho mise**.
- Ach cha bhi mi a' bruidhinn **ri iadsan** anns a' Ghàidhlig tòrr
- Uaireannan tha na tidsearan a' cleachdadh *phrases* chan eil fios **aig sinne** air.

Ìre na h-àrd-sgoile:
- Airson, tha i, nuair a tha i air tadhail bhon taigh, gun ... bràthran **aig i**.
- 'S urrainn dhut a' faighinn *conversation* **còmhla ri iad**.
- Bidh mi a' bruidhinn Gàidhlig **ri iadsan**.
- Tha facail ann a bheil, a tha rud beag **mu dheidhinn iad**.

4) A' cleachdadh ainmearan gnìomhaireach + riochdairean pearsanta gu ceart

Am measg nan sgoilearan air fad cha robh ach triùir no ceathrar comasach air ainmearan gnìomhaireach ann an cothlamadh ri riochdairean pearsanta a chleachdadh gu ceart, le gam/gad/msaa air beulaibh an ainmeir. Bhiodh e a' mhòr-chuid de sgoilearan (bun-sgoile agus àrd-sgoile) a' cleachdadh riochdairean anns an tuiseal àbhaisteach air cùlaibh an ainmeir a-mhàin.

Ìre na bun-sgoile:
- Uill, bidh mi **a' cluinntinn iad** uaireannan, ach ... chan eil, chan eil mi **a' cluinntinn iad** fad an latha.
- Bidh mi **a' faicinn ise** uabhasach fhèin tòrr.
- Bidh feadhainn de daoine **a' faighinn e** doirbh agus feadhainn de daoine **a' faighinn e** furasta.

- Bidh thu dìreach a' *pick*eadh rudan an-àirde, a thoirt rudan an-àirde, agus dìreach **a' cleachdadh iad.**

Ìre na h-àrd-sgoile:
- Bidh na tidsearan **a' ceartachadh thu.**
- Bidh sinn **a' faicinn iad** dhà no trì triopan sa bhliadhna.
- Tha e dìreach uabhasach furasta, carson bha thu **a'** dèanamh e nuair a bha thu òg, *so* tha fios agad, dè tha thu ag ràdh agus dè tha thu a' dèanamh.
- Tha e ... cànan aig an Gàidheil agus bidh iad **a' bruidhinn e** anns an Alba.

Mar a chithear sna h-eisimpleirean gu h-ìosal, cha robh cuid de na beagan sgoilearan a chleachd an gleus-cainnt seo gu ceart an-còmhnaidh cinnteach nas motha, is iad a' dol eadar a bhith ga dhèanamh ceart aon mhionaid agus ceàrr an ath mhionaid (aig amannan le bhith a' cleachdadh an riochdaire dà thuras san aon ghleus-cainnt):

Ìre na bun-sgoile:
- Tha mi 's dòcha nas fheàrr leatha, airson 's toil leam a bhith **ga** dhèanamh, so tha mi mar *improvement* nuair a tha mi a' dèanamh **iad.**
- Agus an uair sin bidh sin tuilleadh *people* **ga**, tuilleadh daoine **ga** ionnsachadh **e.**

Ìre na h-àrd-sgoile:
- Oir tha i dìreach **ga** h-ionnsachadh **e.**
- Tha e **gam** chuideachadh, airson tha mi, tha thu, ...tha mi a' cur **e** ceart.

5) Trioblaidean leis a' ghleus-cainnt 'cas mu seach' (le ainmear no riochdaire)

B' e duilgheadas gramataigeach eile a chaidh a mhothachadh an gleus-cainnt 'cas mu seach'. A-rithist, cha robh ach triùir no ceathrar sgoilearan comasach air seantansan a leithid 'Bha mi airson X a dhèanamh' a ràdh gu ceart, fhad 's a bhiodh a' mhòr-chuid aca a' dol leis an dòigh cheàrr, gun a bhith ag iomlaid a' ghnìomhair is a' chùisear *(*Bha mi airson a' dèanamh X)* agus le bhith a' cleachdadh foirm ceàrr den ghnìomhair sa chiad dol-a-mach. Far an robh riochdaire a' gabhail àite an ainmeir, cha d' fhuaireadh eisimpleirean ceart ach bho dhithis.

Ìre na bun-sgoile:
- Tha mo Mamaidh ag iarraidh **ag ionnsachadh Gàidhlig.**
- Tha feum agad **a' cleachdadh rudan** mar sin.

- Bha mi ag iarraidh **a' bruidhinn Gàidhlig**.
- Tha mi a' smaointinn feumaidh tòrr daoine eile **a' bruidhinn e**.
- Faodaidh mi dìreach **ag ràdh** sa Ghàidhlig.
- Tha e math **a'** dèanamh e nas cumanta.

Ìre na h-àrd-sgoile:
- Airson **a' cumail an cànan** …ann.
- Tha mi a' smaoineachadh gu bheil iad a' teagasg airson **toirt cothrom dhuinne** a' faighinn mar a' Ghàidhlig againn cofhurtail.
- Ma tha faclan ùra againn, feumaidh sinn **a' cur iad** ann an *jotter*.
- Bidh iad ag iarraidh **ga bhruidhinn**.
- Bha mo Mhamaidh ag iarraidh mi **a' dèanamh e**.

6) A' cleachdadh *airson* no *carson* an àite *a chionn 's/air sgàth 's/oir* msaa

Air adhbharan nach eil buileach soilleir aig an ìre-sa, bhiodh cha mhòr a h-uile aon de na h-agallaichean (bun-sgoile is àrd-sgoile) a' cleachdadh *airson* + IND (foirm neo-eisimeileach den ghnìomhair) mar cho-cheanglaiche adhbharach far am bu chòir *a chionn 's* + DEP /*air sgàth 's* + DEP /*oir* + IND a bhith. Mhothaicheadh buidheann bheag am measg sgoilearan bhon dà ìre sgoile a chanadh fiù 's *carson* anns na co-theacsaichean sin, .i. a' cleachdadh riochdaire na ceist fhèin mar thoiseach na freagairt.

Ìre na bun-sgoile:
- *A bheil beachd agad carson a tha sin?*
  … Carson **maybe** tha iad a' dol gu sgoil Gàidhlig no rudeigin mar sin.
- Ach cha bhi mi a' bruidhinn ri iadsan anns a' Ghàidhlig tòrr, **airson cha** …tha mo phiuthar agus mo bràthair a' bruidhinn Gàidhlig, ach chan eil mo Mamaidh.
- **Airson** ma chan eil fhios againn air facal Gàidhlig.

Ìre na h-àrd-sgoile:
- Tha Gàidhlig … *fifty-fifty* riumsa, chan eil fhios 'am. **Carson,** chan eil … is toil leam e … agus cha toil leam e.
- Tha e dìreach uabhasach furasta, **carson bha** thu a' dèanamh e nuair a bha thu òg, *so* tha fios agad, dè tha thu ag ràdh agus dè tha thu a' dèanamh.
- **Airson** tha i, nuair a tha i air tadhal bhon taigh, gun … bràithrean aig i.
- Chan eil fhios agamsa, **airson** càite am bi mi … a' fuireach.

B' iad sin na prìomh sia seòrsaichean mhearachdan a chaidh a mhothachadh anns an dàta is a chaidh a thaghadh airson a' phàipeir seo, air sgàth 's gun robh iad cho cumanta is cho cunbhalach ann an cainnt na cloinne. Dh'fhaodadh a' phuing a thogail gun cluinnear cuid de na 'mearachdan' no structaran neo-àbhaisteach bho fhileantaich nas aosta cuideachd, bho àm gu àm, agus tha sin fìor, gu h-àraidh airson a leithid 'tha mi a' dèanamh e', 'airson iadsan' agus 'airson' mar cho-cheanglaiche adhbharach. Ge-tà, don luchd-labhairt sin,'s e tionndaidhean cànain a th' annta, a thèid a chleachdadh airson cuideam a bharrachd, ann an cabhag no air adhbharan eile gun ullachadh (*spontaneous*) agus, gu dearbh, bidh iad comasach air na structaran ceart a chleachdadh agus bidh iad gan cleachdadh a' chuid a bu mhotha den ùine.[4] Bha cùisean eadar-dhealaichte am measg na cloinne, far an deach na gleusan-cainnt neo-àbhaisteach sin a chleachdadh gu cunbhalach agus, le àireamh glè mhòr de na sgoilearan, chaidh fiù 's an cleachdadh a-mhàin, gun luaidh air structar sam bith eile. Cha robh coltas anns na h-eisimpleirean sin gum b' e taghadh no 'tubaist' a bh' ann, ach dìreach àbhaist nan dòighean-bruidhinn.

Fhuaireadh geàrr-chunntas air iomadh eisimpleir de mhearachdan sa phàirt seo. 'S e an ath cheist a-nis, dè tha an luchd-teagaisg a' dèanamh mu mhearachdan den t-seòrsa sin, is ciamar a tha iad a' feuchainn ri dèanamh cinnteach gun tuig na sgoilearan am mearachdan is gun tog iad gleusan-cainnt ann an cruth ceart?

Thèid am pàirt seo thairis air beachdan an luchd-teagaisg air dòighean ceartachaidh. Mhothaicheadh gun robh mì-chinnt nam measg mu dè bhiodh èifeachdach a thaobh ceartachaidh agus, aig an aon àm, taiceil don chloinn, gun a bhith gan dì-mhisneachadh nan cuid sgilean Gàidhlig. B' e an dragh a bu mhotha a chaidh ainmeachadh leis na tidsearan gur dòcha nach biodh na sgoilearan airson a' Ghàidhlig a bhruidhinn idir, nan robh iad air an ceartachadh fad an t-siubhail (cf. Vásquez is Harvey, 2010, Lyster, 2004).

A rèir an luchd-teagaisg (16 dhiubh uile-gu-lèir) ris an deach agallamhan a chumail, cha robh poileasaidh aig gin de na sgoiltean a thaobh ceartachaidh no stiùireadh eile air a' chùis. Bheirear sùil a-nis air modhan ceartachaidh mar a thèid an cleachdadh leotha, a rèir an cuid fhaireachdainnean is an cuid tuigse phearsanta. An uair sin, chithear geàrr-chunntas air beachdan agus draghan an luchd-teagaisg co-cheangailte ris na dòighean ceartachaidh sin.

Modhan obrach

Bhiodh mòran am measg an luchd-teagaisg gu math faiceallach gun a bhith a' ceartachadh a h-uile càil ann an cainnt na cloinne, air eagal 's gun cailleadh a' chlann am misneachd. Air sgàth an dragha sin, bidh mòran thidsearan a' cleachdadh *recasts*, an dà chuid airson briathrachas agus gràmar:

NT-BS[5]
> an rud a tha mise a' dèanamh, … tha e ceart gu leòr leis an fheadhainn bheaga a bhith dìreach, nuair a tha iad a' bruidhinn, nuair a tha iad ag ràdh rudeigin ceàrr, bidh mise ag ràdh am facal ceart, dìreach cuiridh mi a-steach e.

Bidh cuid dhiubh dìreach a' mìneachadh puing gràmair gu luath, don chlas air fad, nan robh cuideigin air structar a chleachdadh gu ceàrr:

NT-BS
> rud a tha iad an-còmhnaidh a' dèanamh, 's e a bhiodh iad ag ràdh 'aig mise' an àite 'agamsa' no 'agam'. Agus … ma tha sin a' tachairt, bidh mi, bidh mi a' dèanamh rudeigin mòr dheth, air sgàth 's gur e rudeigin a tha tòrr dhaoine a' faighinn ceàrr, chan, cha bhi mi ag ràdh 'O, thuirt thusa sin ceàrr! Èist a h-uile duine!', dìreach uaireannan, canaidh mi, 'ceart, feumaidh sinn uile cuimhneachadh nuair a tha thu a' bruidhinn mu dheidhinn rudeigin a th' agad, 's e 'agam', chan e 'aig mise'.

Thuirt dithis gum biodh iad a' toirt air a' chloinn an gleus-cainnt a bha ceàrr a ràdh a-rithist: bhiodh aonan a' toirt *prompts* dhaibh airson sin (*elicitation* tro ath-aithris le beàrn), agus bhiodh an tè eile a' cur cheistean (sanas for-chànanach), gus an obraicheadh an neach-bruidhinn fhèin a-mach na bha ceàrr:

NT-BS
> Ma chanas cuideigin … 'aice' an àite 'aige', rudeigin mar sin, cheartaichinn sin anns a' bhad. Chanainn, *you know,* 'an e nighean a th' ann a shin, no an e balach ann a shin?'

B' e dòigh obrach eile a chaidh ainmeachadh a bhith a' ceartachadh còmhradh dìreach aig amannan, le barrachd fòcas air leigeil don chloinn bruidhinn sa Ghàidhlig gun stad a chur orra. Thuirt cuid eile fiù 's nach biodh iad a' ceart-achadh mhearachdan ach ann an sgrìobhadh a-mhàin:

NT-AS[6]
> A' ceartachadh rudan sgrìobhaidh ceart gu leòr, ach … chan eil mi a-riamh a' ceartachadh mearachdan … gràmar nuair a tha iad ga bhruidhinn.

Bha diofar bheachdan aig an luchd-teagaisg air a bhith a' ceartachadh na cloinne idir sa chiad àite. Thuirt cuid nach robh iad a' cur cus cuideam air, m.e. briathrachas sònraichte: b' fheàrr leotha gum bi a' chlann a' mìneachadh rudeigin ann an Gàidhlig idir, fiù 's ann am facail shìmplidh agus le mearachdan nan cuid gràmair, an àite na tidsearan a bhith a' cur maille orra le briathran mionaideach agus ceartachadh ann am meadhan còmhraidh.

NT-BS
> [A]ig a' fìor thoiseach nuair a tha iad a-staigh sa … na clasaichean

beaga bìodach ann a shin, 's e *really* ag iarraidh orra a bhith ga, ga bruidhinn. Chan eil thu ag iarraidh a bhith cus, cus de, *you know, pressure* orra, fhios agad, a' faighinn a h-uile càil ceart.

Ge-tà, sheall mòran am measg an luchd-teagaisg mothachadh air duilgheadasan na cloinne ann an gràmar agus dragh nach robhar a' dèanamh gu leòr an-dràsta airson an cuideachadh. Bha an fheadhainn seo den bheachd nach robh *recasts* a-mhàin ag obrachadh math gu leòr gus sgilean gràmair na cloinne a leasachadh:

NT-BS

[R]ud a chaidh a ràdh rium, 's e, uill, ma tha thu a … a' bruidhinn riutha leis a' ghràmar cheart gum bu chòir iad sin a thogail, … ach chan eil fhios 'am, cha robh mi a' faireachdainn gun robh sin ag obair idir. Agus … bha, bha mi a' faireachdainn gun robh, ann an dòigh, tha mi a' faireachdainn gu bheil feum againne air barrachd comhairle mu, a thaobh ciamar a bu chòir dhuinn gràmar a dhèanamh leotha….

Air sgàth 's chan e, chan e pàirt mhòr dhen, dhen churraicealam, mar gum biodh, a th' ann.

A rèir coltais, bidh còmhraidhean am measg cuid den luchd-teagaisg mu dheidhinn sin, ann an cuid de na sgoiltean, agus iad a' beachdachadh air na b' urrainn dhaibh dèanamh gus na modhan obrach sin a leasachadh. Ge-tà, 's e cuspair duilich a bh' ann dhaibh, gun stiùireadh bho muigh, gu h-àiridh leis gun robh iad mì-chinnteach cuideachd a thaobh na h-ìre de chomasan a bu chòir a bhith aig a' chloinn aig diofar aoisean.

Chunnacas an sin gu bheil gu leòr obair leasachaidh a dhìth a thaobh modhan ceartachaidh ann am FMG agus, gu h-àraidh, barrachd stiùiridh don luchd-teagaisg air diofar dhòighean-obrach co-cheangailte ri sin agus air cho èifeachdach is a tha iad ann an diofar cho-theacsaichean ionnsachaidh. Thàinig e am bàrr cuideachd gu bheil na tidsearan fhèin ag iarraidh trèanadh is stiùireadh air a' chùis, seach gu bheil iad air fhaicinn nach eil sgilean cànanach na cloinne cho math is a b' urrainn dhaibh a bhith, a dh'aindeoin na tha iad air feuchainn airson a' chlann a chumail ceart.

Tha seo gar toirt air ais don deasbad a chaidh a thaisbeanadh san ro-ràdh agus na diofar dhòighean anns am b' urrainnear a bhith ri ceartachadh ann am bogadh cànain. 'S e buannachd mhòr a th' ann do FMG gu bheil uiread rannsachaidh air a dhèanamh mar-thà air a' chuspair sin ann an dùthchannan eile. Gabhaidh togail air na toraidhean sin sa bhad, gun a bhith a' dol air ais gu toiseach-tòiseachadh na cùise le rannsachadh gu tur ùr.

Seach gun tog e ceann gun robh duilgheadasan gramataigeach aig mòran cloinne ann am FMG, ged a bha iad reusanta fileanta agus glè mhath air sgilean tuigse sa Ghàidhlig, agus, aig an aon àm, gun tuirt a' mhòr-chuid den luchd-teagaisg nach biodh iad ach ri ceartachadh no fios air ais mì-dhìreach (*recasts*, faic tràchdas (ii) gu h-àrd), gheibhear am beachd nach eil am modh obrach sin èifeachdach gu leòr. Tha an toradh sin a' dol leis na fhuair an luchd-rannsachaidh a thaobh tràchdas (i) a-mach, a thaobh sgilean gramataigeach luchd-ionnsachaidh agus gum biodh buaidh na bu mhotha aig fios air ais dìreach air leasachadh nan sgilean sin (Ellis, 2013; Lyster et al., 2013; Lyster is Ranta, 2013; Nicholas, Lightbown is Spada, 2001; Seedhouse, 1997). Chaidh diofar theannaidhean a chur air adhart leotha a mhìnicheas carson, nam beachdsan, nach eil *recasts* cho èifeachdach ri fios air ais dìreach ann an co-theagsa tocail gràmair tro bhogadh, agus 's ann a tha na teannaidhean sin fìor bhuntainneach don tsuidheachadh ann am FMG cuideachd.

'S e an duilgheadas as cudromaiche le *recasts*, mar a chaidh ainmeachadh le Nicholas, Lightbown is Spada (2001), gu bheil teansa mhath ann nach mothaich an luchd-ionnsachaidh gun deach an ceartachadh idir. A chionn 's gun tèid *recasts* a chleachdadh ann an dà dhòigh ann an còmhradh sa chlas, 's e sin airson ceartachadh falaichte, ach, cuideachd, airson daingneachadh susbaint (*recast* eu-cheartachail, *ibid.*), chan urrainnear a bhith cinnteach an tog a' chlann a' mhearachd a chaidh a chur ceart idir. Airson ceartachadh a tharraing às an *recast*, dh'fheumadh iad dol tro phròiseas cognatach gu math fillte: (i) ag aithneachadh gun do chleachd an tidsear gleus-cainnt ann an cruth beagan eadar-dhealaichte, (ii) a' dèanamh às nach b' e dìreach roghainn eile a bh' ann is nach robh an dà chruth ceart, (iii) ag obrachadh a-mach dè an diofar a bh' ann eadar na dhà gu mionaideach agus, mar sin, dè a' mhearachd a bha iad air a dhèanamh agus (iv) a' cur nan cuimhne gus nach tachair i a-rithist (faic cuideachd Lyster, 2004). Ach, leis gun tèid *recasts* a ràdh mar as trice ann an tòna molaidh, airson an neach-bruidhinn a bhrosnachadh gus cumail a' dol a bhruidhinn, tha cunnart ann gun tog an luchd-ionnsachaidh am pàirt susbainteach den *recast* a-mhàin is gun gabh iad ris mar mholadh is mar dhaingneachadh air susbaint an ràdh aca fhèin, an àite a bhith a' cnuasachadh air a chruth (Ellis, Loewen, is Erlam, 2006; Nicholas, Lightbown is Spada, 2001).

A bharrachd air sin, ma thèid *recasts* a chleachdadh, chan fhaigh an neach-bruidhinn an cothrom a bhith ri fèin-cheartachadh (mar a gheibheadh iad tro *prompts*) no fiù 's a bhith ag ràdh cruth ceart a' ghleus-cainnte i fhèin. Ge-tà, bhiodh sin glè chuideachail don phròsas ionnsachaidh aice, oir tha e fada nas coltaiche gun cuimhnich luchd-ionnsachaidh air a' chruth cheart ma tha iad fhèin ga chur an cèill gu spreigeach, an àite a bhith ga chluinntinn a-mhàin ann an labhairt cuideigin eile, gu fulangach (faic Ellis, Loewen, is Erlam, 2006; Lyster, 2002 is 2004; Lyster is Ranta, 1997).

Sheall iomadh neach-rannsachaidh gum bi tidsearan glè thric a' dol le *recasts* mar fhios air ais an àite cuimseachadh air cruth, ge-tà, dìreach mar a chunnacas am measg an luchd-teagaisg ann am FMG. 'S e pàirt den adhbhar dha sin nach eil iad a' faighinn stiùireadh domhainn air a' chùis is air na diofar roghainnean ceartachaidh, agus ma gheibh iad fiosrachadh idir, gu bheil glè thric rabhadh ga thogail ann gum b' urrainn do dh'fhios air ais dìreach a bhith a' dèanamh cron do mhisneachd an luchd-bruidhinn (Ellis, 2013). Ach, mar a chaidh sealltainn san deasbad eadar-nàiseanta seo, aig diofar ìrean agus ann an iomadh co-theacsa ionnsachaidh, bidh na diofar sheòrsaichean de dh'fhios air ais dìreach a' toirt deagh bhuaidh mhaireannach air gràmar an luchd-ionnsachaidh – agus, a rèir an rannsachaidh, nas doimhne agus nas maireannaiche na fios air ais mì-dhìreach – agus ma nithear an ceartachadh seo ann an dòigh chùramach, nach dèanar cron air 'sruth' a' chonaltraidh sa chlas no air misneachd nan sgoilearan (faic Lyster, Saito is Sato, 2013; Lyster, 2002; Lyster is Ranta, 1997). Glè thric, tha an luchd-ionnsachaidh ag iarraidh a bhith buileach ceart agus an cuid cainnte a bhith air a cumail ceart tron tidsear – mhothaicheadh gum fàs an seasamh sin nas treasa le aois nan sgoilearan – agus dh'fhaodadh e barrachd cron a dhèanamh don mhisneachd aca a bhith a' cumail fios air ais èifeachdach bhuapasan (Lyster, Saito is Sato, 2013).

Mar sin, tha mi a' moladh an seo gu bheil e deatamach agus èiginneach gun tèid an t-eòlas eadar-nàiseanta seo a thoirt a-steach agus a chur ri trèanadh leantainneach an luchd-teagaisg ann am FMG. Tha mi an dòchas gur e seo aon dòigh a dh'fhaodadh luchd-rannsachaidh a bhith a' cuideachadh an luchd-teagaisg ann an leasachadh foghlam tro mheadhan na Gàidhlig, le bhith a' solarachadh is a' measadh mhodhan obrach a chuidicheas ri Gàidhlig na cloinne a thoirt am feabhas anns an àm ri teachd.

Notaichean

1 Chithear an aon trioblaid am measg sgoilearan ann an Èirinn san latha an-diugh, mar a thaisbein Pétervàry *et al.* (2014) san rannsachadh aca air dà-chànanas anns a' Ghaeltacht. Faic cuideachd Harris is Cummins (2013) airson barrachd fiosrachaidh air sgilean sgoilearan ann an Gàidhlig na h-Èireann, a' gabhail a-steach diofar shuidheachaidhean is co-theacsaichean ionnsachaidh. Airson iomradh air buaidh modhan teagaisg air sgilean cànain sgoilearan anns a' Chuimris, faic Williams (1997) agus airson fòcas sònraichte air an duilgheadas a bhith a' teagasg luchd-bruidhinn C1 is C2 san aon seòmar-teagaisg, Lewis (2006).

2 Gu sònraichte leis gur e feadhainn fìor bhunaiteach a bh' anns a' mhòr-chuid, stèidhichte gu làidir is gu domhainn sa chànain, mar an diofar eadar gleusan-cainnt le *tha* vs. *'s e*.

3 Clann a thog a' Ghàidhlig tro stèidheachdan sgoile (sgoil-àraich, bun-sgoil msaa) mar dhàrna cànain (C2), le bhith air an teagasg tro mheadhan na cànain (seach a

bhith ga h-ionnsachadh mar chuspair).
4 Aon phuing a tha sònraichte annasach mu 'airson' + IND mar cho-cheanglaiche adhbharach, 's e gum b' e sin an *aon* cho-cheanglaiche adhbharach a chleachd cha mhòr a h-uile aon de na sgoilearan san rannsachadh seo. Ged a tha taghadh cho mòr dhiubh anns a' Ghàidhlig agus ged nach eil e idir coltach gun cleachd an luchd-teagaisg 'airson' san t-seagh sin mar *default*, cha do chuir a' mhòr-chuid de na sgoilearan gin de na co-cheanglaichean adhbharach as cumanta gu feum.
5 NT-BS 'Neach-teagaisg aig ìre na bun-sgoile'.
6 NT-AS 'Neach-teagaisg aig ìre na hàrd-sgoile'.

Tùsan

Ammar, Ahlem (2008). 'Prompts and recasts: Differential effects on second language morphosyntax'. *Language Teaching Research*, Iml. 12, Àir. 2, tdd. 183–210.
Baker, Colin (1992). *Attitudes and Language*, Clevedon: Multilingual Matters.
Bell, Susan, et al. (2014). *Dlùth is Inneach: Linguistic and Institutional Foundations for Gaelic Corpus Planning*. Glaschu: Soillse.
Dorian, Nancy C. (1981). *Language Death: The Life Cycle of a Scottish Gaelic Dialect*, Philadelphia: University of Pennsylvania Press.
Dorian, Nancy C. (1994). 'Comment: Choices and Values in Language Shift and Its Study'. *International Journal of the Sociology of Language*, Iml. 110, tdd. 113–24.
Ellis, Rod (2013). 'Corrective feedback in teacher guides and SLA'. *Iranian Journal of Language Teaching Research*, Iml. 1, No. 3, tdd. 1–18.
Ellis, Rod, Loewen, Shawn is Erlam, Rosemary (2006). 'Implicit and explicit corrective feedback and the acquisition of L2 grammar'. *Studies in Second Language Acquisition*, Iml. 28, tdd. 339–68.
Goo, Jaemyung, is Mackey, Alison (2013). 'The case against the case against recasts'. *Studies in Second Language Acquisition*, Iml. 35, tdd. 127–65.
Harris, John, is Cummins, Jim (2013). 'Issues in all-Irish education: Strengthening the case for comparative immersion', ann an David Singleton et al. (deas.), *Current Multilingualism*, tdd. 69–97. Berlin: De Gruyter.
Lewis, W. G. (2006). 'Welsh-medium primary education: the challenges and opportunities of the twenty-first century', ann an Colin Baker et al. (deas.), Welsh-medium and Bilingual Education, tdd. 20–36. Bangor: School of Education, University of Wales.
Lyster, Roy (2002). 'Negotiation in immersion teacher–student interaction'. *International Journal of Educational Research*, Iml. 37, No. 3, tdd. 237–53.
Lyster, Roy (2004). 'Differential effects of prompts and recasts in form-focused instruction'. *Studies in Second Language Acquisition*, Iml. 26, tdd. 399–432.
Lyster, Roy, is Ranta, Leila (1997). 'Corrective feedback and learner uptake'. *Studies in Second Language Acquisition*, Iml. 19, Àir. 1, tdd. 37–66.
Lyster, Roy, is Ranta, Leila (2013). 'Counterpoint Piece: The Case for Variety in Corrective Feedback Research'. *Studies in Second Language Acquisition*, Iml. 35, tdd. 167–84.
Lyster, Roy, Saito, Kazuya, is Sato, Masatoshi (2013). 'Oral corrective feedback in second language classrooms'. *Language Teaching*, Iml. 46, Àir. 1, tdd. 1–40.
Nicholas, Howard, Lightbown, Patsy M. is Spada, Nina (2001). 'Recasts as feedback to language learners'. *Language Learning*, Iml. 51, tdd. 719–58.
NicLeòid, Sìleas L. (2015). *A' Ghàidhlig agus Beachdan nan Sgoilearan: cothroman*

leasachaidh ann am foghlam tro mheadhan na Gàidhlig. Slèite: Clò Ostaig.

O'Hanlon, Fiona (2013). 'Celtic-medium education and language maintenance in Scotland and Wales: language use, ability and attitudes at the primary to secondary school stage', ann an Nancy McGuire agus Colm Ó Baoill (deas.), *Rannsachadh na Gàidhlig 6*, tdd. 323–54. Obar Dheathain: An Clò Gàidhealach.

Oliver, James (2006). 'Where is Gaelic? Revitalisation, language, culture and identity', ann an Wilson McLeod (deas.), *Revitalising Gaelic in Scotland: Policy, Planning and Public Discourse*, tdd. 155–68. Dùn Èideann: Dunedin Academic Press.

Péterváry, Tamás, et al. (2014). *Iniúchadh ar an gCumas Dátheangach: An sealbhú teanga i measc ghlúin óg na Gaeltachta / Assessment of Bilingual Competence: Language acquisition among people in the Gaeltacht*. Baile Átha Cliath: An Chomhairle um Oideachas Gaeltachta agus Gaelscolaíochta.

Seedhouse, Paul (1997). 'The case of the missing "no": The relationship between pedagogy and interaction'. *Language Learning*, Iml. 47, Àir. 3, tdd. 547–83.

Stiùbhart, Mòrag (2011). 'Cainnt nan Deugairean', ann an Richard A. V. Cox is Timothy Currie Armstrong (deas.), *A' cleachdadh na Gàidhlig: slatan-tomhais ann an dìon cànain sa choimhearsnachd*, tdd. 275–82. Slèite: Clò Ostaig.

Swain, Merrill, is Lapkin, Sharon (1995). 'Problems in output and the cognitive processes they generate: A step towards second language learning'. *Applied Linguistics*, Iml. 16, Àir. 3, tdd. 371–91.

Truscott, John (1999). 'What's wrong with oral grammar correction'. *Canadian Modern Language Review/La Revue canadienne des langues vivantes*, Iml. 55, tdd. 437–56.

Vásquez, Camilla, is Harvey, Jane (2010). 'Raising teachers' awareness about corrective feedback through research replication'. *Language Teaching Research*, Iml. 14, Àir. 4, tdd. 421–43.

Williams, Seimon (1997). 'The Use of Welsh and English as the Medium of Instruction'. Pàipear air a leughadh aig British Educational Research Association Annual Conference, York, 11–14 Sultain.